DEBATING TEXTS

Readings in Twentieth-Century Literary Theory and Method

edited by

Rick Rylance

University of Toronto Press

Toronto and Buffalo

Canadian Cataloguing in Publication Data
Main entry under title:

  Debating texts

Includes bibliographical references and index.
ISBN 0-8020-5768-3 (bound). — ISBN 0-8020-6682-8 (pbk.)

1. Criticism.   2. Literature — History and criticism.
I. Rylance, Rick.

PN81.R95   1987   801'.95   C87-093755-3

First published in Canada and the United States by

University of Toronto Press 1987

Toronto and Buffalo

Contents

Acknowledgements

The editor and publishers are grateful to the following for permission to reprint copyright material:

Faber and Faber Ltd and Harcourt Brace Jovanovich Inc for 'Tradition and the Individual Talent' from *Selected Essays* by T. S. Eliot, reprinted by permission; the authors' estates and Chatto and Windus for extracts from *Revaluation* by F. R. Leavis and *Lectures in America* by F. R. Leavis and Q. D. Leavis; Cleanth Brooks for 'Irony as a Principle of Structure', © Cleanth Brooks 1951; the University of Nebraska Press for extracts from *Russian Formalist Criticism: Four Essays*, edited and translated by Lee T. Lemon and Marion J. Reis, copyright © 1965 by the University of Nebraska Press; Editions Gallimard and the University of Miami Press for Mary Elizabeth Meek's translation of 'The Nature of the Linguistic Sign' from *Problems in General Linguistics* by Emile Benveniste, original French edition © Editions Gallimard 1966; Editions du Seuil and Northwestern University Press for 'What is Criticism?' and 'The Imagination of the Sign' from Roland Barthes' *Critical Essays* in Richard Howard's translation, original French edition © Editions du Seuil, 1964; Stephen Heath and Fontana Paperbacks for the translations of 'The Struggle With The Angel' and 'From Work to Text' from *Image-Music-Text* by Roland Barthes, © Stephen Heath 1977; The University of Minnesota Press for an extract from 'The Dead-End of Formalist Criticism' from *Blindness and Insight: Essays in the Rhetoric of Contemporary Criticism* by Paul De Man, © The University of Minnesota Press; The University of Chicago Press and Routledge & Kegan Paul Ltd for Alan Bass's translation of 'Structure, Sign and Play in the Discourse of the Human Sciences' from *Writing and Difference* by Jacques Derrida, © University of Chicago Press 1978; A. D. Peters and Co Ltd for an extract from *The Classic* by Frank Kermode, reprinted by permission; The University of Chicago Press and Stanley Fish for 'Interpreting the *Variorum*', © The University of Chicago 1976; The University of Chicago Press and E. D. Hirsch for 'The Politics of Theories of Interpretation', © The University of Chicago 1982; Oxford University Press for 'The Text, the Poem and the Problem of Historical Method' reprinted by permission from *The Beauty of Inflections: Literary Investigations in Historical Method and Theory* by Jerome J. McGann (1985), © Jerome J. McGann 1985, and for 'The Multiplicity of Writing' from *Marxism and Literature* by Raymond Williams (1977), © Oxford University Press 1977, reprinted by permission; Lawrence and Wishart Ltd for an extract from 'Preface' to *A Contribution to the Critique of Political Economy* from *Selected Works* by Karl Marx and Frederick Engels; New Left Books for 'Base and Superstructure in Marxist Cultural Theory' from *Problems in Materialism and Culture* by Raymond Williams © New Left Books 1980; Terry Eagleton and New Left Books for an extract from *Criticism and Ideology: A Study in Marxist Literary*

Theory, © Terry Eagleton 1975, 1976; Elaine Showalter for 'Towards a Feminist Poetics', © Elaine Showalter 1979; Yale University Press and Sandra M. Gilbert for an extract from chapter 8 of *The Madwoman in the Attic: The Woman Writer and the Nineteenth-Century Literary Imagination* by Sandra M. Gilbert and Susan Gubar, © Yale University Press 1979; Rachel Blau DuPlessis for 'For the Etruscans', © Rachel Blau DuPlessis, 1984, reprinted by permission of the author.

Introduction

Interest in the theory of literary criticism is increasing in all sectors of higher education. For some, it must be said, this is a regrettable development, for they feel that critical theory distracts attention from the freshness of the individual's response to literary works. Others, however, find the idea that we encounter these works in such an open and independently-minded way difficult to accept. For them (and this is my own view) literary works arrive on our cognitive doorsteps in context. These contexts may be institutional, in the sense that literary works are frequently read in highly specific and controlling situations, most usually within a set syllabus and for examination. But these contexts are also intellectual and methodological, for the choices we make about which works to study, which critical methods we bring to bear, and what aims and purposes we have in view for such an activity, must have a determining impact on the conclusions we form about our reading. At all events, it is certainly the case that at different times, and for different reasons, critics have urged attention on particular critical procedures, and that in turn these have had effects on the institutional study of literature. When critics or educational policy makers propose such procedures they are engaging in activities of a theoretical kind.

Here is an example of such a theoretical activity. In 1828 Professor Thomas Dale introduced a lecture series at the University of London in this way:

> in all my Lectures, more particularly when treating upon that glorious and inexhaustible subject, the LITERATURE of our country — I shall esteem it my duty — and I trust I shall find it my delight — to inculcate lessons of virtue, through the medium of the masters of our language. Nor to those parents who are acquainted with the earlier productions of English literature will such a declaration appear superfluous or misplaced. *They* know, that the gems with which it is so copiously adorned, sometimes require to be abstracted with careful hand; lest they should convey pollution with the foul mass of daring profaneness or disgusting wantonness in which they are too often incrusted. *They* at least, therefore, will appreciate my motive, when I declare that . . . never will I suffer the eye of inexperienced youth to be dazzled by the brilliancy of genius, when its broad lustre obscures the deformity of vice . . .
>
> (quoted by D. J. Palmer, *The Rise of English Studies*, p. 20)

Dale defines an *object* for criticism (the 'masters' and 'gems' of the language), a *purpose* ('to inculcate lessons of virtue'), and a *method* (abstraction and exhibition 'with a careful hand'). He answers, therefore, some basic questions which are fundamental components of any critical theory: *what* is it we study in English? *Why* do we study it? *How* do we go about it? (Here by a kind of censorship.)

Dale's answers were confident and functional in the early-Victorian phase of the history of English studies in Britain. Nowadays, though, it is unlikely that they would command much agreement among teachers and students of literature who may reject his didactic purposes, or scorn the looseness of his definitions (what is a gem? what is virtue?). What is less easy to do however, for all of us, is to formulate satisfying answers of our own to such questions. Nevertheless they require careful attention, particularly in a contemporary institutional context where funds are increasingly hard to come by and educational policy is a matter of lively public concern. When questions are asked about the study of literature it would seem best to know what we are about.

The present range of theoretical and methodological options available to literary critics is very large. This is partly because the issues engaged by such apparently simple questions as those mentioned above are very complex. It is not easy nowadays (and in truth it never really was) to read literary works and engage in criticism of them without a sense of the wider ethical, social and philosophic issues involved in such an activity. In addition, criticism of late has become more conceptually rigorous and sometimes demandingly technical in some of its procedures. As a result it is sometimes studied independently from the more usual kinds of critical activity in courses specifically devoted to theoretical questions.

The aim of this book is to provide an accessible, introductory selection of critical texts and information about supporting theories and contexts from this century. I have selected this material in accordance with what I believe to be a common perception of the leading influential schools, though clearly any selection involves omissions and choices of emphasis which may not accord with all senses of this complex history. For example, only passing reference is made to psychoanalysis, and there is no consideration of drama; but space is limited and choices have to be made. The materials are arranged roughly chronologically, but are weighted towards contemporary arguments which interconnect in many ways. Debates and arguments do not develop in neat pigeon-holes or discrete historical time-slots, as the introductions make clear. Comment on literary structuralism, for instance, has not been confined to the introduction to Section 3, for the resonances of it are felt in the work represented in all succeeding sections.

Some other criteria of selection have been used. Because the book is primarily aimed at the student beginning his or her encounter with theory, and because such a reader, by training and convention, more usually reads criticism to learn about literary works, each section includes an example of the close application of theoretical principles to a piece of writing. By and large I have tried to choose these pieces so that the reader does not have to be familiar with a wide range of diverse literary material before beginning each one; thus *Wuthering Heights* features prominently. I have chosen this work because interpretations of it vary so enormously. In other cases I have chosen essays which address literary works whose texts are given in the essays, or which will require relatively little other reading. The book is, in this way, designed to be as self-contained as possible. This has been a strong consideration because of the constraints on students' budgets. Though this orientation towards literary commentary, and the limited focus, may be thought to beg some theoretical questions, it will have advantages for teaching purposes. I have also tried to print entire essays or sections from books whenever possible. When the original has been edited this is clearly noted in the points of information at the beginning of each section and is marked by asterisks in the text.

I do not see this book as separated from the contexts of its uses. I imagine it being used in classrooms, or as a basis for other forms of discussion, where questions will be asked, explanations demanded and given, debates conducted, and arguments offered. For the reader without such a context, I hope there is enough basic information and guides to further reading to encourage exploration. Much of this material is difficult, and for many it will be new and perhaps unexpected. But it repays close attention and engages fundamental questions about our activities as readers and commentators on that body of material we call literature. Above all, this book is about debate.

In compiling a book such as this one has many debts to pay, above all to those whose work is included in it. Formal acknowledgements are made on a separate page, but I owe much informal thanks to many; first of all to Isobel Armstrong, Deborah Cartmell, Simon Dentith, Aleid Fokkema, Eamonn Hughes, Jokhim Meikle, Bill Myers, Jon Stone and many others in the Leicester University staff-postgraduate seminar group with and from whom I learnt so much over many years from 1976. I owe particular thanks also to Jane Aaron and Kelvin Everest with whom I taught critical theory at Leicester. Other friends — Ed Esche, Elaine Hobby, Martin Stannard — have aided and abetted in several ways. Peter Fisher kindly helped me with the translations from Latin and Greek. Nora Crook, Kelvin Everest, Kate Flint and Nigel Wheale read the introductions and their comments were more than helpful. Jon Stone worked on the proofs and index. Remaining errors are mine. Finally John Skelton and Ray Cunningham at the Open University Press have been splendidly encouraging throughout.

My part in this work is dedicated to my Mum and Dad, and to Judith, as ever.

A note on further reading

Specific, selected further reading is given at the close of the introductions to each section, and there is a checklist of full references at the end. There are also a number of other works which readers may find generally helpful. These contain reference to most of the lines of thinking represented in this anthology.

M.H. Abrams, *A Glossary of Literary Terms,* 4th edn. (1981)
Terry Eagleton, *Literary Theory: An Introduction* (1983)
D.W. Fokkema and Elrud Kunne-Ibsch, *Theories of Literature in the Twentieth Century* (1977)
Jeremy Hawthorn, ed., *Criticism and Critical Theory* (1984)
Ann Jefferson and David Robey, eds., *Modern Literary Theory: A Comparative Introduction,* 2nd edn. (1986)
K.K. Ruthven, *Critical Assumptions* (1979)
Hilda Schiff, ed., *Contemporary Approaches to English Studies* (1977)
Raman Selden, *A Reader's Guide to Contemporary Literary Theory* (1985)
Raymond Williams, *Keywords: A Vocabulary of Culture and Society*, 2nd edn. (1983)

Section One

THE FORCE OF TRADITION

1. T. S. Eliot, 'Tradition and the Individual Talent' (1919)
2. F. R. Leavis, from 'Wordsworth' (1936)
3. Q. D. Leavis, from 'A Fresh Approach to *Wuthering Heights*' (1969)

Points of information

1. 'Tradition and the Individual Talent' first appeared in *The Egoist*. It is reprinted here from Eliot's *Selected Essays* (1932). F. R. Leavis's 'Wordsworth' is reprinted from *Revaluation* (1936). Q. D. Leavis's essay first appeared in F. R. and Q. D. Leavis, *Lectures in America* (1969).

2. The quotation in section II of Eliot's essay comes from Tourneur's *The Revenger's Tragedy*, III, 5. The Greek used as an epigraph to section III means: 'The mind is doubtless more divine and less subject to passion'. It comes from Aristotle, *De Anima*.

3. About seven pages have been omitted from the opening of F. R. Leavis's essay on Wordsworth. They deal with the question of Wordsworth's 'philosophy', and with some comments by William Empson on Wordsworth from his *Seven Types of Ambiguity* (1930).

4. Q. D. Leavis's essay has been heavily edited to about a third of its original length. In the third extract here Mrs Leavis makes a comparison between *Wuthering Heights* and Henri-Pierre Roché's novel *Jules et Jim* (1953).

It is now widely acknowledged that the most influential critics in Britain in the earlier part of this century were the American ex-patriate poet T. S. Eliot

1

(1888–1965) and two Cambridge academics I. A. Richards (1893–1979) and F. R Leavis (1895–1978). The work of these writers has diverse features and emphases but each contributed in a major way to a shift in thinking within literary studies during the early decades. They gave a fresh impetus to criticism and a corporate sense of identity, purpose and direction.

Two features of this movement for change can be highlighted initially. The first concerns the new avant-garde literary practice now known as 'modernism' of which Eliot's 1922 poem *The Waste Land* is generally taken to be representative. Fragmentary in form and time scheme, cosmopolitan, allusive and highly self-conscious about its literariness and literary antecedents, *The Waste Land*, and similar writing by Pound, Joyce, Yeats, Woolf and many others, set new challenges and possibilities before critics and readers. At the same time many of these writers, in critical essays, reviews and polemical pieces, revised the terms of debate and the standards and norms by way of which literary argument was conducted. Eliot's 'Tradition and the Individual Talent', written in 1919 as he was preparing *The Waste Land*, is one example of this new critical writing.

The second feature was the rise in prestige and intellectual vitality of English as an academic discipline in British education from around the turn of the century. The reasons for this are numerous and complex. They include: worries about the standards of British education in comparison with Britain's leading trading rivals, principally Germany and the United States; increasing demands for education by women; and the need to spread newly-vitalised conceptions of English culture through a social system which was felt to be increasingly fragmented and culturally dispersed. The anxiety felt by influential thinkers on all these questions was heightened by the crisis of the First World War. In addition there was a powerful nineteenth-century line of thought which had stressed the same alarm about the predicament of traditional English culture in a rapidly industrialising nation. Prominent here is the poet, educationalist and literary and cultural critic Matthew Arnold, whose work has some resemblance in outlook to that of Eliot, Richards and Leavis. It can be most easily sampled in his essays 'The Function of Criticism at the Present Time' (1864) and 'The Study of Poetry' (1880). Arnold and others had argued for the centrality of the study of poetry in the spiritual vacuum produced by industrialisation and the collapse of religion as a national cultural bond.

In this context young and adventurous critics and writers such as Eliot, Richards and Leavis had an intellectual and disciplinary opportunity to reshape English critical practice by giving it greater conceptual rigour and a more pointed ethical and social urgency. Whilst *The Waste Land* grimly fastened upon what Eliot saw as the signs of post-war cultural collapse, his essays spoke for the force of tradition and the need for an a-historical 'impersonality' to adjudicate its standards and dimensions.

Richards, too, in *Science and Poetry* (1926) wrote of the weakening of tradition and moral authority and the new need for moral and psychological order. Following Arnold, Richards saw the hope for such a new cultural training in the study of poetry. The reading of poetry would enable standards to be set, and sponsor a wise reflectiveness and emotional equilibrium which could overcome spiritual chaos. Slightly later F. R. Leavis juxtaposed the worlds of 'Mass Civilisation and Minority Culture' (the title of his 1930 pamphlet) and sought a way to moral and cultural health through the literary traditions of the latter. These were preferred to the corrupt and corrupting business of daily life in an advanced industrial culture with its emphasis on the machine, commercialism, advertising, the new electronic communications systems and the best-seller. Through all of these, in mass civilisation, citizens' experiences and responses were degraded and their values distorted. In an influential reading of Eliot in his *New Bearings in English Poetry* (1932), Leavis saw *The Waste Land* as a poem which implicitly harked back to the pre-industrial, 'organic' communities of rural life 'rooted in the soil'. Leavis's preferences in this respect can also be detected in his account of Wordsworth which is printed here.

The criticism of this period, then, was marked by a sharp sense of crisis and a responding missionary spirit. These critics bemoaned the present and with it aspects of the cultural heritage which had led to it. The result was a potent, attractive, tough-minded reconceptualisation of literary studies which quickly found followers and partisans. The Leavis circle, especially, through its journal *Scrutiny* (1932–1953) and in its connections with the educational world at large, went a considerable way to forming the literary standards, values and methods for several succeeding generations of teachers and students in Britain — though in some respects both F. R. Leavis and, especially, his wife Q. D. Leavis (1907–1981) were frustrated in their academic careers at Cambridge.

A number of themes were persistently developed in this work: the importance of 'the tradition' (the singular noun is important) which transmitted historical experiences and values; the committed, humanistic emphasis — in the Leavises particularly — on moral and spiritual judgement and the 'life-enhancing' possibilities of fine, engaged literary writing; and the objectivity ('impersonality' in Eliot's essay) of the chosen critical method as the critic encounters passages in close reading, a method Richards called 'practical criticism'. All of these demanded attention and it is important in this respect to take full measure of the tone and style of the pieces printed here. They declare their commitments forcefully. In his essay here Eliot uses scientific metaphors and analogies. He stresses the hard work necessary for the attainment of the sense of tradition, and he insists upon a closely-focused objectivity (criticism is to be 'directed not upon the poet but upon the poetry'). The effect is to give a rigour and status to criticism it might otherwise have been thought to lack.

Some of Eliot's formulations in this essay are teasingly provocative, even ambiguous. It is difficult, for instance, to understand what is meant by a 'historical sense' which is both 'timeless and temporal'; and it is, notoriously, even harder to work through the precise terms of the extended metaphor which compares the activity of a poet's mind to the actions of gases and platinum in a catalyst. But these are all matters for discussion.

It is not an exaggeration to claim that the three critics mentioned here (though Richards is not represented in the selection), and those who worked with them to develop and refine their emphases and techniques, redefined literary criticism for this century. They formed new answers to those questions of 'what', 'why' and 'how' mentioned in the introduction. They had urgent cultural reasons for undertaking and valuing literary criticism in a general cultural context. They developed a massively influential method of analysis in 'practical criticism' (whose advantages, and perhaps limitations, can be sampled in Leavis's essay on Wordsworth), which could be used in demonstration of wider arguments. And they also redefined the object of study, drawing up a 'canon' of major writers for central attention. Some writers, temporarily, suffered in this process, like Milton or Shelley, and others received greater and greater attention as forming the significant 'lines' through the tradition. Meanwhile, as a shadow to this ruthless selective process, certain writers received little or no attention.

Leavis's books, particularly, promoted certain writers, even whole periods, in a large overhauling 'revaluation' of the canon. Leavis's *Revaluation: Tradition and Development in English Poetry* (1936), from which the essay on Wordsworth comes, established the landmarks of 'the tradition' in English poetry, and his *The Great Tradition* (1948) performed a similar exercise for the novel. There were five great novelists who 'mattered' (Austen, George Eliot, James, Conrad and Lawrence); that is, they spoke through their qualities to the particular cultural needs of the present English condition and beyond that to crucial, permanent values. Though in later years both the Leavises extended this severe selection to include others — most notably Dickens and, as here, Emily Brontë — the patterns and tactics of analysis and the controlling assumptions about cultural and literary value remained broadly consistent.

Further reading:

Eliot's literary and cultural criticism is most readily available in *Selected Prose of T. S. Eliot,* ed. Frank Kermode (1975), which contains a helpful introduction and notes. I. A. Richards's two principal books are *Principles of Literary Criticism* (1924) and *Practical Criticism* (1929). The Leavises were prolific writers; a beginning can be made with F. R. Leavis's *New Bearings in English Poetry* (1932); *Revaluation* (1936); *The Great Tradition* (1948); and *The Common Pursuit* (1952), a collection of essays. His short essay 'Mass Civilisation and Minority Culture' is reprinted in his *Education and the University* (1943) and provides a brief introduction to his general cultural thought. Q. D. Leavis's work on the English novel is brought together in volume one of her *Collected Essays*, ed. G. Singh (1983). Her important contribution to the 'mass civilisation' argument is *Fiction and the Reading Public* (1932), a pathbreaking doctoral dissertation supervised in Cambridge by Richards.

Several studies set out the social and intellectual contexts of this early British criticism. Chris Baldick, *The Social Mission of English Criticism, 1848–1932* (1983) is excellent; see also Brian Doyle, 'The Hidden History of English Studies' in *Re-Reading English,* ed. Peter Widdowson (1982); D. J. Palmer, *The Rise of English Studies* (1965); Patrick Parrinder, *Authors and Authority; A Study of English Literary Criticism and It's Relation to Culture 1750–1900* (1977); Raymond Williams, *Culture ad Society 1780–1950* (1958).

On individual writers Pamela McCallum's *Literature and Method: Towards a Critique of I. A. Richards, T. S. Eliot and F. R. Leavis* (1983) and Vincent Buckley's appreciative *Poetry and Morality: Studies in the Criticism of Matthew Arnold, T. S. Eliot and F. R. Leavis* (1959) are useful. There is much Eliot criticism and reference is generally made to both his literary and cultural criticism. There are specific essays on his literary criticism by John Casey in his *The Language of Criticism* (1966) and by John Chalker in *Eliot in Perspective*, ed., Graham Martin (1970). See also the piece by Terry Eagleton in Section 6. Eliot's later ideas are discussed by Lucy McDiarmid in *Saving Civilisation: Yeats, Eliot and Auden Between the Wars* (1984).

There is a recent biography of him by Peter Ackroyd, *T. S. Eliot* (1984).

Francis Mulhern's *The Moment of 'Scrutiny'* (1979) is the most thorough account of the Leavises' intellectual millieu and influence. There are also interesting and illuminating pieces in Denys Thompson, ed., *The Leavises: Recollections and Impressions* (1984). John Harvey's 'Leavis: An Appreciation', printed there, is an elegant, sympathetic assessment. Bernard Bergonzi, 'Leavis and Eliot: The Long Road to Rejection', *Critical Quarterly,* 26 (1984) examines relations between the two. Frank Kermode's piece in Section 4 responds, in part, to Q. D. Leavis's account of *Wuthering Heights*, as, in less detail, does that by Gilbert and Gubar in Section 7.

1

T. S. Eliot,
'Tradition and the Individual Talent'

I

In English writing we seldom speak of tradition, though we occasionally apply its name in deploring its absence. We cannot refer to 'the tradition' or to 'a tradition'; at most, we employ the adjective in saying that the poetry of So-and-so is 'traditional' or even 'too traditional'. Seldom, perhaps, does the word appear except in a phrase of censure. If otherwise, it is vaguely approbative, with the implication, as to the work approved, of some pleasing archaeological reconstruction. You can hardly make the word agreeable to English ears without this comfortable reference to the reassuring science of archaeology.

Certainly the word is not likely to appear in our appreciations of living or dead writers. Every nation, every race, has not only its own creative, but its own critical turn of mind; and is even more oblivious of the shortcomings and limitations of its critical habits than of those of its creative genius. We know, or think we know, from the enormous mass of critical writing that has appeared in the French language the critical method or habit of the French; we only conclude (we are such unconscious people) that the French are 'more critical' than we, and sometimes even plume ourselves a little with the fact, as if the French were the less spontaneous. Perhaps they are; but we might remind ourselves that criticism is as inevitable as breathing, and that we should be none the worse for articulating what passes in our minds when we read a book and feel an emotion about it, for criticising our own minds in their work of criticism. One of the facts that might come to light in this process is our tendency to insist, when we praise a poet, upon those aspects of his work in which he least resembles anyone else. In these aspects or parts of his work we pretend to find what is individual, what is the peculiar essence of the man. We dwell with satisfaction upon the poet's difference from his predecessors, especially his immediate predecessors; we endeavour to find something that can be isolated in order to be enjoyed. Whereas if we approach a poet without this prejudice we shall often find that not only the best, but the most individual parts of his work may be those in which the dead poets, his ancestors, assert their immortality most vigorously. And I do not mean the impressionable period of adolescence, but the period of full maturity.

Yet if the only form of tradition, of handing down, consisted in following the ways of the immediate generation before us in a blind or timid adherence to its successes, 'tradition' should positively be discouraged. We have seen many such simple currents soon lost in the sand; and novelty is better than repetition. Tradition is a matter of much wider significance. It cannot be inherited, and if you want it you must obtain it by great labour. It involves, in the first place, the historical sense, which we may call nearly indispensable to anyone who would continue to be a poet beyond his twenty-fifth year; and the historical sense involves a perception, not only of the pastness of the past, but of its presence; the historical sense compels a man to write not merely with his own generation in his bones, but with a feeling that the whole of the literature of Europe from Homer and within it the whole of the literature of his own country has a simultaneous existence and composes a simultaneous order. This historical sense, which is a sense of the timeless as well as of the temporal and of the timeless and of the temporal together, is what makes a writer traditional. And it is at the same time what makes a writer most acutely conscious of his place in time, of his own contemporaneity.

No poet, no artist of any art, has his complete meaning alone. His significance, his appreciation is the appreciation of his relation to the dead poets and artists. You cannot value him alone; you must set him, for contrast and comparison, among the dead. I mean this as a principle of aesthetic, not merely historical, criticism. The necessity that he shall conform, that he shall cohere, is not onesided; what happens when a new work of art is created is something that happens simultaneously to all the works of art which preceded it. The existing monuments form an ideal order among themselves, which is modified by the introduction of the new (the really new) work of art among them. The existing order is complete before the new work arrives; for order to persist after the supervention of novelty, the *whole* existing order must be, if ever so slightly, altered; and so the relations, proportions, values of each work of art toward the whole are readjusted; and this is conformity between the old and the new. Whoever has approved this idea of order, of the form of European, of English literature will not find it preposterous that the past should be altered by the present as much as the present is directed by the past. And the poet who is aware of this will be aware of great difficulties and responsibilities.

In a peculiar sense he will be aware also that he must inevitably be judged by the standards of the past. I say judged, not amputated, by them; not judged to be as good as, or worse or better than, the dead; and certainly not judged by canons of dead critics. It is a judgment, a comparison, in which two things are measured by each other. To conform merely would be for the new work not really to conform at all; it would not be new, and would therefore not be a work of art. And we do not quite say that the new is more valuable because it fits in; but its fitting in is a test of its value — a test, it is true, which can only be slowly and cautiously applied, for we are none of us infallible judges of conformity. We say: it appears to conform, and is perhaps individual, or it appears individual, and may conform; but we are hardly likely to find that it is one and not the other.

To proceed to a more intelligible exposition of the relation of the poet to the past: he can neither take the past as a lump, an indiscriminate bolus, nor can he form himself wholly on one or two private admirations, nor can he form himself wholly upon one preferred period. The first course is inadmissible, the second is an important experience of youth, and the third is a pleasant and highly desirable supplement. The poet must be very conscious of the main current, which does not at all flow invariably through the most distinguished reputations. He must be quite aware of the obvious fact that art never improves, but that the material of art is never quite the same. He must be aware that the mind of Europe — the mind of his own country — a mind which he learns in time to be much more important than his own private mind — is a mind which changes, and that this change is a development which abandons nothing *en route*, which does not superannuate either Shakespeare, or Homer, or the rock drawing of the Magdalenian draughtsmen. That this development, refinement perhaps, complication certainly, is not, from the point of view of the artist, any improvement. Perhaps not even an improvement from the point of view of the psychologist or not to the extent which we imagine; perhaps only in the end based upon a complication in economics and machinery. But the diference between the present and the past is that the conscious present is an awareness of the past in a way and to an extent which the past's awareness of itself cannot show.

Someone said: 'The dead writers are remote from us because we *know* so much more than they did'. Precisely, and they are that which we know.

I am alive to a usual objection to what is clearly part of my programme for the *métier* of poetry. The objection is that the doctrine requires a ridiculous amount of erudition (pedantry), a claim which can be rejected by appeal to the lives of poets in any pantheon. It will even be affirmed that much learning deadens or perverts poetic sensibility. While, however, we persist in believing that a poet ought to know as much as will not encroach upon his necessary receptivity and necessary laziness, it is not desirable to confine knowledge to whatever can be put into a useful shape for examinations, drawing-rooms, or the still more pretentious modes of publicity. Some can absorb knowledge, the more tardy must sweat for it. Shakespeare acquired more essential history from Plutarch than most men could from the whole British Museum. What is to be insisted upon is that the poet must develop or procure the consciousness of the past and that he should continue to develop this consciousness throughout his career.

What happens is a continual surrender of himself as he is at the moment to something which is more valuable. The progress of an artist is a continual self-sacrifice, a continual extinction of personality.

There remains to define this process of depersonalisation and its relation to the sense of tradition. It is in this depersonalisation that art may be said to approach the condition of science. I therefore invite you to consider, as a suggestive analogy, the action which takes place when a bit of finely filiated platinum is introduced into a chamber containing oxygen and sulphur dioxide.

II

Honest criticism and sensitive appreciation is directed not upon the poet but upon the poetry. If we attend to the confused cries of the newspaper critics and the susurrus of popular repetition that follows, we shall hear the names of poets in great numbers; if we seek not Blue-book knowledge but the enjoyment of poetry, and ask for a poem, we shall seldom find it. I have tried to point out the importance of the relation of the poem to other poems by other authors, and suggested the conception of poetry as a living whole of all the poetry that has ever been written. The other aspect of this Impersonal theory of poetry is the relation of the poem to its author. And I hinted, by an analogy, that the mind of the mature poet differs from that of the immature one not precisely in any valuation of 'personality', not being necessarily more interesting, or having 'more to say', but rather by being a more finely perfected medium in which special, or very varied, feelings are at liberty to enter into new combinations.

The analogy was that of the catalyst. When the two gases previously mentioned are mixed in the presence of a filament of platinum, they form sulphurous acid. This combination takes place only if the platinum is present; nevertheless the newly formed acid contains no trace of platinum, and the platinum itself is apparently unaffected: has remained inert, neutral, and unchanged. The mind of the poet is the shred of platinum. It may partly or exclusively operate upon the experience of the man himself; but, the more perfect the artist, the more completely separate in him will be the man who suffers and the mind which creates; the more perfectly will the mind digest and transmute the passions which are its material.

The experience, you will notice, the elements which enter the presence of the transforming catalyst, are of two kinds: emotions and feelings. The effect of a work of art upon the person who enjoys it is an experience different in kind from any experience not of art. It may be formed out of one emotion, or may be a combination of several; and various feelings, inhering for the writer in particular words or phrases or images, may be added to compose the final result. Or great poetry may be made without the direct use of any emotion whatever: composed out of feelings solely. Canto XV of the *Inferno* (Brunetto Latini) is a working up of the emotion evident in the situation; but the effect, though single as that of any work of art, is obtained by considerable complexity of detail. The last quatrain gives an image, a feeling attaching to an image, which 'came', which did not develop simply out of what precedes, but which was probably in suspension in the poet's mind until the proper combination arrived for it to add itself to. The poet's mind is in fact a receptacle for seizing and storing up numberless feelings, phrases, images, which remain there until all the particles which can unite to form a new compound are present together.

If you compare several representative passages of the greatest poetry you see how great is the variety of types of combination, and also how completely any semi-ethical criterion of 'sublimity' misses the mark. For it is not the 'greatness', the intensity, of the emotions, the components, but the intensity of the artistic process, the pressure, so to speak, under which the fusion takes place, that counts. The episode of Paolo and Francesca employs a definite emotion, but the intensity of the poetry is something quite different from whatever intensity in the supposed experience it may give the impression of. It is no more intense, furthermore, than Canto XXVI, the voyage of Ulysses, which has not the direct dependence upon an emotion. Great variety is possible in the process of transmutation of emotion: the murder of Agamemnon, or the agony of Othello, gives an artistic effect apparently closer to a possible original than the scenes from Dante. In the *Agamemnon,* the artistic emotion approximates to the emotion of an actual spectator; in *Othello* to the emotion of the protagonist himself. But the difference between art and the event is always absolute; the combination which is the murder of Agamemnon is probably as complex as that which is the voyage of Ulysses. In either case there has been a fusion of elements. The ode of Keats contains a number of feelings which have nothing particular to do with the nightingale, but which the nightingale, partly perhaps because of its attractive name, and partly because of its reputation, served to bring together.

The point of view which I am struggling to attack is perhaps related to the metaphysical theory of the substantial unity of the soul: for my meaning is, that the poet has, not a 'personality' to express, but a particular medium, which is only a medium and not a personality, in which impressions and experiences combine in peculiar and unexpected ways. Impressions and experiences which are important for the man may take no place in the poetry, and those which become important in the poetry may play quite a negligible part in the man, the personality.

I will quote a passage which is unfamiliar enough to be regarded with fresh attention in the light — or darkness — of these observations:

> And now methinks I could e'en chide myself
> For doating on her beauty, though her death
> Shall be revenged after no common action.
> Does the silkworm expend her yellow labours
> For thee? For thee does she undo herself?
> Are lordships sold to maintain ladyships
> For the poor benefit of a bewildering minute?
> Why does yon fellow falsify highways,
> And put his life between the judge's lips,
> To refine such a thing — keeps horse and men
> To beat their valours for her? . . .

In this passage (as is evident if it is taken in its context) there is a combination of positive and negative emotions: an intensely strong attraction toward beauty and an equally intense fascination by the ugliness which is contrasted with it and which destroys it. This balance of contrasted emotion is in the dramatic situation to which the speech is pertinent, but that situation alone is inadequate to it. This is, so to speak, the structural emotion, provided by the drama. But the whole effect, the dominant tone, is due to the fact that a number of floating feelings, having an affinity to this emotion by no means superficially evident, have combined with it to give us a new art emotion.

It is not in his personal emotions, the emotions provoked by particular events in his life, that the poet is in any way remarkable or interesting. His particular emotions may be simple, or crude, or flat. The emotion in his poetry will be a very complex thing, but not with the complexity of the emotions of people who have very complex or unusual emotions in life. One error, in fact, of eccentricity in poetry is to seek for new human emotions to express; and in this search for novelty in the wrong place it discovers the perverse. The business of the poet is not to find new emotions, but to use the ordinary ones and, in working them up into poetry, to express feelings which are not in actual emotions at all. And emotions which he has never experienced will serve his turn as well as those familiar to him. Consequently, we must believe that 'emotion recollected in tranquillity' is an inexact formula. For it is neither emotion, nor recollection, nor, without distortion of meaning, tranquility. It is a concentration, and a new thing resulting from the concentration, of a very great number of experiences which to the practical and active person would not seem to be experiences at all; it is a concentration which does not happen consciously or of deliberation. These experiences are not 'recollected', and they finally unite in an atmosphere which is 'tranquil' only in that it is a passive attending upon the event. Of course this is not quite the whole story. There is a great deal, in the writing of poetry, which must be conscious and deliberate. In fact, the bad poet is usually unconscious where he ought to be conscious, and conscious where he ought to be unconscious. Both errors tend to make him 'personal'. Poetry is not a turning loose of emotion, but an escape from emotion, it is not the expression of personality, but an escape from personality. But, of course, only those who have personality and emotions know what it means to want to escape from these things.

III
ὁ δὲ νοῦς ἴσως θειότερόν τι καὶ ἀπαθές ἐστιν.

This essay proposes to halt at the frontier of metaphysics or mysticism, and confine itself to such practical conclusions as can be applied by the responsible person interested in poetry. To divert interest from the poet to the poetry is a laudable aim: for it would conduce to a juster estimation of actual poetry, good and bad. There are many people who appreciate the expression of sincere emotion in verse, and there is a smaller number of people who can appreciate technical excellence. But very few know when there is an expression of *significant* emotion, emotion which has its life in the poem and not in the history of the poet. The emotion of art is impersonal. And the poet cannot reach this impersonality without surrendering himself wholly to the work to be done. And he is not likely to know what is to be done unless he lives in what is not merely the present, but the present moment of the past, unless he is conscious, not of what is dead, but of what is already living.

2
F. R. Leavis,
from 'Wordsworth'

***He had, if not a philosophy, a wisdom to communicate. The mistake encouraged by Coleridge is understandable, and we can see how *The Recluse* should have come to be projected — see, too, that the petering out of the enterprise in that long life does not prove essential failure (though it proves the enterprise misconceived). It may be said, fairly, that Wordsworth went on tinkering with *The Prelude* through his life instead of completing the great 'philosophic poem' because, as he had in the end tacitly to recognize, his resources weren't adequate to the ambition — he very obviously hadn't enough material. But it must also be said that in letting the ambition lapse he was equally recognizing its superfluity: his real business was achieved. His wisdom is sufficiently presented in the body of his living work.

What he had for presentment was a type and a standard of human normality, a way of life; his preoccupation with sanity and spontaneity working at a level and in a spirit that it seems appropriate to call religious. His philosophising (in the sense of the Hartleian studies and applications) had not the value he meant it to have; but it is an expression of his intense moral seriousness and a mode of the essential discipline of contemplation that gave consistency and stability to his experience. Wordsworth, we know, is the 'poet of Nature,' and the associations of the term 'Nature' here are unfortunate, suggesting as it does a vaguely pantheistic religion-substitute. If this is all Wordsworth has to offer, or if, as Mr Empson, expressing (apparently) very much this notion of him, states, he 'had no inspiration other than his use when a boy of the mountains as a totem or father-substitute,' then (the world being what it is) one may save one's irony for other things than his supersession, as the presiding genius of Lakeland, by Mr Hugh Walpole. But Wordsworth himself, in the famous passage that, 'taken from the conclusion of the first book of *The Recluse*', he offers 'as a kind of *Prospectus* of the design and scope of the whole Poem', proposes something decidedly different when he stresses 'the Mind of Man' as

> My haunt, and the main region of my song.

And Wordsworth here, as a matter of fact, is critically justified. Creative power in him, as in most great poets, was accompanied by a high degree of critical consciousness in the use of it. His critical writings give a good view of his creative preoccupations; and both his main preoccupation and his achievement are fairly intimated by this passage from the *Letter to John Wilson*:

You have given me praise for having reflected faithfully in my Poems the feelings of human nature. I would fain hope that I have done so. But a great Poet ought to do more than this; he ought, to a certain degree, to rectify men's feelings, to give them new compositions of feelings, to render their feelings more sane, pure, and permanent, in short, more consonant to nature, that is, to eternal nature, and the great moving spirit of things. He ought to travel before men occasionally as well as at their sides.

'Nature' in the phrase 'poet of Nature' can hardly be made to take on the force suggested here; that is why the description is so unacceptable. Wordsworth's preoccupation was with a distinctively human naturalness, with sanity and spiritual health, and his interest in mountains was subsidiary. His mode of preoccupation, it is true, was that of a mind intent always upon ultimate sanctions, and upon the living connexions between man and the extra-human universe; it was, that is, in the same sense as Lawrence's was, religious.

If the association of Wordsworth's name with Lawrence's seems incongruous, as it may reasonably do, the following passage, nevertheless, is very well known:

> For I must tread on shadowy ground, must sink
> Deep — and, aloft ascending, breathe in worlds
> To which the heaven of heavens is but a veil.
> All strength — all terror, single or in bands,
> That ever was put forth in personal form —
> Jehovah — with his thunder, and the choir
> Of shouting Angels, and the empyreal thrones —
> I pass them unalarmed. Not Chaos, not
> The darkest pit of lowest Erebus,
> Nor aught of blinder vacancy, scooped out
> By help of dreams — can breed such fear and awe
> As fall upon us often when we look
> Into our Minds, into the Mind of Man —
> My haunt, and the main region of my song.

This, perhaps, may not extravagantly be allowed to recall Lawrence's preoccupation with the deep levels, the springs, of life, the illimitable mystery that wells up into consciousness (cf. 'This is the innermost symbol of man: alone in the darkness of the cavern of himself, listening to the soundlessness of inflowing fate'). It is possible, at any rate, to rest too easily satisfied with the sense one commonly has of Wordsworth as of a tranquil surface reflecting the sky. How little a 'wise passiveness' (the purpose of which being in Lawrence's words — and there is point in applying words of Lawrence here — 'so that that which is perfectly ourselves can take place in us') is mere passiveness the lines quoted above from the *The Recluse* sufficiently convey.

But the main effect of bringing Wordsworth and Lawrence together must, of course, be contrast. And the contrast that is proposed by Lawrence's notoriety is a violent one. His preoccupation with sex is vulgarly both misconceived and overemphasized; nevertheless, no one would dispute that it is an essential characteristic. Wordsworth's poetry, on the other hand, is remarkable for exhibiting the very opposite of such a preoccupation — for that is perhaps the best way of putting the case, which may be very easily misrepresented or misapprehended. Shelley, for instance, in *Peter Bell the Third,* says:

> But from the first 'twas Peter's drift

> To be a kind of moral eunuch;
> He touched the hem of Nature's shift,
> Felt faint — and never dared uplift
> The closest, all-concealing tunic.

Peter Bell the Third contains some very good criticism of Wordsworth, but this stanza tells us more about Shelley — it is of him that that kind of 'feeling faint' is characteristic. Shelley, indeed, is unwittingly illustrating the difference between himself and Wordsworth that he intends to be commenting on.

It is the difference constituting so large an element in the contrast felt, at a glance, when passages of Wordsworth and Shelley are juxtaposed. There is an obvious contrast in movement; or rather, of Shelley's eager, breathless hurry — his verse always seems to lean forward, so that it must run in order not to fall — with Wordsworth's static contemplation ('I gazed and gazed . . .'). But the immediately relevant prompting is to description in terms of temperature: if Wordsworth, as Shelley says, is 'cold' (which is truer in suggestion than 'felt faint', and hardly congruous with it), Shelley himself seems fevered. And the effect of warmth derives very largely from the pervasiveness in Shelley's verse of caressing, cherishing, fondling, and, in general, sensuously tender suggestions, explicit and implicit, more and less subtle. To bring these under the general head of the 'erotic' may seem arbitrary, yet an examination of Shelley's work will show the relation between the 'gentle odours' of this first stanza of *The Question* and the subsequent image of embracing, so significantly inappropriate, to be representative:

> I dreamed that, as I wandered by the way,
>   Bare Winter suddenly was changed to Spring,
> And gentle odours led my steps astray,
>   Mixed with a sound of waters murmuring
> Along a shelving bank of turf, which lay
>   Under a copse, and hardly dared to fling
> Its green arms round the bosom of the stream,
> But kissed it and then fled, as thou mightest in dream.

At any rate, one of the most remarkable facts about Wordsworth's poetry is the virtual absence from it of this whole set of associations and suggestions, and it is this absence that Shelley, when he calls Wordsworth 'cold', is remarking upon; this is the fact, however perceived, that evokes that 'moral eunuch' — 'A solemn and unsexual man', says Shelley, later in the poem. The nature of the fact neither Shelley nor, in his psychoanalytics about Wordsworth's poetic decline, Mr Herbert Read recognises. The pathological efficacy that Mr Read ascribes to the episode of Annette Vallon is discredited by the peculiarity just noted: such an absence of the erotic element hardly suggests repression. It suggests that, whatever reason Wordsworth may have had for choosing not to deal in 'animated description of the pleasures of love', he had no need of subconscious relief and covert outlets.

There are, in fact, no signs of morbid repression anywhere in Wordsworth's poetry. And his various prose remarks about love plainly come from a mind that is completely free from timidity or uneasiness. The phrase just quoted may be found in the *Letter to John Wilson* (1800). Discussing there the limiting bents and pre-possessions that disqualify different readers, 'some,' says Wordsworth, 'cannot tolerate a poem with a ghost or any supernatural agency in it; others would shrink from an animated description of the pleasures of love, as from a thing carnal and libidinous; some cannot bear to see delicate and refined feelings ascribed to men in low conditions of society. . . .' To take an illustration from a later period of his life, in the *Letter to a Friend of Robert Burns* he pronounces: 'The poet, trusting to primary instincts, luxuriates among the felicities of love and wine; nor does he shrink from the company of the passion of love, though immoderate. . . .'

Sex, nevertheless, in spite of this pronouncement, is virtually absent from Wordsworth's poetry. The absence no doubt constitutes a limitation, a restriction of interest; but it constitutes at the same time an aspect of Wordsworth's importance. The point of this remark depends on another striking difference between Wordsworth and both Lawrence and Shelley; on the characteristic of his own poetry that Wordsworth indicates here: 'I have said that poetry is the spontaneous overflow of powerful feelings: it takes its origin from emotion recollected in tranquillity. . . .' Wordsworth here describes the withdrawn, contemplative collectedness of his poetry — 'Thus devoted, concentrated in purpose,' and the double description has been elucidated earlier in the *Preface*:

> Not that I always began to write with a distinct purpose formally conceived; but habits of meditation have, I trust, so prompted and regulated my feelings, that my descriptions of such objects as strongly excite those feelings, will be found to carry along with them a *purpose*. If this opinion be erroneous, I can have little right to the name of a Poet. For all good poetry is the spontaneous overflow of powerful feelings: and though this be true, Poems to which any value can be attached were never produced on any variety of subjects but by a man who, being possessed of more than usual organic sensibility, had also thought long and deeply. For our continued influxes of feeling are modified and directed by our thoughts, which are indeed the representatives of all our past feelings; and, as by contemplating the relation of these general representatives to each other, we discover what is really important to men, so . . .

Spontaneity, that is, as Wordsworth seeks it, involves no cult of the instinctive and primitive at the expense of the rationalized and civilized; it is the spontaneity supervening upon complex development, a spontaneity engaging an advanced and delicate organisation. He stands for a distinctly human naturalness; one, that is, consummating a discipline, moral and other. A poet who can bring home to us the possibility of such a naturalness should today be found important. In Wordsworth's poetry the possibility is offered us realised — realised in a mode central and compelling enough to enforce the bearing of poetry upon life, the significance of this poetry for actual living. The absence both of the specifically sexual in any recognizable form and of any sign of repression serves to emphasize this significance, the significance of this achieved naturalness, spontaneous, and yet the expression of an order and the product of an emotional and moral training.

No one should, after what has been said, find it necessary to impute to the critic at this point, or to suppose him to be applauding in Wordsworth, a puritanic warp. Wordsworth was, on the showing of his poetry and everything else, normally and robustly human. The selectiveness and the habit of decorum involved in 'recollection in tranquillity' were normal and, in a wholly laudatory sense of the word, conventional; that is, so endorsed by common usage as to be natural. The poetic process engaged an organisation that had, by his own account, been determined by an upbringing in a congenial social environment, with its wholesome simple pieties and the traditional sanity of its moral culture, which to him were nature. He may have been a 'Romantic,' but it would be misleading to think of him as an individualist. The implicit social and moral preoccupation of his self-communings in solitude, his recollecting in tranquillity, is fairly suggested by this, from the *Letter to John Wilson*:

> I return then to the question, please whom? or what? I answer, human nature as it has been and ever will be. But, where are we to find the best measure of this? I answer, from within; by stripping our own hearts naked, and by looking out of ourselves towards men who lead the simplest lives, and most according to nature; men who have never known false refinements, wayward and artificial desires, false criticisms, effeminate habits of thinking and feeling, or who having known these things have outgrown them. This latter class is the most to be depended upon, but it is very small in number.

This, of course, is in a sense commonplace about Wordsworth. Yet it would appear to be very easy, in a confusion of anecdotage and criticism, biography and poetry, to slip into giving the observation that he was self-centred a wholly uncritical and misleading effect.

> He had as much imagination
>   As a pint-pot; — he never could
> Fancy another situation
>   From which to dart his contemplation
>   Than that wherein he stood.

Shelley here again notes a striking difference between himself and Wordsworth. He could hardly be expected to note — what is not the commonplace it ought to be — that the self-projecting and ardently altruistic Shelley is, in the comparison, the narrowly limited and the egoist (which term, it may be added, applies with less injustice to Milton than to Wordsworth). Wordsworth, it is true, has no dramatic gift, and compared with Shakespeare's, the range of interests he exhibits is narrow. But he exhibits also in his poetry, as an essential characteristic, an impersonality unknown to Shelley.

This characteristic (consider the capacity and the habit it implies) is closely associated with the social-moral centrality insisted on above. The insistence will no doubt be challenged; it is at any rate time to take account of the aspect of Wordsworth stressed by Dr Bradley in his well-known essay (see *Oxford Lectures on Poetry*). Wordsworth is often spoken of as a 'mystic,' and the current valuation would appear to rest his greatness largely upon the 'visionary movements' and 'spots of time'. Wordsworth himself undoubtedly valued the 'visionary' element in his experience very highly, and it is important to determine what significance he attributes to it. In this passage from Book II of *The Prelude* he is as explicit as he ever is:

> and, at that time,
> Have felt whate'er there is of power in sound
> To breathe an elevated mood, by form
> Or image unprofaned; and I would stand,
> Beneath some rock, listening to sounds that are
> The ghostly language of the ancient earth,
> Or make their dim abode in distant winds.
> Thence did I drink the visionary power.
> I deem not profitless these fleeting moods
> Of shadowy exultation: not for this,
> That they are kindred to our purer mind

> And intellectual life; but that the soul,
> Remembering how she felt, but what she felt
> Remembering not, retains an obscure sense
> Of possible sublimity, to which,
> With growing faculties she doth aspire,
> With faculties still growing, feeling still
> That whatsoever point they gain, they still
> Have something to pursue.

It would be difficult to suggest anything more elusive than this possibility which the soul glimpses in 'visionary' moments and,

> Remembering how she felt, but what she felt
> Remembering not,

retains an 'obscure sense' of.[1] Perhaps it will be agreed that, though Wordsworth no doubt was right in feeling that he had something to pursue, the critic here is in a different case. If these 'moments' have any significance for the critic (whose business it is to define the significance of Wordsworth's poetry), it will be established, not by dwelling upon or in them, in the hope of exploring something that lies hidden in or behind their vagueness, but by holding firmly on to that sober verse in which they are presented.

How strong are the eighteenth-century affinities of this verse Mr Nichol Smith brings out when, in his introduction to *The Oxford Book of Eighteenth Century Verse,* he quotes a piece of Akenside and suggests rightly that it might have passed for Wordsworth. Wordsworth's roots were deep in the eighteenth century. To say this is to lay the stress again — where it ought to rest — on his essential sanity and normality.

But though he is so surely and centrally poised, the sureness had nothing of complacency about it. It rests consciously over unsounded depths and among mysteries, itself a mystery. This recognition has its value in the greater validity of the poise — in a kind of sanction resulting. So, too, Wordsworth's firm hold upon the world of common perception is the more notable in one who knows of 'fallings from us, vanishings, blank misgivings' ('when the light of sense goes out'), and is capable of recording such moments as when

> I forgot,
> That I had bodily eyes, and what I saw
> Appear'd like something in myself, a dream,
> A prospect in my mind.[2]

The point of stressing Wordsworth's normality and sanity in dealing with such passages as this comes out when we turn from it to, say, Shelley's *Mont Blanc* or compare *Mont Blanc* with Wordsworth's *Simplon Pass.*

If anyone demands a more positive valuation of the 'visionary moments' in Wordsworth (disputing, perhaps, the complete representatives of the 'shadowy' passage quoted above), it may be granted that they sometimes signify a revitalizing relaxation of purpose, of moral and intellectual effort, in a surrender to

> The gravitation and the filial bond
> Of nature, that connect him with the world.

For if Wordsworth was too inveterately human and moral for the 'Dark Gods' (how incongruous a phrase in connexion with him!) to be invoked here, he none the less drew strength from his sense of communion with the non-human universe.

'Dark Gods,' some readers will have commented, is indeed an incongruous phrase in connexion with Wordsworth. And it is now time to qualify the present account of him, as it stands now, by taking note of criticisms that it will have provoked from a quarter opposite to that saluted in the last paragraph. Does not, for instance, the formula, 'recollection in tranquillity,' apply to Wordsworth's poetry with a limiting effect that has as yet not been recognized? Is the tranquillity of this wisdom really at all close to any 'spontaneous overflow of powerful feelings'? Are the feelings, as recollected, so very powerful?

It has to be admitted that the present of this poetry is, for the most part, decidedly tranquil and that the emotion — anything in the nature of strong excitement or disturbance — seems to belong decidedly to the past. If, as might be said, the strength of the poetry is that it brings maturity and youth into relation, the weakness is that the experience from which it draws life is confined mainly to youth, and lies at a distance. What, an intelligent contemporary reader might have asked at the creative period, will happen as youth recedes? What did happen we know, in any case, and the fact of the decline may reasonably be held to have a bearing on the due estimate of Wordsworth's wisdom.

In the discussion above of the distinctive characteristics of his poetry 'poise' has received some emphasis; further inquiry is necessary in the direction that the term suggests. There is, relevant to this inquiry, a significant passage in Book I of *The Excursion*:

> From his native hills
> He wandered far; much did he see of men,
> Their manners, their enjoyments, and pursuits,
> Their passions and their feelings; chiefly those
> Essential and eternal in the heart,
> That, 'mid the simpler forms of rural life,
> Exist more simple in their elements,
> And speak a plainer language. In the woods,
> A lone Enthusiast, and among the fields,
> Itinerant in this labour, he had passed
> The better portion of his time; and there
> Spontaneously had his affections thriven
> Amid the bounties of the year, the peace
> And liberty of nature; there he kept
> In solitude and solitary thought
> His mind in a just equipoise of love.
> Serene it was, unclouded by the cares
> Of ordinary life; unvexed, unwarped
> By partial bondage. In his steady course,
> No piteous revolutions had he felt,
> No wild varieties of joy and grief
> Unoccupied by sorrow of its own,
> His heart lay open; and by nature tuned
> And constant disposition of his thoughts
> To sympathy with man, he was alive
> To all that was enjoyed where'er he went,
> And all that was endured; for in himself

> Happy, and quiet in his cheerfulness,
> He had no painful pressure from without
> That made him turn aside from wretchedness
> With coward fears. He could *afford* to suffer
> With those whom he saw suffer.

The Wanderer as described here would seem to be very much what the intelligent reader imagined above might have expected Wordsworth to become. Indeed, the description is, fairly obviously, very much in the nature of an idealised self-portrait. If Wordsworth, even when well embarked on *The Excursion*, was not quite this, this clearly is what he would have liked to be. That he should have wished to be this is significant. That he should have needed to wish it is the great difference between himself and the Wanderer. For Wordsworth's course had not been steady; he sought the Wanderer's 'equipoise' just because of the 'piteous revolutions' and the 'wild varieties of joy and grief' that he had so disturbingly known. The Wanderer could not have written Wordsworth's poetry; it emerges out of Wordsworth's urgent personal problem; it is the answer to the question: 'How, in a world that has shown itself to be like this, is it possible to go on living?'

Behind, then, the impersonality of Wordsworth's wisdom there is an immediately personal urgency. Impelling him back to childhood and youth — to their recovery in a present of tranquil seclusion — there are the emotional storms and disasters of the intervening period, and these are also implicitly remembered, if not 'recollected', in the tranquillity of his best poetry. In so far as his eyes may fairly be said to 'avert their ken from half of human fate,' extremely painful awareness of this half is his excuse. For if his problem was personal, it was not selfishly so, not merely self-regarding; and it is also a general one: if (and how shall they not?) the sensitive and imaginative freely let their 'hearts lie open' to the suffering of the world, how are they to retain any health or faith for living? Conflicting duties seem to be imposed (for it is no mere blind instinct of self-preservation that is in question). Wordsworth is not one of the few great tragic artists, but probably not many readers will care to censure him for weakness or cowardice. His heart was far from 'unoccupied by sorrow of its own,' and his sense of responsibility for human distress and his generously active sympathies had involved him in emotional disasters that threatened his hold on life. A disciplined limiting of contemplation to the endurable, and, consequently, a withdrawal to a reassuring environment, became terrible necessities for him.

It is significant that (whatever reason Wordsworth may have had for putting it there) the story of Margaret should also, following, as it does, close upon the description of the Wanderer, appear in Book 1 of *The Excursion*. It seems to me the finest thing that Wordsworth wrote, and it is certainly the most disturbingly poignant. The poignancy assures us with great force that the Wanderer, for all his familiarity with the Preface to the *Lyrical Ballads*, is not Wordsworth — not, at any rate, the poet; and it clearly bears a significant relation to the early date of composition: Wordsworth began *Margaret; or, The Ruined Cottage* — the substance of this part of Book 1 of *The Excursion* — in 1795 and finished it in 1797. At this period he was, we have reason to believe, striving towards his 'equipoise' with great difficulty; striving, because of his great need.

The difficulty does not merely appear in the poignancy of the poetry, which contrasts so with the surrounding verse; it gets its implicit comment in the by-play between Wordsworth and the Wanderer. At a painful point in the story 'the Wanderer paused' (l. 592):

> 'Why should we thus, with an untoward mind,
> And in the weakness of humanity,
> From natural wisdom turn our hearts away;
> To natural comfort shut our eyes and ears;
> And, feeding on disquiet, thus disturb
> The calm of nature with our restless thoughts?'

Wordsworth gladly acquiesced:

> That simple tale
> Passed from my mind like a forgotten sound.

But it refused to be dismissed; it rose insistently up through the distracting idle talk:

> In my own despite
> I thought of that poor Woman as one
> Whom I had known and loved.

No doubt the particular memory of Annette asserts itself here, but that recognition (or guess) makes it all the more important to give due weight to the corrective hint thrown out by the Wanderer a little later:

> ''Tis a common tale,
> An ordinary sorrow of man's life . . .'

— Wordsworth at this date cannot easily afford to suffer with those whom he sees suffer.

   That is very apparent in the way 'that Woman's sufferings' (which had 'seemed present') are, at the end of the story, distanced. Wordsworth, 'in the impotence of grief', turns to trace, around the Cottage, the 'secret spirit of humanity' that 'still survives'

> 'mid the calm oblivious tendencies
> Of nature, 'mid her plants, and weeds, and flowers
> And silent overgrowings . . .

The 'old Man,' with consummate poetic skill, endorses those tendencies:

> Why then should we read
> The forms of things with an unworthy eye?
> She sleeps in the calm earth, and peace is here.
> I well remember that those very plumes,
> Those weeds, and the high spear-grass on that wall,
> By mist and silent rain-drops silvered o'er,
> As once I passed, into my heart conveyed
> So still an image of tranquillity,
> So calm and still, and looked so beautiful
> Amid the uneasy thoughts which filled my mind,
> That what we feel of sorrow and despair
> From ruin and from change, and all the grief
> That passing shows of Being leave behind,
> Appeared an idle dream . . .

Michael was written in 1800 — three years later. Wordsworth here has no need to withdraw his mind from the theme to a present 'image of tranquillity'. The things of which he speaks never 'seem present' in this story; they are seen always as belonging, in their moving dignity, to the past. 'Recollection' holds them at such a distance that serenity, for all the pathos, never falters; and an idealising process, making subtle use of the mountain background, gives to 'human suffering' a reconciling grandeur. *Michael*, of course, is only one poem (and an exceptionally fine one), but the implied representative significance of this comparison with *Margaret* is justly implied. When in the characteristic good poetry of Wordsworth painful things are dealt with, we find them presented in modes, more and less subtle, that are fairly intimated by his own phrase (the context[3] of which is very relevant):

> Remov'd and to a distance that was fit.

In *Michael* Wordsworth is very much more like the Wanderer. What, the contemporary reader already invoked may be imagined as asking, will be the next phase in the development? What will happen as youth, where lie the emotional sources of his poetry — 'the hiding-place of my power' — and young manhood, which, in the way suggested, provides the creative pressure and incitement, recede further and further into the past, and the 'equipoise' becomes a settled habit? The answer appears plainly enough in the description of the Wanderer — in that complacent 'partial bondage' and in that curiously italicized '*afford*': one may come to afford too easily. The equipoise settles towards inertness:

> I long for a repose that ever is the same.

The *Ode to Duty* (1805) from which this line comes would, of course, be cited by many as going with the patriotic sonnets of these years to prove that Wordsworth, so far from subsiding in the way suggested, had acquired a new 'inspiration', a new source of energy. The *Ode*, no doubt, is an impressive performance; but it may be ventured that few to whom Wordsworth matters would grieve much if some very inferior bard were proved to have written it. As for the sonnets, their quality is a comment on the value to the poet of his new inspiration: the worst of them (look, for instance, at 'It is not to be thought of . . .') are lamentable claptrap, and the best, even if they are distinguished declamation, are hardly distinguished poetry. And the association in general of these patriotic moral habits with a settled addiction to Miltonizing has to be noted as (in the poet of the *Lyrical Ballads*) significant.

It is not that these new attitudes, and the process by which he settled into them, are not wholly respectable. There was never anything incompatible between the 'natural piety' that his poetry cherishes and celebrates and the immemorial pieties and loyalties centring in the village church (see his reference to the 'Village Steeple' in Book X of *The Prelude*, 1805–6; l. 268). The transition was easy. But when he made it his days ceased to be 'bound each to each' back to childhood. No longer could he say:

> The days gone by
> Come back upon me from the dawn almost
> Of life: the hiding-places of my power
> Seem open . . .

The Wordsworth who in the *Ode to Duty* spoke of the 'genial sense of youth' as something he happily surrendered had seen the hiding-places of his power close. The 'equipoise' had lost its vitality; the exquisitely fine and sensitive organisation of the poet no longer informed and controlled his pen. The energy of the new patriotic moral interests, far from bringing the poet new life, took the place of creative sensibility, and confirmed and ensured its loss.

In fact, the new power belongs, it might be said, not to the 'hiding-places' — it has no connexion with them — but to the public platform (a metaphor applying obviously to the patriotic development, with which, it should be noted, the religious is not accidentally associated): the public voice is a substitute for the inner voice, and engenders an insensitiveness to this — to its remembered (or, at least, to its recorded) burden and tone. For the sentiments and attitudes of the patriotic and Anglican Wordsworth do not come as the intimately and particularly realised experience of an unusually and finely conscious individual; they are external, general, and conventional; their quality is that of the medium they are proffered in, which is insensitively Miltonic, a medium not felt into from within as something at the nerve-tips, but handled from outside. This is to question, not their sincerity, but their value and interest; their representativeness is not of the important kind. The relation to poetry may be gathered from the process to which, at their dictation, Wordsworth subjected *The Prelude*: in the pursuit of formal orthodoxy he freely falsified and blunted the record of experience.

This process is forecast in the *Immortality Ode*, the essential purpose of which is to justify it. Criticism of Stanza VIII ('Mighty Prophet! Seer blest!') has been permissible, even correct, since Coleridge's time. But the empty grandiosity apparent there is merely the local manifestation of a general strain, a general factitiousness. The *Ode* (1803–6) belongs to the transition at its critical phase and contains decided elements of the living. But these do not lessen the dissatisfaction that one feels with the movement — the movement that makes the piece an ode in the Grand Style; for, as one reads, it is in terms of the movement that the strain, the falsity, first asserts itself. The manipulations by which the changes of mood are indicated have, by the end of the third stanza, produced an effect that, in protest, one describes as rhythmic vulgarity (for Dryden to do this kind of thing is quite another matter). The effort towards the formal ode is, clearly, the effort towards the formal attitude (Wordsworth himself being the public in view), and the strain revealed in technique has an obvious significance. What this is it hardly needs Stanza VI to proclaim:

> . . . even with something of a Mother's mind
> And no unworthy aim,
> The homely Nurse doth all she can
> To make her Foster-child, her Inmate Man,
> Forget the glories he hath known,
> And that imperial palace whence he came.

There is no suggestion of 'that imperial palace' in the relevant parts of *The Prelude*, and 'Foster-child' patently falsifies the feeling towards 'Earth' ('the gravitation and the filial bond') recorded there.

Notes

1. Cf. . . . in such strength
   > Of usurpation, when the light of sense
   > Goes out, but with a flash that has revealed
   > This invisible world, doth greatness make abode,
   > There harbours; whether we be young or old,
   > Our destiny, our being's heart and home,
   > Is with infinitude, and only there;
   > With hope it is, hope that can never die,
   > Effort, and expectation, and desire,
   > And something evermore about to be.
   >> *The Prelude*, Book VI, ll. 599–608 (1805–6).

2. *The Prelude*, Book II, ll. 342–52 (1805–6).

3. *The Prelude*, Book VIII, l. 305.

Q. D. Leavis,
from 'A Fresh Approach to Wuthering Heights'

I would first like to clear out of the way the *confusions* of the plot and note the different levels on which the novel operates at different times. It seems clear to me that Emily Brontë had some trouble in getting free of a false start — a start which suggests that we are going to have a regional version of the sub-plot of *Lear* (Shakespeare being generally the inspiration for those early nineteenth-century novelists who rejected the eighteenth-century idea of the novel). In fact, the Lear-world of violence, cruelty, unnatural crimes, family disruption and physical horrors remains the world of the household at Wuthering Heights, a characteristic due not to sadism or perversion in the novelist (some of the physical violence is quite unrealised) but to the Shakespearian intention. The troubles of the Earnshaws started when the father brought home the boy Heathcliff (of which he gives an unconvincing explanation and for whom he shows an unaccountable weakness) and forced him on the protesting family; Heathcliff 'the cuckoo' by intrigue soon ousts the legitimate son Hindley and, like Edmund, Gloucester's natural son in *Lear*, his malice brings about the ruin of two families (the Earnshaws and the Lintons, his rival getting the name Edgar by attraction from *Lear*). Clearly, Heathcliff was originally the illegitimate son and Catherine's half-brother, which would explain why, though so attached to him by early associations and natural sympathies, Catherine never really thinks of him as a possible lover either before or after marriage;[1] it also explains why all the children slept in one bed at the Heights till adolescence, we gather (we learn later from Catherine (Chapter XII) that being removed at puberty from this bed became a turning-point in her inner life, and this is only one of the remarkable insights which *Wuthering Heights* adds to the Romantic poets' exploration of childhood experience). The favourite Romantic theme of incest therefore must have been the impulsion behind the earliest conception of *Wuthering Heights*. Rejecting this story for a more mature intention, Emily Brontë was left with hopeless inconsistencies on her hands, for while Catherine's feelings about Heathcliff are never sexual (though she feels the bond of sympathy with a brother to be more important to her than her feelings for her young husband), Heathcliff's feelings for her are always those of a lover. As Heathcliff has been written out as a half-brother, Catherine's innocent refusal to see that there is anything in her relation to him incompatible with her position as a wife, becomes preposterous and the impropriety which she refuses to recognize is translated into social terms — Edgar thinks the kitchen the suitable place for Heathcliff's reception by Mrs Linton while she insists on the parlour. Another trace of the immature draft of the novel is the fairy-tale opening of the Earnshaw story, where the father, like the merchant in *Beauty and the Beast*, goes off to the city promising to bring his children back the presents each has commanded: but the fiddle was smashed and the whip lost so the only present he brings for them is the Beast himself, really a 'prince in disguise' (as Nelly tells the boy he should consider himself rightly); Catherine's tragedy then was that she forgot her prince and he was forced to remain the monster, destroying her; invoking this pattern brought in much more from the fairy-tale world of magic, folk-lore and ballads, the oral tradition of the folk, that the Brontë children learnt principally from their nurses and their servant Tabby.[2] This element surges up in Chapter XII, the important scene of Catherine's illness, where the dark superstitions about premonitions of death, about ghosts and primitive beliefs about the soul, come into play so significantly; and again in the excessive attention given to Heathcliff's goblin-characteristics and especially to the prolonged account of his uncanny obsession and death. That this last should have an air of being infected by Hoffmann too is not surprising in a contemporary of Poe's; Emily is likely to have read Hoffmann when studying German at the Brussels boarding-school and certainly read the ghastly supernatural stories by James Hogg and others in the magazines at home. It is a proof of her immaturity at the time of the original conception of *Wuthering Heights* that she should express real psychological insights in such inappropriate forms.

But this originally naïve and commonplace subject — the Romantics' image of childhood in conflict with society — becomes something that in this novel is neither superficial nor theoretic because the interests of the responsible novelist gave it, as we have seen above, a new insight, and also a specific and informed sociological content. The theme is here very firmly rooted in time and place and richly documented: we cannot forget that Gimmerton and the neighbourhood are so bleak that the oats are always green there three weeks later than anywhere else, and that old Joseph's Puritan preachings accompany his 'overlaying his large Bible with dirty bank-notes, the produce of the day's transactions' at market; and we have a thoroughly realistic account of the life indoors and outdoors at Wuthering Heights as well as at the gentleman's residence at the Grange. In fact, there would be some excuse for taking this, the pervasive and carefully maintained sociological theme which fleshes the skeleton, for the real novel. This novel, which could be extracted by cutting away the rest, was deliberately built, to advance a thesis, on the opposition between Wuthering Heights and Thrushcross Grange, two different cultures of which the latter inevitably supersedes the former. The point about dating this novel as ending in 1801 (instead of its being contemporary with the Brontës' own lives) — and much trouble was taken to keep the dates, time-scheme and externals such as legal data, accurate[3] — is to fix its happenings at a time when the old rough farming culture based on a naturally patriarchal family life, was to be challenged, tamed and routed by social and cultural changes that were to produce the Victorian class consciousness and 'unnatural' ideal of gentility.[4]

The inspiration for this structure, based on a conflict between, roughly speaking, a wholesome primitive and natural unit of a healthy society and its very opposite, felt to be an unwholesome refinement of the parasitic 'educated', comes from observation — in the Brontës' youth and county the old order visibly survived. But the clue to making such perceptions and sympathies into a novel was found, I suspect, in Scott, whose novels and poetry were immensely admired by Charlotte and Emily. His own sympathies were with the wild rough Border-farmers, not only because they represented a romantic past of balladry. He felt that civilisation introduced there entailed losses more than gains, and a novel where — before, with characteristic lack of staying power, he divagated from a serious theme into tushery — he made some effort to express this, *The Black Dwarf*, has long been known as the source for surnames used in *Wuthering Heights*. Scott's Earnscliffe (= Eaglescliff) and Ellieslaw suggested Heathcliff and Earnshaw no doubt, but more important is their suggesting, it seems to me, that Emily Brontë found part of her theme in that novel's contrast between a weak, corrupt, refined upper-class, and the old-style Border farmers' 'natural' or socially primitive way of life in which feuds and violence were a recognised part of the code (though trans-acted for the most part strictly according to rule and tradition and quite compatible with good-humour and a generous humanity); there, the rich and great live in their castles, are treacherous, and come to grief, the rough Borderers, eking out sub-sistence farming by hunting, suffer drastic ups and downs with hardihood and survive; the setting is on the moors and hills, and an essential element in establishing the primitive social condition of the Borderers is the superstition and folk-lore believed in by them all. Now the Yorkshire moors with the hardy yeomen farmers of pre-Victorian times who had lived thereabouts and whose histories Tabby used to tell the Brontë children[5] in her broad dialect, must have seemed to them not essentially different from Scott's Border farmers. Emily and Charlotte were genuinely attached to their moorland country but Scott's example was what made it usable for them as literature and gave it rich associations, so it is natural that in her first attempt at a novel Emily should draw on even a poor fiction like *The Black Dwarf* to give meaning and purpose to her feelings about what was happening or had happened recently to the world she lived in. It is proof of her development out of her daydream world of the Gondals that she was thus interested in the real world and roused to the need to inquire into the true nature of the change, perhaps as a way to alert her own (Early Victorian) generation to what this was. From being a self-indulgent storytelling, *Wuthering Heights* thus became a responsible piece of work, and the writer thought herself into the positions, outlooks, sufferings and tragedies of the actors in these typical events as an *artist.****

Now, not only does Catherine Earnshaw behave similarly and often identically [to Kate, the heroine of Roché's *Jules et Jim*], she has even the same disgust for her husband's bookishness, which she identifies as the source of his weakness or inadequacy. It is true the Lintons seem to shrink from healthy outdoor life and prefer to get their ideas about life from literature (in Isabella's case leading to her disastrous infatuation with Heathcliff conceived as a sensitive, noble Byronic soul — Catherine knows better); and that Wordsworth's mistrust of books and meddling intellect apparently gives respectable support to Catherine's attitude. But it is also apparent that Catherine feels her husband's intellectual tastes to be rivals — when intolerably provoked by her he retires to his studies, and it is this she thinks of when, on what she feels to be her death-bed, she envisages him with great bitterness as ' "offering prayers of thanks to God for restoring peace to his house, and going back to his *books*!" '. The Emily Brontë who kneaded the dough with a German book propped up before her cannot be supposed to endorse Catherine's hostility to learning; and though we must beware of identifying the novelist's attitude to Catherine with Nelly's, yet in general she endorses Nelly's shrewd analysis of Catherine's behaviour. Unlike Nelly however the novelist though concerned to diagnose does not blame Catherine, because she understands, as Nelly cannot, why a Catherine can hardly help behaving as she does. But she is as far as possible from admiring Catherine; being a woman, Emily Brontë has none of Roché's fascinated respect for his Kate as a force of nature. The woman novelist does not believe that all women share these characteristics more or less and are unfeminine without them, in fact, she takes pains to show that these characteristics are incompatible with what is required of a wife and mother. On the other hand, Roché's strength lies in being able to evoke a civilisation made by the efforts of men which is indestructible by Woman. The friendship between the two men who have been students together and have in common a devotion to literature and the arts, though they are of different nationalities, a friendship which, to make the point clear, is shown as surviving even their fighting on opposite sides in the first World War as well their being in love with the same woman — this is the point in which *Jules et Jim* is more subtle than *Wuthering Heights*, where the ill-will between Edgar and Heathcliff is dramatically commonplace. (Of course their hostility was necessary also in the sociological context of the novel where Edgar's assurance of class superiority and the unfeeling social contempt Heathcliff is exposed to in adolescence condition Heathcliff to become the Frankenstein monster we are introduced to by Mr Lockwood at the opening of the novel. Even so, Emily Brontë struggles to suggest some deeper truths than the situation seems to hold: for instance, Heathcliff's protestation to Nelly that he is superior to mere rivalry for Catherine's love — ' "had he been in my place and I in his, though I hated him with a hatred that turned my life to gall, I never would have raised a hand against him. I never would have banished him from her society as long as she desired his. . . . I would have died by inches before I touched a single hair of his head!" ')

Over and above their hostility, Catherine deliberately foments trouble between them as part of her need for violence and domination; and the scene where she locks the three of them in and then throws the key on the fire, putting her delicate (though by no means cowardly) husband at the mercy of the brutal Heathcliff, and humiliating him by her insults, disloyalty and indifference to what happens to him, is extremely painful reading. She has no moral sensibility to comprehend that he is stricken not by cowardice but by her attitude to him. In these ways she behaves quite as insufferably as Kate but unlike her she is offset in the context of the novel by many other and very different feminine natures and dispositions, this point being driven home in the second half where the younger Catherine, with similar drives and temptations to her mother's, is able to profit by experience and get a moral education from her sufferings because she is also her father's daughter. It is the men who strike one as making a consistently poor showing in *Wuthering Heights* — not only Heathcliff and his odious son Linton but the generally callous Joseph, the misguided older Earnshaw, his drunken son Hindley, the crude youth Hareton, the conceited narrator Lockwood, and even Edgar Linton who is imprisoned in class and for all his civilised virtues ineffective. But in spite of these inevitable differences in prejudice by a male and a female novelist, there is a wide agreement in Roché's and Emily Brontë's investigations into 'what people call love'. Both isolate the striking irrationality that impels the heroine of each to destroy her own possibility of happiness, both note that the only kind of love a woman like Catherine or Kate can feel is death-centred. A surprising insight of Emily Brontë's is that apportioning moral blame is impossible.***

This episode (Chap. VIII, that is) not only leads inevitably to Catherine's self-destruction; it is recalled by contrast when we read the scene in Chapter XI where Nelly goes up to the Heights to see how her foster-child Hareton is getting on and to warn his father, her old playmate Hindley, against Heathcliff. Full of tender reminiscences of their joint childhood, she comes on the child Hareton, whom she at first takes for his father a generation ago, to find, to her horror and ours, that he has forgotten his foster-mother completely and, schooled by Heathcliff, greets her with curses and stones. With the most admirable restraint she suppresses her natural reactions, even grief, to try to do something for the child's welfare. Recalling Catherine's behaviour ('wicked aunt Cathy') to the same child, we realise that Catherine's kind of femininity is neither exhaustive of the possibilities of Woman nor really typical. And Nelly's adult and selflessly maternal behaviour prepares us for her foster-child's, the younger Catherine's, evolution away from the possibilities of repeating her mother's disaster, though Cathy is shown to have similar impulses and in some ways nearly as unfortunate an upbringing (she is everyone's idol at the Grange). Cathy achieves the self-knowledge and wisdom that bring her to a successful coming of age as a woman with which the novels ends. Roché's novel and Truffaud's film with equal and unnecessary pessimism show Kate's daughter committed in childhood to an instinctive repetition of the mother's attitudes. Their message seems to be *'Così fan tutte'*.

It is quite otherwise in *Wuthering Heights,* where a careful integrity of observation and a finer, more informed insight, are apparent. We may note the care taken to make conventional moral judgments impossible (its original readers would have been only too inclined to make them) by showing always the psychological reasons for certain kinds of behaviour, so that there is nothing mysterious or incredible about Catherine or even, in essentials, about Heathcliff. And it is important to realise that the principal events are made to take place in the early adolescence of all the main actors, when they are so young as to be at the mercy of their impulses. Also (as we should have realized even if the actors and actions were not transmitted to us through the critical medium of Mr Lockwood who is so conscious of being stuck in a half-savage country) the time is the eighteenth century and the place remote and northern. The unconscious brutality of the family doctor who, telling Hindley that his wife is dying, adds: 'It can't be helped. And besides, you should have known better than to choose such a rush of a lass!' is an early index of the northern plain speaking that is proud of putting sense in place of feeling.[6] (Zillah fills this post in the second half of the novel.) But after the shock this gives us, we realise it is truth and an important truth in the world of the Heights. A farmer's wife, especially in such testing conditions, needed to be robust to do what was required and provide healthy children. By choosing a delicate lass Hindley was flouting traditional wisdom (as the doctor points out) — fatally. He had gone to college (we now see why he was made to) and acquired an unsuitable taste in women, for which he must now pay; Nature is ruthless too. And in such ways the sociological element or setting of the book is indispensable, in reinforcing these radical truths on which life has to be built.***

And these elements which give depth to the novel are enclosed in a sociological whole which serves as the framework of a parable or moral fable of extended interest. Think of what the household at the Heights comprised, with old Joseph, who refuses his portion of Christmas fare on principle and deplores even the hymns Nelly sings because they sound like 'songs', raising the voice of the traditional Puritanism (though wise as well as harsh); while Nelly offsets him with her equally traditional pagan enjoyment of life, of folk-song and ballad as well as of rearing babies and sympathising with love-affairs. ' "This is 'Faery Annie's Wedding' — a bonny tune — it goes to a dance" ' is Nelly's mischievous reply to Joseph's groans that ' "Aw cannut oppen t'Blessed Book, bud yah set up them glories tuh Sattan." ' Yet they are equally indispensable, Joseph as devoted farmer and Nelly as nurse and housemother. And in another respect Joseph is indispensable too: one of his functions is to offer his own, a rigid religious, interpretation of all events as they happen, so that he sees Heathcliff's life, for example, as a drama of the wicked man whose soul the Devil in due course inevitably collects — for which judgment he falls on his knees beside the corpse to thank God. This is not of course the novelist's view, but it registers her understanding of an important moral vein in the English tradition, one which has fed both folk and 'literary' literature. The novelist is careful to show that Isabella's and the two Catherines' contemptuous attitudes to Joseph are not justified, though their dislike of him is understandable. His piety, for instance, is not hypocrisy as they assume, but a true natural piety expressed in the only idiom he commands other than his everyday dialect — it is the traditional language of Puritanism, of course, as when he calls food 't'precious gifts uh God' — and his sour disapproval of both Isabella and Cathy on the grounds that they are idle inmates where everyone else works, is as reasonable and sound as his anger at Catherine's effect on young Heathcliff which has caused the lad to carelessly leave the gate open so that the pony gets into the cornfield. His duty to the farm, to his master, and to God's laws, are not separate duties in his mind but form together a rule of life. In fact, a Shakespearean character.[7] The whole social pattern provided for us by the farm-house at the Heights, with its house-place shared by master and man, is created for us as something to be respected, and regretted when it is superseded, whatever its limitations.***

I would make a plea, then, for criticism of *Wuthering Heights* to turn its attention to the human core of the novel, to recognize its truly human centrality. How can we fail to see that the novel is based on an interest in, concern for, and knowledge of, real life? We cannot do it justice, establish what the experience of reading it really is, by making analyses of its lock and window imagery, or by explaining it as being concerned with children of calm and children of storm, or by putting forward such bright ideas as that '*Wuthering Heights* might be viewed at long range as a variant of the demon-lover motif' (*The Gates of Horn*, H. Levin) or that 'Nelly Dean is Evil' — these are the products of an age which conceives literary criticism as either a game or an industry, not as a humane study. To learn anything of this novel's true nature we must put it into the category of novels it belongs to — I have specified *Women in Love* and *Jules et Jim* and might add *Anna Karenina* and *Great Expectations* — and recognise its relation to the social and literary history of its own time. The human truths *Wuthering Heights* is intended to establish are, it is necessary to admit, obscured in places and to varying degrees by discordant trimmings or leftovers from earlier writings or stages of its conception; for these, stylistic and other evidence exists in the text. Nor could we expect such complexity and such technical skill to have been achieved in a first novel otherwise; it is necessary to distinguish what is genuine complexity from what is merely confusion. That there is the complexity of accomplished art we must feel in the ending, ambiguous, impersonal, disquieting but final. And when we compare the genius devoted to creating Nelly Dean, Joseph, Zillah, Frances, Lockwood, the two Catherines, and to setting them in significant action, with the very perfunctory attention given to Heathcliff and Hareton as wholes (attention directed only when these two are wheeled out to perform necessary parts at certain points in the exposition of the theme to which — like Isabella and Edgar Linton — they are subsidiary) then we can surely not misinterpret the intention and the nature of the achievement of *Wuthering Heights*.

Notes:

1. The speech (Chap. IX) in which Catherine explains to Nelly why she couldn't marry Heathcliff — on social grounds — belongs to the sociological *Wuthering Heights*. But even then she intends, she declares, to keep up her old (sisterly) relations with him, to help him get on in the world — ' to *rise*' as she significantly puts it in purely social terms.
2. Tabby had, Mrs Gaskell reports, 'known the "bottom" or valley in those primitive days when the faeries frequented the margin of the "beck" on moonlight nights, and had known folk who had seen them. But that was when there were no mills in the valleys, and when all the woodspinning was done by hand in the farm-houses round. "It wur the factories as had driven 'em away", she said.'
3. v.C.P. Sanger's *The Structure of 'Wuthering Heights'* (a Hogarth Press pamphlet).
4. Other pre-Victorian novelists noted and resented the effects on children too. In the original preface to her children's classic *Holiday House* (1839), Catherine Sinclair wrote: 'In these pages the author has endeavoured to paint that species of noisy, frolicsome, mischievous children, now almost extinct, wishing to preserve a sort of fabulous remembrance of days long past, when young people were like wild horses on the prairies, rather than like well-broken hacks on the road.'
5. Mrs Gaskell says she told 'of bygone days of the countryside; old ways of living, former inhabitants, decayed gentry who had melted away, and whose places knew them no more; family tragedies, and dark superstitious dooms; and in telling these things, without the least consciousness that there might ever be anything requiring to be softened down, would give at full length the bare and simple details.' This is evidence of external, real life, sources for *Wuthering Heights* which cannot be dismissed.
6. The economy and impersonality with which this point is made, and the complexity of apprehension — so that what seems gratuitously wounding is seen to be also natural (i.e. necessary) in the context of such a way of life — contrasts, greatly to Emily's advantage, with Charlotte's raw reaction to the same Yorkshire plain-speaking, as seen in *Shirley*. There Emily's sister presents a whole family (drawn from life), given the typical name of 'the Yorkes', to show the hurtful effect of this much-vaunted 'out-spokenness'; Charlotte has the father and mother 'told off' by both heroines, making an obtrusively personal episode which is not integral to the novel. Charlotte, that is, could see only the disagreeable effects of this northern characteristic, whereas Emily understood and made clear the reasons why it came about and prevailed, since, as she shows, it made for survival originally, though of course unnecessary to the Linton class now.
7. It is characteristic of *Wuthering Heights* that though Emily Brontë sees how old Joseph affects her Catherines and Isabellas, she makes it clear that she is perfectly aware that there are other points of view from which he makes a better showing — he has dignity, utility and even higher virtues, and an unprejudiced examination of all he says and does himself (ignoring what others say of him) proves this. But concentration on the 'metaphysical' account of *Wuthering Heights* has lost sight of the realistic novel it really is. And when I say 'Shakespearean' I mean also that Joseph is an indication of his creator's indebtedness to Shakespeare for novelistic method and technique that she could have learnt nowhere else.

Section Two

VERSIONS OF FORMALISM

1. Cleanth Brooks, 'Irony as a Principle of Structure' (1951)
2. Victor Shklovsky, from 'Art as Technique' (1917)
3. Boris Tomashevsky, from 'Thematics' (1925)

Points of information

1. Cleanth Brooks's essay, originally published in 1949, is reprinted in this version from *Literary Opinion in America*, ed., Morton D. Zabel. The extracts from the essays by Shklovsky and Tomashevsky are translated by Lee T. Lemon and Marion J. Reis and reprinted from their *Russian Formalist Criticism: Four Essays*.

2. About five pages from the beginning of Shklovsky's essay have been omitted. They deal mainly with the immediate Russian context.

3. Only about a tenth of Tomashevsky's 'Thematics' is printed here. Lemon and Reis translate about half of it.

This section illustrates two contrasting conceptions of the functions and properties of literary language: that developed by the American 'New Critics' of the 1940s and 1950s, and certain ideas explored by Russian literary theorists in the 1910s and 1920s. This group is usually known as the 'Russian Formalists'. In turning their attention to questions of literary language both groups of critics address basic theoretical questions: how do we define literary as opposed to other language uses? By what criteria do we assess success or quality in literary works? How do we describe the structure of whole literary works?

Both of these schools have been called 'formalist' — usually by opponents —

31

and it might be as well to begin by considering what we mean by this. In general critical usage, form is distinguished from content. In fact though, such distinctions are difficult to maintain in any absolute way, for it is as hard to imagine a formless content as it is to imagine contentless form. Nevertheless the two poles of the argument have, in various ways, always caused controversy, and certain persistent methodological problems follow from allowing the distinction. Should critics primarily attend to the significant human or social content of a work, or to its powers of organisation and arrangement which, in a very old line of critical thinking, are held to be the sources of its beauty, pleasure and success? Furthermore, is an adequate account of a work to be had on the basis of its internal properties only, or is it necessary to take into account the extrinsic contexts of its production (publishing, social, biographical or other), or indeed of its reception by readers who may be centuries from its original writing? Other, related questions follow from this. Are the properties of a work stable and timeless in the sense of being able to be understood in the same way and with equal facility across time? To what extent can it be claimed that literary analyses are objective, or are they coloured by the choices and preferences of the critic? Such questions are persistent and will run through all subsequent sections.

Within the maze of questions such as these both American New Criticism and Russian Formalism claimed to be objective, even scientific. Both groups were eager to boost criticism's professional standing and methodological rigour. Both centred attention on the literary language of texts and tried to describe their internal properties and relations. It was in the precise definition of literary language, they believed, that the key to objectivity lay. Nevertheless, their accounts are radically at odds in spirit and conceptual procedure.

Chronologically, Russian Formalism preceded the New Criticism, though the American movement outlasted the Russian and was dominant in American critical thinking for several decades. The New Criticism is dealt with first because of the continuities of approach and outlook between it and those writers represented in Section 1. The Russian Formalists, in turn, offer conceptual departures from traditional Anglo-American thinking and look forward to some recent developments.

The collective term New Criticism originally referred to the work of a group of critics and poets based in the American South. John Crowe Ransom (whose book of 1941 *The New Criticism* named the movement), Robert Penn Warren, Allen Tate and Cleanth Brooks were the principal figures. Many of the original New Critics were Christians and held firm political convictions of a conservative kind associated with the 'organic' agrarian communities of the South. There are therefore some lines of connection between them and, for instance, T. S. Eliot's conservative Christianity and the Leavises' account of the importance of rural organicism in British history.

The New Critical movement, however, included other important critics, like R. P. Blackmur, W. K. Wimsatt and the European emigré René Wellek, who are not so easily classified but who shared the Southerners' literary commitments. These are perhaps most thoroughly codified in Wellek and Austin Warren's influential *Theory of Literature* (1949). The New Critics shared several critical beliefs with the writers introduced in Section 1. They too believed in the objective method of close reading or 'practical criticism' and were quick to rule certain approaches out of court. Wimsatt and Monroe Beardsley's two celebrated essays 'The Intentional Fallacy' and 'The Affective Fallacy' (1946) were centrally important statements.

'The Intentional Fallacy' essay argues that the cause of a poem (the New Critics almost always speak of poetry, primarily lyric poetry), that is the poet's intentions, is not in itself a standard for the assessment of a poem's meanings. Authors often have conflicting intentions; they revise their work; and decisive documentation is not in most cases available. Equally, concentration on reader's responses (the 'Affective Fallacy') opens up a distracting critical relativism which is incapable of responding reliably to the words on the page or establishing firm standards for judgement or appreciation.

Wimsatt and Beardsley urge a concentration on 'the poem itself', and the assumption of an internal or 'dramatic' speaker who, to all intents and purposes is to be separated from the historical individual the writer (compare Eliot's 'extinction of personality'). Poetry in this sense constitutes an autonomous realm and any individual poem is a free-standing and self-sustaining entity. Though the content of a poem enacts a human situation, this situation is taken from its original context and writers and readers are able to commune across time unproblematically. The New Critics were fond of metaphors for literature drawn from the visual or plastic arts which encouraged integrative conceptions of literary works. Poems are like urns (Brooks), icons (Wimsatt), pieces of architecture (Ransom and Brooks), or abstract paintings (Ransom). In other words they are like things which, at first sight, do not seem to change over time. Wimsatt and Beardsley close their essay on 'The Affective Fallacy' with a ringing echo of Keats's poem 'Ode on a Grecian Urn': 'in short, though cultures have changed and will change, poems remain and explain'. This poem is itself revealingly and symptomatically analysed in Cleanth Brooks's influential *The Well Wrought Urn* (1947).

Wimsatt and Beardsley's essays are closely-argued accounts of several founding New Critical principles which can be seen to be at work also in the essay here by Cleanth Brooks (b. 1906). If the poem is to be considered as in some senses historically autonomous, it is also at the same time uniquely coherent and integrated. It is, for interpretive purposes, self sufficient and hence particularly amenable to the techniques of analysis developed by practical criticism. Following Eliot and Richards, the New Critics emphasised tight literary organisation and the 'associated sensibility' (Eliot's concept of 'dissociation of sensibility', from his important essay of 1921 'The Metaphysical Poets', was widely adopted by many critics). Poems enacted the true complexities of emotional life, but at the same time offered suitably satisfying integrations of experience. They are formed by 'patterns of resolved stresses' (Brooks). In the essay printed here these conceptions are related to the use of irony. In the movement as a whole the rich texture of poetic language, which cannot be restated or paraphrased, is further held to act as a forceful counterweight to the 'abstract' and reductionist languages of science and pure 'statement'. The New Criticism was thus a thoroughly committed humanism concerned, as were the Leavises, to defend the impressive qualities of finely-rendered human situations which were available in their highest forms through the special qualities of excellent literary uses of language. It was in this sense that they defined the special properties of that language.

Russian Formalist conceptions of literary language contrast markedly with these ideas. They too emphasised the need for rigorously objective descriptions of language performances and structures in literary texts to place criticism on an 'objective' footing. However, rather than elaborating models of coherence and integration, the Formalist critics stressed the dynamic and disruptive character of literary language. This is strikingly brought out in the concept of 'defamiliarisation' ('ostrananie' in Russian) developed here in the essay by Victor Shklovsky (b. 1893). In Formalist criticism readers are to be shaken out of their complacent, familiar modes of perception and confronted with fresh ways of seeing by the defamiliarising strategies of literary works.

In one sense this was also the aim of the New Criticism which in some versions saw successful poems as reinvigorating responses to complex emotional and cognitive situations as against the 'easy habituations' (Brooks) of the modern mass media. But whereas the American critics saw this process as one conducted between superior and inferior cultural levels, the Russian Formalists saw it as a characteristic, and in effect value-free, dynamic of all modes of writing. They noted the ways 'high' literary writers responded to and adopted 'low' forms, and that it was extremely difficult to make absolute hierarchical distinctions between the two; for very often 'high' and 'low' forms coexist in the same works. The use made of mystery stories and 'who-dun-its' by nineteenth-century novelists like Dickens would be an example from English writing, as would Emily Brontë's use of gothic and popular romance conventions in *Wuthering Heights*.

The Formalists were excited by the collisions of different genres and styles and held that it was in the friction between modes of writing that exciting literary possibilities were realised. The process worked both ways: 'high' writing could defamiliarise 'low', but equally 'low' could reinvigorate the postures and stale conventions of 'high'. For instance, at the end of the eighteenth century, Wordsworth challenged prevailing conceptions of correct poetic style in his and Coleridge's *Lyrical Ballads*. He introduced popular ballad forms into his work and the 'language of conversation of the middle and lower classes of society' ('Advertisement'). His 'Advertisement' and 'Preface' to the *Ballads* reveal the self-conscious decision he took in doing so, as well as the anxiety he felt about it. In Russia, at the time of the 1917 Revolution when the Formalists were at work, such ideas reflected aspects of contemporary artistic practice in both literary and visual art. There are links between the Formalists and Russian Futurism.

Russian Formalist conceptions of literary power and development, then, are essentially based on conflict models, and they produced ideas on the evolution of literary history which can be sharply contrasted with the tradition-based models of the writers represented in Section 1. Literary history, in their view, moves forward in zig-zags with complex rejections and adaptations. Yury Tynyanov, an early Formalist critic, wrote in 1921 that there 'is no continuing direct line; there is rather a departure, a pushing away from the known point — a struggle . . . Any literary succession is first of all a struggle, a destruction of old values and a reconstruction of old elements'. These ideas anticipate, and in some senses have provoked, significant later developments in the West with the introduction of more complex awarenesses of the varieties of writing which might be considered available for literary kinds of analysis. In addition recent work has reconsidered questions of literary history and the formation of 'traditions' (see the second piece by Raymond Williams in Section 6 and the introduction to Section 7). Nevertheless it should be stressed that the focus of Formalist analysis remains upon the literary, and the relationship between form and content is a difficult area for Formalist theory.

The Russian Formalists met criticism in their own time. The label 'formalist' was given to imply limitation. For more socially-engaged writers, like Trotsky in *Literature and Revolution* (1924), the Formalists were distracted from encountering the content of works and hence the specific urgencies of the history being made around them. And it is certainly true that the problem of 'literariness' and the self-governing rules of the literary system and its developments preoccupied them. They spotlighted the 'device' — as in Shklovsky's essay here — as the means by which literary form was 'roughened' and the processes of literary structures were revealed. They valued works which exposed their 'devices' most thoroughly and which tend to look eccentric to tradition-based models of literary history and evaluation. For example Shklovsky considered Laurence Sterne's remarkable parodic novel *Tristram Shandy* (1759–67) to be the 'most typical novel in world literature', and formalist techniques would have abundant material to work with in an analysis of *Wuthering Heights* or *The Waste Land*.

The devices of literature can be found in the very texture of the language used (striking diction, the deployment of rhythms, unusual combinations of elements or rhetorical figures), or they could be discovered in broader structural arrangements, particularly in narrative for which Boris Tomashevsky (1890–1957) offers a descriptive vocabulary in his arrestingly original essay here. The Formalists were not primarily interested in the referential capacities of literary language. Shklovsky unilaterally proclaims that art is '*a way of experiencing the artfulness of an object; the object is not important.*' However is describing the function of a device as essentially cognitive — it defamiliarises habitual perception — he seems to read-mit some aspects of content. The examples he gives only reinforce the difficulty, and the problem is a persistent one for all formalist–inclined criticism.

The bulk of Russian Formalist criticism was produced by two groups, the Moscow Linguistic Circle (founded 1915) and the 1916 St Petersburg 'Society for the Study of Poetic Language' (OPOJAZ). It flourished during the early years of the Revolution. In the late 1920s it was forced into abrupt retreat as Stalinism took its grip on Russian culture and some of its most able theorists moved to Prague. Thereafter the influence of Formalism can be seen in literary structuralism (Section 3), and, in an alternative direction, in the more socially engaged work of Mikhail Bakhtin which is not represented here.

Further Reading:

The writings of whole movements are extensive, particularly of one so durable as the New Criticism, but works by principal New Critics include:

Cleanth Brooks, *The Well Wrought Urn* (1947) and *Modern Poetry and the Tradition* (1948). The latter contains a reading of *The Waste Land*. Brooks has also published, with W. K. Wimsatt, a four-volume *Literary Criticism: A Short History* (1957). Volume 4 covers the modern period and includes essays on Eliot and Richards. John Crowe Ransom's two principal books are *The World's Body* (1938) and *The New Criticism* (1941). W. K. Wimsatt's *The Verbal Icon* (1954) includes the essays on the intentional and affective fallacies, and these are also reprinted in David Lodge, ed., *Twentieth-Century Literary Criticism*. René Wellek and Austin Warren's *Theory of Literature* (1949) is central. Wellek's *Concepts of Criticism* (1963) contains a useful essay on 'Concepts of Form and Structure in Twentieth-Century Criticism'.

There are two anthologies of Russian Formalist criticism translated into English: *Russian Formalist Criticism: Four Essays* , ed. L. T. Lemon and M. J. Reis (1965), and *Readings in Russian Poetics: Formalist and Structuralist Views*, ed. L. Matejka and K. Pomorska (1971).

David Robey's essay on the New Criticism in Jefferson and Robey, eds., *Modern Literary Theory* (1986), is a good introductory account, but there are many commentaries and responses. (This book also contains a useful essay on Russian Formalism.) John Fekete, *The Critical Twilight* (1977) examines the social bearings and contexts of the New Critical movement. Murray Kreiger, *The New Apologists for Poetry* (1956) is one contemporary response. Lionel Trilling's essay 'The Meaning of a Literary Idea', in his *The Liberal Imagination* (1951), interestingly engages with some New Critical ideas, as does E. D. Hirsch's *Validity in Interpretation* (see Section 5). For specific consideration of Cleanth Brooks see Lewis P. Simpson, ed., *The Possibilities of Order: Cleanth Brooks and his Work* (1976). Also of interest are the accounts given from present perspectives by Catherine Belsey, *Critical Practice* (1980), ch. 1, and Frank Lentricchia, *After the New Criticism* (1980). Finally, René Wellek has written a retrospective defence, 'The New Criticism: Pro and Contra', which is in his *The Attack on Literature and Other Essays* (1982). This collection also includes an essay on Russian Formalism with which Wellek had early connections.

Perhaps the best short introduction to Russian Formalism is Boris Eichenbaum's 1926 review essay 'The Theory of the "Formal Method"'. Eichenbaum was a leading member of the OPOJAZ group. The essay is reprinted in both the anthologies noted above. The most detailed study of the movement is Victor Erlich, *Russian Formalism: History-Doctrine* (1965). There is a useful short essay by Tzvetan Todorov, 'Some Approaches to Russian Formalism' in *Russian Formalism: A Collection of Articles and Texts in Translation,* ed. S. Bann and J. E. Bowlt (1973). Several lively recent studies introduce Russian Formalist ideas in connection with other bodies of thought: Fredric Jameson, *The Prison-House of Language* (1972), Terence Hawkes, *Structuralism and Semiotics* (1977) and Tony Bennett, *Formalism and Marxism* (1979). Bennett's book gives some information on the Bakhtin school. E. M. Thompson, *Russian Formalism and Anglo-American New Criticism* (1971) deals with the relationships between the two.

1

Cleanth Brooks,
'Irony as a Principle of Structure'

One can sum up modern poetic technique by calling it the rediscovery of metaphor and the full commitment to metaphor. The poet can legitimately step out into the universal only by first going through the narrow door of the particular. The poet does not select an abstract theme and then embellish it with concrete details. On the contrary, he must establish the details, must abide by the details, and through his realization of the details attain to whatever general meaning he can attain. The meaning must issue from the particulars; it must not seem to be arbitrarily forced upon the particulars. Thus, our conventional habits of language have to be reversed when we come to deal with poetry. For here it is the tail that wags the dog. Better still, here it is the tail of the kite — the tail that makes the kite fly — the tail that renders the kite more than a frame of paper blown crazily down the wind.

The tail of the kite, it is true, seems to negate the kite's function: it weights down something made to rise; and in the same way, the concrete particulars with which the poet loads himself seem to deny the universal to which he aspires. The poet wants to 'say' something. Why, then, doesn't he say it directly and forthrightly? Why is he willing to say it only through his metaphors? Through his metaphors, he risks saying it partially and obscurely, and risks not saying it at all. But the risk must be taken, for direct statement leads to abstraction and threatens to take us out of poetry altogether.

The commitment to metaphor thus implies, with respect to general theme, a principle of indirection. With respect to particular images and statements, it implies a principle of organic relationship. That is, the poem is not a collection of beautiful or 'poetic' images. If there really existed objects which were somehow intrinsically 'poetic,' still the mere assemblage of these would not give us a poem. For in that case, one might arrange bouquets of these poetic images and thus create poems by formula. But the elements of a poem are related to each other, not as blossoms juxtaposed in a bouquet, but as the blossoms are related to the other parts of a growing plant. The beauty of the poem is the flowering of the whole plant, and needs the stalk, the leaf, and the hidden roots.

If this figure seems somewhat highflown, let us borrow an analogy from another art: the poem is like a little drama. The total effect proceeds from all the elements in the drama, and in a good poem, as in a good drama, there is no waste motion and there are no superfluous parts.

In coming to see that the parts of a poem are related to each other organically, and related to the total theme indirectly, we have come to see the importance of *context*. The memorable verses in poetry — even those which seem somehow intrinsically 'poetic' — show on inspection that they derive their poetic quality from their relation to a particular context. We may, it is true, be tempted to say that Shakespeare's 'Ripeness is all' is poetic because it is a sublime thought, or because it possesses simple eloquence; but that is to forget the context in which the passage appears. The proof that this is so becomes obvious when we contemplate such unpoetic lines as 'vitality is all,' 'serenity is all,' 'maturity is all,' — statements whose philosophical import in the abstract is about as defensible as that of 'ripeness is all.' Indeed, the common place word 'never' repeated five times becomes one of the most poignant lines in *Lear*, but it becomes so because of the supporting context. Even the 'meaning' of any particular item is modified by the context. For what is said is said in a particular situation and by a particular dramatic character.

The last instances adduced can be most properly regarded as instances of 'loading' from the context. The context endows the particular word or image or statement with significance. Images so charged become symbols; statements so charged become dramatic utterances. But there is another way in which to look at the impact of the context upon the part. The part is modified by the pressure of the context.

Now the *obvious* warping of a statement by the context we characterize as 'ironical.' To take the simplest instance, we say 'this is a fine state of affairs,' and in certain contexts the statement means quite the opposite of what it purports to say literally. This is sarcasm, the most obvious kind of irony. Here a complete reversal of meaning is effected: effected by the context, and pointed, probably, by the tone of voice. But the modification can be most important even though it falls far short of sarcastic reversal, and it need not be underlined by the tone of voice at all. The tone of irony can be effected by the skillful disposition of the context. Gray's *Elegy* will furnish an obvious example.

> Can storied urn or animated bust
> Back to its mansion call the fleeting breath?
> Can Honour's voice provoke the silent dust,
> Or Flatt'ry soothe the dull cold ear of death?

In its context, the question is obviously rhetorical. The answer has been implied in the characterisation of the breath as fleeting and of the ear of death as dull and cold. The form is that of a question, but the manner in which the question has been asked shows that it is no true question at all.

These are obvious instances of irony, and even on this level, much more poetry is ironical than the reader may be disposed to think. Many of Hardy's poems and nearly all of Housman's, for example, reveal irony quite as definite and overt as this. Lest these examples, however, seem to specialise irony in the direction of the sardonic, the reader ought to be reminded that irony, even in its obvious and conventionally recognised forms, comprises a wide variety of modes: tragic irony, self-irony, playful, arch, mocking, or gentle irony, etc. The body of poetry which may be said to contain irony in the ordinary senses of the term stretches from *Lear*, on the one hand, to 'Cupid and Campaspe Played,' on the other.

What indeed would be a statement wholly devoid of an ironic potential — a statement that did not show any qualification of the context? One is forced to offer statements like 'Two plus two equals four,' or 'The square on the hypotenuse of a right triangle is equal to the sum of the squares on the two sides.' The meaning of these statements is unqualified by any context; if they are true, they are equally true in any possible context.[1] These statements are properly abstract, and their terms are pure denotations. (If 'two' or 'four' actually happened to have connotations for the fancifully minded, the connotations would be quite irrelevant: they do not participate in the meaningful structure of the statement.)

But connotations are important in poetry and do enter significantly into the structure of meaning which is the poem. Moreover, I should claim also — as a corollary of the foregoing proposition — that poems never contain abstract statements. That is, any 'statement' made in the poem bears the pressure of the context and has its meaning modified by the context. In other words, the statements made — including those which appear to be philosophical generalisations — are to be read as if they were speeches in a drama. Their relevance, their propriety, their rhetorical force, even their meaning, cannot be divorced from the context in which they are imbedded.

The principle I state may seem a very obvious one, but I think that it is nonetheless very important. It may throw some light upon the importance of the term *irony* in modern criticism. As one who has certainly tended to overuse the term *irony* and perhaps, on occasion, has abused the term, I am closely concerned here. But I want to make quite clear what that concern is: it is not to justify the term *irony* as such, but rather to indicate why modern critics are so often tempted to use it. We have doubtless stretched the term too much, but it has been almost the only term available by which to point to a general and important aspect of poetry.

Consider this example: The speaker in Matthew Arnold's 'Dover Beach' states that the world, 'which seems to lie before us like a land of dreams . . . hath really neither joy nor love nor light. . . .' For some readers the statement will seem an obvious truism. (The hero of a typical Hemingway short story or novel, for example, will say this, though of course in a rather different idiom.) For other readers, however, the statement will seem false, or at least highly questionable. In any case, if we try to 'prove' the proposition, we shall raise some very perplexing metaphysical questions, and in doing so, we shall certainly also move away from the problems of the poem and, finally, from a justification of the poem. For the lines are to be justified in the poem in terms of the context: the speaker is standing beside his loved one, looking out of the window on the calm sea, listening to the long withdrawing roar of the ebbing tide, and aware of the beautiful delusion of moonlight which 'blanches' the whole scene. The 'truth' of the statement, and of the poem itself, in which it is imbedded, will be validated, not by a majority report of the association of sociologists, or a committee of physical scientists, or of a congress of metaphysicians who are willing to stamp the statement as proved. How is the statement to be validated? We shall probably not be able to do better than to apply T. S. Eliot's test: does the statement seem to be that which the mind of the reader can accept as coherent, mature, and founded on the facts of experience? But when we raise such a question, we are driven to consider the poem as drama. We raise such further questions as these: Does the speaker seem carried away with his own emotions? Does he seem to oversimplify the situation? Or does he, on the other hand, seem to have won to a kind of detachment and objectivity? In other words, we are forced to raise the question as to whether the statement grows properly out of a context; whether it acknowledges the pressures of the context; whether it is 'ironical' — or merely callow, glib, and sentimental.

I have suggested elsewhere that the poem which meets Eliot's test comes to the same thing as I. A. Richards' 'poetry of synthesis' — that is, a poetry which does not leave out what is apparently hostile to its dominant tone, and which, because it is able to fuse the irrelevant and discordant, has come to terms with itself and is invulnerable to irony. Irony, then, in this further sense, is not only an acknowledgement of the pressures of a context. Invulnerability to irony is the stability of a context in which the internal pressures balance and mutually support each other. The stability is like that of the arch: the very forces which are calculated to drag the stones to the ground actually provide the principle of support — a principle in which thrust and counterthrust become the means of stability.

In many poems the pressures of the context emerge in obvious ironies. Marvell's 'To His Coy Mistress' or Raleigh's 'Nymph's Reply' or even Gray's 'Elegy' reveal themselves as ironical, even to readers who use irony strictly in the conventional sense.

But can other poems be subsumed under this general principle, and do they show a comparable basic structure? The test case would seem to be presented by the lyric, and particularly the simple lyric. Consider, for example, one of Shakespeare's songs:

> Who is Silvia: what is she
>   That all our swains commend her?
> Holy, fair, and wise is she;
>   The heavens such grace did lend her,
> That she might admired be.
>
> Is she kind as she is fair?
>   For beauty lives with kindness.
> Love doth to her eyes repair,
>   To help him of his blindness,
> And, being help'd, inhabits there.
>
> Then to Silvia let us sing,
>   That Silvia is excelling;
> She excels each mortal thing
>   Upon the dull earth dwelling:
> To her let us garlands bring.

On one level the song attempts to answer the question 'Who is Silvia?' and the answer given makes her something of an angel and something of a goddess. She excels each mortal thing 'Upon the dull earth dwelling.' Silvia herself, of course, dwells upon that dull earth, though it is presumably her own brightness which makes it dull by comparison. (The dull earth, for example, yields bright garlands which the swains are bringing to her.) Why does she excel each mortal thing? Because of her virtues ('Holy, fair, and wise is she'), and these are a celestial gift. She is heaven's darling ('The heavens such grace did lend her').

Grace, I suppose, refers to grace of movement, and some readers will insist that we leave it at that. But since Silvia's other virtues include holiness and wisdom, and since her grace has been lent from above, I do not think that we can quite shut out the theological overtones. Shakespeare's audience would have found it even more difficult to do so. At any rate, it is interesting to see what happens if we are aware of these overtones. We get delightful richness, and we also get something very close to irony.

The motive for the bestowal of grace — that she might admired be — is oddly untheological. But what follows is odder still, for the love that 'doth to her eyes repair' is not, as we might expect, Christian 'charity' but the little pagan god Cupid ('Love doth to her eyes repair, / To help him of his blindness.') But if Cupid lives in her eyes, then the second line of the stanza takes on another layer of meaning. 'For beauty lives with kindness' becomes not merely a kind of charming platitude — actually often denied in human experience. (The Petrarchan lover, for example, as Shakespeare well knew, frequently found a beautiful and *cruel* mistress.) The second line, in this context, means also that the love god lives with the kind Silvia, and indeed has taken these eyes that sparkle with kindness for his own.

Is the mixture of pagan myth and Christian theology, then, an unthinking confusion into which the poet has blundered, or is it something wittily combined? It is certainly not a confusion, and if blundered into unconsciously, it is a happy mistake. But I do not mean to press the issue of the poet's self-consciousness (and with it, the implication of a kind of playful irony). Suffice it to say that the song is charming and delightful, and that the mingling of elements is proper to a poem which is a deft and light-fingered attempt to suggest the quality of divinity with which lovers perennially endow maidens who are finally mortal. The touch is light, there is a lyric grace, but the tone is complex, nonetheless.

I shall be prepared, however, to have this last example thrown out of court since Shakespeare, for all his universality, was a contemporary of the metaphysical poets, and may have incorporated more of their ironic complexity than is necessary or normal. One can draw more innocent and therefore more convincing examples from Wordsworth's Lucy poems.

> She dwelt among the untrodden ways
>   Beside the springs of Dove,
> A maid whom there were none to praise
>   And very few to love;
>
> A violet by a mossy stone
>   Half hidden from the eye!
> Fair as a star, when only one
>   Is shining in the sky.
>
> She lived unknown, and few could know
>   When Lucy ceased to be;
> But she is in her grave, and, oh,
>   The difference to me.

Which is Lucy really like — the violet or the star? The context in general seems to support the violet comparison. The violet, beautiful but almost unnoticed, already half hidden from the eye, is now, as the poem ends, completely hidden in its grave, with none but the poet to grieve for its loss. The star comparison may seem only vaguely relevant — a conventional and here a somewhat anomalous compliment. Actually, it is not difficult to justify the star comparison: to her lover's eyes, she is the solitary star. She has no rivals, nor would the idea of rivalry, in her unselfconscious simplicity, occur to her.

The violet and the star thus balance each other and between themselves define the situation: Lucy was, from the viewpoint of the great world, unnoticed, shy, modest, and half hidden from the eye, but from the standpoint of her lover, she is the single star, completely dominating that world, not arrogantly like the sun, but sweetly and modestly, like the star. The implicit contrast is that so often developed ironically by John Donne in his poems where the lovers, who amount to nothing in the eyes of the world, become, in their own eyes, each the other's world — as in 'The Good-Morrow,' where their love makes 'one little room an everywhere,' or as in 'The Canonization,' where the lovers drive into the mirrors of each other's eyes the 'towns, countries, courts' — which make up the great world; and thus find that world in themselves. It is easy to imagine how Donne would have exploited the contrast between the violet and the star, accentuating it, developing the irony, showing how the violet was really like its antithesis, the star, etc.

Now one does not want to enter an Act of Uniformity against the poets. Wordsworth is entitled to his method of simple juxtaposition with no underscoring of the ironical contrast. But it is worth noting that the contrast with its ironic potential is there in his poem. It is there in nearly all of Wordsworth's successful lyrics. It is certainly to be found in 'A slumber did my spirit seal.'

> A slumber did my spirit seal;
>   I had no human fears:
> She seemed a thing that could not feel
>   The touch of earthly years.
>
> No motion has she now, no force;
>   She neither hears nor sees,
> Rolled round in earth's diurnal course,
>   With rocks, and stones, and trees.

The lover's insensitivity to the claims of mortality is interpreted as a lethargy of spirit — a strange slumber. Thus the 'human fears' that he lacked are apparently the fears normal to human beings. But the phrase has a certain pliability. It could mean fears *for* the loved one as a mortal human being; and the lines that follow tend to warp the phrase in this direction: it does not occur to the lover that he needs to fear for one who cannot be touched by 'earthly years.' We need not argue that Wordsworth is consciously using a witty device, a purposed ambiguity; nor need we conclude that he is confused. It is enough to see that Wordsworth has developed, quite 'normally,' let us say, a context calculated to pull 'human fears' in opposed directions, and that the slightest pressure of attention on the part of the reader precipitates an ironical effect.

As we move into the second stanza, the potential irony almost becomes overt. If the slumber has sealed the lover's spirit, a slumber, immersed in which he thought it impossible that his loved one could perish, so too a slumber has now definitely sealed *her* spirit: 'No motion has she now, no force; / She neither hears nor sees.' It is evident that it is her unnatural slumber that has waked him out of his. It is curious to speculate on what Donne or Marvell would have made of this.

Wordsworth, however, still does not choose to exploit the contrast as such. Instead, he attempts to suggest something of the lover's agonised shock at the loved one's present lack of motion — of his response to her utter and horrible inertness. And how shall he suggest this? He chooses to suggest it, not by saying that she lies as quiet as marble or as a lump of clay; on the contrary, he attempts to suggest it by imagining her in violent motion — violent, but imposed motion, the same motion indeed which the very stones share, whirled about as they are in earth's diurnal course. Why does the image convey so powerfully the sense of something inert and helpless? Part of the effect, of course, resides in the fact that a dead lifelessness is suggested more sharply by an object's being whirled about by something else than by an image of the object in repose. But there are other matters which are at work here: the sense of the girl's falling back into the clutter of things, companioned by things chained like a tree to one particular spot, or by things completely inanimate, like rocks and stones. Here, of course, the concluding figure leans upon the suggestion made in the first stanza, that the girl once seemed something not subject to earthly limitations at all. But surely, the image of the whirl itself is important in its suggestion of something meaningless — motion that mechanically repeats itself. And there is one further element: the girl, who to her lover seemed a thing that could not feel the touch of earthly years, is caught up helplessly into the empty whirl of the earth which measures and makes time. She is touched by and held by earthly time in its most powerful and horrible image. The last figure thus seems to me to summarise the poem — to offer to almost every facet of meaning suggested in the earlier lines a concurring and resolving image which meets and accepts and reduces each item to its place in the total unity.

Wordsworth, as we have observed above, does not choose to point up specifically the ironical contrast between the speaker's former slumber and the loved one's present slumber. But there is one ironical contrast which he does stress: this is the contrast between the two senses in which the girl becomes insulated against the 'touch of earthly years.' In the first stanza, she 'could not feel / The touch of earthly years' because she seemed divine and immortal. But in the second stanza, now in her grave, she still does not 'feel the touch of earthly years,' for, like the rocks and stones, she feels nothing at all. It is true that Wordsworth does not repeat the verb 'feels'; instead he writes 'She neither *hears* nor *sees*.' But the contrast, though not commented upon directly by any device of verbal wit, is there nonetheless, and is bound to make itself felt in any sensitive reading of the poem. The statement of the first stanza has been literally realized in the second, but its meaning has been ironically reversed.

Ought we, then, to apply the term *ironical* to Wordsworth's poem? Not necessarily. I am trying to account for my temptation to call such a poem ironical — not to justify my yielding to the temptation — least of all to insist that others so transgress. Moreover, Wordsworth's poem seems to me admirable, and I entertain no notion that it might have been more admirable still had John Donne written it rather than William Wordsworth. I shall be content if I can make a much more modest point: namely, that since both Wordsworth and Donne are poets, their work has at basis a similar structure, and that the dynamic structure — the pattern of thrust and counterthrust — which we associate with Donne has its counterpart in Wordsworth. In the work of both men, the relation between part and part is organic, which means that each part modifies and is modified by the whole.

Yet to intimate that there are potential ironies in Wordsworth's lyric may seem to distort it. After all, is it not simple and spontaneous? With these terms we encounter two of the critical catchwords of the nineteenth century, even as *ironical* is in danger of becoming a catchword of our own period. Are the terms *simple* and *ironical* mutually exclusive? What after all do we mean by *simple* or by *spontaneous*? We may mean that the poem came to the poet easily and even spontaneously: very complex poems may — indeed have — come just this way. Or the poem may seem in its effect on the reader a simple and spontaneous utterance: some poems of great complexity possess this quality. What is likely to cause trouble here is the intrusion of a special theory of composition. It is fairly represented as an intrusion since a theory as to how a poem is written is being allowed to dictate to us how the poem is to be read. There is no harm in thinking of Wordsworth's poem as simple and spontaneous unless these terms deny complexities that actually exist in the poem, and unless they justify us in reading the poem with only half our minds. A slumber ought not to seal the *reader's* spirit as he reads this poem, or any other poem.

I have argued that irony, taken as the acknowledgment of the pressures of context, is to be found in poetry of every period and even in simple lyrical poetry. But in the poetry of our own time, this pressure reveals itself strikingly. A great deal of modern poetry does use irony as its special and perhaps its characteristic strategy. For this there are reasons, and compelling reasons. To cite only a few of these reasons: there is the breakdown of a common symbolism; there is the general scepticism as to universals; not least important, there is the depletion and corruption of the very language itself, by advertising and by the mass-produced arts of radio, the moving picture, and pulp fiction. The modern poet has the task of rehabilitating a tired and drained language so that it can convey meanings once more with force and with exactitude. This task of qualifying and modifying language is perennial; but it is imposed on the modern poet as a special burden. Those critics who attribute the use of ironic techniques to the poet's own bloodless sophistication and tired scepticism would be better advised to refer these vices to his potential readers, a public corrupted by Hollywood and the Book of the Month Club. For the modern poet is not addressing simple primitives but a public sophisticated by commercial art.

At any rate, to the honor of the modern poet be it said that he has frequently succeeded in using his ironic techniques to win through to clarity and passion. Randall Jarrell's 'Eighth Air Force' represents a success of this sort.

> If, in an odd angle of the hutment,
> A puppy laps the water from a can
> Of flowers, and the drunk sergeant shaving
> Whistles *O Paradiso!* — shall I say that man
> Is not as men have said: a wolf to man?
>
> The other murderers troop in yawning;
> Three of them play Pitch, one sleeps, and one
> Lies counting missions, lies there sweating
> Till even his heart beats: One; One; One.
> *O murderers!* . . . Still, this is how it's done:
>
> This is a war. . . . But since these play, before they die,
> Like puppies with their puppy; since, a man,
> I did as these have done, but did not die —

> I will content the people as I can
> And give up these to them: Behold the man!
>
> I have suffered, in a dream, because of him,
> Many things; for this last saviour, man,
> I have lied as I lie now. But what is lying?
> Men wash their hands, in blood, as best they can:
> I find no fault in this just man.

There are no superfluous parts, no dead or empty details. The airmen in their hutment are casual enough and honest enough to be convincing. The raw building is domesticated: there are the flowers in water from which the mascot, a puppy, laps. There is the drunken sergeant, whistling an opera aria as he shaves. These 'murderers,' as the poet is casually to call the airmen in the next stanza, display a touching regard for the human values. How, then, can one say that man is a wolf to man, since these men 'play before they die, like puppies with their puppy.' But the casual presence of the puppy in the hutment allows us to take the stanza both ways, for the dog is a kind of tamed and domesticated wolf, and his presence may prove on the contrary that the hutment is the wolf den. After all, the timber wolf plays with its puppies.

The second stanza takes the theme to a perfectly explicit conclusion. If three of the men play pitch, and one is asleep, at least one man is awake and counts himself and his companions murderers. But his unvoiced cry 'O murderers' is met, countered, and dismissed with the next two lines: '. . . Still this is how it's done: / This is a war. . . .'

The note of casuistry and cynical apology prepares for a brilliant and rich resolving image, the image of Pontius Pilate, which is announced specifically in the third stanza:

> I will content the people as I can
> And give up these to them: Behold the man!

Yet if Pilate, as he is first presented, is a jesting Pilate, who asks 'What is truth?' it is a bitter and grieving Pilate who concludes the poem. It is the integrity of Man himself that is at stake. Is man a cruel animal, a wolf, or is he the last saviour, the Christ of our secular religion of humanity?

The Pontius Pilate metaphor, as the poet uses it, becomes a device for tremendous concentration. For the speaker (presumably the young airman who cried 'O murderers') is himself the confessed murderer under judgement, and also the Pilate who judges, and, at least as a representative of man, the saviour whom the mob would condemn. He is even Pilate's better nature, his wife, for the lines 'I have suffered, in a dream, because of him, / Many things' is merely a rearrangement of *Matthew* 27:19, the speech of Pilate's wife to her husband. But this last item is more than a reminiscence of the scriptural scene. It reinforces the speaker's present dilemma. The modern has had high hopes for man; are the hopes merely a dream? Is man incorrigible, merely a cruel beast? The speaker's present torture springs from that hope and from his reluctance to dismiss it as an empty dream. This Pilate is even harder-pressed than was the Roman magistrate. For he must convince himself of this last saviour's innocence. But he has lied for him before. He will lie for him now.

> Men wash their hands, in blood, as best as they can:
> I find no fault in this just man.

What is the meaning of 'Men wash their hands, in blood, as best they can'? It can mean: Since my own hands are bloody, I have no right to condemn the rest. It can mean: I know that man can love justice, even though his hands are bloody, for there is blood on mine. It can mean: Men are essentially decent: they try to keep their hands clean even if they have only blood in which to wash them.

None of these meanings cancels out the others. All are relevant, and each meaning contributes to the total meaning. Indeed, there is not a facet of significance which does not receive illumination from the figure.

Some of Jarrell's weaker poems seem weak to me because they lean too heavily upon this concept of the goodness of man. In some of them, his approach to the theme is too direct. But in this poem, the affirmation of man's essential justness by a Pilate who contents the people as he washes his hands in blood seems to me to supply every qualification that is required. The sense of self-guilt, the yearning to believe in man's justness, the knowledge of the difficulty of so believing — all work to render accurately and dramatically the total situation.

It is easy at this point to misapprehend the function of irony. We can say that Jarrell's irony pares his theme down to acceptable dimensions. The theme of man's goodness has here been so qualified that the poet himself does not really believe in it. But this is not what I am trying to say. We do not ask a poet to bring his poem into line with our personal beliefs — still less to flatter our personal beliefs. What we do ask is that the poem dramatize the situation so accurately, so honestly, with such fidelity to the total situation that it is no longer a question of our beliefs, but of our participation in the poetic experience. At his best, Jarrell manages to bring us, by an act of imagination, to the most penetrating insight. Participating in that insight, we doubtless become better citizens. (One of the 'uses' of poetry, I should agree, is to make us better citizens.) But poetry is not the eloquent rendition of the citizen's creed. It is not even the accurate rendition of his creed. Poetry must carry us beyond the abstract creed into the very matrix out of which, and from which, our creeds are abstracted. That is what 'Eighth Air Force' does. That is what, I am convinced, all good poetry does.

For the theme in a genuine poem does not confront us as abstraction — that is, as one man's generalisation from the relevant particulars. Finding its proper symbol, defined and refined by the participating metaphors, the theme becomes a part of the reality in which we live — an insight, rooted in and growing out of concrete experience, many-sided, three-dimensional. Even the resistance to generalization has its part in this process — even the drag of the particulars away from the universal — even the tension of opposing themes — play their parts. The kite properly loaded, tension maintained along the kite string, rises steadily *against* the thrust of the wind.

Note

1. This is not to say, of course, that such statements are not related to a particular 'universe of discourse.' They are indeed, as are all statements of whatever kind. But I distinguish here between 'context' and 'universe of discourse.' 'Two plus two equals four' is not dependent on a special

dramatic context in the way in which a 'statement' made in a poem is. Compare 'two plus two equals four' and the same 'statement' as contained in Housman's poem:

> — To think that two and two are four
>   And neither five nor three
> The heart of man has long been sore
>   And long 'tis like to be.

2
Victor Shklovsky,
from 'Art as Technique'

***If we start to examine the general laws of perception, we see that as perception becomes habitual, it becomes automatic. Thus, for example, all of our habits retreat into the area of the unconsciously automatic; if one remembers the sensations of holding a pen or of speaking in a foreign language for the first time and compares that with his feeling at performing the action for the ten thousandth time, he will agree with us. Such habituation explains the principles by which, in ordinary speech, we leave phrases unfinished and words half expressed. In this process, ideally realised in algebra, things are replaced by symbols. Complete words are not expressed in rapid speech; their initial sounds are barely perceived. Alexander Pogodin offers the example of a boy considering the sentence 'The Swiss mountains are beautiful' in the form of a series of letters: *T, S, m, a, b.*[1]

This characteristic of thought not only suggests the method of algebra, but even prompts the choice of symbols (letters, especially initial letters). By this 'algebraic' method of thought we apprehend objects only as shapes with imprecise extensions; we do not see them in their entirety but rather recognize them by their main characteristics. We see the object as though it were enveloped in a sack. We know what it is by its configuration, but we see only its silhouette. The object, perceived thus in the manner of prose perception, fades and does not leave even a first impression; ultimately even the essence of what it was is forgotten. Such perception explains why we fail to hear the prose word in its entirety (see Leo Jakubinsky's article[2]) and, hence, why (along with other slips of the tongue) we fail to pronounce it. The process of 'algebrization,' the over-automatization of an object, permits the greatest economy of perceptive effort. Either objects are assigned only one proper feature — a number, for example — or else they function as though by formula and do not even appear in cognition:

> I was cleaning a room and, meandering about, approached the divan and couldn't remember whether or not I had dusted it. Since these movements are habitual and unconscious I could not remember and felt that it was impossible to remember — so that if I had dusted it and forgot — that is, had acted unconsciously, then it was the same as if I had not. If some conscious person had been watching, then the fact could be established. If, however, no one was looking, or looking on unconsciously, if the whole complex lives of many people go on unconsciously, then such lives are as if they had never been.[3]

And so life is reckoned as nothing. Habitualization devours works, clothes, furniture, one's wife, and the fear of war. 'If the whole complex lives of many

48

people go on unconsciously, then such lives are as if they had never been.' And art exists that one may recover the sensation of life; it exists to make one feel things, to make the stone *stony*. The purpose of art is to impart the sensation of things as they are perceived and not as they are known. The technique of art is to make objects 'unfamiliar,' to make forms difficult, to increase the difficulty and length of perception because the process of perception is an aesthetic end in itself and must be prolonged. *Art is a way of experiencing the artfulness of an object; the object is not important.*

The range of poetic (artistic) work extends from the sensory to the cognitive, from poetry to prose, from the concrete to the abstract: from Cervantes' Don Quixote — scholastic and poor nobleman, half consciously bearing his humiliation in the court of the duke — to the broad but empty Don Quixote of Turgenev; from Charlemagne to the name 'king' [in Russian 'Charles' and 'king' obviously derive from the same root, *korol*]. The meaning of a work broadens to the extent that artfulness and artistry diminish; thus a fable symbolises more than a poem, and a proverb more than a fable. Consequently, the least self-contradictory part of Potebnya's theory is his treatment of the fable, which, from his point of view, he investigated thoroughly. But since his theory did not provide for 'expressive' works of art, he could not finish his book. As we know, *Notes on the Theory of Literature* was published in 1905, thirteen years after Potebnya's death. Potebnya himself completed only the section on the fable.[4]

After we see an object several times, we begin to recognize it. The object is in front of us and we know about it, but we do not see it[5] — hence we cannot say anything significant about it. Art removes objects from the automatism of perception in several ways. Here I want to illustrate a way used repeatedly by Leo Tolstoy, that writer who, for Merezhkovsky at least, seems to present things as if he himself saw them, saw them in their entirety, and did not alter them.

Tolstoy makes the familiar seem strange by not naming the familiar object. He describes an object as if he were seeing it for the first time, an event as if it were happening for the first time. In describing something he avoids the accepted names of its parts and instead names corresponding parts of other objects. For example, in 'Shame' Tolstoy 'defamiliarises' the idea of flogging in this way: 'to strip people who have broken the law, to hurl them to the floor, and to rap on their bottoms with switches,' and, after a few lines, 'to lash about on the naked buttocks.' Then he remarks:

> Just why precisely this stupid, savage means of causing pain and not any other — why not prick the shoulders or any part of the body with needles, squeeze the hands or the feet in a vise, or anything like that?

I apologise for this harsh example, but it is typical of Tolstoy's way of pricking the conscience. The familiar act of flogging is made unfamiliar both by the description and by the proposal to change its form without changing its nature. Tolstoy uses this technique of 'defamiliarisation' constantly. The narrator of 'Kholstomer,' for example, is a horse, and it is the horse's point of view (rather than a person's) that makes the content of the story seem unfamiliar. Here is how the horse regards the institution of private property:

> I understood well what they said about whipping and Christianity. But then I was absolutely in the dark. What's the meaning of 'his own,' 'his colt'? From these phrases I

saw that people thought there was some sort of connection between me and the stable. At the time I simply could not understand the connection. Only much later, when they separated me from the other horses, did I begin to understand. But even then I simply could not see what it meant when they called me 'man's property.' The words 'my horse' referred to me, a living horse, and seemed as strange to me as the words 'my land,' 'my air,' 'my water.'

But the words made a strong impression on me. I thought about them constantly, and only after the most diverse experiences with people did I understand, finally, what they meant. They meant this: In life people are guided by words, not by deeds. It's not so much that they love the possibility of doing or not doing something as it is the possibility of speaking with words, agreed on among themselves, about various topics. Such are the words 'my' and 'mine,' which they apply to different things, creatures, objects, and even to land, people, and horses. They agree that only one may say 'mine' about this, that or the other thing. And the one who says 'mine' about the greatest number of things is, according to the game which they've agreed to among themselves, the one they consider the most happy. I don't know the point of all this, but it's true. For a long time I tried to explain it to myself in terms of some kind of real gain, but I had to reject that explanation because it was wrong.

Many of those, for instance, who called me their own never rode on me — although others did. And so with those who fed me. Then again, the coachman, the veterinarians, and the outsiders in general treated me kindly, yet those who called me their own did not. In due time, having widened the scope of my observations, I satisfied myself that the notion 'my,' not only in relation to us horses, has no other basis than a narrow human instinct which is called a sense of or right to private property. A man says 'this house is mine' and never lives in it; he only worries about its construction and upkeep. A merchant says 'my shop,' 'my dry goods shop,' for instance, and does not even wear clothes made from the better cloth he keeps in his own shop.

There are people who call a tract of land their own, but they never set eyes on it and never take a stroll on it. There are people who call others their own, yet never see them. And the whole relationship between them is that the so-called 'owners' treat the others unjustly.

There are people who call women their own, or their 'wives,' but their women live with other men. And people strive not for the good in life, but for goods they can call their own.

I am now convinced that this is the essential difference between people and ourselves. And therefore, not even considering the other ways in which we are superior, but considering just this one virtue, we can bravely claim to stand higher than men on the ladder of living creatures. The actions of men, at least those with whom I have had dealings, are guided by *words* — ours, by deeds.

The horse is killed before the end of the story, but the manner of the narrative, its technique, does not change:

Much later they put Serpukhovsky's body, which had experienced the world, which had eaten and drunk, into the ground. They could profitably send neither his hide, nor his flesh, nor his bones anywhere.

But since his dead body, which had gone about in the world for twenty years, was a great burden to everyone, its burial was only a superfluous embarrassment for the people. For a long time no one had needed him; for a long time he had been a burden on all. But nevertheless, the dead who buried the dead found it necessary to dress this bloated body, which immediately began to rot, in a good uniform and good boots; to lay it in a good new coffin with new tassels at the four corners, then to place this new coffin in another of lead and ship it to Moscow; there to exhume ancient bones and at just that spot, to hide this putrefying body, swarming with maggots, in its new uniform and clean boots, and to cover it over completely with dirt.

Thus we see that at the end of the story Tolstoy continues to use the technique even though the motivation for it (the reason for its use) is gone.

In *War and Peace* Tolstoy uses the same technique in describing whole battles as if battles were something new. These descriptions are too long to quote; it would be necessary to extract a considerable part of the four-volume novel. But Tolstoy uses the same method in describing the drawing room and the theater:

> The middle of the stage consisted of flat boards; by the sides stood painted pictures representing trees, and at the back a linen cloth was stretched down to the floor boards. Maidens in red bodices and white skirts sat on the middle of the stage. One, very fat, in a white silk dress, sat apart on a narrow bench to which a green pasteboard box was glued from behind. They were all singing something. When they had finished, the maiden in white approached the prompter's box. A man in silk with tight-fitting pants on his fat legs approached her with a plume and began to sing and spread his arms in dismay. The man in the tight pants finished his song alone; then the girl sang. After that both remained silent as the music resounded; and the man, obviously waiting to begin singing his part with her again, began to run his fingers over the hand of the girl in the white dress. They finished their song together, and everyone in the theater began to clap and shout. But the men and women on stage, who represented lovers, started to bow, smiling and raising their hands.
>
> In the second act there were pictures representing monuments and openings in the linen cloth representing the moonlight, and they raised lamp shades on a frame. As the musicians started to play the bass horn and counter-bass, a large number of people in black mantles poured onto the stage from right and left. The people, with something like daggers in their hands, started to wave their arms. Then still more people came running out and began to drag away the maiden who had been wearing a white dress but who now wore one of sky blue. They did not drag her off immediately, but sang with her for a long time before dragging her away. Three times they struck on something metallic behind the side scenes, and everyone got down on his knees and began to chant a prayer. Several times all of this activity was interrupted by enthusiastic shouts from the spectators.

The third act is described:

> . . . But suddenly a storm blew up. Chromatic scales and chords of diminished sevenths were heard in the orchestra. Everyone ran about and again they dragged one of the bystanders behind the scenes as the curtain fell.

In the fourth act, 'There was some sort of devil who sang, waving his hands, until the boards were moved out from under him and he dropped down.'[6]

In *Resurrection* Tolstoy describes the city and the court in the same way; he uses a similar technique in 'Kreutzer Sonata' when he describes marriage — 'Why, if people have an affinity of souls, must they sleep together?' But he did not defamiliarise only those things he sneered at:

> Pierre stood up from his new comrades and made his way between the campfires to the other side of the road where, it seemed, the captive soldiers were held. He wanted to talk with them. The French sentry stopped him on the road and ordered him to return. Pierre did so, but not to the campfire, not to his comrades, but to an abandoned, unharnessed carriage. On the ground, near the wheel of the carriage, he sat cross-legged in the Turkish fashion, and lowered his head. He sat motionless for a long time, thinking.

More than an hour passed. No one disturbed him. Suddenly he burst out laughing with his robust, good natured laugh — so loudly that the men near him looked around, suprised at his conspicuously strange laughter.

'Ha, ha, ha,' laughed Pierre. And he began to talk to himself. 'The soldier didn't allow me to pass. They caught me, barred me. Me — me — my immortal soul. Ha, ha, ha,' he laughed with tears starting in his eyes.

Pierre glanced at the sky, into the depths of the departing, playing stars. 'And all this is mine, all this is in me, and all this is I,' thought Pierre. 'And all this they caught and put in a planked enclosure.' He smiled and went off to his comrades to lie down to sleep.[7]

Anyone who knows Tolstoy can find several hundred such passages in his work. His method of seeing things out of their normal context is also apparent in his last works. Tolstoy described the dogmas and rituals he attacked as if they were unfamiliar, substituting everyday meanings for the customarily religious meanings of the words common in church ritual. Many persons were painfully wounded; they considered it blasphemy to present as strange and monstrous what they accepted as sacred. Their reaction was due chiefly to the technique through which Tolstoy perceived and reported his environment. And after turning to what he had long avoided, Tolstoy found that his perceptions had unsettled his faith.

The technique of defamiliarisation is not Tolstoy's alone. I cited Tolstoy because his work is generally known.

Now, having explained the nature of this technique, let us try to determine the approximate limits of its application. I personally feel that defamiliarisation is found almost everywhere form is found. In other words, the difference between Potebnya's point of view and ours is this: An image is not a permanent referent for those mutable complexities of life which are revealed through it; its purpose is not to make us perceive meaning, but to create a special perception of the object — *it creates a 'vision' of the object instead of serving as a means for knowing it.*

The purpose of imagery in erotic art can be studied even more accurately; an erotic object is usually presented as if it were seen for the first time. Gogol, in 'Christmas Eve,' provides the following example:

Here he approached her more closely, coughed, smiled at her, touched her plump, bare arm with his fingers, and expressed himself in a way that showed both his cunning and his conceit.

'And what is this you have, magnificent Solokha?' and having said this, he jumped back a little.

'What? An arm, Osip Nikiforovich!' she answered.

'Hmm, an arm! *He, he, he!*' said the secretary cordially, satisfied with his beginning. He wandered about the room.

'And what is this you have, dearest Solokha?' he said in the same way, having approached her again and grasped her lightly by the neck, and in the very same way he jumped back.

'As if you don't see, Osip Nikiforovich!' answered Solokha, 'a neck, and on my neck a necklace.'

'Hmm! On the neck a necklace! *He, he, he!*' and the secretary again wandered about the room, rubbing his hands.

'And what is this you have, incomparable Solokha?' . . . It is not known to what the secretary would stretch his long fingers now.

And Knut Hamsun has the following in 'Hunger': 'Two white prodigies appeared from beneath her blouse.'

Erotic subjects may also be presented figuratively with the obvious purpose of leading us away from their 'recognition.' Hence sexual organs are referred to in terms of lock and key,[8] or quilting tools,[9] or bow and arrow, or rings and marlinspikes, as in the legend of Stavyor, in which a married man does not recognise his wife, who is disguised as a warrior. She proposes a riddle:

> 'Remember, Stavyor, do you recall
> How we little ones walked to and fro in the street?
> You and I together sometimes played with a marlinspike —
> You had a silver marlinspike,
> But I had a gilded ring?
> I found myself at it just now and then,
> But you fell in with it ever and always.'
> Says Stavyor, son of Godinovich,
> 'What! I didn't play with you at marlinspikes!'
> Then Vasilisa Mikulichna: 'So he says.
> Do you remember, Stavyor, do you recall,
> Now must you know, you and I together learned to
>   read and write;
> Mine was an ink-well of silver,
> And yours a pen of gold?
> But I just moistened it a little now and then,
> And I just moistened it ever and always.'[10]

In a different version of the legend we find a key to the riddle:

> Here the formidable envoy Vasilyushka
> Raised her skirts to the very navel,
> And then the young Stavyor, son of Godinovich,
> Recognized her gilded ring. . . .[11]

But defamiliarisation is not only a technique of the erotic riddle — a technique of euphemism — it is also the basis and point of all riddles. Every riddle pretends to show its subject either by words which specify or describe it but which, during the telling, do not seem applicable (the type: 'black and white and ''red'' — read — all over') or by means of odd but imitative sounds ('''Twas brillig, and the slithy toves/Did gyre and gimble in the wabe').[12]

Even erotic images not intended as riddles are defamiliarised ('boobies,' 'tarts,' 'piece,' etc.). In popular imagery there is generally something equivalent to 'trampling the grass' and 'breaking the guelder-rose.' The technique of defamiliarisation is absolutely clear in the widespread image — a motif of erotic affectation — in which a bear and other wild beasts (or a devil, with a different reason for nonrecognition) do not recognise a man.[13]

The lack of recognition in the following tale is quite typical:

A peasant was plowing a field with a piebald mare. A bear approached him and asked, 'Uncle, what's made this mare piebald for you?'

'I did the piebalding myself.'

'But how?'

'Let me, and I'll do the same for you.'

The bear agreed. The peasant tied his feet together with a rope, took the ploughshare from the two-wheeled plough, heated it on the fire, and applied it to his flanks. He made the bear piebald by scorching his fur down to the hide with the hot ploughshare. The man untied the bear, which went off and lay down under a tree.

A magpie flew at the peasant to pick at the meat on his shirt. He caught her and broke one of her legs. The magpie flew off to perch in the same tree under which the bear was lying. Then, after the magpie, a horsefly landed on the mare, sat down, and began to bite. The peasant caught the fly, took a stick, shoved it up its rear, and let it go. The fly went to the tree where the bear and the magpie were. There all three sat.

The peasant's wife came to bring his dinner to the field. The man and his wife finished their dinner in the fresh air, and he began to wrestle with her on the ground.

The bear saw this and said to the magpie and the fly, 'Holy priests! The peasant wants to piebald someone again.'

The magpie said, 'No, he wants to break someone's legs.'

The fly said, 'No, he wants to shove a stick up someone's rump.'[14]

The similarity of technique here and in Tolstoy's 'Kholstomer,' is, I think, obvious.

Quite often in literature the sexual act itself is defamiliarised; for example, the *Decameron* refers to 'scraping out a barrel,' 'catching nightingales,' 'gay wool-beating work,' (the last is not developed in the plot). Defamiliarisation is often used in describing the sexual organs.

A whole series of plots is based on such a lack of recognition; for example, in Afanasyev's *Intimate Tales* the entire story of 'The Shy Mistress' is based on the fact that an object is not called by its proper name — or, in other words, on a game of nonrecognition. So too in Onchukov's 'Spotted Petticoats,' tale no. 525, and also in 'The Bear and the Hare' from *Intimate Tales*, in which the bear and the hare make a 'wound.'

Such constructions as 'the pestle and the mortar,' or 'Old Nick and the infernal regions' (*Decameron*), are also examples of the technique of defamiliarisation. And in my article on plot construction I write about defamiliarisation in psychological parallelism. Here, then, I repeat that the perception of disharmony in a harmonious context is important in parallelism. The purpose of parallelism, like the general purpose of imagery, is to transfer the usual perception of an object into the sphere of new perception — that is, to make a unique semantic modification.

In studying poetic speech in its phonetic and lexical structure as well as in its characteristic distribution of words and in the characteristic thought structures compounded from the words, we find everywhere the artistic trademark — that is, we find material obviously created to remove the automatism of perception; the author's purpose is to create the vision which results from that deautomatized perception. A work is created 'artistically' so that its perception is impeded and the greatest possible effect is produced through the slowness of the perception. As a result of this lingering, the object is perceived not in its extension in space, but, so to speak, in its continuity. Thus 'poetic language' gives satisfaction. According to Aristotle, poetic language must appear strange and wonderful; and, in fact, it is often actually foreign: the Sumerian used by the Assyrians, the Latin of Europe during the Middle Ages, the Arabisms of the Persians, the Old Bulgarian of Russian literature, or the elevated, almost literary language of folk songs. The common archaisms of poetic language, the intricacy of the sweet new style [*dolce stil nuovo*],[15] the obscure style of the language of Arnaut Daniel with the 'roughened' [*harte*] forms *which make pronunciation difficult* — these are used in much the same way. Leo Jakubinsky has demonstrated the principle of phonetic 'roughening' of poetic language in the particular case of the repetition of identical sounds. The language of poetry is, then, a difficult, roughened, impeded language. In a few special instances the language of poetry approximates the language of prose, but this does not violate the principle of 'roughened' form.

> Her sister was called Tatyana.
> For the first time we shall
> Wilfully brighten the delicate
> Pages of a novel with such a name.

wrote Pushkin. The usual poetic language for Pushkin's contemporaries was the elegant style of Derzhavin; but Pushkin's style, because it seemed trivial then, was unexpectedly difficult for them. We should remember the consternation of Pushkin's contemporaries over the vulgarity of his expressions. He used the popular language as a special device for prolonging attention, just as his contemporaries generally used Russian words in their usually French speech (see Tolstoy's examples in *War and Peace*).

Just now a still more characteristic phenomenon is under way. Russian literary language, which was originally foreign to Russia, has so permeated the language of the people that it has blended with their conversation. On the other hand, literature has now begun to show a tendency towards the use of dialects (Remizov, Klyuyev, Essenin, and others,[16] so unequal in talent and so alike in language, are intentionally provincial) and of barbarisms (which gave rise to the Severyanin group[17]). And currently Maxim Gorky is changing his diction from the old literary language to the new literary colloquialism of Leskov.[18] Ordinary speech and literary language have thereby changed places (see the work of Vyacheslav Ivanov and many others). And finally, a strong tendency, led by Khlebnikov, to create a new and properly poetic language has emerged. In the light of these developments we can define poetry as *attenuated, tortuous* speech. Poetic speech is *formed speech*. Prose is ordinary speech — economical, easy, proper, the goddess of prose [*dea prosae*] is a goddess of the accurate, facile type, of the 'direct' expression of a child. I shall discuss roughened form and retardation as the general *law* of art at greater length in an article on plot construction.[19]

Nevertheless, the position of those who urge the idea of the economy of artistic energy as something which exists in and even distinguishes poetic language seems, at first glance, tenable for the problem of rhythm. Spencer's description of rhythm would seem to be absolutely incontestable:

> Just as the body in receiving a series of varying concussions, must keep the muscles ready to meet the most violent of them, as not knowing when such may come: so, the mind in receiving unarranged articulations, must keep its perspectives active enough to recognise the least easily caught sounds. And as, if the concussions recur in definite order, the body may husband its forces by adjusting the resistance needful for each concussion; so, if the syllables be rhythmically arranged, the mind may economise its energies by anticipating the attention required for each syllable.[20]

This apparently conclusive observation suffers from the common fallacy, the confusion of the laws of poetic and prosaic language. In *The Philosophy of Style* Spencer failed utterly to distinguish between them. But rhythm may have two functions. The rhythm of prose, or of a work song like 'Dubinushka,' permits the members of the work crew to do their necessary 'groaning together' and also eases the work by making it automatic. And, in fact, it is easier to march with music than without it, and to march during an animated conversation is even easier, for the walking is done unconsciously. Thus the rhythm of prose is an important automatizing element; the rhythm of poetry is not. There is 'order' in art, yet not a single column of a Greek temple stands exactly in its proper order; poetic rhythm is similarly disordered rhythm. Attempts to systematize the irregularities have been made, and such attempts are part of the current problem in the theory of rhythm. It is obvious that the systematization will not work, for in reality the problem is not one of complicating the rhythm but of disordering the rhythm — a disordering which cannot be predicted. Should the disordering of rhythm become a convention, it would be ineffective as a device for the roughening of language. But I will not discuss rhythm in more detail since I intend to write a book about it.

Notes:

1. Alexander Pogodin, *Yazyk, kak tvorchestvo* [*Language as Art*] (Kharkov, 1913), p. 42. [The original sentence was in French, '*Les montaignes de la Suisse sont belles,*' with the appropriate initials.]
2. Jakubinsky, *Sborniki*, I (1916).
3. Leo Tolstoy's *Diary*, entry dated February 29, 1897. [The date is transcribed incorrectly; it should read March 1, 1897.]
4. Alexander Potebnya, *Iz lektsy po teorii slovesnosti* [*Lectures on the Theory of Language*] (Kharkov, 1914).
5. Victor Shklovsky, *Voskresheniye slova* [*The Resurrection of the Word*] (Petersburg, 1914).
6. The Tolstoy and Gogol translations are ours. The passage occurs in Vol. II, Part 8, Chap. 9 of the edition of *War and Peace* published in Boston by the Dana Estes Co. in 1904–1912. *Translator's note.*
7. Leo Tolstoy, *War and Peace*, IV, Part 13. Chap. 14. *Translator's note.*
8. [Dimitry] Savodnikov, *Zagadki russkovo naroda* [*Riddles of the Russian People*] (St. Petersburg, 1901), Nos. 102–107.
9. *Ibid.*, Nos. 588–591.
10. A. E. Gruzinsky, ed., *Pesni, sobrannye P*[*avel*] *N. Rybnikovym* [*Songs Collected by P. N. Rybnikov*] (Moscow, 1909–1910), No. 30.
11. *Ibid.*, No. 171.
12. We have supplied familiar English examples in place of Shklovsky's word-play. Shklovsky is saying that we create words with no referents or with ambiguous referents in order to force attention to the objects represented by the similar sounding words. By making the reader go through the extra step of interpreting the nonsense word, the writer prevents an automatic response. A toad is a toad, but 'tove' forces one to pause and think about the beast. *Translator's note.*
13. E. R. Romanov, 'Besstrashny barin,' *Velikorusskiye skazki* (Zapiski Imperskovo Russkovo Geograficheskovo Obschestva, XLII, No. 52). Belorussky sbornik, 'Spravyadlivy soldat' ['The Intrepid Gentleman,' *Great Russian Tales* (Notes of the Imperial Russian Geographical Society, XLII, No. 52). White Russian Anthology, 'The Upright Soldier' (1886–1912)].
14. D[mitry] S. Zelenin, *Velikorusskiye skazki Permskoy gubernii* [*Great Russian Tales of the Permian Province* (St. Petersburg, 1913)], No. 70.
15. Dante, *Purgatorio*, 24:56 Dante refers to the new lyric style of his contemporaries. *Translator's note.*
16. Alexy Remizov (1877–1957) is best known as a novelist and satirist; Nicholas Klyuyev (1885–1937) and Sergey Essenin (1895–1925) were 'peasant poets.' All three were noted for their faithful reproduction of Russian dialects and colloquial language. *Translator's note.*
17. A group noted for its opulent and sensuous verse style. *Translator's note.*
18. Nicholas Leskov (1831–1895), novelist and short story writer, helped popularise the *skaz*, or yarn, and hence, because of the part dialect peculiarities play in the *skaz*, also altered Russian literary language. *Translator's note.*
19. Shklovsky is probably referring to his *Razvyortyvaniye syuzheta* [*Plot Development*] (Petrograd, 1921). *Translator's note.*
20. Herbert Spencer, *The Philosophy of Style* [(Humboldt Library, Vol XXXIV; New York, 1882), p. 169. The Russian text is slightly shortened from the original].

3

Boris Tomashevsky,
from 'Thematics'

***2. Story and Plot

A theme has a certain unity and is composed of small thematic elements arranged in a definite order.

We may distinguish two major kinds of arrangement of these thematic elements: (1) that in which causal-temporal relationships exist between the thematic elements, and (2) that in which the thematic elements are contemporaneous, or in which there is some shift of theme without internal exposition of the causal connections. The former are *stories* (tales, novels, epics); the latter have no 'story,' they are 'descriptive' (e.g., descriptive and didactic poems, lyrics, and travel books such as Karamzin's *Letters of a Russian Traveller* or Goncharov's *The Frigate Pallas*).

We must emphasise that a story requires not only indications of time, but also indications of cause. Time indicators may occur in telling about a journey, but if the account is only about the sights and not about the personal adventures of the travelers, we have exposition without story. The weaker the causal connections, the stronger the purely chronological connection. As the story line becomes weaker, we move from the novel to the chronicle, to a simple statement of the sequence of events (*The Childhood Years of Bagrov's Grandson*[1]).

Let us take up the notion of the story, the aggregate of mutually related events reported in the work. No matter how the events were originally arranged in the work and despite their original order of introduction, in practice the story may be told in the actual chronological and causal order of events.

Plot is distinct from story. Both include the same events, but in the plot the events *are arranged* and connected according to the orderly sequence in which they were presented in the work.[2]

The idea expressed by the theme is the idea that *summarizes* and unifies the verbal material in the work. The work as a whole may have a theme, and at the same time each part of a work may have its own theme. The development of a work is a process of diversification unified by a single theme. Thus Pushkin's 'The Shot' develops the story of the narrator's meetings with Silvio and the Count, and the story of the conflict between the two men. The story of life in the regiment and the country is developed, followed by the first part of the duel between Silvio and the Count, and the story of their final encounter.

After reducing a work to its thematic elements, we come to parts that are irreducible, the smallest particles of thematic material: 'evening comes,' 'Raskolnikov kills the old woman,' 'the hero dies,' 'the letter is received,' and so on. The theme

57

of an irreducible part of a work is called the *motif*; each sentence, in fact, has its own motif.

It should be noted that the meaning of 'motif,' as used in historical poetics — in comparative studies of migratory plots (for example, in the study of the *skaz* [or yarn][3]) — differs radically from its meaning here, although they are usually considered identical. In comparative studies a motif is a thematic unit which occurs in various works (for example, 'the abduction of the bride,' 'the helpful beast' — that is, the animal that helps the hero solve his problem — etc.). These motifs move in their entirety from one plot to another. In comparative poetics, reduction to the smaller elements is not important; what is important is only that within the limits of the given genre these 'motifs' are always found in their complete forms. Consequently, in comparative studies one must speak of motifs that have remained intact historically, that have preserved their unity in passing from work to work, rather than of 'irreducible' motifs. Nevertheless, many motifs of comparative poetics remain significant precisely because they are also motifs in our theoretical sense.

Mutually related motifs form the thematic bonds of the work. From this point of view, the story is the aggregate of motifs in their logical, causal-chronological order; the plot is the aggregate of those same motifs but having the relevance and the order which they had in the original work. The place in the work in which the reader learns of an event, whether the information is given by the author, or by a character, or by a series of indirect hints — all this is irrelevant to the story. But the aesthetic function of the plot is precisely this bringing of an arrangement of motifs to the attention of the reader. Real incidents, not fictionalized by an author, may make a story. A plot is wholly an artistic creation.

Usually there are different kinds of motifs within a work. By simply retelling the story we immediately discover what may be *omitted* without destroying the coherence of the narrative and what may not be omitted without disturbing the connections among events. The motifs which cannot be omitted are *bound motifs*; those which may be omitted without disturbing the whole causal-chronological course of events are *free motifs*.

Although only the bound motifs are required by the story, free motifs (digressions, for example) sometimes dominate and determine the construction of the plot. These incidental motifs (details, etc.) are presented so that the tale may be told artistically; we shall return later to the various functions they perform. Literary tradition largely determines the use of free motifs, and each literary school has its characteristic stock; however, bound motifs are usually distinguished by their 'vitality' — that is, they appear unchanged in the works of various schools. Nevertheless, literary tradition clearly plays a significant role in the development of the story (for example, the stories of typical novels of the 1840's and '50's are about the disasters of a petty official — e.g., Gogol's 'The Greatcoat,' Dostoevsky's *Poor People*; in the 1820's the stories were usually about the unfortunate love of a European for a foreigner — e.g., Pushkin's *Captive of the Caucasus* and *The Gypsies*).***

Motifs which change the situation are *dynamic motifs*; those which do not are *static*. Consider, for example, Pushkin's 'Mistress into Maid.' Although Alexey Berestov loves Akulina, his father is arranging his marriage to Liza Muromskaya. Alexey, unaware that Akulina and Liza are one and the same person, objects to the

marriage thrust upon him by his father. He goes to have it out with Liza and discovers that she is Akulina, so the situation changes — Alexey's objections to the
marriage vanish. The discovery that Akulina and Liza are the same person is a
dynamic motif.

Free motifs are usually static, but not all static motifs are free. Thus we assume
that if a murder is necessary to the progress of the story, one of the characters must
have a revolver. The motif of the revolver, as the reader becomes aware of it, is
both static and bound — bound because without the revolver the murder could
not be committed. This situation occurs in Ostrovsky's *The Poor Bride*.

Descriptions of nature, local color, furnishings, the characters, their persona-
lities, and so on — these are typically static motifs. The actions and behavior of the
main characters are typically dynamic motifs.

Dynamic motifs are motifs which are central to the story and which keep it
moving; in the plot, on the other hand, static motifs may predominate.

From the point of view of the story, motifs are easily ranked according to their
importance. Dynamic motifs are most important, then motifs which prepare their
way, then motifs defining the situation, and so on. The relative importance of a
motif to the story may be determined by retelling the *story* in abridged form, then
comparing the abridgement with the more fully developed narrative.***

3. Motivation

The system of motifs comprising the theme of a given work must show some kind of
artistic unity. If the individual motifs, or a complex of motifs, are not sufficiently
suited to the work, if the reader feels that the relationship between certain com-
plexes of motifs and the work itself is obscure, then that complex is said to be superfluous. If all the parts of the work are badly suited to one another, the work is
incoherent. That is why the introduction of each separate motif or complex of motifs
must be *motivated*. The network of devices justifying the introduction of individual
motifs or of groups of motifs is called *motivation*.

The devices of motivation are so numerous and varied that they must be
classified:

(1) The principle of *compositional motivation* refers to the economy and usefulness
of the motifs. Separate motifs may characterize either objects (stage properties)
brought to the reader's attention or the activities of the characters (episodes). Not a
single property may remain unused in the telling, and no episode may be without
influence on the situation. Chekhov referred to just such compositional motivation
when he stated that if one speaks about a nail beaten into a wall at the beginning of a
narrative, then at the end the hero must hang himself on that nail.

A prop, in this case a weapon, is used in precisely this way in Ostrovsky's *The
Poor Bride*. The third act set includes 'a revolver hung on the tapestry over the
divan.' At first this detail of the setting seems a simple, concrete feature
characterizing Karandyshev's way of life. In the sixth scene attention is directed
towards this detail:

ROBINSON: (looking at the tapestry) What do you have here?
KARANDYSHEV: Cigars.
R.:   No, what's hanging up there? Is this real?
K.:   What do you mean 'real'? This is a Turkish weapon.

The dialogue continues and the speakers ridicule the weapon; then the motif narrows until a remark is made about the worthlessness of the pistol:

> K.:   But in what way is it worthless? This pistol, for example . . . (he takes the pistol from the wall).
>
> PARATOV: (taking the pistol from him) This pistol?
>
> K.:   Ah, be careful — it shoots.
>
> P.:   Don't be afraid. It's just as dangerous whether it fires or not. All the same, it won't fire. Shoot at me from five paces; I'll let you.
>
> K.:   Well — no. This pistol may be loaded.
>
> P.:   So — it will do to hammer nails into the wall.
>
> (Throws the pistol on the table.)

At the end of the act the fleeing Karandyshev takes the pistol from the table; in the fourth act he shoots Larissa with it.

Here compositional considerations motivate the introduction of the pistol motif. Because it prepares the audience for the final moments of the play, the pistol is an indispensable part of the denouement. This is the first kind of compositional motivation. A second type of compositional motivation occurs when motifs are used as devices of characterization, but these motifs must be appropriate to the story. Thus in the same play, *The Poor Bride*, the motif of the burgundy prepared and adulterated by a shady wine merchant for cheap sale typifies the poverty of Karandyshev's daily life and prepares for the departure of Larissa.

Details which show character may be integrated with the action either by psychological analogy (e.g. moonlight nights for love scenes and lightning and thunder for scenes of death or evil in novels) or by contrast (the motif of indifferent nature). In *The Poor Bride*, when Larissa dies, the singing of a Gypsy chorus is heard from the restaurant door.

We have still to consider the possibility of misleading motivation; props and episodes may be used to distract the reader's attention from the real situation. This happens frequently in detective novels, where a series of details is given in order to lead the reader (and a group of characters — for example, Watson or the police in Conan Doyle) up a blind alley. The author forces the reader to expect an ending inconsistent with the facts of the case. Techniques of misleading motivation occur chiefly in works created against the background of a major literary tradition; the reader naturally interprets each detail according to the conventions of the tradition. The deception is discovered at the end, and the reader is convinced that all such details were introduced merely to support the final surprises.

Misleading motivation (the play upon generally known literary rules firmly entrenched in tradition and used by the author in other than their traditional ways) is indispensable for parody.

(2) *Realistic motivation.* We demand an element of 'illusion' in any work. No matter how convention-filled and artistic it is, our perception of it must be accompanied by a feeling that what happens in it is 'real.' The naive reader feels this with extraordinary force and may try to verify the authencity of the statements, perhaps even to make certain that the characters existed. Pushkin, after completing *The History of the Pugachyov Rebellion*, published *The Captain's Daughter* in the form of the memoirs of Grinyov and concluded with this epilogue:

> The manuscript of Peter Andreyevitch Grinyov was given to us by one of his grand-children who had learned that we were occupied with a work concerning the times his

grandfather described. We decided, with the family's permission, to publish it separately.

Pushkin creates the illusion of a real Grinyov and his memoirs, supported in detail by a well-know personal fact of Pushkin's life — his historical study of the history of Pugachyov. The illusion is further supported by the opinions and convictions expressed by Grinyov, which differ in many ways from opinions expressed by Pushkin himself.

For more experienced readers the need for realistic illusion expresses itself as a demand for 'lifelikeness.' Although firmly aware of the fictitious nature of the work, the experienced reader nevertheless demands some kind of conformity to reality, and finds the value of the work in this conformity. Even readers fully aware of the laws of aesthetic structure may not be psychologically free from the need for such illusion. As a result, each motif must be introduced as a *probable* motif in the given situation. But since the laws of plot construction have nothing in common with probability, any introduction of motifs is a compromise between objective reality and literary tradition. We will not mention the utter absurdity of many of the more traditional techniques for introducing motifs. To show the irreconcilability of these absurd traditional techniques with realistic motivation we should have to parody them. See, for example, *Vampuk*, the famous parody of operatic productions which humorously presents a selection of lampoonable traditional operatic situations. This parody is still included in the repertory of The Distorted Mirror.[4]

Accustomed to the techniques of adventure novels, we overlook the absurdity of the fact that the rescue of the hero always occurs five minutes before his seemingly inevitable death; the audience of ancient comedy or the comedy of Molière overlooks the fact that in the last act all the characters turn out to be close relatives (the motif of recognition by the family, as in Molière's *The Miser*. The same situation occurs in Beaumarchais' comedy *The Marriage of Figaro*, but by that time the technique is already dead and so it may be parodied. Nevertheless, the extent to which this motif has survived in dramatic literature is shown by Ostrovsky's *The Guilty Are Without Blame*, where at the end of the play the heroine recognises the hero as her lost son.) This motif of the recognition of kinship was exceptionally suitable for the ending (kinship reconciles interests, drastically changing the situation), and so became firmly entrenched in the tradition. The explanation that in antiquity the discovery of a lost son and mother was a common event quite misses the mark; it was common only on the stage, in the rigidly conventional nature of literary form.

When traditional means of introducing motifs are debunked during the development of new schools of poetry, of the two kinds of motivation used by the old school (the traditional and the realistic) only the realistic remains after the traditional declines. That is why any literary school which opposes an older aesthetic always produces manifestoes in one form or another about 'faithfulness to life' or 'adherence to reality.' So Boileau wrote in the seventeenth century, defending the young classicism against the traditions of the old French literature; so in the eighteenth century the encyclopedists defended the less elevated genres (the domestic novel and the bourgeois drama) against the old canons; so in the nineteenth century the romantics, in the name of 'lifelikeness' and faithfulness to 'unadorned nature,' rose up against the orthodoxy of the earlier classicism. Succeeding groups even called themselves 'Naturalists.' In general the nineteenth century abounded in schools whose very names hint at realistic techniques of motivation — 'Realism,' 'Naturalism,' 'the Nature School,' 'Populism,' and so on. In our time the Symbolists replaced the Realists in the name of some kind of transnaturalism (*de realibus ad realiora*, from the real to the more real) a fact which did not prevent the appearance of Acmeism — which demanded greater attention to the *material* and the *concrete* — and Futurism — which initially rejected aestheticism, desiring at its start to repeat the 'original' creative process, and which in its second stage definitely exploited 'lower' processes — e.g., realistic motifs.

From school to school we hear the call to 'Naturalism.' Why, then, has a 'completely naturalistic school' not been founded, one which would be the ultimate Naturalism? — because the name 'Realist' is attached to each school (and to none). Naive literary histories use 'Realist' as the highest praise of a writer; 'Pushkin is a Realist' is a typical historical-literary cliché that does not take into account how the word was used in Pushkin's time. This explains the ever present antagonism of the new school for the old — that is, the exchange of old and obvious conventions for new, less obvious ones within the literary pattern. On the other hand, this also shows that realistic material in itself does not have artistic structure and that the formation of an artistic structure requires that reality be reconstructed according to aesthetic laws. Such laws are always, considered in relation to reality, conventional.

Thus, while the source of realistic motivation is either a naive faith or a demand for illusion, neither prevents the development of literary fantasies. Although folk tales frequently arise among people who believe in the real existence of witches and goblins, their continued existence depends upon some kind of conscious illusion in which a mythological system or fantastic view of the world (i.e., an assumption not really warranted as possible) is present as an illusory hypothesis. On such hypotheses H. G. Wells builds his fantasies — fantasies that are made to seem real not by some mythological system, but by some kind of assumption usually contrary to the laws of nature. (Perelman, in his interesting *Journey to the Planets*, criticises such fantastic novels because of their unreal assumptions.)

It is curious that in sophisticated literary media influenced by a demand for realistic motivation, fantasies are usually open to a double interpretation. They may be accepted both as real events and as fantasies. In the introduction to Alexey Tolstoy's novel, *The Vampire*, which is an unusually clear example of fantasy, Vladimir Solovyev wrote:

> The real interest and significance of the *fantastic* in literature is contained in the belief that everything that happens in the world, and especially everything that happens in the life of man — except that for which the cause is proximate and obvious — still depends on some other kind of causation. This other causation is more profound and more universal, but to make up for that it is less clear. And this is the distinguishing characteristic of the genuinely fantastic; it is never, so to speak, in full view. Its presence must never compel belief in a mystic interpretation of a vital event; it must rather point, or *hint*, at it. In the really fantastic, the external, formal possibility of a simple explanation or ordinary and commonplace connections among the phenomena always remains. This external explanation, however, finally loses its internal probability. All the individual details must seem ordinary, and only their relation to the whole pattern must point to another cause.

If we remove the touch of idealism the philosopher Solovyev gives these words, they contain a satisfactorily precise formulation of the techniques of the fantastic narrative viewed from the norm of realistic motivation. The tales of Hoffmann, the novels of Mrs. Radcliffe, etc., use the technique. Sleep, delirium, optical or other illusions, and so on, are the usual motifs which permit the possibility of double interpretation. (See Bryusov's collection of stories, *The Axis of the Globe*, in this connection.)

Realistic motivation explains why nonliterary materials — that is, themes having real significance outside the limits of the artistic imagination — are introduced into the work of art. Thus in historical novels historical figures are brought onto the scene with this or that interpretation of the historical events, as in Tolstoy's *War and Peace*. The entire report on the military strategy of the Battle of Borodino and the burning of Moscow reminds one of the debates in specialists' journals. More modern works which depict familiar, everyday life raise questions about the moral, social, political, and other orders; themes whose vitality is outside literature are introduced by a single word. Even in conventional parodies, where we see a deliberate display of techniques, we must ultimately discuss questions of poetics. Thus the so-called 'laying bare' of a device (its use without the motivation which traditionally accompanies it) is an indication of the literariness of the literary work, something not unlike the play within a play (that is, a dramatic work in which the spectacle is presented as an element of the story, as in Hamlet's staging of a play or the final scene in Alexandre Dumas' *Kean; ou Désordre et génie*, and so on).

(3) *Artistic motivation.* As I said, the use of a motif results from a compromise between realistic illusion and the demands of the artistic structure. Not everything borrowed from reality is fit for the work of art, as Lermontov noted when he wrote about the journalistic prose of his contemporaries in 1840:

> Whose portraits do they depict?
> Where do they hear their conversations?
> *Yet if they had really happened —*
> *We simply would not want to hear them.*

Boileau said much the same in his play on words, '*le vrai peut quelquefois n'être pas vraisemblable*' ('Sometimes the truth may not seem true'), understanding by '*vrai*' realistic motivation, and by '*vraisemblable*' artistic motivation.

A system of realistic motivation quite often includes a denial of artistic motivation. The usual formula is, 'If this had happened in a novel, my hero would have done such and such, but since it really happened, here are the facts . . . .' But the denial of the literary form in itself asserts the laws of artistic composition.

Each realistic motif must somehow be inserted into the structure of the narrative and be illuminated by a particular part of it. The very selection of realistic themes must be justified artistically.

Usually quarrels between new and old literary groups arise over artistic motivation. The old, tradition-oriented group generally denies the artistry of the new literary form. This is shown, for example, in poetic diction, where the use of individual words must be in accord with firmly established literary traditions (tradition, which produces the distinction between prosaic and poetic words, strictly forbids their use together).

I consider the device of *defamiliarisation* to be a special instance of artistic motivation. The introduction of nonliterary material into a work, if it is to be aesthetic, must be justified by a new and individual interpretation of the material. The old and habitual must be spoken of as if it were new and unusual. One must speak of the ordinary as if it were unfamiliar.

Techniques of defamiliarising ordinary things are usually justified because the objects are distorted through the mental processes of a character who is not familiar with them. A well-known example of Leo Tolstoy's use of the technique occurs in *War and Peace* when he describes the council of war at Fils. He introduces a little peasant girl who watches the council and, like a child, interprets what is done and said without understanding it. Tolstoy uses precisely the same method of interpreting human relationships in 'Kholstomer,' where he presents them through the hypothetical psychology of a horse. (See 'Kashtanka,' in which Chekhov gives as much of the psychology of a dog as is necessary to defamiliarise the narrative; Korolenko's 'The Blind Musician,' which interprets the life of the seeing through the psychology of the blind, is of the same type.)

Swift uses these methods of defamiliarisation extensively in *Gulliver's Travels* in order to present a satirical picture of the European social-political order. Gulliver, arriving in the land of the Houyhnhnms (horses endowed with reason), tells his master (a horse) about the customs of the ruling class in human society. Compelled to tell everything with the utmost accuracy, he removes the shell of euphemistic phrases and fictitious traditions which justify such things as war, class strife, parliamentary intrigue, and so on. Stripped of their verbal justification and thereby defamiliarised, these topics emerge in all their horror. Thus criticism of the political system — nonliterary material — is artistically motivated and fully involved in the narrative.

As a specific example of such defamiliarisation, I shall cite Pushkin's treatment of the duel in *The Captain's Daughter*. As early as 1830, Pushkin wrote in the *Literary Gazette*:

> People in high society have their own modes of thought, their peculiar prejudices, which are incomprehensible to other classes. How do you explain the duel of two French officers to a peace-loving Eskimo? The delicacy of the officers would seem quite strange to him, and he would hardly be wrong.

Pushkin later used this observation in *The Captain's Daughter*. In the third chapter Mironovaya, the Captain's wife, tells Grinyov why Shvabrin was transferred from the guard to an outlying garrison:

> 'Shvabrin was transferred to us five years ago after a murder. God knows what kind of sin he committed. You see, he rode out of the city with a lieutenant, and they took their swords and jabbed at one another, and he began to stab the lieutenant, even though two witnesses were present.'

Later, in the fourth chapter, when Shvabrin challenges Grinyov to a duel, the latter turns to a garrison lieutenant and invites him to second the affair:

> 'You are pleased to say,' he answered, 'that you intend to kill Alexey Ivanovich, and you wish me to witness it? Is that it? May I ask?'
> 'Precisely so.'
> 'Good heavens, Peter Andreyich! What do you think you're doing?
> You've had words with Alexey Ivanovich? So what? Abuse doesn't stick. He curses you, and you swear back at him. He hits you in the kisser, you hit him on one ear — then two, then three, then you part. And then we see to it that you make up later.'

As a result of all this conversation, Grinyov is categorically refused:

> 'You may say what you like, but if I am to get mixed up in this business it will be only to go to Ivan Kuzmich and tell him, as my duty requires, that a crime against the public interest is being plotted in this fortress.'

In the fifth chapter, Savelyich's comments further defamiliarise the subject of dueling with swords:

> 'Not I, but the damned Frenchman, started it all. He taught you to jab people with iron spits and to stamp your feet, as if jabbing and dancing could defend you from a vicious man.'

The result of this comic defamiliarisation is that the idea of dueling is presented in a fresh, unusual form. Here the defamiliarisation is comic, underlined by the diction ('He hits you in the kisser,' — the vulgarism 'kisser' characterizes the speech of the lieutenant about a rough scuffle; it does not at all describe Grinyov's face. 'You hit him on one ear — then two, then three' — counts the number of blows, not ears. Such a clash of words creates the comic effect). But the technique of defamiliarisation is, to be sure, not always comic.***

Notes:

1. A volume of reminiscences by Sergey Aksakov, published in 1858. *Translator's note.*
2. In brief, the story is 'the action itself,' the plot, 'how the reader learns of the action.'
3. Possibly the nearest equivalent of *skaz* is 'yarn.' Technically, a *skaz* is a story in which the manner of telling (normal speech patterns of the narrator — dialect, pronunciation, grammatical peculiarities, pitch patterns, etc.) is as important to the effect as the story itself. For a description of the American equivalent of the *skaz*, see Samuel Clemens' widely reprinted 'How to Tell a Story.' *Translator's note.*
4. The Distorted Mirror was a Petersburg theater which staged parodies. *Vampuk, the African Bride: A Formal Opera in All Respects* was staged there in 1908; the term *Vampuk* was later applied to anything outlandish. *Translator's note.*

Section Three

THE ANALYSIS OF STRUCTURE AND MEANING

Points of information

1. 'The Nature of the Linguistic Sign' was originally published in *Acta Linguistica* I (Copenhagen, 1939). It is reprinted here from Benveniste's *Problems in General Linguistics* (1966), trans. Mary Elizabeth Meek (1971). The two Greek words on p. 79 mean 'nature' and 'position', though the context determines their precise sense.

2. Barthes' 'What is Criticism?' and 'The Imagination of the Sign' are reprinted from his *Critical Essays* (1964), trans. Richard Howard (1972). Both essays contain reference to an array of names significant in French cultural debate in the 1960s. From the point of view of the overall argument perhaps the most significant is Gustave Lanson, who is referred to in 'What is Criticism?'. Lanson (1857–1934) was a French literary historian whose work became standard. He thus represents for Barthes the academic orthodoxy against which he was reacting. The German word 'Abgrund' in the penultimate paragraph of 'The Imagination of the Sign' means 'abyss' or 'chasm'.

3. 'The Struggle With The Angel' was originally published in *Analyse Structurale et exégèse biblique* (1971). It is reprinted here from *Image-Music-Text*, ed. and trans. Stephen Heath (1977).

4. Paul De Man's 'The Dead-End of Formalist Criticism' was first published, in French, in the journal *Critique*. It is reprinted here from his *Blindness and Insight*, 2nd edn. (1983) and is translated by Wlad Godzich. About four pages have been omitted from the end of the essay. They suggest three 'avenues for reflection' on the study of poetics.

Each of the writers whose work is printed in this section is responding, in various ways, to that movement in twentieth-century thought known as 'structuralism' whose influence has been seen by many as marking a decisive shift of interest and focus in literary criticism. Structuralism's intellectual range is enormous. At its broadest it can be said to engage with any structured activity whose laws it proposes to uncover. Thus its influence is felt in a wide range if disciplines from the 'hard' sciences, such as physics or biology, to the humanities where its applications are most contentious. Within literary criticism, however, it is primarily as a theory of language that its effects have been most powerful. The extrapolations made from this theory of language are seen by its opponents to threaten the humanistic core of literary studies.

Though its main endeavours were focused elsewhere, the Anglo-American criticism introduced in Sections 1 and 2 nevertheless had a particular and supporting view of language. In these kinds of criticism language tends to be seen as an unproblematic, humanistic fact, a 'living principle' in F. R. Leavis's phrase; thus in *Revaluation* Leavis can write of the 'sinewy and living nerve of English' as though language were itself a person. Though the special qualities of literary language-use require a heightened sense of complex verbal organisation, attention in the end rests upon the subtle, resonant messages about undifferentiated human experience which literary works deliver. Language, though it invigorates artists, is in the end broadly obedient to them.

In structuralist thought, however, language is seen as neither humanly-centred nor unproblematic. It is a structure with its own internal rules which govern its operation and it is considered theoretically distinct from the uses to which it is put in any given case. In extreme and extended versions (as for instance in some marxist or psychoanalytic adaptations of structuralism) it is seen as a socially-constructed system which coerces language users and imposes pre-established patterns of understanding upon them. Language, in this sense, in an autonomous entity and is not compliant, ultimately, either to the world it allegedly represents or to language users as individuals. Further, all cultural activities, from political processes to literary works, are conditioned by complex structures which can be analysed in their turn as though they worked like a language. Linguistic theory thus provides the basic analytic model for structuralism in the humanities and social sciences.

There are two traditions of structuralist thought on language, though they share major emphases. These are: an American tradition which includes the work of Leonard Bloomfield, Edward Sapir and, most famously, Noam Chomsky; and a European tradition which stems from the work of the Swiss linguist Ferdinand de

Saussure (1857–1913). The American tradition has tended to stress the structures of grammar and syntax, whereas the European has emphasised the analysis of linguistic units, for example individual words. It is the latter — Saussurean — tradition which has had the most direct influence on literary theory.

Saussure's *Course in General Linguistics* (1916) has been seen as one of the path-breaking books of twentieth-century thought, though in fact the text of the *Course* was not written by Saussure himself but compiled, after his death, by two of his students from lecture notes. The *Course* made a radical break from the dominant ideas of nineteenth-century linguistics (which had primarily been concerned with historical philology — the study of the etymological relationships between languages) and established the intellectual basis on which language could be understood as a functioning structure rather than a historically shifting set of discrete facts. In retrospect connections can be made between Saussure's thought and significant new ideas in other branches of knowledge, as the article by Emile Benveniste printed here indicates. Historically, though, the response to Saussure's work was gradual. Whilst it was slowly absorbed into the mainstream of linguistic thought, its significance for other, related areas of intellectual inquiry was not fully explored until the 1960s and 70s. From the point of view of literary studies, what we understand as 'structuralism' is the work of a group of (primarily French) thinkers who applied the principles on which Saussure's work is based directly to other areas, including the study of literature and popular culture; or who adapted these ideas in relationship with other bodies of thought such as psychoanalysis and marxism; or who explored their consequences and implications at 'purely' theoretical or philosophical levels. Aspects of these developments will be outlined in the introductions to subsequent sections.

Structuralism as a movement, then, is strongly interdisciplinary, in contrast to some of the lines of thinking introduced in the first two sections. However in order to understand these theoretical developments it is necessary to have some grasp of the underlying linguistic ideas on which structuralism is based. What follows is an introduction to some Saussurean terms and ideas which are regularly used in literary studies by critics whose work has been influenced by structuralist thought. Clearly it is not possible to introduce structural linguistics — or even Saussure — thoroughly, but readers will need to understand certain features of his work. For a more exacting account of these ideas Jonathan Culler's *Saussure* (1976) is very helpful, as, more generally, is Culler's *Structuralist Poetics* (1975) and the books by Hawkes, Jameson, Lepschy, Robey, Scholes and Sturrock mentioned in the Further Reading.

At the heart of Saussure's work are several essential theoretical distinctions. To begin with he distinguishes between the *diachronic* and the *synchronic* axes of language. The diachronic axis is constituted by the evolution of a language over time, whilst the synchronic axis is constituted by the state of a language at any given moment. The *Course in General Linguistics* is almost entirely preoccupied with the synchronic axis; that is with the formal relationships that obtain within a language between its various parts and which enable it to function as a means of communication. Saussure is primarily interested, then, in describing the rather abstract, formal conditions which enable language to mean anything at all. To this end he makes a further distinction between what he calls *langue* and what he calls *parole*.

Langue refers to the general system of a language, whereas *parole* refers to any utterance made possible by that system. For example, each of us 'knows' the English language system in the 1980s, and, though we are not conscious of it as a totality, its rules and forms permit any act of communication, any *parole*, to take place within it, as for instance in the writing and reading of this introduction. Again, however, within the terms of this distinction, Saussure paid little attention to *parole* and emphasised *langue*, the enabling formal system. Though at various points in the *Course* Saussure is at pains not to rule out of account the contingencies of language use and change, the value of his work for subsequent theorists is to be found in the spotlighting of the rather static, formal character of language. In structuralist accounts *langue* always has functional priority. Any given utterance is made possible by the language system which pre-exists the activities of any language user.

How, then, is *langue* organised? Structural linguistics breaks language down into its functional units. Every language is made up of sound, but not every possible sound is functional within a given language. It is possible for an English speaker to make many sounds, but not all of these sounds are functional (ie meaningful) in English. Those that are functional are called 'phonemes' and a language organises these systematically by rules of combination and differentiation to form strings of meaningful utterance: sounds form words, and words form sentences, and so on in a rule-governed way. The technical term for this is a 'phonological' system, and every language employs such a system though these systems will of course differ from one language to another.

Structuralist analysis then is very careful to distinguish between the various levels at which a language may be analysed, but the basic point is clear. Each linguistic unit derives its function (that is its meaning) from its relationship to the rest of the system. No part of language, at the level of *langue*, is a free-standing entity which means something just by itself. And this has startling implications if for instance we think of the words we give to things, that is, the way language as it were 'labels' the world.

Saussure calls these words *signs*. Any sign, according to Saussure, comprises two elements. These are the *signifier* and the *signified*. The signifier is the material element (the combination of phonemes), and the signified is the mental concept attached to it. The relationship between these two is said to be 'arbitrary'. That is, there is no reason in nature why this thing you are reading should be given the signifier 'book'; it could be given any other signifier (within the phonological rules of English), as long as nothing else was designated by that signifier. In other words, the relationship between the signifier and the signified is a *differential* one within the system. We call this thing 'book' to differentiate it from 'volume', 'newspaper', 'magazine' or indeed any other sign in the language. Again the general point is that it is the system which generates meaning, not the individual unit. This theoretical point is vital because Saussure's concept of the sign entails a further distinction, though the *Course* itself never quite makes this clear (see Benveniste). The mental concept, the signified, is theoretically distinct from the *referent*, or the object outside consciousness for which the sign stands. Signs are not simply welded to the things of the world and so derive their meanings from them. Rather our conceptual schemas, based on language, divide up the world according to their structural character, and our labelling (and hence comprehension) of the world is derived from systems which operate largely independently of the individuals who participate in these systems. The theory is complex and demanding but, once understood, it's not difficult to see the value of these ideas for the study of litera-ture, or indeed any other mode of representation within a culture (myth, for instance, or advertising). For example we might think about the ways in which women are portrayed in, say, poetry where the literary conventions appropriate to that language system offers certain highly stylised and even stereotyped signs to designated femininity. The same point of course could also be made about the representation of male behaviour and characteristics. Structuralist analysis is thus capable of revealing the systematic ways of designation and understanding which every culture possesses.

Clearly these perspectives extend Saussure's thought beyond linguistics proper and they are complex and disputed areas which are given extensive consideration in this and subsequent sections. But Saussure's essential point about language is clear. Language, in his phrase, is a system of 'differences without positive terms'. The reason why we call one animal a 'cat' and another a 'rat', for example, is not because there is something about each animal which spontaneously suggests that these signifiers be used for them. Rather, because they are different conceptual entities, they required different signifiers to mark their differences. There is nothing, theoretically, in the language system itself which would prohibit swopping one signifier for the other so that 'cat' became 'rat' and vice versa. However, after the event as it were, these signs do acquire associations. A rat, for instance, may be associated with vermin or viciousness, whilst a cat — in certain periods and cultures at least — is associated with other quite different and more pleasant things. It is important to take the point, though, that these associated qualities may by no means refer to 'real' attributes. Cats, too, can be vicious, but it hard to imagine James Cagney saying 'You dirty cat!'. These considerations would make such a swopping of signifiers extremely difficult in practice. It would require, indeed, a shift in the whole language system for each individual unit in it is related differentially to all others.

In Saussure's work, then, language (*langue*) is relational and differential. The technical term for this is 'diacritical'. Each linguistic item is linked in opposition to all others and the whole is organised by the overall structure and not by the unique appropriateness of the items to the 'things' they conceptually indicate. It remains now to describe how Saussure theorises the combinations of these items in utterances. Here he distinguishes between the *syntagmatic axis* and the *paradigmatic* or *associative axis*. The syntagmatic axis is, as it were, the horizontal plane, the rules of combination through time as in the rules of combination for phonemes or the syntactical rules which govern the construction of sentences. This latter aspect has been most thoroughly developed by American linguists, especially Chomsky who posits deep language structures embedded in the mind which control syntactical transformations, though his ideas in this respect are disputed (see Further Reading).

The paradigmatic or associative axis concerns the individual units within the sentence; that is the range of items which might take the place of any of the items that have in fact been selected. The speaker or writer thus choses amongst an uncountable number of possible candidates to fill any given 'slot'. These choices are limited formally by the phonological or syntactical rules, but any given word, say, might call up a host of associations. These might be associated through their linguistic forms ('cat' might be associated with 'hat' as well as 'rat'), or conceptually; thus 'hat' might be associated with 'bonnet' and so on. Clearly this latter group can be highly idiosyncratic or culture-bound. 'Bonnet', for instance, may summon up other signs relating to 'femininity' or even 'Scottish-ness' — though in each of these cases the language user would draw, some would feel, upon a highly insulting and restrictive cultural-verbal paradigm.

The idea of paradigmatic sets of signs has been used in psychotherapy in 'word association' tests and, indeed, there is an influential psychoanalytic version of structuralist thought associated with Jacques Lacan which explores the relationships between Saussure's linguistic ideas and Freud's roughly contemporary thought. 'Modernist' art, another phenomenon contemporary with Saussure's work, is also seen by some as exploiting the resources of paradigmatic sets. For instance, Eliot's *The Waste Land* has no obvious formal narrative or 'syntagmatic' shape, but it can be read as organised by associations and resemblances between its various parts. Roman Jakobson (see below) offered a further influential version of the syntagmatic/paradigmatic opposition when he related them to the rhetorical figures of metonymy and metaphor respectively. Jakobson held that forms of writing could then be classified on the basis of their use of these figures. David Lodge has explored these ideas further in his book *The Modes of Modern Writing* (1977). Finally, Roland Barthes' essay 'The Imagination of the Sign', printed here, also uses paradigmatic and syntagmatic as two terms in a typology of modern artistic practice.

Structuralist thinking, then, can offer a highly sophisticated and flexible means of analysing cultural phenomena which relates individual features to the organising structures of which they are a part. Its goal is the identification of the functional features of systems of meaning. Though its methodological model and conceptual apparatus is that of Saussure's linguistics, the material to which it can be applied need not itself be immediately language-based. Indeed, Saussure himself looked forward to a general science of 'semiology' (the study of sign systems) of which linguistics would only be one area. Thus Claude Lévi-Strauss has examined the structures of mythological systems amongst tribal peoples on the model of language. He breaks down into its constituent units ('mythemes') material which is apparently incoherent to the outside observer. He then conceptually reassembles it to display its functional, differential workings. The advantage of this method is that it doesn't translate 'alien' mythologies into western terms, but simply displays its machinery. Or so it is claimed. Structuralist concepts have also been applied to the analysis of visual material, particularly film where Lacanian psychoanalysis has been important. For literary studies Roland Barthes' essay 'What is Criticism?' offers the suggestion that one goal of criticism is to lay bare the complex structural relationships through which meaning is made possible in literary texts, though as a corollary of this position he also insists that critics reveal their own interpretive systems.

Structuralist thought, throughout, stresses the *functional*. It is not interested in details for themselves but only insofar as they contribute to — and are contained within — the overall system of meaning. Thus it will not be interested in isolating one feature as beautiful or moving; nor will it be primarily interested in the situation or place (for instance) to which literary works seem to refer; nor will it be interested in the discussion of characters in a novel or play as though these characters were 'real' people. Rather what it will be interested in are the particular *representations* of places or people. These representations will then be analysed in terms of the structural rules by which they are organised, and hence have meaning and significance within a culture.

This will be clear if one thinks of character stereotypes, for example that villains have black hats and heroes white. Black and white here refer not to what such 'people' 'really' wear, but to the conventional, oppositional structure which gives them their meanings in this case. These meanings are dependent on a relational and oppostional system because neither colour would have any meaning without the other. At this level of example structuralism's insights perhaps seem commonplace, but structuralist thought would go further and claim that even in those cases where characters seem to be 'drawn from life' our sense of their 'reality' is in fact only a product of an organising system of meaning, though in this case an immensely more sophisticated and complex one. (For further consideration of the question of 'realism' in literature see the introduction to Section 4.) It is the business of criticism, then, to reveal the structural workings of these representations of, for example, people. It is because it apparently has 'scientific' aspirations, and because it denies interest in literary characters as people, or literary situations as immediately human situations, that structuralism is considered to be anti-humanist and has provoked much opposition in many quarters of the literary world.

In theory structuralism is indifferent to the kind of material it addresses. Because all cultural products are structurally organised (they have meaning), structuralist analysis can go to work on anything. It is not troubled by the cultural 'value' of this material as were some of the critics in Sections 1 and 2. Indeed Roland Barthes' *Mythologies* is an excellent place to begin acquaintance with structuralist work. *Mythologies* lucidly and wittily engages with popular cultural products and activities (film, menus, tourism, sport, washing powders and so on) drawing out their structural workings and their larger cultural meanings. Its delighted, but sardonic, engagement with these things — in the late 1950s — makes a refreshing contrast to the rather sour jeremiads on popular culture put forward by some British and American critics in the same decade. One interesting aspect of *Mythologies* is its highly ironic sense of literature itself, or rather the literary system, in essays such as 'The Writer on Holiday'. For of course the understanding of literature's place within culture can be as much a part of the critic's business as the analysis of individual works. 'What is Criticism?', for instance, challenges the place criticism assumes for itself; more directly, it challenges the objective, disinterested stance older critics have assumed. All criticism in Barthes' view should make clear the methodological choices is makes amongst the (opposed) range available, for these choices structure any individual critical act.

Of the pieces printed here only Barthes' 'The Struggle With The Angel' attempts anything like a full-blooded structuralist analysis of a piece of text, and even that is complicated by Barthes' own gradual withdrawal from specifically structuralist commitments (see the introduction to Section 4). A great deal of early structuralist work was preoccupied with reconstituting criticism under the new theoretical lights, often by attacking its opponents in response to attacks on it in the highly-charged climate of Parisian intellectual culture in the late 1950s and early

60s when structuralism began generally to develop Saussure's ideas. (Some of these early arguments have been replayed in Britain in the 1980s.) 'The Struggle' indicates some of the analytic procedures which structuralist criticism uses. It is an analysis of a piece of narrative, and narrative analysis has been home-ground for structuralism. This is a project it has resumed from Russian Formalism, and Barthes' essay here might be interestingly compared with Tomashevsky's in Section 2. Details of other structuralist work on narrative is given in the Further Reading.

One other element of structuralist theory needs to be mentioned and this spotlights the connections between structuralism and Russian Formalism. One of the first developments of Saussure's ideas was undertaken by a group of linguists in Prague in the 1930s. Several of these were Russian emigrés who had previously been members of the Formalist groups. Most·prominent amongst them was Roman Jakobson, who later emigrated again to the USA. Jakobson's work on the language texture of literature has been important for the development of structuralist and linguistic approaches to literature. Jakobson was interested in language functions; that is the properties of language that are put to the fore ('foregrounded') in different kinds of language use. These are functional in relation to the discursive purposes of the language type. One of the six functions Jakobson identified was the 'poetic', and he thus took up again the Formalist concern with defining the qualities of specifically literary language. Jakobson's argument is complex, and he develops it in some considerable technical detail in a variety of studies. There isn't space here to attend to it in any detail, but sources and commentaries are noted in the Further Reading. Jakobson's work can be thought to be adjacent to structuralist concerns because again it is concerned with establishing a precise description of the verbal structures which govern a work's meanings.

Finally, the essays in this section also include two resisting voices to some structuralist ambitions which look forward and backward to earlier and subsequent sections. The essay by Emile Benveniste (1902–1976) points up some of the central innovative features of Saussure's theory of the linguistic sign, but he also adds some cautionary thoughts about its exorbitant extension into philosophical territory. This is relevant to the material in Section 4. Paul De Man (1919–1984), on the other hand, anticipates some of these developments. De Man was in his later career one of the leading lights of American 'deconstruction' which is an influential post-structuralist development (see Section 4). In this early essay, he reconsiders the assumptions about literary language made by the Anglo-American tradition of 'practical criticism'. It is interesting that in doing so he couples Barthes' early structuralist work with the analytic ambitions of practical criticism. For De Man the density of signification achieved by literature will always defeat attempts by critics to thoroughly describe it. The theoretical consequences of this belief will become clear in Section 4. His focus on William Empson, as an alternative voice, also reminds us that it is problematic to tidy national or period critical styles into discrete categories. Empson's major work was contemporary with that of the Leavises, and takes its impetus from I. A. Richards.

Further reading:

There are two translations available of Saussure's *Course in General Linguistics*, by Wade Baskin (1959) and Roy Harris (1983). There is also an excellent short introduction to his work by Jonathan Culler, *Saussure* (1976). Further consideration is given in Giulio Lepschy, *A Survey of Structural Linguistics* (1970) which also examines work in the American tradition. John Lyons, *Chomsky* (1970) is also to be recommended.

There are several useful anthologies dealing with semiotics and structuralist thought in various disciplines: Jacques Ehrmann, ed., *Structuralism* (1970); Michael Lane, ed., *Structuralism: A Reader* (1970); David Robey, ed., *Structuralism: An Introduction* (1974); Marshall Blonsky, ed., *On Signs: A Semiotics Reader* (1985); and Robert E. Innes, ed., *Semiotics: An Introductory Anthology* (1986). Robey's anthology includes an essay by Tzvetan Todorov on Henry James.

John Sturrock, *Structuralism* (1986) is a lucid, sympathetic introduction. Jean Piaget, *Structuralism* (1968) mainly examines structuralism in the sciences.

Roland Barthes' *Mythologies* (1957) should be read especially, from a theoretical perspective, the concluding essay 'Myth Today' which relates his analytic practice to the underlying linguistic model. It is also to be found with a number of other essays from *Mythologies*, and much else, in *Barthes: Selected Writings*, ed. Susan Sontag (1983). See also his *Elements of Semiology* (1964) and his *Critical Essays* (1964). For other work by Barthes and studies of it see the Further Reading to Section 4. Tony Bennett *et al.* eds., *Culture, Ideology and Social Process: A Reader* (1981) is an anthology of work on popular culture which includes some structuralist material.

There are four introductory accounts of structuralism which are helpful for students of literature: Fredric Jameson, *The Prison-House of Language* (1972); Robert Scholes, *Structuralism in Literature: An Introduction* (1974); Jonathan Culler, *Structuralist Poetics* (1975); and Terence Hawkes, *Structuralism and Semiotics* (1977). All have very useful bibliographies.

Roman Jakobson's essay on the 'poetic function', 'Linguistics and Poetics', is in *Style in Language*, ed., Thomas Sebeok (1960). A guide to and application of Jakobson's work is to be found in David Lodge, *The Modes of Modern Writing* (1977). See also F. W. Galen, *Historic Structures: The Prague School Project, 1928–1946* (1985). Lodge's *Working With Structuralism* (1981) contains some moderate applications of structuralist principles.

Elizabeth Wright, *Psychoanalytic Criticism: Theory in Practice* (1984) introduces structuralist and post-structuralist psychoanalytic theory for the literature student and will guide further reading in this area. Edmund Leach, *Lévi-Strauss* (1970) is a helpful introduction to his work. Lévi-Strauss's own *Structural Anthropology*, vol. 1, (1958) contains an influential analysis of the Oedipus myth which is relevant to literary studies.

For structuralist work on narrative translated into English see: Vladimir Propp, *Morphology of the Folktale* (1928) (Propp was a member of the Russian Formalist group); Barthes, 'Introduction to the Structural Analysis of Narratives' (1966) (to be found in both the Heath and Sontag collections of his work); Gerard Genette, *Figures of Literary Discourse* (1966–69) and *Narrative Discourse: An Essay in Method* (1972). See also Lodge, *The Modes of Modern Writing*.

Finally, for stimulating critiques from marxist perspectives of structuralist theories of language and their extension into other domains of analysis, see: Robert Weimann, *Structure and Society in Literary History* (1977); Raymond Williams, *Marxism and Literature* (1977), especially Part 1, ch. 3; and Sebastiano Timpanaro, 'Structuralism and its Successors', in his *On Materialism* (1980).

1

Emile Benveniste,
'The Nature of the Linguistic Sign'

The idea of the linguistic sign, which is today asserted or implied in most works of general linguistics, came from Ferdinand de Saussure. And it was as an obvious truth, not yet explicit but nevertheless undeniable in fact, that Saussure taught that the nature of the sign is *arbitrary*. The formula immediately commanded attention. Every utterance concerning the essence of language or the modalities of discourse begins with a statement of the arbitrary character of the linguistic sign. The principle is of such significance that any thinking bearing upon any part of linguistics whatsoever necessarily encounters it. That it is cited everywhere and always granted as obvious are two good reasons for seeking at least to understand the sense in which Saussure took it and the nature of the proofs which show it.

In the *Cours de linguistique générale,*[1] this definition is explained in very simple statements. One calls *sign* 'the total resultant of the association of a signifier (= sound image) and what is signified (= concept) . . .' 'The idea of ''sister'' is not linked by any inner relationship to the succession of sounds *s-ö-r* which serves as its signifier in French; that it could be represented equally by just any other sequence is proved by differences among languages and by the very existence of different languages: the signified ''ox'' has as its signifier *b-ö-f* on one side of the border and *o-k-s* (Ochs) on the other' (p. 102 [pp. 67–68]). This ought to establish that 'The bond between the signifier and the signified is arbitrary,' or, more simply, that 'the linguistic sign is arbitrary' (p. 67). By 'arbitrary,' the author means that 'it is *unmotivated*, i.e., arbitrary in that it actually has no natural connection with the signified' (p. 103 [p. 69]). This characteristic ought then to explain the very fact by which it is verified: namely, that expressions of a given notion vary in time and space and in consequence have no necessary relationship with it.

We do not contemplate discussing this conclusion in the name of other principles or by starting with different definitions. The question is whether it is consistent and whether, having accepted the bipartite nature of the sign (and we do accept it), it follows that the sign should be characterized as arbitrary. It has just been seen that Saussure took the linguistic sign to be made up of a signifier and signified. Now — and this is essential — he meant by 'signifier,' the *concept*. He declared in so many words (p. 100 [p. 66]) that the 'linguistic sign unites, not a thing and a name, but a concept and a sound image.' But immediately afterward he stated that the nature of the sign is arbitrary because it 'actually has no natural connection with the signified' (p. 69). It is clear that the argument is falsified by an unconscious and surreptitious recourse to a third term which was not included in the initial definition. This third term is the thing itself, the reality. Even though Saussure said that the idea of 'sister' is not connected to the signifier *s-ö-r*, he was not thinking any the less of the *reality* of the notion. When he spoke of the difference between *b-ö-f* and *o-k-s*, he was referring in spite of himself to the fact that these two terms applied to the same *reality*. Here, then, is the *thing*, expressly excluded at first from the definition of the sign, now creeping into it by a detour, and permanently installing a contradiction there. For if one states in principle — and with reason — that language is *form*, not *substance*. (p. 163 [p. 113]), it is necessary to admit — and Saussure asserted it plainly — that linguistics is exclusively a science of forms. Even more imperative is the necessity for leaving the 'substance,' *sister* or *ox*, outside the realm of the sign. Now it is only if one thinks of the animal *ox* in its concrete and 'substantial' particularity, that one is justified in considering 'arbitrary' the relationship between *böf* on the one hand and *oks* on the other to the same reality. There is thus a contradiction between the way in which Saussure defined the linguistic sign and the fundamental nature which he attributed to it.

Such an anomaly in Saussure's close reasoning does not seem to me to be imputable to a relaxation of his critical attention. I would see instead a distinctive trait of the historical and relativist thought of the end of the nineteenth century, an inclination often met with in the philosophical reflection of comparative thought. Different people react differently to the same phenomenon. The infinite diversity of attitudes and judgements leads to the consideration that apparently nothing is necessary. From the universal dissimilarity, a universal contingency is inferred. The Saussurian concept is in some measure dependent on this system of thought. To decide that the linguistic sign is arbitrary because the same animal is called *bœuf* in one country and *Ochs* elsewhere, is equivalent to saying that the notion of mourning is arbitrary because in Europe it is symbolized by black, in China by white. Arbitrary, yes, but only under the impassive regard of Sirius or for the person who limits himself to observing from the outside the bond established between an objective reality and human behavior and condemns himself thus to seeing nothing in it but contingency. Certainly with respect to a same reality, all the denominations have equal value; that they exist is thus the proof that none of them can claim that the denomination in itself is absolute. This is true. It is only too true and thus not very instructive. The real problem is far more profound. It consists in discerning the inner structure of the phenomenon of which only the outward appearance is perceived, and in describing its relationship with the ensemble of manifestations on which it depends.

And so it is for the linguistic sign. One of the components of the sign, the sound image, makes up the signifier; the other, the concept, is the signified. Between the signifier and the signified, the connection is not arbitrary; on the contrary, it is *necessary*. The concept (the 'signified') *bœuf* is perforce identical in my consciousness with the sound sequence (the 'signifier') *böf*. How could it be otherwise? Together the two are imprinted on my mind, together they evoke each other under any circumstance. There is such a close symbiosis between them that the concept of *bœuf* is like the soul of the sound image *böf*. The mind does not contain empty forms, concepts without names. Saussure himself said:

> Psychologically our thought — apart from its expression in words — is only a shapeless and indistinct mass. Philosophers and linguists have always agreed in recognizing that without the help of signs we would be unable to make a clear-cut, consistent distinction

between two ideas. Without language, thought is a vague, uncharted nebula. There are no preexisting ideas, and nothing is distinct before the appearance of language (p. 161 [pp. 111–112]).

Conversely, the mind accepts only a sound form that incorporates a representation identifiable for it; if it does not, it rejects it as unknown or foreign. The signifier and the signified, the mental representation and the sound image, are thus in reality the two aspects of a single notion and together make up the ensemble as the embodier and the embodiment. The signifier is the phonic translation of a concept; the signified is the mental counterpart of the signifier. This consubstantiality of the signifier and the signified assures the structural unity of the linguistic sign. Here again we appeal to Saussure himself for what he said of language:

> Language can also be compared with a sheet of paper: thought is the front and the sound the back; one cannot cut the front without cutting the back at the same time; likewise in language, one can neither divide sound from thought nor thought from sound; the division could be accomplished only abstractedly, and the result would be either pure psychology or pure phonology (p. 163 [p. 113]).

What Saussure says here about language holds above all for the linguistic sign in which the primary characteristics of language are incontestably fixed.

One now sees the zone of the 'arbitrary,' and one can set limits to it. What is arbitrary is that one certain sign and no other is applied to a certain element of reality, and not to any other. In this sense, and only in this sense, is it permissible to speak of contingency, and even in so doing we would seek less to solve the problem than to point it out and then to take leave of it temporarily. For the problem is none other than the famous φύσει or Θέσει? and can only be resolved by decree. It is indeed the metaphysical problem of the agreement between the mind and the world transposed into linguistic terms, a problem which the linguist will perhaps one day be able to attack with results but which he will do better to put aside for the moment. To establish the relationship as arbitrary is for the linguist a way of defending himself against this question and also against the solution which the speaker brings instinctively to it. For the speaker there is a complete equivalence between language and reality. The sign overlies and commands reality; even better, it *is* that reality (*nomen/omen*, speech taboos, the magic power of the word, etc.). As a matter of fact, the point of view of the speaker and of the linguist are so different in this regard that the assertion of the linguist as to the arbitrariness of designations does not refute the contrary feeling of the speaker. But, whatever the case may be, the nature of the linguistic sign is not at all involved if one defines it as Saussure did, since the essence of this definition is precisely to consider only the relationship of the signifier and the signified. The domain of the arbitrary is thus left outside the extension of the linguistic sign.

It is thus rather pointless to defend the principle of the 'arbitrariness of the sign' against the objection which could be raised from onomatopoeia and expressive words (Saussure, pp. 103–104 [pp. 69–70]). Not only because their range of use is relatively limited and because expressivity is an essentially transitory, subjective, and often secondary effect, but especially because, here again, whatever the reality is that is depicted by the onomatopoeia or the expressive word, the allusion to that reality in most cases is not immediate and is only admitted by a symbolic convention analogous to the convention that sanctions the ordinary signs of the system.

We thus get back to the definition and the characteristics which are valid for all signs. The arbitrary does not exist here either, except with respect to the pheno-menon or to the *material* object, and does not interfere with the actual composition of the sign.

Some of the conclusions which Saussure drew from the principle here discussed and which had wide effect should now be briefly considered. For instance, he demonstrated admirably that one can speak at the same time of the mutability and immutability of the sign; mutability, because since it is arbitrary it is always open to change, and immutability, because being arbitrary it cannot be challenged in the name of a rational norm. 'Language is radically powerless to defend itself against the forces which from one moment to the next are shifting the relationship between the signified and the signifier. This is one of the consequences of the arbitrary nature of the sign' (p. 112 [p. 75]). The merit of this analysis is in no way diminished, but on the contrary is reinforced, if one states more precisely the rela-tionship to which it in fact applies. It is not between the signifier and the signified that the relationship is modified and at the same time remains immutable; it is between the sign and the object; that is, in other terms, the objective *motivation* of the designation, submitted, as such, to the action of various historical factors. What Saussure demonstrated remains true, but true of the *signification*, not the sign.

Another problem, no less important, which the definition of the sign concerns directly, is that of *value*, in which Saussure thought to find a confirmation of his views: '. . . the choice of a given slice of sound to name a given idea is completely arbitrary. If this were not true, the notion of value would be compromised, for it would include an externally imposed element. But actually values remain entirely relative, and that is why the bond between the sound and the idea is radically arbitrary' (p. 163 [p. 113]). It is worth the trouble to take up in succession the several parts of this argument. The choice that invokes a certain sound slice for a certain idea is not at all arbitrary; this sound slice would not exist without the corresponding idea and vice versa. In reality, Saussure was always thinking of the representation of the *real object* (although he spoke of the 'idea') and of the evidently unnecessary and unmotivated character of the bond which united the sign to the *thing* signified. The proof of this confusion lies in the following sentence in which I have underlined the characteristic part: 'If this were not true, the notion of value would be compromised *since it would include an externally imposed element.*' It is indeed an 'externally imposed element,' that is, the *objective* reality which this argument takes as a pole of reference. But if one considers the sign in itself and insofar as it is the carrier of value, the arbitrary is necessarily eliminated. For — the last proposi-tion is the one which most clearly includes its own refutation — it is quite true that values remain entirely 'relative' but the question is how and with respect to what. Let us state this at once: value is an element of the sign; if the sign taken in itself is not arbitrary, as we think to have shown, it follows that the 'relative' character of the value cannot depend on the 'arbitrary' nature of the sign. Since it is necessary to leave out of account the conformity of the sign to reality, all the more should one consider the value as an attribute only of the *form*, not of the substance. From then on, to say that the values are 'relative' means that they are relative *to each other*. Now, is that not precisely the proof of their *necessity*? We deal no longer here with the isolated sign but with language as a system of signs, and no one has conceived of and described the systematic economy of language as forcefully as Saussure. Whoever says system says arrangement or conformity of parts in a structure which transcends and explains its elements. Everything is so *necessary* in it that modifications of the whole and of details reciprocally condition one another. The relativity of values is the best proof that they depend closely upon one another in the synchrony of a system which is always being threatened, always being restored. The point is that all values are values of opposition and are defined only by their difference. Opposed to each other, they maintain themselves in a mutual relationship of necessity. An opposition is, owing to the force of circumstances, subtended by necessity, as it is necessity which gives shape to the opposition. If language is something other than a fortuitous conglomeration of erratic notions and sounds uttered at random, it is because necessity is inherent in its structure as in all structure.

It emerges, then, that the role of contingency inherent in language affects denomination insofar as denomination is a phonic symbol of reality and affects it in its relationship with reality. But the sign, the primordial element in the linguistic system, includes a signifier and a signified whose bond has to be recognized as *necessary*, these two components being consubstantially the same. *The absolute character of the linguistic sign* thus understood commands in its turn the dialectical *necessity* of values of constant opposition, and forms the structural principle of language. It is perhaps the best evidence of the fruitfulness of a doctrine that it can engender a contradiction which promotes it. In restoring the true nature of the sign in the internal conditioning of the system, we go beyond Saussure himself to affirm the rigour of Saussure's thought.

Note:

1. Cited here from the first edition, Lausanne — Paris, 1916. (Ferdinand de Saussure, *Course in General Linguistics*, Wade Baskin trans. [New York, 1959]. The page numbers in square brackets refer to this translation.)

2

Roland Barthes,
'What is Criticism?'

It is always possible to prescribe major critical principles in accord with one's ideological situation, especially in France, where theoretical models have a great prestige, doubtless because they give the practitioner an assurance that he is participating at once in a combat, a history, and a totality; French criticism has developed in this way for some fifteen years, with various fortunes, within four major 'philosophies.' First of all, what is commonly — and questionably — called existentialism, which has produced Sartre's critical works, his *Baudelaire*, his *Flaubert*, the shorter articles on Proust, Mauriac, Giraudoux, and Ponge, and above all his splendid *Genet*. Then Marxism: we know (the argument is already an old one) how sterile orthodox Marxism has proved to be in criticism, proposing a purely mechanical explanation of works or promulgating slogans rather than criteria of values; hence it is on the 'frontiers' of Marxism (and not at its avowed centre) that we find the most fruitful criticism: Lucien Goldmann's work explicitly owes a great deal to Lukacs; it is among the most flexible and the most ingenious criticism which takes social and political history as its point of departure. And then psychoanalysis; in France today, the best representative of Freudian criticism is Charles Mauron, but here too it is the 'marginal' psychoanalysis which has been most fruitful; taking its departure from an analysis of substances (and not of works), following the dynamic distortions of the image in a great number of poets, Bachelard has established something of a critical school, so influential that one might call French criticism today, in its most developed form, a criticism of Bachelardian inspiration (Poulet, Starobinski, Richard). Finally structuralism (or to simplify to an extreme and doubtless abusive degree: formalism): we know the importance, even the vogue of this movement in France since Lévi-Strauss has opened to it the methods of the social sciences and a certain philosophical reflection; few critical works have as yet resulted from it, but they are in preparation, and among them we shall doubtless find, in particular, the influence of linguistic models constructed by Saussure and extended by Jakobson (who himself, early in his career, participated in a movement of literary criticism, the Russian formalist school): it appears possible, for example, to develop an entire literary criticism starting from the two rhetorical categories established by Jakobson: metaphor and metonymy.

As we see, this French criticism is at once 'national' (it owes little or nothing to Anglo-American criticism, to Spitzer and his followers, to the Croceans) and contemporary (one might even say 'faithless'): entirely abosorbed in a certain ideological present, it is reluctant to acknowledge any participation in the critical tradition of Sainte-Beuve, Taine, or Lanson. This last model nonetheless raises a special problem for our contemporary criticism. The work, method, and spirit of Lanson, himself a prototype of the French professor, has controlled, through countless epigones, the whole of academic criticism for fifty years. Since the (avowed) principles of this criticism are rigour and objectivity in the establishment of facts, one might suppose that there is no incompatibility between Lansonism and the ideological criticisms, which are all criticisms of interpretation. However, though the majority of French critics today are themselves professors, there is a certain tension between interpretive criticism and positivist (academic) criticism. This is because Lansonism is itself an ideology; not content to demand the application of the objective rules of all scientific investigation, it implies certain general convictions about man, history, literature, and the relations between author and work; for example, the psychology of Lansonism is utterly dated, consisting essentially of a kind of analogical determinism, according to which the details of a work must *resemble* the details of a life, the soul of a character must *resemble* the soul of the author, etc. — a very special ideology, since it is precisely in the years following its formulation that psychoanalysis, for example, has posited contrary relations, relations of denial, between a work and its author. Indeed, philosophical postulates are inevitable; Lansonism is not to be blamed for its prejudices but for the fact that it conceals them, masks them under the moral alibi of rigour and objectivity: ideology is smuggled into the baggage of scientism like contraband merchandise.

If these various ideological principles are possible at the same time (and for my part, in a certain sense I subscribe to each of them at the same time), it is doubtless because an ideological choice does not constitute the Being of criticism and because 'truth' is not its sanction. Criticism is more than discourse in the name of 'true' principles. It follows that the capital sin in criticism is not ideology but the silence by which it is masked: this guilty silence has a name: *good conscience*, or again, *bad faith*. How could we believe, in fact, that the work is an object exterior to the psyche and history of the man who interrogates it, an object over which the critic would exercise a kind of extraterritorial right? By what miracle would the profound communication which most critics postulate between the work and its author cease in relation to their own enterprise and their own epoch? Are there laws of creation valid for the writer but not for the critic? All criticism must include in its discourse (even if it is in the most indirect and modest manner imaginable) an implicit reflection on itself; every criticism is a criticism of the work *and* a criticism of itself. In other words, criticism is not at all a table of results or a body of judgements, it is essentially an activity, i.e., a series of intellectual acts profoundly committed to the historical and subjective existence (they are the same thing) of the man who performs them. Can an activity be 'true'? It answers quite different requirements.

Every novelist, every poet, whatever the detours literary theory may take, is presumed to speak of objects and phenomena, even if they are imaginary, exterior and anterior to language: the world exists and the writer speaks: that is literature. The object of criticism is very different; the object of criticism is not 'the world' but a discourse, the discourse of someone else: criticism is discourse upon a discourse; it is a second language, or a *metalanguage* (as the logicians would say), which operates on a first language (or *language object*). It follows that the critical language must deal with two kinds of relations: the relation of the critical language to the language of the author studied, and the relation of this language object to the world. It is the 'friction' of these two languages which defines criticism and perhaps gives it a great resemblance to another mental activity, logic, which is also based on the distinction between language object and metalanguage.

For if criticism is only a metalanguage, this means that its task is not at all to discover 'truths,' but only 'validities.' In itself, a language is not true or false, it is or is not valid: valid, i.e., constitutes a coherent system of signs. The rules of literary language do not concern the conformity of this language to reality (whatever the claims of the realistic schools), but only its submission to the system of signs the author has established (and we must, of course, give the word *system* a very strong sense here). Criticism has no responsibility to say whether Proust has spoken 'the truth,' whether the Baron de Charlus was indeed the Count de Montesquiou, whether Françoise was Céleste, or even, more generally, whether the society Proust described reproduces accurately the historical conditions of the nobility's disappearance at the end of the nineteenth century; its role is solely to elaborate a language whose coherence, logic, in short whose *systematics* can collect or better still can 'integrate' (in the mathematical sense of the word) the greatest possible quantity of Proustian language, exactly as a logical equation tests the validity of reasoning without taking sides as to the 'truth' of the arguments it mobilizes. One can say that the criticial task (and this is the sole guarantee of its universality) is purely formal: not to 'discover' in the work or the author something 'hidden,' 'profound,' 'secret,' which hitherto passed unnoticed (by what miracle? Are we more perspicacious than our predecessors?), but only to adjust the language his period affords him (existentialism, Marxism, psychoanalysis) to the language, i.e., the formal system of logical constraints elaborated by the author according to his own period. The 'proof' of a criticism is not of an 'alethic' order (it does not proceed from truth), for critical discourse — like logical discourse, moreover — is never anything but tautological: it consists in saying ultimately, though placing its whole being within that delay, what thereby is not insignificant: Racine is Racine, Proust is Proust; critical 'proof,' if it exists, depends on an aptitude not to *discover* the work in question but on the contrary to *cover* it as completely as possible by its own language.

Thus we are concerned, once again, with an essentially formal activity, not in the esthetic but in the logical sense of the term. We might say that for criticism, the only way of avoiding 'good conscience' or 'bad faith' is to take as a moral goal not the decipherment of the work's meaning but the reconstruction of the rules and constraints of that meaning's elaboration; provided we admit at once that a literary work is a very special semantic system, whose goal is to put 'meaning' in the world, but not 'a meaning'; the work, at least the work which ordinarily accedes to critical scrutiny — and this is perhaps a definition of 'good' literature — the work is never entirely non-signifying (mysterious or 'inspired'), and never entirely clear; it is, one may say, a *suspended* meaning: it offers itself to the reader as an avowed signifying system yet withholds itself from him as a signified object. This disappointment of meaning explains on the one hand why the literary work has so much power to ask the world questions (undermining the assured meanings which ideologies, beliefs, and common sense seem to possess), yet without ever answering them (there is no great work which is 'dogmatic'), and on the other hand why it offers itself to endless decipherment, since there is no reason for us ever to stop speaking of Racine or Shakespeare (unless by a disaffection which will itself be a language): simultaneously an insistent proposition of meaning and a stubbornly fugitive meaning, literature is indeed only a *language*, i.e., a system of signs; its being is not in its message but in this 'system.' And thereby the critic is not responsible for reconstructing the work's message but only its system, just as the linguist is not responsible for deciphering the sentence's meaning but for establishing the formal structure which permits this meaning to be transmitted.

It is by acknowledging itself as no more than a language (or more precisely, a metalanguage) that criticism can be — paradoxically but authentically — both objective and subjective, historical and existential, totalitarian and liberal. For on the one hand, the language each critic chooses to speak does not come down to him from Heaven; it is one of the various languages his age affords him, it is objectively the end product of a certain historical ripening of knowledge, ideas, intellectual passions — it is a *necessity*; and on the other hand, this necessary language is chosen by each critic as a consequence of a certain existential organisation, as the exercise of an intellectual function which belongs to him in his own right, an exercise in which he puts all his 'profundity,' i.e., his choices, his pleasures, his resistances, his obsessions. Thus begins, at the heart of the critical work, the dialogue of two histories and two subjectivities, the author's and the critic's. But this dialogue is egoistically shifted toward the present: criticism is not an 'homage' to the truth of the past or to the truth of 'others' — it is a construction of the intelligibility of our own time.

3

Roland Barthes,
'The Imagination of the Sign'

Every sign includes or implies three relations. To start with, an interior relation which unites its signifier to its signified; then two exterior relations: a virtual one that unites the sign to a specific reservoir of other signs it may be drawn from in order to be inserted in discourse; and an actual one that unites the sign to other signs in the discourse preceding or succeeding it. The first type of relation appears clearly in what is commonly called a *symbol*; for instance, the Cross 'symbolizes' Christianity, red 'symbolizes' a prohibition to advance; we shall call this first relation, then, a *symbolic* relation, though we encounter it not only in symbols but also in signs (which are, roughly speaking, purely conventional symbols). The second type of relation implies the existence, for each sign, of a reservoir or organised 'memory' of forms from which it is distinguished by the smallest difference necessary and sufficient to effect a change of meaning; in *lupum*, the element *-um* (which is a sign, and more precisely a morpheme) affords its meaning of 'accusative case' only insofar as it is opposed to the (virtual) remainder of the declension (*-us, -i, -o,* etc.); red signifies prohibition only insofar as it is *systematically* opposed to green and yellow (of course, if there were no other colour but red, red would still be opposed to the absence of colour); this second type of relation is therefore that of the system, sometimes called paradigm; we shall therefore call it a *paradigmatic* relation. According to the third type of relation, the sign is no longer situated with regard to its (virtual) 'brothers,' but with regard to its (actual) 'neighbours'; in *homo homini lupus, lupus* maintains certain connections with *homo* and with *homini*; in garment systems, the elements of an outfit are associated according to certain rules: to wear a sweater and a leather jacket is to create, between these two garments, a temporary but signifying association, analogous to the one uniting the words of a sentence; this level of association is the level of the syntagm, and we shall call the third relation the *syntagmatic relation*.

Now it seems that when we consider the signifying phenomenon (and this interest may proceed from very different horizons), we are obliged to focus on one of these three relations more than on the other two; sometimes we 'see' the sign in its symbolic aspect, sometimes in its systematic aspect, sometimes in its syntagmatic aspect; this is occasionally the result of mere ignorance of the other relations: symbolism has long been blind to the formal relations of the sign; but even when the three relations have been defined (for example, in linguistics), each school tends to base its analysis on one of the sign's dimensions: one vision overflows the whole of the signifying phenomenon, so that we may speak, apparently, of different semiological consciousnesses (I refer, of course, to the consciousness of the analyst, not of the user, of the sign). Now, on the one hand, the choice of a dominant relation implies a certain ideology; and, on the other hand, one might say that each consciousness of the sign (symbolic, paradigmatic, and syntagmatic) corresponds to a certain moment of reflection, either individual or collective: structuralism, in particular, can be defined historically as the passage from symbolic consciousness to paradigmatic consciousness: there is a history of the sign, which is the history of its 'consciousnesses.'

The symbolic consciousness sees the sign in its profound, one might almost say its geological, dimension, since for the symbolic consciousness it is the tiered arrangement of signifier and signified which constitutes the symbol; there is a consciousness of a kind of vertical relation between the Cross and Christianity: Christianity is *under* the Cross, as a profound mass of beliefs, values, practices, more or less disciplined on the level of its form. The verticality of the relation involves two consequences: on the one hand, the vertical relation tends to seem solitary: the symbol seems to stand by itself in the world and even when we assert that it is abundant, it is abundant in the fashion of a 'forest' — i.e., by an anarchic juxtaposition of profound relations which communicate, so to speak, only by their roots (by what is signified); and on the other hand, this vertical relation necessarily appears to be an analogical relation: to some degree the form resembles the content, as if it were actually produced by it, so that the symbolic consciousness may sometimes mask an unacknowledged determinism: thus there is a massive privilege of resemblance (even when we emphasize the inadequate character of the sign). The symbolic consciousness has dominated the sociology of symbols and of course a share of psychoanalysis in its early stages, though Freud himself acknowledged the inexplicable (nonanalogical) character of certain symbols; this moreover was the period when the very word *symbol* prevailed; during all this time, the symbol possessed a mythic prestige, the glamour of 'richness': the symbol was rich, hence it could not be reduced to a 'simple sign' (today we may doubt the sign's 'simplicity'): its form was constantly exceeded by the power and the movement of its content; indeed, for the symbolic consciousness, the symbol is much less a (codified) form of communication than an (affective) instrument of participation. The word *symbol* has now gone a little stale; we readily replace it by *sign* or *signification*. This terminological shift expresses a certain crumbling of the symbolic consciousness, notably with regard to the analogical character of signifier and signified; nonetheless the symbolic consciousness remains typical, insofar as its analytical consideration is not interested in the formal relations of signs, for the symbolic consciousness is essentially the rejection of form; what interests it in the sign is the signified: the signifier is always a determined element.

Once the forms of two signs are compared, or at least perceived in a somewhat comparative manner, a certain paradigmatic consciousness appears; even on the level of the classical symbol, the least subtle of signs, if there is some occasion to perceive the variation of two symbolic forms, the other dimensions of the sign are immediately discovered; as in the case, for instance, of the opposition between *Red Cross* and *Red Crescent*: on the one hand, *Cross* and *Crescent* cease to entertain a 'solitary' relation with what they respectively signify (Christianity and Islam), they are included in a stereotyped syntagm; and, on the other hand, they form between themselves an interplay of distinctive terms, each of which corresponds to

a different signified: the paradigm is born. The paradigmatic consciousness therefore defines meaning not as the simple encounter of signifier and signified, but,
according to Merleau-Ponty's splendid expression, as a veritable 'modulation of
coexistence'; it substitutes for the bilateral relation of the symbolic consciousness a
quadrilateral or more precisely a homological relation. It is the paradigmatic consciousness which permitted Lévi-Strauss to reconceive the problem of totemism:
whereas the symbolic consciousness vainly seeks the 'dimensional,' more or less
analogical characters which unite a signifier (the totem) to a signified (the clan), the
paradigmatic consciousness establishes a homology (as Lévi-Strauss calls it)
between the relation of two totems and that of two clans. Naturally, by retaining in
the signified only its demonstrative role (it designates the signifier and makes it
possible to locate the terms of the opposition), the paradigmatic consciousness
tends to empty it: but it does not thereby empty the signification. It is obviously the
paradigmatic consciousness which has permitted (or expressed) the extraordinary
development of phonology, a science of exemplary paradigms (*marked/non-marked*):
it is the paradigmatic consciousness which, through the work of Lévi-Strauss,
defines the structuralist threshold.

The syntagmatic consciousness is a consciousness of the relations which unite
signs on the level of discourse itself, i.e., essentially a consciousness of the constraints, tolerances, and liberties of the sign's associations. This consciousness has
marked the linguistic endeavours of the Yale school and, outside linguistics, the
investigations of the Russian formalist school, notably those of Propp in the
domain of the Slavic folk tale (hence we may expect that it will eventually illuminate analysis of the major contemporary 'narratives,' from the *fait-divers* to the
popular novel). But this is not the only orientation of the syntagmatic consciousness; of the three, it is certainly the syntagmatic consciousness which most readily
renounces the signified: it is more a structural consciousness than a semantic one,
which is why it comes closest to practice: it is the syntagmatic consciousness which
best permits us to imagine operational groups, 'dispatchings,' complex classifications: the paradigmatic consciousness permits the fruitful return from decimalism
to binarism; but it is the syntagmatic consciousness which actually permits us to
conceive cybernetic 'programs,' just as it has permitted Propp and Lévi-Strauss to
reconstruct the myth-'series.'

Perhaps we shall some day be able to return to the description of these semantic
consciousnesses, attempt to link them to a history; perhaps we shall some day be
able to create a semiology of the semiologists, a structural analysis of the structuralists. All we are endeavouring to say here is that there is probably a genuine
imagination of the sign; the sign is not only the object of a particular knowledge,
but also the object of a vision, analogous to the vision of the celestial spheres in
Cicero's *Somnium Scipionis* or related to the molecular representations used by
chemists; the semiologist *sees* the sign moving in the field of signification, he
enumerates its valences, traces their configuration: the sign is, for him, a sensuous
idea. Of the three (still fairly technical) consciousnesses discussed here, we must
presume an extension toward much wider types of imagination, which we may find
mobilized in many other objects than the sign.

The symbolic consciousness implies an imagination of depth; it experiences the
world as the relation of a superficial form and a many-sided, massive, powerful
Abgrund, and the image is reinforced by a very intense dynamics: the relation of

form and content is ceaselessly renewed by time (history), the superstructure overwhelmed by the infrastructure, without our ever being able to grasp the structure itself. The paradigmatic consciousness, on the contrary, is a formal imagination; it *sees* the signifier linked, as if in profile, to several virtual signifiers which it is at once close to and distinct from: it no longer sees the sign in its depth, it sees it in its perspective; thus the dynamics attached to this vision is that of a summons: the sign is chosen from a finite organised reservoir, and this summons is the sovereign act of signification: imagination of the surveyor, the geometrician, the owner of the world who finds himself at his ease on his property, since man, in order to signify, has merely to choose from what is presented to him already prestructured either by his brain (in the binarist hypothesis), or by the material finitude of forms. The syntagmatic imagination no longer sees the sign in its perspective, it *foresees* it in its extension: its antecedent or consequent links, the bridges it extends to other signs; this is a 'stemmatous' imagination of the chain or the network; hence the dynamics of the image here is that of an arrangement of mobile, substitutive parts, whose combination produces meaning, or more generally a new object; it is, then, a strictly fabricative or even *functional* imagination (the word is conveniently ambiguous, since it refers both to the notion of a variable relation and to that of a usage).

Such are (perhaps) the three imaginations of the sign. We may doubtless attach to each of them a certain number of different creations, in the most diverse realms, for nothing constructed in the world today escapes meaning. To remain in the realm of recent intellectual creation, among the works of the profound (symbolic) imagination, we may cite biographical or historical criticism, the sociology of 'visions,' the realist or introspective novel, and in a general way, the 'expressive' arts or languages, postulating the signified as sovereign, extracted either from an interiority or from a history. The formal (or paradigmatic) imagination implies an acute attention to the *variation* of several recurrent elements; thus this type of imagination accommodates the dream and oneiric narratives, powerfully thematic works and those whose esthetic implies the interplay of certain commutations (Robbe-Grillet's novels, for example). The functional (or syntagmatic) imagination nourishes, lastly, all those works whose fabrication, by arrangement of discontinuous and mobile elements, constitutes the spectacle itself: poetry, epic theatre, serial music, and structural compositions, from Mondrian to Butor.

4

Roland Barthes,
'The Struggle With The Angel: Textual
Analysis of Genesis *32:22–32'*

(22) And he rose up that night, and took his two wives, and his two women-servants, and his eleven sons, and passed over the ford Jabbok. (23) And he took them, and sent them over the brook, and sent over that he had. (24) And Jacob was left alone; and there wrestled a man with him until the breaking of the day. (25) And when he saw that he prevailed not against him, he touched the hollow of his thigh; and the hollow of Jacob's thigh was out of joint as he wrestled with him. (26) And he said, Let me go, for the day breaketh. And he said, I will not let thee go, except thou bless me. (27) And he said unto him, What is thy name? And he said, Jacob. (28) And he said, Thy name shall be called no more Jacob, but Israel: for as a prince hast thou power with God and with men, and hast prevailed. (29) And Jacob asked him, and said, Tell me, I pray thee, thy name. And he said, Wherefore is it thou dost ask after my name? And he blessed him there. (30) And Jacob called the name of the place Peniel: for I have seen God face to face, and my life is preserved. (31) And as he passed over Penuel the sun rose upon him, and he halted upon his thigh. (32) Therefore the children of Israel eat not of the sinew which shrank, which is upon the hollow of the thigh, unto this day: because he touched the hollow of Jacob's thigh in the sinew that shrank. (*Authorised Version*)

The clarifications — or precautionary remarks — which will serve as an introduction to the following analysis will in fact be largely negative. First of all, it must be said that I shall not be giving any preliminary exposition of the principles, perspectives and problems of the structural analysis of narrative. That analysis is not a science nor even a discipline (it is not taught), but, as part of the newly developing semiology, it nevertheless represents an area of research which is becoming well known, so much so that to set out its prolegomena on the occasion of every fresh analysis[1] would be to run the risk of producing an impression of useless repetition. Moreover, the structural analysis presented here will not be very pure. I shall indeed be referring in the main to the principles shared by all those semiologists concerned with narrative and, to finish, I shall even show how the piece under discussion lends itself to an extremely classic and almost canonical structural analysis, this orthodox consideration (orthodox from the point of view of the structural analysis of narrative) is all the more justified in that we shall be dealing with a mythical narrative that may have entered writing (entered Scripture) via an oral tradition. At the same time, however, I shall allow myself every so often (and perhaps continuously on the quiet) to direct my investigations towards an analysis with which I am more at home, textual analysis ('textual' is used with reference to the contemporary theory of the *text*, this being understood as production of *signifiance* and not as philological object, custodian of the Letter). Such an analysis endeavours to 'see' each particular text in its difference — which does not mean in its ineffable individuality, for this difference is 'woven' in familiar codes; it conceives the text as taken up in an *open* network which is the very infinity of language, itself structured without closure; it tries to say no longer *from where* the text comes (historical criticism), nor even *how* it is made (structural analysis), but how it is unmade, how it explodes, disseminates — by what coded paths it *goes off*. Finally, the last of these precautionary remarks and intended to forestall any disappointment, there is no question in what follows of a methodological confrontation between structural or textual analysis and exegesis, this lying outside my competence.[2] I shall simply analyse the text of *Genesis* 32 (traditionally called 'Jacob's struggle with the angel') as though I were at the first stage of a piece of research (which is indeed the case). What is given here is not a 'result' nor even a 'method' (which would be too ambitious and would imply a 'scientific' view of the text that I do not hold), but merely a 'way of proceeding'.

I. Sequential Analysis

Structural analysis embraces roughly three types or three objects of analysis, or again, if one prefers, comprises three tasks. 1) The inventorization and classification of the 'psychological', biographical, characterical and social attributes of the characters involved in the narrative (age, sex, external qualities, social situation or position of importance, etc.) Structurally, this is the area of indices (notations, of infinitely varied expression, serving to transmit a signified — as, for example, 'irritability', 'grace', 'strength' — which the analyst names in his metalanguage; it being understood that the metalinguistic term may very well not figure directly in the text — as indeed is generally the case — which will not employ 'irritability' or 'grace' or whatever. If one establishes a homology between narrative and (the linguistic) sentence, then the indice corresponds to the adjective, to the *epithet* (which, let us not forget, was a figure of rhetoric). This is what we might call *indicial analysis*. 2) The inventorization and classification of the *functions* of the characters; what they do according to their narrative status, in their capacity as subject of an action that remains constant: the Sender, the Seeker, the Emissary, etc. In terms of the sentence, this would be the equivalent of the *present participle* and is that *actantial analysis* of which A. J. Greimas was the first to provide the theory. 3) The inventorization and classification of the *actions*, the plane of the *verbs*. These narrative actions are organized in sequences, in successions apparently ordered according to a pseudo-logical schema (it is a matter of a purely empirical, cultural logic, a product of experience — even if ancestral — and not of reasoning). What we have here is thus *sequential analysis*.

Our text lends itself, if in fact briefly, to indicial analysis. The contest it describes can be read as an indice of Jacob's strength (attested in other episodes of the chronicle of this hero's exploits) and that indice leads towards an anagogical meaning which is the (invincible) strength of God's Elect. Actantial analysis is also possible, but as the text is essentially made up of seemingly contingent actions it is better to work mainly on a sequential (or actional) analysis of the episode, being prepared in conclusion to add one or two remarks concerning the actantial. I shall divide the text (without, I think, forcing things) into three sequences: 1. the Crossing, 2. the Struggle, 3. the Namings.

1. *The Crossing* (v. 22–24). Let us straightaway give the schema of the sequences of this episode, a schema which is twofold or at least, as it were, 'strabismic' (what is at stake here will be seen in a moment):

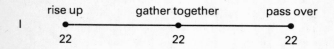

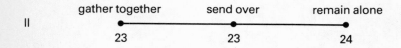

It can be noted at once that structurally *rise up* is a simple *operator for beginning*; one might say, putting things quickly, that by *rise up* is to be understood not only that Jacob starts moving but also that the discourse *gets underway*. The beginning of a narrative, of a discourse, of a text, is an extremely sensitive point — *where to begin?* the *said* must be torn from the *not-said*, whence a whole rhetoric of beginning *markers*. The most important thing, however, is that the two sequences (or subsequences) seem to be in a state of redundancy (which is perhaps usual in the discourse of the period: a piece of information is given and then repeated; but the rule here is reading, not the historical and philological determination of the text: we are reading the text not in its 'truth' but in its 'production' — which is not its 'determination'). Paradoxically moreover (for redundancy habitually serves to homogenize, to clarify and assure a message), when read after two millennia of Aristotelian rationalism (Aristotle being the principal theoretician of classic narrative) the redundancy of the two sub-sequences creates an abrasion, a grating of readability. The sequential schema, that is, can be read in two ways: 1) Jacob himself crosses over the ford — if need be after having made several trips back and forth — and thus the combat takes place on the left bank of the flood (he is coming from the North) *after he has definitively crossed over*; in this case, *send over* is read *cross over himself*; 2) Jacob sends over but does not himself cross over; he fights on the right bank of the Jabbok *before crossing over*, in a rearguard position. Let us not look for some *true* interpretation (perhaps our very hesitation will appear ridiculous in the eyes of the exegetes); rather, let us consume two different pressures of readability: 1) if Jacob remains alone *before* crossing the Jabbok, we are led towards a 'folkloric' reading of the episode, the mythical reference then being overwhelming which has it that a trial of strength (as for example with a dragon or the guardian spirit of a river) must be imposed on the hero *before* he clears the obstacle, *so that* — once victorious — he can clear it; 2) if on the contrary Jacob having crossed over (he and his tribe), he remains alone on the good side of the flood (the side of the country to which he wants to go), then the passage is without structural finality while acquiring on the other hand a religious finality: if Jacob is alone, it is no longer to settle the question of and obtain the crossing but in order that he be *marked* with solitude (the familiar *setting apart* of the one chosen by God). There is a historical circumstance which increases the undecidability of the two interpretations. Jacob's purpose is to return home, to enter the land of Canaan: given this, the crossing of the River Jordan would be easier to understand than that of the Jabbok. In short, we are confronted with the crossing of a spot that is neutral. The crossing is crucial if Jacob has to win it over the guardian of the place, indifferent if what is important is the solitude, the mark of Jacob. Perhaps we have here the tangled trace of two stories, or at least of two narrative instances: the one, more 'archaic' (in the simple stylistic sense of the term), makes of the crossing itself an ordeal; the other, more 'realist', gives a 'geographical' air to Jacob's journey by mentioning the places he goes through (without attaching any mythical value to them).

If one carries back on to this twofold sequence the pattern of subsequent events, that is the Struggle and the Naming, the dual reading continues, coherent to the end in each of its two versions. Here again is the diagram:

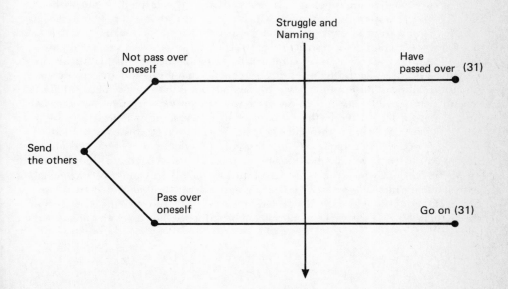

If the Struggle stands between the 'not pass over' and the 'have passed over' (the folklorizing, mythical reading), then the mutation of the Names corresponds to the very purpose of every etymological saga; if on the contrary the Struggle is only a stage between a position of immobility (of meditation, of election) and a movement of setting off again, then the mutation of the Name has the value of a spiritual rebirth (of 'baptism'). All of which can be summarised by saying that in this first episode there is sequential readability but cultural ambiguity. No doubt the theologian would grieve at this indecision while the exegete would acknowledge it hoping for some element of fact or argument that would enable him to put an end to it. The textual analyst, judging by my own impression, savours such *friction* between two intelligibilities.

2. *The Struggle* (v. 24–29). For the second episode we have once again to start from a complication (which is not to say a doubt) of readability — remember that textual analysis is founded on *reading* rather than on the objective structure of the text, the latter being more the province of structural analysis. This complication stems from the interchangeable character of the pronouns which refer to the two opponents in the combat: a style which a purist would describe as *muddled* but whose lack of sharpness doubtless posed no problem for Hebrew syntax. Who is 'a man'? Staying within verse 25, is it 'a man' who does not succeed in getting the better of Jacob or Jacob who cannot prevail over this someone? Is the 'he' of 'he prevailed not against him' (25) the same as the 'he' of 'And he said' (26)? Assuredly everything becomes clear in the end but it requires in some sort a retro-active reasoning of a syllogistic kind: you have vanquished God. He who is speaking to you is he whom you vanquished. Therefore he who is speaking to you is God. The identification of the opponents is oblique, the readability is *diverted* (whence occasionally commentaries which border on total misunderstanding; as for example: 'He wrestles with the Angel of the Lord and, thrown to the ground, obtains from him the certainty that God is with him').

Structurally, this amphibology, even if subsequently clarified, is not without significance. It is not in my opinion (which is, I repeat, that of a reader today) a simple complication of expression due to an unpolished, archaizing style; it is bound up with a paradoxical structure of the contest (paradoxical when compared with the stereotypes of mythical combat). So as to appreciate this paradox in its structural subtlety, let us imagine for a moment an endoxical (and no longer para-doxical) reading of the episode: A wrestles with B but fails to get the better of him; to gain victory at all costs, A then resorts to some exceptional strategy, whether an unfair and forbidden blow (the forearm chop in wrestling matches) or a blow which, while remaining within the rules, supposes a secret knowledge, a 'dodge' (the 'ploy' of the Jarnac blow[3]). *In the very logic of the narrative* such a blow, generally described as 'decisive', brings victory to the person who administers it: the emphatic mark of which this blow is structurally the object cannot be reconciled with its being ineffective — by the very god of narrative it *must* succeed. Here, however, the opposite occurs: the decisive blow fails; A, who gave the blow, is not the victor; which is the structural paradox. The sequence then takes an unexpected course:

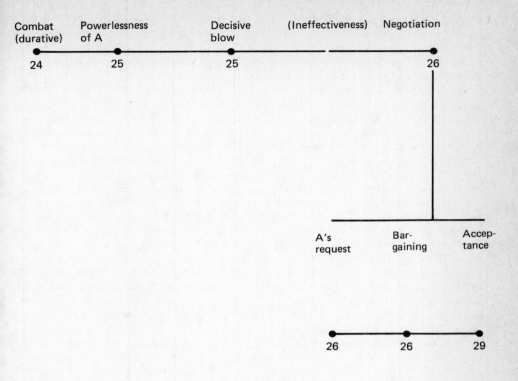

It will be noted that A (it matters little from the point of view of the structure if this be *someone, a man, God* or *the Angel*) is not strictly speaking vanquished but *held in check*. For this to be seen as a defeat, the adjunction of a *time limit* is needed: this is the breaking of day ('for the day breaketh' 26), a notation which picks up verse 24 ('until the breaking of day') but now in the explicit context of mythical structure. The theme of the nocturnal combat is structurally justified by the fact that at a certain moment, fixed in advance (as is the rising of the sun, as is the duration of a boxing match), the rules of the combat will no longer obtain, the structural play will come to an end, as too the supernatural play (the 'demons' withdraw at dawn). Thus we can see that it is within a quite 'regular' combat that the sequence sets up an unexpected readability, a logical surprise: the person who has the knowledge, the secret, the special ploy, is nevertheless defeated. The sequence itself, however actional, however anecdotal it may be, functions to *unbalance* the opponents in the combat, not only by the unforeseen victory of the one over the other, but above all (let us be fully aware of the *formal* subtlety of this surprise) by the illogical, *inverted*, nature of the victory. In other words (and here we find an eminently structural term, well known to linguists), the combat, as it is reversed in its unexpected development, *marks* one of the combatants: the weakest defeats the strongest, *in exchange for which* he is marked (on the thigh).

It is plausible (moving somewhat away from pure structural analysis and approaching textual analysis, vision *without barriers* of meanings) to fill out this schema of the mark (of the disequilibrium) with contents of an ethnological kind. The structural meaning of the episode, once again, is the following: a situation of balance (the combat at its outset) — and such a situation is a prerequisite for any marking (ascesis in Ignatius of Loyola for instance functions to establish the *indifference* of the will which allows the manifestation of the divine mark, the choice, the election) — is disturbed by the unlikely victory of one of the participants: there is an inversion of the mark, a counter-mark. Let us turn then to the family configuration. Traditionally, the line of brothers is in principle evenly balanced (they are all situated on the same level in relation to the parents); this equality of birth is normally unbalanced by the right of primogeniture: the eldest is marked. Now in the story of Jacob, there is an inversion of the mark, a counter-mark: it is the younger who supplants the elder (*Genesis* 27:36), taking his brother by the heel in order to reverse time; it is Jacob, the younger, who marks himself. Since Jacob has just obtained a mark in his struggle with God, one can say in a sense that A (God) is the substitute of the elder brother, once again beaten by the younger. The conflict with Esau is *displaced* (every symbol is a *displacement*; if the 'struggle with the angel' is symbolic, then it has displaced something). Commentary — for which I am insufficiently equipped — would at this point doubtless have to widen the interpretation of the *inversion of the mark*, by placing it either in a historico-economic context — Esau is the eponym of the Edomites and there were economic ties between the Edomites and the Israelites; figured here perhaps is an overthrow of the alliance, the start of a new league of interests? — or in the field of the symbolic (in the psychoanalytical sense of the term) — the Old Testament seems to be less the world of the Fathers than that of the Enemy Brothers, the elder are ousted in favour of the younger; in the myth of the Enemy Brothers Freud pointed to the theme of *the smallest difference*: is not the blow on the thigh, on the thin sinew, just such a *smallest difference?* Be that as it may, in this world God marks the young, acts against nature: his (structural) function is to constitute a *counter-marker*.

To conclude discussion of this extremely rich episode of the Struggle, of the Mark, I should like to add a remark as semiologist. We have seen that in the binary opposition of the combatants, which is perhaps the binary opposition of the Brothers, the younger is marked both by the reversal of the anticipated distribution of strengths and by a bodily sign, the touch on the thigh, the halting (not without recalling Oedipus, Swollen Foot, the Lame One). A mark is creative of meaning. In the phonological representation of language, the 'equality' of the paradigm is unbalanced in favour of a marked element by the presence of a trait absent from its correlative and oppositional term. By marking Jacob (Israel), God (or the Narrative) permits an anagogical development of meaning, creates the formal operational conditions of a new 'language', the election of Israel being its 'message'. God is a logothete, a founder of a language, and Jacob is here a 'morpheme' of the new language.

3. *The Namings or Mutations* (v. 27–32). The object of the final sequence is the exchange of names, that is to say the promotion of new statuses, new powers. Naming is clearly related to Blessing: to bless (to accept the homage of a kneeling suppliant) and to name are both suzerain acts. There are two namings:

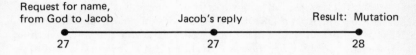

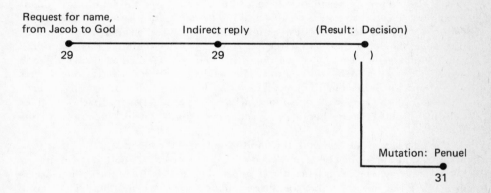

The mutation bears on Names, but in fact it is the entire episode which functions as *the creation of a multiple trace* — across Jacob's body, the status of the Brothers, Jacob's name of the place, the kind of food (creation of an alimentary taboo: the whole story can also be interpreted *a minimo* as the mythical foundation of a taboo). The three sequences that have been analysed are homological; what is in question in each is a *change* — of place, parental line, name, alimentary rite; all this keeping very close to an activity of language, a transgression of the rules of meaning.

Such is the sequential (or actional) analysis of our text. As has been seen, I have tried to remain always on the level of the structure, that is to say of the systematic correlation of the terms denoting an action. If I have chanced to mention certain possible meanings, the purpose has not been to discuss the probability of those meanings but rather to show how the structure 'disseminates' contents — which each reading can make its own. My object is not the philological or historical document, custodian of a truth to be discovered, but the volume, the *signifiance* of the text.

II. Structural Analysis

The structural analysis of narrative being in part already constituted (by Propp, Lévi-Strauss, Greimas, Bremond), I wish to conclude — putting myself even more in the background — by confronting the text under discussion with two modes of structural analysis so as to demonstrate the interest of these two modes, though my own work has a somewhat different orientation:[4] Greimas's actantial analysis and Propp's functional analysis.

1. *Actantial analysis*. The actantial grid worked out by Greimas[5] — to be used, as he himself says, with prudence and flexibility — divides the characters, the actors, of a narrative into six formal classes of actants, defined by what they do according to narrative status and not by what they are psychologically (thus one actant may combine several characters just as a single character may combine several actants; an actant may also be figured by an inanimate entity). The 'struggle with the angel' forms a very familiar episode in mythical narratives: the overcoming of an obstacle, the Ordeal. As far as the particular episode is concerned (things might perhaps be different over the whole set of Jacob's exploits), the actants are 'filled' as follows: Jacob is the *Subject* (subject of the demand, the quest, the action); the *Object* (of the same demand, quest, action) is the crossing of the guarded and forbidden place, the flood, the Jabbok; the *Sender*, who sets in circulation the stake of the quest (namely the crossing of the flood), is obviously God; the *Receiver* is Jacob again (two actants are here present in a single figure); the *Opponent* (the one or ones who hinder the Subject in his quest) is God himself (it is he who, mythically, guards the crossing); the *Helper* (the one or ones who aid the Subject) is Jacob who provides help to himself through his own, legendary, strength (an indicial trait, as was noted).

The paradox, or at very least the anomic nature of the formulation, can be seen at once: that the subject be confounded with the receiver is banal; that the subject be his or her own helper is less usual (it generally occurs in 'voluntarist' narratives or novels); but that the sender be the opponent is very rare and there is only one type of narrative that can present this paradoxical form — narratives relating an act of blackmail. If the opponent were only the (provisional) holder of the stake, then of course there would be nothing extraordinary: it is the opponent's role to have and defend ownership of the object that the hero wants to obtain (as with the dragon guarding a place to be crossed). Here however, as in every blackmail, God, at the same time that he guards the flood, also dispenses the mark, the privilege. The actantial form of the text is thus far from conciliatory: structurally, it is extremely audacious — which squares well with the 'scandal' represented by God's defeat.

2. *Functional Analysis*. Propp was the first to establish the structure of the folktale, by dividing it into its *functions* or narrative acts.[6] The functions, according to Propp, are stable elements, limited in number (some thirty or so) and always identical in their concatenation, even if occasionally certain functions are absent from this or that narrative. It so happens — as will be seen in a moment — that our text fulfills perfectly a section of the functional schema brought to light by Propp who would have been unable to imagine a more convincing application of his discovery.

In a preparatory section of the folktale (as analysed by Propp) there necessarily occurs an absence of the hero, something already the case in the tale of Jacob: Isaac sends Jacob far from his homeland to Laban (*Genesis* 28: 2 and 5). Our episode effectively begins at the fifteenth of Propp's narrative functions and can be coded in the following manner, showing at each stage the striking parallelism between Propp's schema and the *Genesis* narrative:

Propp and the folktale	*Genesis*
15. Transference from one place to another (by bird, horse, ship, etc.)	Set out from the North, from the Aramaeans, from the house of Laban, Jacob journeys home, to his father's house (29: 1, Jacob sets out)
16. combat between the Villain and the Hero	This is the sequence of the Struggle (32: 24–27)
17. The hero is branded, 'marked' (generally it is a matter of a mark on the body, but in other cases it is simply the gift of a jewel, of a ring)	Jacob is marked on the thigh (32: 25–32)
18. Victory of the Hero, defeat of the Villain	Jacob's victory (32: 26)
19. Liquidation of the misfortune or lack: the misfortune or lack had been established in the initial absence of the Hero: this absence is repaired	Having succeeded in crossing Penuel (32: 31), Jacob reaches Schechem in Canaan (33: 18)

There are other parallels. In Propp's function 14, the hero acquires the use of a magical object; for Jacob this talisman is obviously the blessing that he surprises his blind father into giving him (*Genesis* 27). Again, function 29 represents the transfiguration of the hero (for example, the Beast transformed into a handsome nobleman); such a transfiguration seems to be present in the changing of the Name (*Genesis* 32:28) and the rebirth it implies. The narrative model stamps God with the role of the Villain (his *structural* role — it is not a question of a psychological role); the fact is that a veritable folktale stereotype can be read in the *Genesis* episode — the difficult crossing of a ford guarded by a hostile spirit. A further similitude between episode and tale is that in both cases character motivations (their reasons for acting) go unnoted, the ellipsis of such notations being not a stylistic element but a pertinent structural characteristic of the narration. Structural analysis in the strict sense of the term would thus conclude emphatically that the 'struggle with the angel' is a true fairytale, since according to Propp all fairytales belong to the same structure, the one he described.

So we can see that what might be called the structural exploitation of the episode is very possible and even imperative. Let me indicate in conclusion, however, that what interests me most in this famous passage is not the 'folkloristic' model but the abrasive frictions, the breaks, the discontinuities of readability, the juxtaposition of narrative entities which to some extent run free from an explicit logical articulation. One is dealing here (this at least is for me the savour of the reading) with a sort of *metonymic montage*: the themes (Crossing, Struggle, Naming, Alimentary Rite) are *combined*, not 'developed'. This abruptness, this asyndetic character of the narrative is well expressed by Hosea (12: 3–4):

> 'He took his brother by the heel in the womb // and by his strength he had power with God.'

Metonymic logic is that of the unconscious. Hence it is perhaps in that direction that one would need to pursue the present study, to pursue the reading of the text — its dissemination, not its truth. Evidently, there is a risk in so doing of weakening the episode's economico-historical force (certainly existent, at the level of the exchanges of tribes and the questions of power). Yet equally in so doing the symbolic explosion of the text (not necessarily of a religious order) is reinforced. The problem, the problem at least posed for me, is exactly to manage not to reduce the Text to a signified, whatever it may be (historical, economic, folkloristic or kerygmatic), but to hold its *signifiance* fully open.

Notes:

1. On this subject (and in relation to exegesis), see R. Barthes, 'L'analyse structurale du récit: à propos d'*Actes* 10–11', in *Exégèse et Herméneutique*, Paris 1971, pp. 181–204.
2. I wish to express my gratitude to Jean Alexandre whose socio-historical, linguistic and exegetical knowledge, together with his intellectual openness, helped me to understand the text analysed here. Many of his ideas are to be found in this analysis and only fear of having distorted them has prevented me from acknowledging them each time they appear.
3. In 1547 Guy de Jarnac won a duel by an unexpected thrust which hamstrung his opponent. (Translator's note)
4. My work on Balzac's story *Sarrasine* (*S/Z*, Paris 1970; [trans. *S/Z*, New York and London 1975]) belongs more to textual than to structural analysis.
5. See specially A. J. Greimas, *Sémantique structurale* and *Du Sens*.
6. V. Propp, *Morphology of the Folktale*. Unfortunately, the word 'function' is always ambiguous; at the beginning of the present piece we used it to define actantial analysis which assesses characters by their roles in the action (precisely their 'function'); in Propp's terminology, there is a shift from character to the action itself, grasped in its *relations* to the actions surrounding it.

5

Paul De Man,

from 'The Dead-End of Formalist Criticism'

As a new generation enters the scene, a certain unease manifests itself in French literary criticism. This uncertainty prevails at once in the concern over funda-mental methodological issues, and in the experimental, or polemical, character of several recent works. Roland Barthes' book-length essay, *Writing Degree Zero*,[1] for example, asserts its own *terrorism*; and Jean-Pierre Richard's two books, *Littérature et Sensation* and *Poésie et Profondeur*,[2] have recourse to a method whose systematic and exclusive use takes on the dimensions of a manifesto, an impression further rein-forced by the author's own preface and that provided by Georges Poulet, both of which stress their opposition to other critical idioms. Explicitly, Poulet and Richard are opposed to Blanchot in the name of a criticism whose initiators would have been Marcel Raymond and Albert Beguin, and whose philosophical under-pinnings would be found in Bachelard, Jean Wahl, and Sartre — a grouping that, in the case of every one of these, requires reservations and qualifications. Implicitly, they are also opposed to the historical and philological scholarship of the universities, from traditional *explication de texte* to the writings of Etiemble, as well as to other current trends: Jean Paulhan's work, Marxist criticism, history of ideas, etc. All of these trends — and there are others — are mutually incompatible.

In the United States, the state of criticism appears more stable. It is well known that since roughly 1935, alongside traditional approaches to criticism such as the historical and the sociological or the biographical and psychological, there has arisen a trend that without constituting a school or even a homogeneous group, nevertheless shares certain premises. These are the authors generally known under the term 'New Critics' (even though, once again, this term does not designate a well-defined group) and they can generally be subsumed under the denomination of 'formalist' criticism — a term we will seek to make more explicit later on. This movement has come to wield considerable influence, in journals and in books, and especially in university teaching; to such an extent that one could legitimately speak of a certain formalist orthodoxy. In some cases, an entire generation has been trained in this approach to literature without awareness of any other.

It is true, though, that at the very moment when it comes into its own, this generation is apt to turn against the training of which it is the product. Recently there have been attacks upon the methods of the prevalent criticism and calls for a clean sweeping away, a new start. It is hard to tell if these are portents of a more general reaction or merely individual and isolated occurrences. But even if it were on the point of being overtaken, formalist criticism would still have made a considerable contribution: on the positive side, by fostering the refinement of analytical and didactic techniques that have often led to remarkable exegeses; on the negative side, by highlighting the inadequacies of the historical approach as it was practiced in the United States. But it is also interesting from the perspective of theory: its internal evolution leads it to put into question the conception of the literary work upon which it was implicitly founded. Its development may well have a premonitory value for the new French criticism just as the latter, especially in the case of Roland Barthes, appears to be moving in the direction of a formalism that, appearances notwithstanding, is not that different from New Criticism. In addition, it also has a certain demonstrative value for ontological criticism, for it proceeds in particularly clear fashion from a theory based upon more or less hidden or unconscious philosophical presuppositions. In its own inadequacy, it brings them out to the surface, and thus leads to authentic ontological questions.

It has been said that all of American formalist criticism originates in the works of the English linguist and psychologist I. A. Richards.[3] As a historical statement such an assertion is questionable, for the mutual relations of American and English criticism are rendered more complex by the existence of purely native strands on both sides; but it is certainly true that Richards's theories have found fertile terrain in the United States, and that all American works of formalist criticism accord him a special status.

For Richards, the task of criticism consists in correctly apprehending the signifying value, or meaning, of the work; an exact correspondence between the author's originary experience and its communicated expression. For the author, the labour of formal elaboration consists in constructing a linguistic structure that will correspond as closely as possible to the initial experience. Once it is granted that such a correspondence is established by the author, it will exist for the reader as well, and what is called communication can then occur.

The initial experience may be anything at all and need not have anything specifically 'aesthetic' about it. Art is justified as the preservation of moments in 'the lives of exceptional people, when their control and command of experience is at its highest degree . . .'[4] The critic's task consists in retracing the author's journey backward: he will proceed from a careful and precise study of the signifying form toward the experience that produced this form. Correct critical understanding is achieved when it reaches the cluster of experiences elicited through reading, insofar as they remain sufficiently close to the experience or experiences the author started out with. It becomes possible then to define a poem, for example, as the series of experiences comprised within such a cluster. Since there are numerous possibilities of error in the carrying out of these analytical tasks, it is Richards's intention to elaborate techniques for avoiding them; but there never is the slightest doubt that in every case a correct procedure can be arrived at.

This theory, which appears to be governed by common sense, implies, in fact, some highly questionable ontological presuppositions, the most basic of which is, no doubt, the notion that language, poetic or otherwise, can *say* any experience, of whatever kind, even a simple perception. Neither the statement 'I see a cat' nor, for that matter, Baudelaire's poem '*Le Chat*' contains wholly the experience of this perception. It can be said that there is a perceptual consciousness of the object and an experience of this consciousness, but the working out of a *logos* of this experience or, in the case of art, of a *form* of this experience, encounters considerable difficulties. Almost immediately the existential status of the experience seems to be in question, and we conclude by considering as constructed that which at first appeared to be given: instead of containing or reflecting experience, language constitutes it. And a theory of constituting form is altogether different from a theory of signifying form. Language is no longer a mediation between two subjectivities but between a being and a non-being. And the problem of criticism is no longer to discover to what experience the form refers, but how it can constitute a world, a totality of beings without which there would be no experience. It is no longer a question of imitation but one of creation; no longer communication but participation. And when this form becomes the object of consideration of a third person who seeks to state the experience of his perception, the least that can be said is that this latest venture into language will be quite distant from the original experience. Between the originary cat and a critic's commentary on Baudelaire's poem, quite a few things have occurred.

Nonetheless, Richards postulates a perfect continuity between the sign and the thing signified.[5] Through repeated association, the sign comes to take the place of the thing signified; and consciousness is consciousness *of* 'the missing part of the sign, or, more strictly, "of" anything which would complete the sign as cause.'[6] The cat is the cause of the consciousness that perceives the cat; when we read the word 'cat,' we are conscious of the sign 'cat' inasmuch as it refers back to the cause of this sign. Richards adds immediately that, for such a consciousness to be specific as experience perforce is, language must achieve a spatial and temporal determination, implying, for example, 'this cat here and now.' But what do the words 'here' and 'now' refer to — not to mention the words 'to be' that are always implied — if not to a general space and time that permit *this* here and this now? Thus the 'cause' of the perception of the sign becomes, at the least, the object plus time and space, with, in addition, a specific causal relation between the object and space and time. When we read the word 'cat,' we are forced to construct an entire universe in order to understand it, whereas direct experience makes no such requirements. We are driven back to the problem of constitution, which does not appear to have arisen for Richards.[7]

Richards insists continually on the fact that criticism does not deal with any given material object but with a consciousness (or an experience) of this object, and he quotes Hume to this effect: 'Beauty is no quality in things themselves; it exists merely in the mind which contemplates them.'[8] Form, as the object of the critic's reflection, is not a thing then but stands as the equivalent of the experience. An object described or painted or sculpted is the object initially given; it is the sign of the experience of a consciousness of that object. However, since form is the imitation of a mental experience in a substance (language, pigment, or marble), it is legitimate for an observer to treat it as a signifying object that refers to a prior mental experience. In this sense, one can speak of a form-object in Richards. And one can also understand his insistent claim that poetic language is purely affective and, therefore, can never lead to cognition, since it has no verifiable referential value in reference to an external object. But for the critic who seeks to apprehend correctly the experience that is conveyed to him, the work itself is an object of cognition insofar as he respects its affective tenor exclusively.

The route may be different, but the starting point is the same for Roland

Barthes. He, too, defines writing, or form, as the faithful reflection of the writer's free and signifying experience. It is true, though, that for him this form is not necessarily an object; when human actions are historically free, form is transparent. It is an object but not an object of reflection. But the moment this freedom is curtailed, the artist's endeavour and his choice of form become problematic; any restriction in the free choice of experience requires a justification of the form selected, an operation whose net effect is the genuine objectification of form. Richards's form-object resulted from the postulate of a perfect continuity of consciousness with its linguistic correlates; Barthes, on the other hand, proceeds from a historical situation. But, from the point of view of criticism, the result is the same, since, in both instances, criticism begins and ends with the study of form. There is, to be sure, a parting of the ways ultimately: for Richards, the next stage would be the working out of a utilitarian morality, while for Barthes it would more likely be revolutionary action. But, for the time being, we are concerned with issues of critical methodology; and it turns out that in the examples that he provides (the uses of the past tense in the novel, of the third person pronoun in Balzac, or of the 'realistic' style of Garaudy — I am leaving aside his *Michelet*) Barthes' analyses are quite close to Richards's and those of his disciples. He could well profit, in fact, from the storehouse of techniques contained in their works in the preparation of his announced History of Writing.

As befits its origins in the pedagogical research Richards conducted at Cambridge University,[9] his method derives much of its influence from its undeniable didactic power. His conception of form permits, at once, the development of a critical vocabulary of an almost scientific power and the elaboration of easily taught analytic techniques possessing the virtues of *explication de texte*, yet not thwarting the freedom of formal imagination. In its suggestion of a balanced and stable moral climate, it is also reassuring criticism. By bringing down poetic language to the level of the language of communication, and in its steadfast refusal to grant aesthetic experience any difference from other human experiences, it is opposed to any attempt to confer upon poetry an excessively exalted function, while still preserving for it the freshness and originality of invention.

But what happens when one studies poetry a little closer following these instructions? A surprising answer is to be found in the work of William Empson, a brilliant student of Richards.[10] Empson, a poet in his own right, and, moreover, a reader of great acuity, applied Richards's principles faithfully to a set of texts drawn mainly, though not exclusively, from Shakespeare and the metaphysical poets of the seventeenth century. From the very first example studied in *Seven Types of Ambiguity*, the results are troubling. It is a line from one of Shakespeare's sonnets. To evoke old age, the poet thinks of winter, more precisely a forest in winter, which, he says, is like:

> Bare ruined choirs, where late the sweet birds sang.[11]

The thought is stated in a metaphor whose perfection is immediately felt. But if it is asked what is the common experience awakened by the forest and the ruined choir, one does not discover just one but an indefinite number. Empson lists a dozen of them and there are many others; it would be impossible to tell which was dominant in the poet's mind or at which we should stop. What the metaphor does is actually the opposite: instead of setting up an adequation between two experiences, and thereby fixing the mind on the repose of an established equation, it deploys the initial experience into an infinity of associated experiences that spring from it. In the manner of a vibration spreading in infinitude from its centre, metaphor is endowed with the capacity to situate the experience at the heart of a universe that it generates. It provides the ground rather than the frame, a limitless anteriority that permits the limiting of a specific entity. Experience sheds its uniqueness and leads instead to a dizziness of the mind. Far from referring back to an object that would be its cause, the poetic sign sets in motion an imaging activity that refers to no object in particular. The 'meaning' of the metaphor is that it does not 'mean' in any definite manner.

This is obviously problematic. For if a simple metaphor suffices to suggest an infinity of initial experiences and, therefore, an infinity of valid readings, how can we live up to Richards's injunction to bring the reader's experience in line with the typical experience ascribed to the author? Can we still speak of communication here, when the text's effect is to transform a perfectly well-defined unity into a multiplicity whose actual number must remain undetermined? Empson's argument, as it proceeds from simple to increasingly complex examples, becomes apparent: a fundamental ambiguity is constitutive of all poetry. The correspondence between the initial experience and the reader's own remains forever problematic because poetry sets particular beings in a world yet to be constituted, as a task to fulfill.

Not all ambiguities are of this basic type. Some are pure signifying forms, condensed means of evoking real adequation, of stating rapidly a perfectly determined mental structure. In such cases, and whatever the degree of complexity of the text, exegesis is primarily a matter of concentration and intelligence, and it is in search of a precise signification. It ends up either with a single reading concealed in the apparent multiplicity, or in a controlled, even when antithetical, superposition of significations to be uncovered. The latter type of ambiguity would be like the proffered 'explication' of Mallarmé's hermetic sonnets as purely erotic or scatological poems — a perfectly legitimate and possible reading in many instances, provided one adds immediately that they are something else and that Mallarmé was striving to achieve precisely this layered presence of different significations. This type of form occurs most frequently in Elizabethan and metaphysical poetry, as indeed in any precious or baroque poetry, and lends itself particularly well to a deciphering along I. A. Richards's line. Some of the more notable achievements of formalist criticism are to be found in this area.

Although Empson does not draw this basic distinction himself, it is clear that five of his seven types of ambiguity fall within this category of controlled pseudo-ambiguity, and that only the first and the last relate to a more fundamental property of poetic language. Any poetic sentence, even one devoid of artifice or baroque subtlety, must, by virtue of being poetic, constitute an infinite plurality of significations all melded into a single linguistic unit: that is the first type. But as Empson's inquiry proceeds, there occurs a visible increase in what he calls the logical disorder of his examples until, in the seventh and last type of ambiguity, the form blows up under our very eyes. This occurs when the text implies not merely distinct signification but significations that, against the will of their author, are mutually exclusive. And here Empson's advance beyond the teachings of his master becomes apparent. For under the outward appearance of a simple list classifying random examples, chapter seven develops a thought Richards never wanted to consider: true poetic ambiguity proceeds from the deep division of Being itself, and poetry does no more than state and repeat this division. Richards did recognize the existence of conflicts, but he invoked Coleridge, not without some simplification, to appeal to the reassuring notion of art as the reconciliation of opposites.[12] Empson's less serene mind is not content with this formula. In a note added to the text, he writes: 'It may be said that the contradiction must somehow form a larger unity if the final effect is to be satisfying. But the onus of reconciliation can be laid very heavily on the receiving end,'[13] that is, on the reader, for the reconciliation does not occur in the text. The text does not resolve the conflict, it *names* it. And there is no doubt as to the nature of the conflict. Empson has already prepared us by saying that it is 'at once an indecision and a structure, like the symbol of the Cross,'[14] and he ends his book on George Herbert's extraordinary poem entitled 'The Sacrifice,' a monologue uttered by Christ upon the cross, whose refrain is drawn from the 'Laments of Jeremiah' (1, 12). 'Is it nothing to you, all ye that pass by? Behold, and see if there be any sorrow like unto my sorrow, which is done unto me, wherewith the Lord hath afflicted me in the day of his fierce anger.'

This conflict can be resolved only by the supreme sacrifice: there is no stronger way of stating the impossibility of an incarnate and happy truth. The ambiguity poetry speaks of is the fundamental one that prevails between the world of the spirit and the world of sentient substance: to ground itself, the spirit must turn itself into sentient substance, but the latter is knowable only in its dissolution into non-being. The spirit cannot coincide with its object and this separation is infinitely sorrowful.

Empson sheds light upon this dialectic, which is that of the unhappy consciousness, through some very well-chosen examples. He begins with Keats's 'Ode to Melancholy;' a very good selection, for Keats lived this tension especially acutely and lived it in its very substance. The growth of his consciousness results most often in a reversal that takes him from a happy and immediate sense impression to a painful knowledge. His sorrow is that of the man who can know substance only as he loses it; for whom any love immediately brings about the death of what is being loved. Empson illustrates this problematic by adducing mystical texts of the seventeenth century which show that spiritual happiness is conceivable only in terms of sensations, of the very substantial joys whose tragic fragility Keats knew so well. Man stands in utter distress before a God whom he risks destroying by wanting to know Him; he feels envy for the natural creature that is the direct emanation of Being. A sonnet by the Jesuit poet Gerard Manley Hopkins states the torture of this indecision. To be sure, George Herbert's serene tone does seem to convey a kind of peaceableness, for he managed in his poem to bring these contradictions and paradoxes side-by-side without occulting their outrageousness; but we must bear in mind that the protagonist here is not man but the Son of God, and that the display of error and human misery has been relegated to the background. We have travelled far from Richards's universe where there never is any error, only misunderstanding. Empson's inquiry, drawn by the very weight of his cogitations to problems that can no longer be ignored, has led him to broader questions. Instead of concentrating on details of poetic form, he will have to reflect henceforth upon the poetic phenomenon as such; a phenomenon that does seem to deserve this kind of attention since it leads, willy-nilly, to unsuspected perspectives upon human complexity.

These broader questions are not addressed in the rather pedestrian last chapter of *Seven Types of Ambiguity*, but they are raised in the book Empson published a few years later. The tone of the exposition, as well as the selection of works commented upon in *Some Versions of Pastoral*, could lead to the supposition that he had undertaken the study of one literary form among others, and that this study could be followed by others in a similar vein, upon the epic tradition, let us say, or the tragic. Nothing could be further from the truth, as a consideration of the central theme of the book, to be found in the commentary on Andrew Marvell's famous 'The Garden' (Chapter IV), makes abundantly clear. The central strophe of the poem happens to name the very problem upon which Empson's previous work ended: the contradictory relations between natural being and the being of consciousness:

> The Mind, that Ocean where each kind
> Does straight its own resemblance find;
> Yet it creates, transcending these,
> Far other worlds, and other Seas,
> Annihilating all that's made
> To a green thought in a green shade.

The dialectical armature of this strophe defines what Empson calls the pastoral convention. It is the movement of consciousness as it contemplates the natural entity and finds itself integrally reflected down to the most peculiar aspects of *phusis*. But a reflection is not an identification, and the simple correspondence of the mind with the natural, far from being appeasing, turns troublesome. The mind recovers its balance only in domination over that which is its complete other. Thus the essentially negative activity of all thought takes place, and poetic thought in particular: 'Annihilating all that's made.' One would be hard pressed to state it any more strongly. However, the recourse to the modifier 'green' to qualify what is then created by thought, reintroduces the pastoral world of innocence, of 'humble, permanent, undeveloped nature which sustains everything, and to which everything must return.'[15] And it is reintroduced at the very moment that this world has been annihilated. It is the freshness, the greenness of budding thought that can evoke itself only through the memory of what it destroys on its way.

What is the pastoral convention, then, if not the eternal separation between the mind that distinguishes, negates, legislates, and the originary simplicity of the natural? A separation that may be lived, as in Homer's epic poetry (evoked by Empson as an example of the universality of its definition), or it may be thought in full consciousness of itself as in Marvell's poem. There is no doubt that the pastoral theme is, in fact, the only poetic theme, that it is poetry itself. Under the deceitful title of a genre study, Empson has actually written an ontology of the poetic, but wrapped it, as is his wont, in some extraneous matter that may well conceal the essential.

In light of this, what is the link between these considerations and the first chapter of the book, entitled 'Proletarian Literature,' which concludes, paradoxically enough, that Marxist thought is pastoral thought disguised. Marxism draws its attractiveness from the reconciliation it promises, in all sincerity to be sure, but with a naive prematurity. 'I do not mean to say,' writes Empson, 'that the

[Marxist] philosophy is wrong; for that matter pastoral is worked from the same philosophical ideas as proletarian literature — the difference is that it brings in the absolute less prematurely.'[16] The pastoral problematic, which turns out to be the problematic of Being itself, is lived in our day by Marxist thought, as by any genuine thought. In motivation, if not in its claims, Marxism is, ultimately, a poetic thought that lacks the patience to pursue its own conclusions to their end; this explains why Empson's book, which is all about separation and alienation, places itself at the outset under the aegis of Marxism; a convergence confirmed by the apparent contradiction of the attraction exerted upon our generation by the problematic of poetry and the solution of Marxism.[17]

Having started from the premises of the strictest aesthetical formalism, Empson winds up facing the ontological question. And it is by virtue of this question that he stands as a warning against certain Marxist illusions. The problem of separation inheres in Being, which means that social forms of separation derive from ontological and meta-social attitudes. For poetry, the divide exists forever. 'To produce pure proletarian art the artist must be one with the worker; this is impossible, not for political reasons, but because the artist never is at one with any public.'[18] This conclusion is grounded in a very thorough study and it is especially difficult to take issue with since it originated in the opposite conviction. It stands as an irrefutable critique by anticipation of Roland Barthes' position, for whom the separation is a phenomenon that admits of precise dating. 'It is because there is no reconciliation in society that language, at once necessary and necessarily oriented, institutes a torn condition for the writer,'[19] writes Barthes, and he has tried, in his *Michelet* and elsewhere, to show the socially imposed abyss that confines the modern writer to an interiority he hates. Such a writer exists in a sort of historical transition, whose boundaries Barthes sets by inventing the myth of a genuinely univocal form in Classicism — but an Empsonian study of Racine would quickly dispose of this illusion — and the future myth of a 'new Adamic world where language would no longer be alienated.'[20] This is a good instance of falling all at once into all the traps of impatient 'pastoral' thought: formalism, false historicism, and utopianism.

The promise held out in Richards's work, of a convergence between logical positivism and literary criticism, has failed to materialize. After the writings of an Empson, little is left of the scientific claims of formalist criticism. All of its basic assumptions have been put into question: the notions of communication, form, signifying experience, and objective precision. And Empson is but an example among others.[21] Their routes may at times have differed, but numerous critics have come to recognise within poetic language the same pluralism and the disorders signalling ontological complexities. Terms such as paradox, tension,and ambiguity abound in American criticism to the point of nearly losing all meaning.
***

Notes:

Translator's note: This article was written for the express purpose of introducing the New Criticim to French readers at the moment that there were some stirrings in French Criticism, but before the advent of Structuralism on the literary scene.

1. Roland Barthes, *Le Degré Zéro de l'Écriture* (Paris: Seuil, 1953); trans. Annette Lavers and Colin Smith, *Writing Degree Zero* (New York: Hill and Wang, 1967).

2. Paris: Editions de Seuil, 1954 and 1955 respectively.

3. Stanley Hyman, *The Armed Vision* (New York: A. A. Knopf, 1948), p. 7.

4. I. A. Richards, *Principles of Literary Criticism* (London: Kegan Paul, Trench, Trubner and Co., 1962), p. 32. Richards's reasons for attaching such an importance to the knowledge of what he calls 'experience' are of a moral order. As a disciple of Bentham's utilitarianism, moral order consists for him in a correctly hierarchised organisation of human needs, and these needs can be evaluated through the study of the 'experiences' of consciousness.

5. This theory is outlined in *Principles of Literary Criticism*, pp. 127ff.

6. *Ibid.*, p. 127.

7. In reference to this problem, one can draw a useful comparison between Richards's analysis and that of the phenomenologist and student of Husserl, Roman Ingarden, in *Das Literarische Kunstwerk* (Halle, 1931; 3rd ed., Tübingen: Max Niemeyer, 1965); trans. George G. Grabowicz, *The Literary Work of Art* (Evanston, Ill.: Northwestern University Press, 1973).

8. Quoted by Richards in *Principles of Literary Criticism*, p. 186.

9. A very instructive narrative of this research appears in the volume published after *Principles of Literary Criticism* entitled *Practical Criticism* (Edinburgh: Edinburgh Press, 1929).

10. I will deal with two of William Empson's works: *Seven Types of Ambiguity* (London: Chatto and Windus, 1930; 2nd revised edition, 1947) and *Some Versions of Pastoral* (London: Chatto and Windus, 1935). A third, and somewhat more technical, work is outside the scope of our study.

11. William Shakespeare, *Sonnets* #73.

12. *Principles of Literary Criticism*, pp. 251ff.

13. *Seven Types of Ambiguity*, note on p. 193.

14. *Ibid.*, p. 192.

15. *Some Versions of Pastoral*, p. 128.

16. *Ibid.*, p. 23.

17. A remark by Heidegger confirms and sheds light on this encounter: 'The fate of the world announces itself in poetry, without already appearing nonetheless as a history of Being. . . . Alienation has become fated on a world-scale. Which is why this destiny must be thought at the outset of the history of Being. What Marx recognized, basing himself upon Hegel, as essentially and significantly the alienation of man, takes root in the fundamentally exiled character of modern man. . . . It is because he had a real experience of this alienation that Marx has attained a profound dimension of history. That is why the Marxist conception of history by far surpasses all of the forms of contemporary historicism.' *Platons Lehre von der Wahrheit; mit einem Brief über den 'Humanismus'* (Bern: A. Francke, 1947), p. 87.

18. *Pastoral*, p. 15.

19. *Degré Zéro de l'Ecriture*, p. 119; in English, p. 83.

20. *Ibid.*, p. 126; in English, p. 88.

21. The French reader unfamiliar with Empson's work should be warned that this has been an interpretation and not an exposition, and that it is, therefore, subject to discussion. I suppose that the author especially, who has always proclaimed his agreement with Richards, would have some difficulty endorsing it.

Section Four

DEVELOPMENTS AFTER STRUCTURALISM

1. Roland Barthes, 'From Work to Text' (1971)
2. Jacques Derrida, 'Structure, Sign and Play in the Discourse of the Human Sciences' (1966)
3. Frank Kermode, '*Wuthering Heights*' (1975)

Points of information

1. Barthes' 'From Work to Text' first appeared in *Revue d'esthétique*. It is reprinted from his *Image-Music-Text*, ed. and trans. Stephen Heath (1977). Derrida's 'Structure, Sign and Play' was a lecture first delivered in 1966. It is reprinted here from Jacques Derrida, *Writing and Difference*, ed. and trans. Alan Bass (1978). Frank Kermode's analysis of *Wuthering Heights* is taken from his *The Classic*.

2. The Latin phrase used by Kermode on p. 145 means 'who completes a hundred years'. It is taken from Horace, *Epistles*, II, 1. The sentence in full is: 'He is ancient and good who completes a hundred years.' The topic of discussion is the reputations of writers.

'Pure' structuralism flourished only briefly in Anglo-American criticism, though some critics such as David Lodge have continued to make use of its insights. By the early 1970s, when important French work was beginning to be translated for English-speaking critics and students, structuralism in France had been overtaken. Some structuralist ideas were adapted by other areas of thought, such as psychoanalysis and marxism, and thus its original basis in linguistics was refocused and extended. At the same time its premises were subject to powerful critiques. Its emphasis on the static (synchronic) language system, for instance, was felt to neglect process and change. Indeed the explanation of linguistic change through time is a major theoretical problem for the Saussurean theory of language. (See the marxist critiques of structuralist linguistics detailed in the Further Reading to Section 3.) Further, certain dissatisfactions were becoming apparent even within structuralism itself. Roland Barthes' career is indicative.

As we have seen, Barthes (1915–80) began with apparently firm allegiances to structuralist techniques and terminology. In 'What is Criticism?' he recommends 'covering' the language of the literary work with the up-to-the-minute language of the critic, in his case the structuralist critic. By the end of the 1960s, however, Barthes had clearly drawn away from these quasi-scientific ambitions — though it has also been argued that he was never fully committed to structuralism, and this might be borne in mind when considering the essays printed in Section 3. Nevertheless, it is certainly true that his critical practice in the 1970s became increasingly to delve deeper and deeper into the rich signifying resources of texts, to the point where any 'covering' theory seemed exhausted by them — rather as Paul De Man describes the defeat of the hopes of practical criticism by the dense multiple significations of literature itself. Barthes' essay 'From Work to Text' printed here outlines, in a typically polemical mode, his move to a conception of literary texts as composed of an endlessly plural signifying practice which defeats analytic restatement or description. The usual name for this conception of multiplicity in meaning is 'textuality'.

The idea of 'textuality' or 'textual playfulness' offered by Barthes and Derrida in this section is crucial to much post-structuralist theory. It is, in its own way, a major development of some of Saussure's original insights into the workings of language. As we have seen, Saussurean linguistics posits a 'diacritical' conception of meaning. Meaning is a function not of reference, but of the differential relationships in the language system. Meaning is thus not anchored in the 'real world' but is a product of the particular language or discursive structure of which its units are a part, as in the example of the black and white hats in the introduction to Section 3. One consequence of this idea is that meaning itself becomes insecure: there are no certain or stable 'truths' in knowledge or belief; all is relational. Thus some structuralist-influenced theories encourage an epistemologically sceptical view of the world (epistemology is the theory of knowledge); and some early structuralist and post-structuralist thought became adept at demonstrating how received, apparently 'natural' and taken-for-granted beliefs were in fact culturally-produced effects of the governing structure. This is apparent in analyses of the transmission of political views and, especially in its early days, much of this work inclined to the political left. Barthes' *Mythologies* (1957), for instance, tackled French political 'myths' at the time of the Algerian war, and the ultra-libertarian radicalism of the late 1960s in Paris has clearly left its mark on some post-structuralist thinking. Though, in politics as so much else, it is difficult to define Barthes' views with any consistency.

One consequence of this line of thought for literary criticism is a distrust of so-called 'realist' modes of writing. Most nineteenth-century novels, for example, appear to insist upon their participation in the 'real' world outside the book. They complexly reflect, say, Dickens's London or George Eliot's West Midlands.

However structuralist-influenced analysis is able to demonstrate that these references are only 'reality effects', part of the larger structure of meanings in the work and not some privileged window onto the world outside language. Their apparent realism only shields particular, partisan views of the world; and this tendency to generalise from the partisan is encouraged by critics who speak in terms of universals: the 'timelessness' of great works, 'the human condition', 'Man' and so forth. The same kind of point can be made about the depiction of human relations. Literary accounts of the relations between the sexes, for instance, can be seen to reflect dominant assumptions about, say, women's roles and potentials and these assumptions are often resumed, perhaps without comment or perhaps with endorsement, in the critical literature. Some feminist critics, therefore, have found this line of thinking useful.

These examples illustrate, in a negative way, the process which post-structuralist critics frequently refer to as 'intertextuality'. Intertextuality is the process whereby meaning is produced from text to text rather than, as it were, between text and world. The relationship between criticism and literature, for example can be seen to be of this kind. Elements from one text are offered to legitimate elements of another. The process though does not stop there, for many critical essays proceed from earlier essays, and it is a common critical ploy to legitimise a reading by way of such reference. The point is that this effort at meaning is vertiginous, and at no point arrives at a position of stability. The whole process cannot at any point insist upon 'truth'. Meaning is passed along indefinitely like the baton in a relay race that never ends; though in this simile of the race-that-never-ends (itself a contradiction perhaps) we would also have to recognise that the baton — the meaning — continually changes its nature as it is passed from hand to hand. This is in a way reminiscent of some Russian Formalist thinking in which literature is seen as developing essentially through its responses to other, earlier literature which it attempts to 'defamiliarise'; in Shklovsky's phrase 'the object [in the world] is not important'.

In many post-structuralist accounts, however, ideas of textuality and intertextuality are causes for rejoicing and not for lament. That 'truths' cannot be maintained is cause for celebration and enjoyment, as in Barthes' essay here. In other versions, as for instance in Derrida's essay, this thinking is used to prise open the false conclusions of assertive discourses which hold that they possess a positive truth about the world. It is not then perhaps surprising that critics such as Barthes have preferred open-ended, inconclusive, 'modernist' writing which doesn't claim a tight referential fit between itself and the world outside discourse. French critics have had their own favourites (some of whom are listed by Barthes in 'The Imagination of the Sign'), but Joyce and Woolf amongst writers in English are often valued. The argument goes that (in Barthes' terminology) such writing is closer to 'text', whereas that of, say, George Eliot is closer to 'work'.

Hard and fast binary distinctions such as work and text, or realist and modernist, are, like form and content, impossible to sustain generally. There are too many compromising instances, and indeed some of Barthes' later work implicitly concedes this. His celebrated *S/Z* (1970), for instance, trawls the apparently endless signifying potential of a Balzac novella to such an extent that a nineteenth-century realist's 'work' looks very much like a modernist's 'text'. Nevertheless it is clear where the general argument tends, which is towards a celebration of signifying plurality and an attack on modes of writing which assert positive truth claims. The most formidable theorist of textuality has been the French philosopher Jacques Derrida (b. 1930) whose work has inspired the recent critical movement known as 'deconstruction' which has been widely influential, especially in the United States, where it has found a kind of home in the so-called 'Yale School' at that university.

Derrida's 'Structure, Sign and Play', printed here, is an early essay — originally a lecture — in which he sets out some of his reservations about structuralism. For of course structuralism too makes truth claims: for example that Saussure's linguistic theories are accurate. Here Derrida takes as his focus Lévi-Strauss's anthropology, but he has elsewhere written about Saussure, most notably in his *Of Grammatology* (1967). His argument with Saussure is well set-out by Christopher Norris and Jonathan Culler (the latter in his essay on Derrida in *Structuralism and Since*, ed. Sturrock). In the essay on Lévi-Strauss, Derrida questions the concept of structure itself and catches Lévi-Strauss in infinitely recessive questions: what structures the structure, and what do we mean by the notion of centre? The structuralists seem, in Derrida's account, to have gone against their own teachings for these concepts seem not to be diacritically conceived. Derrida is expert at turning texts against themselves in this way, and exploring the contradictions in pieces of writing so as to 'deconstruct' their foundations. In doing so he has developed a distinctive battery of terms, though explanation of these is best left to the guides given in the Further Reading. As is indicated in the first part of this essay, Derrida ambitiously wishes to put into question the assumptions which he sees as governing the mainstream traditions of philosophical thought (the ruling 'epistémé') in the West.

Like much post-structuralist theory Derrida's texts are demanding reading; their verbal texture, in effect, reflects their concerns. For, if the view is offered that there are no stable meanings, it becomes contradictory to insist (and Derrida doesn't) on the unshakeable conceptual precision of one's own. Rather criticism of this kind becomes at its best a volatile, richly-suggestive, provocative performance. Deconstructionist critics, for instance, insist on the arbitrariness of the boundaries built between kinds of writing, for all writing is involved in the freeplay of textuality. This being the case it would be absurd to recognise a distinction between literature and criticism in literary studies, and some recent critics, especially in the United States, have begun to explore the creative possibilities of criticism in this new, free-wheeling mode. (See the introduction to Section 7 for further comment.)

Because deconstruction is particularly adroit at teasing out contradictions in pieces of writing it has been ready to go to work on other, more assertive, kinds of literary criticism. Paul De Man's essay in Section 3 is an early instance of this and De Man has become the doyen of American literary deconstruction. In his work literature itself appears as the *ne plus ultra* of writing, the place where conventional efforts to establish firm meanings most apparently fail, and an infinitely-ambiguous, endlessly-differential freeplay of meaning starts. Literature, it is argued, always defeats attempts at positive interpretive statement beyond the most crashingly banal. This would certainly rule out the confident claims to spiritual and human centrality made on behalf of literary texts by some of the earlier Anglo-American critics represented in Sections 1 and 2. For this reason, deconstruction and some other post-structuralist theory has been described as a joyous scepticism which delights in the nullity of meaning and therefore by extension, opponents think, all positive human endeavour.

In the final piece printed here, Frank Kermode (b. 1919) goes some way down the same road as De Man, though his is a less committed response to structuralist and post-structuralist theory. Indeed Kermode is on record as not being overly sympathetic to recent, absolutist forms of deconstruction. He sees it as a mono-lithic theory 'entirely absorbed in demonstrating its own validity', which is a curious state of affairs for a theory which revels in differences. (See the 'Prologue' to his *Essays on Fiction*.) Nevertheless Kermode's analysis of *Wuthering Heights*, con-ducted from his encounter with the new continental theory, is a close and intel-ligent engagement with the complexities of a literary text which seems continually to compromise and evade positive interpretive efforts. Kermode, in part, sets his account of the novel against those of other critics; and the book from which it comes challenges our received sense of what constitutes the literary classic. It is again illustration of the way meaning builds, through refusal and partial acceptance, on other meaning. Like much post-structuralist criticism it finds the interpreter's own difficulties mirrored in the concerns of the literary text itself. To what extent, in such a 'textual' world of indefiniteness and plurality, we can begin to speak of 'valid' interpretations of literary works is the subject of the next section.

Further Reading

A very useful place to begin reading in the transition from structuralism to post-structuralism is *The Structuralist Controversy*, ed. Richard Macksey and Eugenio Donato (1972). This collects the proceedings of the 1966 conference at which Derrida delivered his 'Structure, Sign and Play' paper. Barthes is another con-tributor. There are also two useful anthologies of post-structuralist literary criticism and theory: *Textual Strategies: Perspectives in Post-structuralist Criticism*, ed. Josué Harari (1979); and *Untying the Text: A Post-structuralist Reader*, ed. Robert Young (1981). *Structuralism and Since*, ed. John Sturrock (1979) is a collection of introductory essays on major post-structuralist thinkers including Barthes and Derrida.

Barthes' theory and criticism in its post-structuralist phase includes *S/Z* (1970) and *The Pleasure of the Text* (1973). See also the collection of essays *Image-Music-Text*, ed. Stephen Heath (1977). *Barthes: Selected Writings*, ed. Susan Sontag (1983) also contains relevant material. There are helpful books on Barthes by Annette Lavers, *Roland Barthes: Structuralism and After* (1982) and Jonathan Culler, *Barthes* (1983). The latter is a good introduction.

Derrida's writings are extensive. Readers new to him could begin with the collection of essays *Writing and Difference* (1978) and the large, demanding *Of Grammatology* (1967). Gayatri Chakravorty Spivak, the translator of the latter, also con-tributes a helpful introduction to it. There is a helpful general introduction to deconstruction by Christopher Norris, *Deconstruction: Theory and Practice* (1982). Jonathan Culler's *The Pursuit of Signs* (1981) and *On Deconstruction: Theory and Criticism after Structuralism* (1983) interestingly and illuminatingly dicuss and explain many issues raised by it. See also Vincent B. Leitch, *Deconstructive Criticism: an Advanced Introduction* (1983).

As might be expected there are several different versions of American deconstruction. Paul De Man's *Allegories of Reading* (1979) and *Blindness and Insight: Essays
in the Rhetoric of Contemporary Criticism* (1983) are justly celebrated. Other leading
American critics influenced by deconstuction include: Geoffrey H. Hartman (see
for instance *Criticism in the Wilderness: The Study of Literature Today* [1980]), J. Hillis
Miller (whose *Fiction and Repetition* [1982] has readings of seven English novels
including *Wuthering Heights*), and Harold Bloom (see Section 7). There is a
collection of essays by these four and Derrida himself in Bloom *et al.*, *Deconstruction
and Criticism* (1979). This focuses on some aspects of Romantic poetry. There is an
excellent discussion of American developments of post-structuralist theory by
Frank Lentricchia, *After the New Criticism* (1980); see also William Ray, *Literary
Meaning: From Phenomenology to Deconstruction* (1984). Ruth Nevo, '*The Waste Land:
Ur-Text of Deconstruction*', *New Literary History*, XIII (1982) is a modestly-
attempted description of the poem's possibilities for a deconstructionist reading.

Several British writers have made use of post-structuralist theory, though often
here it is used in tandem with marxist, feminist or psychoanalytic theory; see, for
example, Rosalind Coward and John Ellis, *Language and Materialism* (1977), Colin
MacCabe, *James Joyce and the Revolution of the Word* (1978), and Catherine Belsey,
Critical Practice (1980). Christopher Butler, *Interpretation, Deconstruction and Ideology*
(1984) is a thoughtful discussion of many of the questions provoked by post-structuralism in relation to literature.

Other books by Frank Kermode which contain material of theoretical interest
include *Romantic Image* (1957), which has comments on the New Criticism; *The
Sense of an Ending* (1966), *The Genesis of Secrecy* (1979), and *Essays on Fiction 1971–82*
(1983).

Other important writers whose work has influenced literary studies include the
philosopher-historian Michel Foucault and the American-based Palestinian critic
and historian (particularly of western attitudes to the Arab world) Edward Said.
These writers favour a more socially-directed version of post-structuralist
thinking. There is an anthology of Foucault's work, *The Foucault Reader*, ed. Paul
Rabinow (1986), and an introduction to it by J. L. Merquior, *Foucault* (1985).
Said's work includes *Beginnings: Intention and Method* (1975), *Orientalism* (1978), and
The World, The Text and the Critic (1983).

1

Roland Barthes,
'From Work to Text'

It is a fact that over the last few years a certain change has taken place (or is taking place) in our conception of language and, consequently, of the literary work which owes at least its phenomenal existence to this same language. The change is clearly connected with the current development of (amongst other disciplines) Linguistics, anthropology, Marxism and psychoanalysis (the term 'connection' is used here in a deliberately neutral way: one does not decide a determination, be it multiple and dialectical). What is new and which affects the idea of the work comes not necessarily from the internal recasting of each of these disciplines, but rather from their encounter in relation to an object which traditionally is the province of none of them. It is indeed as though the *interdisciplinarity* which is today held up as a prime value in research cannot be accomplished by the simple confrontation of specialist branches of knowledge. Interdisciplinarity is not the calm of an easy security; it begins *effectively* (as opposed to the mere expression of a pious wish) when the solidarity of the old disciplines breaks down — perhaps even violently, via the jolts of fashion — in the interests of a new object and a new language neither of which has a place in the field of the sciences that were to be brought peacefully together, this unease in classification being precisely the point from which it is possible to diagnose a certain mutation. The mutation in which the idea of the work seems to be gripped must not, however, be over-estimated: it is more in the nature of an epistemological slide than of a real break. The break, as is frequently stressed, is seen to have taken place in the last century with the appearance of Marxism and Freudianism: since then there has been no further break, so that in a way it can be said that for the last hundred years we have been living in repetition. What History, our History, allows us today is merely to slide, to vary, to exceed, to repudiate. Just as Einsteinian science demands that *the relativity of the frames of reference* be included in the object studied, so the combined action of Marxism, Freudianism and structuralism demands, in literature, the relativization of the relations of writer, reader and observer (critic). Over against the traditional notion of the *work*, for long — and still — conceived of in a, so to speak, Newtonian way, there is now the requirement of a new object, obtained by the sliding or over-turning of former categories. That object is the *Text*. I know the word is fashionable (I am myself often led to use it) and therefore regarded by some with suspicion, but that is exactly why I should like to remind myself of the principal propositions at the intersection of which I see the Text as standing. The word 'proposition' is to be understood more in a grammatical than in a logical sense: the following are not argumentations but enunciations, 'touches', approaches that consent to remain metaphorical. Here then are these propositions; they concern method, genres, signs, plurality, filiation, reading and pleasure.

1. The Text is not to be thought of as an object that can be computed. It would be futile to try to separate out materially works from texts. In particular, the tendency must be avoided to say that the work is classic, the text avant-garde; it is not a question of drawing up a crude honours list in the name of modernity and declaring certain literary productions 'in' and others 'out' by virtue of their chronological situation: there may be 'text' in a very ancient work, while many products of contemporary literature are in no way texts. The difference is this: the work is a fragment of substance, occupying a part of the space of books (in a library for example), the Text is a methodological field. The opposition may recall (without at all reproducing term for term) Lacan's distinction between 'reality' and 'the real': the one is displayed, the other demonstrated; likewise, the work can be seen (in bookshops, in catalogues, in exam syllabuses), the text is a process of demonstration, speaks according to certain rules (or against certain rules); the work can be held in the hand, the text is held in language, only exists in the movement of a discourse (or rather, it is Text for the very reason that it knows itself as text); the Text is not the decomposition of the work, it is the work that is the imaginary tail of the Text; or again, *the Text is experienced only in an activity of production*. It follows that the Text cannot stop (for example on a library shelf); its constitutive movement is that of cutting across (in particular, it can cut across the work, several works).

2. In the same way, the Text does not stop at (good) Literature; it cannot be contained in a hierarchy, even in a simple division of genres. What constitutes the Text is, on the contrary (or precisely), its subversive force in respect of the old classifications. How do you classify a writer like Georges Bataille? Novelist, poet, essayist, economist, philosopher, mystic? The answer is so difficult that the literary manuals generally prefer to forget about Bataille who, in fact, wrote texts, perhaps continuously one single text. If the Text poses problems of classification (which is furthermore one of its 'social' functions), this is because it always involves a certain experience of limits (to take up an expression from Philippe Sollers). Thibaudet used already to talk — but in a very restricted sense — of limit-works (such as Chateaubriand's *Vie de Rancé*, which does indeed come through to us today as a 'text'); the Text is that which goes to the limit of the rules of enunciation (rationality, readability, etc.). Nor is this a rhetorical idea, resorted to for some 'heroic' effect: the Text tries to place itself very exactly *behind* the limit of the *doxa* (is not general opinion — constitutive of our democratic societies and powerfully aided by mass communications — defined by its limits, the energy with which it excludes, its *censorship*?). Taking the word literally, it may be said that the Text is always *paradoxical*.

3. The Text can be approached, experienced, in reaction to the sign. The work closes on a signified. There are two modes of signification which can be attributed to this signified: either it is claimed to be evident and the work is then the object of a literal science, of philology, or else it is considered to be secret, ultimate, something to be sought out, and the work then falls under the scope of a hermeneutics, of an interpretation (Marxist, psychoanalytic, thematic, etc,); in short, the work itself functions as a general sign and it is normal that it should represent an institutional category of the civilization of the Sign. The Text, on the contrary, practises the

infinite deferment of the signified, is dilatory; its field is that of the signifier and the signifer must not be conceived of as 'the first stage of meaning', its material vestibule, but, in complete opposition to this, as its *deferred action*. Similarly, the *infinity* of the signifer refers not to some idea of the ineffable (the unnameable signified) but to that of a *playing*; the generation of the perpetual signifier (after the fashion of a perpetual calender) in the field of the text (better, of which the text is the field) is realised not according to an organic progress of maturation or a hermeneutic course of deepening investigation, but, rather, according to a serial movement of disconnections, overlappings, variations. The logic regulating the Text is not comprehensive (define 'what the work means') but metonymic; the activity of associations, contiguities, carryings-over coincides with a liberation of symbolic energy (lacking it, man would die); the work — in the best of cases — is *moderately* symbolic (its symbolic runs out, comes to a halt); the Text is *radically* symbolic: *a work conceived, perceived and received in its integrally symbolic nature is a text*. Thus is the Text restored to language; like language, it is structured but off-centred, without closure (note, in reply to the contemptuous suspicion of the 'fashionable' sometimes directed at structuralism, that the epistemological privilege currently accorded to language stems precisely from the discovery there of a paradoxical idea of structure: a system with neither close nor centre).

4. The Text is plural. Which is not simply to say that it has several meanings, but that it accomplishes the very plural of meaning: an *irreducible* (and not merely an acceptable) plural. The Text is not a co-existence of meanings but a passage, an overcrossing; thus it answers not to an interpretation, even a liberal one, but to an explosion, a dissemination. The plural of the Text depends, that is, not on the ambiguity of its contents but on what might be called the *stereographic plurality* of its weave of signifiers (etymologically, the text is a tissue, a woven fabric). The reader of the Text may be compared to someone at a loose end (someone slackened off from any imaginary); this passably empty subject strolls — it is what happened to the author of these lines, then it was that he had a vivid idea of the Text — on the side of a valley, a *oued* flowing down below (*oued* is there to bear witness to a certain feeling of unfamiliarity); what he perceives is multiple, irreducible, coming from a disconnected, heterogeneous variety of substances and perspectives: lights, colours, vegetation, heat, air, slender explosions of noises, scant cries of birds, children's voices from over on the other side, passages, gestures, clothes of inhabitants near or far away. All these *incidents* are half-identifiable: they come from codes which are known but their combination is unique, founds the stroll in a difference repeatable only as difference. So the Text: it can be it only in its difference (which does not mean its individuality), its reading is semelfactive (this rendering illusory any inductive-deductive science of texts — no 'grammar' of the text) and nevertheless woven entirely with citations, references, echoes, cultural languages (what language is not?), antecedent or contemporary, which cut across it through and through in a vast stereophony. The intertextual in which every text is held, it itself being the text-between of another text, is not to be confused with some origin of the text: to try to find the 'sources', the 'influences' of a work, is to fall in with the myth of filiation; the citations which go to make up a text are anonymous, untraceable, and yet *already read*: they are quotations without inverted commas. The work has nothing disturbing for any monistic philosophy (we know that there are opposing examples of these); for such a philosophy, plural is the Evil.

Against the work, therefore, the text could well take as its motto the words of the man possessed by demons (*Mark* 5:9): 'My name is Legion: for we are many.' The plural of demoniacal texture which opposes text to work can bring with it fundamental changes in reading, and precisely in areas where monologism appears to be the Law: certain of the 'texts' of Holy Scripture traditionally recuperated by theological monism (historical or anagogical) will perhaps offer themselves to a diffraction of meanings (finally, that is to say, to a materialist reading), while the Marxist interpretation of works, so far resolutely monistic, will be able to materialize itself more by pluralizing itself (if, however, the Marxist 'institutions' allow it).

5. The work is caught up in a process of filiation. Are postulated: a *determination* of the work by the world (by race, then by History), a *consecution* of works amongst themselves, and a *conformity* of the work to the author. The author is reputed the father and the owner of his work: literary science therefore teaches *respect* for the manuscript and the author's declared intentions, while society asserts the legality of the relation of author to work (the '*droit d'auteur*' or 'copyright', in fact of recent date since it was only really legalised at the time of the French Revolution). As for the Text, it reads without the inscription of the Father. Here again, the metaphor of the Text separates from that of the work: the latter refers to the image of an *organism* which grows by vital expansion, by 'development' (a word which is significantly ambiguous, at once biological and rhetorical); the metaphor of the Text is that of the *network*; if the Text extends itself, it is as a result of a combinatory systematic (an image, moreover, close to current biological conceptions of the living being). Hence no vital 'respect' is due to the Text: it can be *broken* (which is just what the Middle Ages did with two nevertheless authoritative texts — Holy Scripture and Aristotle); it can be read without the guarantee of its father, the restitution of the inter-text paradoxically abolishing any legacy. It is not that the Author may not 'come back' in the Text, in his text, but he then does so as a 'guest'. If he is a novelist, he is inscribed in the novel like one of his characters, figured in the carpet; no longer privileged, paternal, aletheological, his inscription is ludic. He becomes, as it were, a paper-author: his life is no longer the origin of his fictions but a fiction contributing to his work; there is a reversion of the work on to the life (and no longer the contrary); it is the work of Proust, of Genet which allows their lives to be read as a text. The word 'bio-graphy' re-acquires a strong, etymological sense, at the same time as the sincerity of the enunciation — veritable 'cross' borne by literary morality — becomes a false problem: the *I* which writes the text, it too, is never more than a paper-*I*.

6. The work is normally the object of a consumption; no demagogy is intended here in referring to the so-called consumer culture but it has to be recognised that today it is the 'quality' of the work (which supposes finally an appreciation of 'taste') and not the operation of reading itself which can differentiate between books: structurally, there is no difference between 'cultured' reading and casual reading in trains. The Text (if only by its frequent 'unreadability') decants the work (the work permitting) from its consumption and gathers it up as play, activity, production, practice. This means that the Text requires that one try to abolish (or at the very least to diminish) the distance between writing and reading, in no way by intensifying the projection of the reader into the work but by joining

them in a single signifying practice. The distance separating reading from writing is historical. In the times of the greatest social division (before the setting up of democratic cultures), reading and writing were equally privileges of class. Rhetoric, the great literary code of those times, taught one to *write* (even if what was then normally produced were speeches, not texts). Significantly, the coming of democracy reversed the word of command: what the (secondary) School prides itself on is teaching to *read* (well) and no longer to write (consciousness of the deficiency is becoming fashionable again today: the teacher is called upon to teach pupils to 'express themselves', which is a little like replacing a form of repression by a misconception). In fact, *reading*, in the sense of consuming, is far from *playing* with the text. 'Playing' must be understood here in all its polysemy: the text itself *plays* (like a door, like a machine with 'play') and the reader plays twice over, playing the Text as one plays a game, looking for a practice which re-produces it, but, in order that that practice not be reduced to a passive, inner *mimesis* (the Text is precisely that which resists such a reduction), also playing the Text in the musical sense of the term. The history of music (as a practice, not as an 'art') does indeed parallel that of the Text fairly closely: there was a period when practising amateurs were numerous (at least within the confines of a certain class) and 'playing' and 'listening' formed a scarcely differentiated activity; then two roles appeared in succession, first that of the performer, the interpreter to whom the bourgeois public (though still itself able to play a little — the whole history of the piano) delegated its playing, then that of the (passive) amateur, who listens to music without being able to play (the gramophone record takes the place of the piano). We know that today post-serial music has radically altered the role of the 'interpreter', who is called on to be in some sort the co-author of the score, completing it rather than giving it 'expression'. The Text is very much a score of this new kind: it asks of the reader a practical collaboration. Which is an important change, for who executes the work? (Mallarmé posed the question, wanting the audience to *produce* the book). Nowadays only the critic executes the work (accepting the play on words). The reduction of reading to a consumption is clearly responsible for the 'boredom' experienced by many in the face of the modern ('unreadable') text, the avant-garde film or painting: to be bored means that one cannot produce the text, open it out, *set it going*.

7. This leads us to pose (to propose) a final approach to the Text, that of pleasure. I do not know whether there has ever been a hedonistic aesthetics (eudæ-monist philosophies are themselves rare). Certainly there exists a pleasure of the work (of certain works); I can delight in reading and re-reading Proust, Flaubert, Balzac even — why not? — Alexandre Dumas. But this pleasure, no matter how keen and even when free from all prejudice, remains in part (unless by some exceptional critical effort) a pleasure of consumption; for if I can read these authors, I also know that I cannot *re-write* them (that it is impossible today to write 'like that') and this knowledge, depressing enough, suffices to cut me off from the production of these works, in the very moment their remoteness establishes my modernity (is not to be modern to know clearly what cannot be started over again?). As for the Text, it is bound to *jouissance*, that is to a pleasure without separation. Order of the signifier, the Text participates in its own way in a social utopia; before History (supposing the latter does not opt for barbarism), the Text achieves, if not the

transparence of social relations, that at least of language relations: the Text is that space where no language has a hold over any other, where languages circulate (keeping the circular sense of the term).

These few propositions, inevitably, do not constitute the articulations of a Theory of the Text and this is not simply the result of the failings of the person here presenting them (who in many respects has anyway done no more than pick up what is being developed round about him). It stems from the fact that a Theory of the Text cannot be satisfied by a metalinguistic exposition: the destruction of meta-language, or at least (since it may be necesary provisionally to resort to meta-language) its calling into doubt, is part of the theory itself: the discourse on the Text should itself be nothing other than text, research, textual activity, since the Text is that *social* space which leaves no language safe, outside, nor any subject of the enunciation in position as judge, master, analyst, confessor, decoder. The theory of the Text can coincide only with a practice of writing.

2
Jacques Derrida,
'Structure, Sign and Play in the Discourse of the Human Sciences'

We need to interpret interpretations more than to interpret things. (Montaigne)

Perhaps something has occurred in the history of the concept of structure that could be called an 'event,' if this loaded word did entail a meaning which it is precisely the function of structural — or structuralist — thought to reduce or to suspect. Let us speak of an 'event,' nevertheless, and let us use quotation marks to serve as a precaution. What would this event be then? Its exterior form would be that of a *rupture* and a redoubling.

It would be easy enough to show that the concept of structure and even the word 'structure' itself are as old as the *epistémé* — that is to say, as old as Western science and Western philosophy — and that their roots thrust deep into the soil of ordinary language, into whose deepest recesses the *epistémé* plunges in order to gather them up and to make them part of itself in a metaphorical displacement. Nevertheless, up to the event which I wish to mark out and define, structure — or rather the structurality of structure — although it has always been at work, has always been neutralised or reduced, and this by a process of giving it a centre or of referring it to a point of presence, a fixed origin. The function of this centre was not only to orient, balance, and organise the structure — one cannot in fact conceive of an unorganised structure — but above all to make sure that the organising principle of the structure would limit what we might call the *play* of the structure. By orienting and organising the coherence of the system, the centre of a structure permits the play of its elements inside the total form. And even today the notion of a structure lacking any centre represents the unthinkable itself.

Nevertheless, the centre also closes off the play which it opens up and makes possible. As centre, it is the point at which the substitution of contents, elements, or terms is no longer possible. At the centre, the permutation or the transformation of elements (which may of course be structures enclosed within a structure) is forbidden. At least this permutation has always remained *interdicted* (and I am using this word deliberately). Thus it has always been thought that the centre, which is by definition unique, constituted that very thing within a structure which while governing the structure, escapes structurality. This is why classical thought concerning structure could say that the centre is, paradoxically, *within* the structure and *outside it*. The centre is at the centre of the totality, and yet, since the centre does

123

not belong to the totality (is not part of the totality), the totality *has its centre elsewhere*. The centre is not the centre. The concept of centred structure — although it represents coherence itself, the condition of the *epistémé* as philosophy or science — is contradictorily coherent. And as always, coherence in contradiction expresses the force of a desire.[1] The concept of centred structure is in fact the concept of a play based on a fundamental ground, a play constituted on the basis of a fundamental immobility and a reassuring certitude, which itself is beyond the reach of play. And on the basis of this certitude anxiety can be mastered, for anxiety is invariably the result of a certain mode of being implicated in the game, of being caught by the game, of being as it were at stake in the game from the outset. And again on the basis of what we call the centre (and which, because it can be either inside or outside, can also indifferently be called the origin or end, *arché* or *telos*), repetitions, substitutions, transformations, and permutations are always *taken* from a history of meaning [*sens*] — that is, in a word, a history — whose origin may always be reawakened or whose end may always be anticipated in the form of presence. This is why one perhaps could say that the movement of any archaeology, like that of any eschatology, is an accomplice of this reduction of the structurality of structure and always attempts to conceive of structure on the basis of a full presence which is beyond play.

If this is so, the entire history of the concept of structure, before the rupture of which we are speaking, must be thought of as a series of substitutions of centre for centre, as a linked chain of determinations of the centre. Successively, and in a regulated fashion, the centre receives different forms or names. The history of metaphysics, like the history of the West, is the history of these metaphors and metonymies. Its matrix — if you will pardon me for demonstrating so little and for being so elliptical in order to come more quickly to my principal theme — is the determination of Being as *presence* in all senses of this word. It could be shown that all the names related to fundamentals, to principles, or to the centre have always designated an invariable presence — *eidos, arché, telos, energeia, ousia* (essence, existence, substance, subject) *alétheia*, transcendentality, consciousness, God, man, and so forth.

The event I called a rupture, the disruption I alluded to at the beginning of this paper presumably would have come about when the structurality of structure had to begin to be thought, that is to say, repeated, and this is why I said that this disruption was repetition in every sense of the word. Henceforth, it became necessary to think both the law which somehow governed the desire for a centre in the constitution of structure, and the process of signification which orders the displacements and substitutions for this law of central presence — but a central presence which has never been itself, has always already been exiled from itself into its own substitute. The substitute does not substitute itself for anything which has somehow existed before it. Henceforth, it was necessary to begin thinking that there was no centre, that the centre could not be thought in the form of a present-being, that the centre had no natural site, that it was not a fixed locus but a function, a sort of nonlocus in which an infinite number of sign-substitutions came into play. This was the moment when language invaded the universal problematic, the moment when, in the absence of a centre or origin, everything became discourse — provided we can agree on this word — that is to say, a system in which the central signified, the original or transcendental signified, is never absolutely present outside a system of differences. The absence of the transcendental signified extends the domain and the play of signification infinitely.

Where and how does this decentring, this thinking the structurality of structure, occur? It would be somewhat naïve to refer to an event, a doctine, or an author in order to designate this occurrence. It is no doubt part of the totality of an era, our own, but still it has always already begun to proclaim itself and begun to *work*. Nevertheless, if we wished to choose several 'names,' as indications only, and to recall those authors in whose discourse this occurrence has kept most closely to its most radical formulation, we doubtless would have to cite the Nietzschean critique of metaphysics, the critique of the concepts of Being and truth for which were substituted the concepts of play, interpretation, and sign (sign without present truth); the Freudian critique of self-presence, that is, the critique of consciousness, of the subject, of self-identity and of self-proximity or self-possession; and, more radically, the Heideggerean destruction of metaphysics, of onto-theology, of the determination of Being as presence. But all these destructive discourses and all their analogues are trapped in a kind of circle. This circle is unique. It describes the form of the relation between the history of metaphysics and the destruction of the history of metaphysics. There is no sense in doing without the concepts of metaphysics in order to shake metaphysics. We have no language — no syntax and no lexicon — which is foreign to this history; we can pronounce not a single destructive proposition which has not already had to slip into the form, the logic, and the implicit postulations of precisely what it seeks to contest. To take one example from many: the metaphysics of presence is shaken with the help of the concept of *sign*. But, as I suggested a moment ago, as soon as one seeks to demonstrate in this way that there is no transcendental or privileged signified and that the domain or play of signification henceforth has no limit, one must reject even the concept and word 'sign' itself — which is precisely what cannot be done. For the signification 'sign' has always been understood and determined, in its meaning, as sign-of, a signifier referring to a signified, a signifier different from its signified. If one erases the radical difference between signifier and signified, it is the word 'signifier' itself which must be abandoned as a metaphysical concept. When Lévi-Strauss says in the preface to *The Raw and the Cooked* that he has 'sought to transcend the opposition between the sensible and the intelligible by operating from the outset at the level of signs,'[2] the necessity, force, and legitimacy of his act cannot make us forget that the concept of the sign cannot in itself surpass this opposition between the sensible and the intelligible. The concept of the sign, in each of its aspects, has been determined by this opposition throughout the totality of its history. It has lived only on this opposition and its system. But we cannot do without the concept of the sign, for we cannot give up this metaphysical complicity without also giving up the critique we are directing against this complicity, or without the risk of erasing difference in the self-identity of a signified reducing its signifier into itself or, amounting to the same thing, simply expelling its signifier outside itself. For there are two heterogenous ways of erasing the difference between the signifier and the signified: one, the classic way, consists in reducing or deriving the signifier, that is to say, ultimately in *submitting* the sign to thought; the other, the one we are using here against the first one, consists in putting into question the system in which the preceding reduction functioned: first and foremost, the opposition between the sensible and the intelligible. For the *paradox* is that the metaphysical reduction of the sign needed the opposition it was reducing. The opposition is systematic with the reduction. And what we are saying here about the sign can be extended to all the concepts and all the sentences of metaphysics, in particular to the discourse on 'structure.' But there are several ways of being caught in this circle. They are all more or less naïve, more or less empirical, more or less systematic, more or less close to the formulation — that is, to the formalization — of this circle. It is these differences which explain the multiplicity of destructive discourse and the disagreement between those who elaborate them. Nietzsche, Freud, and Heidegger, for example, worked within the inherited concepts of metaphysics. Since these concepts are not elements or atoms, and since they are taken from a syntax and a system, every particular borrowing brings along with it the whole of metaphysics. This is what allows these destroyers to destroy each other reciprocally — for example, Heidegger regarding Nietzsche, with as much lucidity and rigour as bad faith and misconstruction, as the last metaphysician, the last 'Platonist.' One could do the same for Heidegger himself, for Freud, or for a number of others. And today no exercise is more widespread.

What is the relevance of this formal schema when we turn to what are called the 'human sciences'? One of them perhaps occupies a privileged place — ethnology. In fact one can assume that ethnology could have been born as a science only at the moment when a decentring had come about: at the moment when European culture — and, in consequence, the history of metaphysics and of its concepts — had been *dislocated*, driven from its locus, and forced to stop considering itself as the culture of reference. This moment is not first and foremost a moment of philosophical or scientific discourse. It is also a moment which is political, economic, technical, and so forth. One can say with total security that there is nothing fortuitous about the fact that the critique of ethnocentrism — the very condition of ethnology — should be systematically and historically contemporaneous with the destruction of the history of metaphysics. Both belong to one and the same era. Now, ethnology — like any science — comes about within the element of discourse. And it is primarily a European science employing traditional concepts, however much it may struggle against them. Consequently, whether he wants to or not — and this does not depend on a decision on his part — the ethnologist accepts into his discourse the premises of ethnocentrism at the very moment when he denounces them. This necessity is irreducible; it is not a historical contingency. We ought to consider all its implications very carefully. But if no one can escape this necessity, and if no one is therefore responsible for giving in to it, however little he may do so, this does not mean that all the ways of giving in to it are of equal pertinence. The quality and fecundity of a discourse are perhaps measured by the critical rigour with which this relation to the history of metaphysics and to inherited concepts is thought. Here it is a question both of a critical relation to the language of the social sciences and a critical responsibility of the discourse itself. It is a question of explicitly and systematically posing the problem of the status of a discourse which borrows from a heritage the resources necessary for the deconstruction of that heritage itself. A problem of *economy* and *strategy*.

If we consider, as an example, the texts of Claude Lévi-Strauss, it is not only because of the privilege accorded to ethnology among the social sciences, nor even because the thought of Lévi-Strauss weighs heavily on the contemporary theoretical situation. It is above all because a certain choice has been declared in the work of Lévi-Strauss and because a certain doctrine has been elaborated there, and precisely, in a *more or less explicit manner*, as concerns both this critique of language and this critical language in the social sciences.

In order to follow this movement in the text of Lévi-Strauss, let us choose as one guiding thread among others the opposition between nature and culture. Despite all its rejuvenations and disguises, this opposition is congenital to philosophy. It is even older than Plato. It is at least as old as the Sophists. Since the statement of the opposition *physis/nomos, physis/techné,* it has been relayed to us by means of a whole historical chain which opposes 'nature' to law, to education, to art, to technics — but also to liberty, to the arbitrary, to history, to society, to the mind, and so on. Now, from the outset of his researches, and from his first book (*The Elementary Structures of Kinship*) on, Lévi-Strauss simultaneously has experienced the necessity of utilizing this opposition and the impossibility of accepting it. In the *Elementary Structures*, he begins from this axiom or definition: that which is *universal* and spontaneous, and not dependent on any particular culture or on any determinate norm, belongs to nature. Inversely, that which depends upon a system of *norms* regulating society and therefore is capable of *varying* from one social structure to another, belongs to culture. These two definitions are of the traditional type. But in the very first pages of the *Elementary Structures* Lévi-Strauss, who has begun by giving credence to these concepts, encounters what he calls a *scandal*, that is to say, something which no longer tolerates the nature/culture opposition he has accepted, something which *simultaneously* seems to require the predicates of nature and of culture. This scandal is the *incest prohibition*. The incest prohibition is universal; in this sense one could call it natural. But it is also a prohibition, a system of norms and interdicts; in this sense one could call it cultural:

> Let us suppose then that everything universal in man relates to the natural order, and is characterized by spontaneity, and that everything subject to a norm is cultural and is both relative and particular. We are then confronted with a fact, or rather, a group of facts, which, in the light of previous definitions, are not far removed from a scandal: we refer to that complex group of beliefs, customs, conditions and institutions described succinctly as the prohibition of incest, which presents without the slightest ambiguity, and inseparably combines, the two characteristics in which we recognise the conflicting features of two mutually exclusive orders. It constitutes a rule, but a rule which, alone among all the social rules, possesses at the same time a universal character.[3]

Obviously there is no scandal except within a system of concepts which accredits the difference between nature and culture. By commencing his work with the *factum* of the incest prohibition, Lévi-Strauss thus places himself at the point at which this difference, which has always been assumed to be self-evident, finds itself erased or questioned. For from the moment when the incest prohibition can no longer be conceived within the nature/culture opposition, it can no longer be said to be a scandalous fact, a nucleus of opacity within a network of transparent significations. The incest prohibition is no longer a scandal one meets with or comes up against in the domain of traditional concepts; it is something which escapes these concepts and cetainly precedes them — probably as the condition of their possibility. It could perhaps be said that the whole of philosophical conceptualization, which is systematic with the nature/culture opposition, is designed to leave in the domain of the unthinkable the very thing that makes this conceptualization possible: the origin of the prohibition of incest.

This example, too cursorily examined, is only one among many others, but nevertheless it already shows that language bears within itself the necessity of its own critique. Now this critique may be undertaken along two paths, in two 'manners.' Once the limit of the nature/culture opposition makes itself felt, one might want to question systematically and rigorously the history of these concepts. This is a first action. Such a systematic and historic questioning would be neither a philological nor a philosophical action in the classic sense of these words. To concern oneself with the founding concepts of the entire history of philosophy, to deconstitute them, is not to undertake the work of the philologist or of the classic historian of philosophy. Despite appearances, it is probably the most daring way of making the beginnings of a step outside of philosophy. The step 'outside philosophy' is much more difficult to conceive than is generally imagined by those who think they made it long ago with cavalier ease, and who in general are swallowed up in metaphysics in the entire body of discourse which they claim to have disengaged from it.

The other choice (which I believe corresponds more closely to Lévi-Strauss's manner), in order to avoid the possibly sterilising effects of the first one, consists in conserving all these old concepts within the domain of empirical discovery while here and there denouncing their limits, treating them as tools which can still be used. No longer is any truth value attributed to them; there is a readiness to abandon them, if necessary, should other instruments appear more useful. In the meantime, their efficacy is exploited, and they are employed to destroy the old machinery to which they belong and of which they themselves are pieces. This is how the language of the social sciences criticises *itself*. Lévi-Strauss thinks that in this way he can separate *method* from *truth*, the instruments of the method and the objective significations envisaged by it. One could almost say that this is the primary affirmation of Lévi-Strauss; in any event, the first words of the *Elementary Structures* are: 'Above all, it is begining to emerge that this distinction between nature and society (''nature'' and ''culture'' seem preferable to us today), while of no acceptable historical significance, does contain a logic, fully justifying its use by modern sociology as a methodological tool.'[4]

Lévi-Strauss will always remain faithful to this double intention: to preserve as an instrument something whose truth value he criticises.

On the one hand, he will continue, in effect, to contest the value of the nature/culture opposition. More than thirteen years after the *Elementary Structures*, *The Savage Mind* faithfully echoes the text I have just quoted: 'The opposition between nature and culture to which I attached much importance at one time . . . now seems to be of primarily methodological importance.' And this methodological value is not affected by its 'ontological' nonvalue (as might be said, if this notion were not suspect here): 'However, it would not be enough to reabsorb particular humanities into a general one. This first enterprise opens the way for others which . . . are incumbent on the exact natural sciences: the reintegration of culture in nature and finally of life within the whole of its physico-chemical conditions.'[5]

On the other hand, still in *The Savage Mind*, he presents as what he calls *bricolage* what might be called the discourse of this method. The *bricoleur*, says Lévi-Strauss, is someone who uses 'the means at hand,' that is, the instruments he finds at his disposition around him, those which are already there, which had not been especially conceived with an eye to the operation for which they are to be used and to which one tries by trial and error to adapt them, not hesitating to change them whenever it appears necessary, or to try several of them at once, even if their form and their origin are heterogenous — and so forth. There is therefore a critique of language in the form of *bricolage*, and it has even been said that *bricolage* is critical language itself. I am thinking in particular of the article of G. Genette, 'Structuralisme et critique littéraire,'published in homage to Lévi-Strauss in a special issue of *L'Arc* (no. 26, 1965), where it is stated that the analysis of *bricolage* could 'be applied almost word for word' to criticism, and especially to 'literary criticism.'

If one calls *bricolage* the necessity of borrowing one's concepts from the text of a heritage which is more or less coherent or ruined, it must be said that every discourse is *bricoleur*. The engineer, whom Lévi-Strauss opposes to the *bricoleur*, should be the one to construct the totality of his language, syntax, and lexicon. In this sense the engineer is a myth. A subject who supposedly would be the absolute origin of his own discourse and supposedly would construct it 'out of nothing,' 'out of whole cloth,' would be the creator of the verb, the verb itself. The notion of the engineer who supposedly breaks with all forms of *bricolage* is therefore a theological idea; and since Lévi-Strauss tells us elsewhere that *bricolage* is mythopoetic, the odds are that the engineer is a myth produced by the *bricoleur*. As soon as we cease to believe in such an engineer and in a discourse which breaks with the received historical discourse, and as soon as we admit that every finite discourse is bound by a certain *bricolage* and that the engineer and the scientist are also species of *bricoleurs*, then the very idea of *bricolage* is menaced and the difference in which it took on its meaning breaks down.

This brings us to the second thread which might guide us in what is being contrived here.

Lévi-Strauss describes *bricolage* not only as an intellectual activity but also as a mythopoetical activity. One reads in *The Savage Mind*, 'Like *bricolage* on the technical plane, mythical reflection can reach brilliant unforeseen results on the intellectual plane. Conversely, attention has often been drawn to the mythopoetical nature of *bricolage*.'[6]

But Lévi-Strauss's remarkable endeavour does not simply consist in proposing, notably in his most recent investigations, a structural science of myths and of mythological activity. His endeavour also appears — I would say almost from the outset — to have the status which he accords to his own discourse on myths, to what he calls his 'mythologicals.' It is here that his discourse on myth, reflects on itself and criticises itself. And this moment, this critical period, is evidently of concern to all the languages which share the field of the human sciences. What does Lévi-Strauss say of his 'mythologicals'? It is here that we rediscover the mythopoetical virtue of *bricolage*. In effect, what appears most fascinating in this critical search for a new status of discourse is the stated abandonment of all reference to a *centre*, to a *subject*, to a privileged *reference*, to an origin, or to an absolute *archia*. The theme of this decentring could be followed throughout the 'Overture' to his last book, *The Raw and the Cooked*. I shall simply remark on a few key points.

1. From the very start, Lévi-Strauss recognises that the Bororo myth which he employs in the book as the 'reference myth' does not merit this name and this treatment. The name is specious and the use of the myth improper. This myth deserves no more than any other its referential privilege: 'In fact, the Bororo myth, which I shall refer to from now on as the key myth, is, as I shall try to show, simply a trans-

formation, to a greater or lesser extent, of other myths originating either in the same society or in neighbouring or remote societies. I could, therefore, have legitimately taken as my starting point any one representative myth of the group. From this point of view, the key myth is interesting not because it is typical, but rather because of its irregular position within the group.'[7]

2. There is no unity or absolute source of the myth. The focus or the source of the myth are always shadows and virtualities which are elusive, unactualizable, and nonexistent in the first place. Everything begins with structure, configuration, or relationship. The discourse on the acentric structure that myth itself is, cannot itself have an absolute subject or an absolute centre. It must avoid the violence that consists in centring a language which describes an acentric structure if it is not to shortchange the form and movement of myth. Therefore it is necessary to forego scientific or philosophical discourse, to renounce the *epistémé* which absolutely requires, which is the absolute requirement that we go back to the source, to the centre, to the founding basis, to the principle, and so on. In opposition to *epistemic* discourse, structural discourse on myths — *mythological* discourse — must itself be *mythomorphic*. It must have the form of that of which it speaks. This is what Lévi-Strauss says in *The Raw and the Cooked*, from which I would now like to quote a long and remarkable passage:

> The study of myths raises a methodological problem, in that it cannot be carried out according to the Cartesian principle of breaking down the difficulty into as many parts as may be necessary for finding the solution. There is no real end to methodological analysis, no hidden unity to be grasped once the breaking-down process has been completed. Themes can be split up *ad infinitum*. Just when you think you have disentangled and separated them, you realise that they are knitting together again in response to the operation of unexpected affinities. Consequently the unity of the myth is never more than tendential and projective and cannot reflect a state or a particular moment of the myth. It is a phenomenon of the imagination, resulting from the attempt at interpretation; and its function is to endow the myth with synthetic form and to prevent its disintegration into a confusion of opposites. The science of myths might therefore be termed 'anaclastic,' if we take this old term in the broader etymological sense which includes the study of both reflected rays and broken rays. But unlike philosophical reflection, which aims to go back to its own source, the reflections we are dealing with here concern rays whose only source is hypothetical . . . . And in seeking to imitate the spontaneous movement of mythological thought, this essay, which is also both too brief and too long, has had to conform to the requirement of that thought and to respect its rhythm. It follows that this book on myths is itself a kind of myth.[8]

This statement is repeated a little farther on: 'As the myths themselves are based on secondary codes (the primary codes being those that provide the substance of language), the present work is put forward as a tentative draft of a tertiary code, which is intended to ensure the reciprocal translatability of several myths. This is why it would not be wrong to consider this book itself as a myth: it is, as it were, the myth of mythology.'[9] The absence of a centre is here the absence of a subject and the absence of an author: 'Thus the myth and the musical work are like conductors of an orchestra, whose audience becomes the silent performers. If it is now asked where the real centre of the work is to be found, the answer is that this is impossible to determine. Music and mythology bring man face to face with potential objects of which only the shadows are actualized . . . . Myths are anonymous.'[10] The musical model chosen by Lévi-Strauss for the composition of his book is apparently justified by this absence of any real and fixed centre of the mythical or mythological discourse.

Thus it is at this point that ethnographic *bricolage* deliberately assumes its myth-opoetic function. But by the same token, this function makes the philosophical or epistemological requirement of a centre appear as mythological, that is to say, as a historical illusion.

Nevertheless, even if one yields to the necessity of what Lévi-Strauss has done , one cannot ignore its risks. If the mythological is mythomorphic, are all discourses on myths equivalent? Shall we have to abandon any epistemological requirement which permits us to distinguish between several qualities of discourse on the myth? A classic, but inevitable question. It cannot be answered — and I believe that Lévi-Strauss does not answer it — for as long as the problem of the relations between the philosopheme or the theorem, on the one hand, and the mytheme or the mythopoem, on the other, has not been posed explicitly, which is no small problem. For lack of explicitly posing this problem, we condemn ourselves to transforming the alleged transgression of philosophy into an unnoticed fault within the philosophical realm. Empiricism would be the genus of which these faults would always be the species. Transphilosophical concepts would be transformed into philosophical naïvetés. Many examples could be given to demonstrate this risk: the concepts of sign, history, truth, and so forth. What I want to emphasise is simply that the passage beyond philosophy does not consist in turning the page of philosophy (which usually amounts to philosophizing badly), but in continuing to read philosophers *in a certain way*. The risk I am speaking of is always assumed by Lévi-Strauss, and it is the very price of this endeavour. I have said that empiricism is the matrix of all faults menacing a discourse which continues, as with Lévi-Strauss in particular, to consider itself scientific. If we wanted to pose the problem of empiricism and *bricolage* in depth, we would probably end up very quickly with a number of absolutely contradictory propositions concerning the status of discourse in structural ethnology. On the one hand, structuralism justifiably claims to be the critique of empiricism. But at the same time there is not a single book or study by Lévi-Strauss which is not proposed as an empirical essay which can always be completed or invalidated by new information. The structural schemata are always proposed as hypotheses resulting from a finite quantity of information and which are subjected to the proof of experience. Numerous texts could be used to demonstrate this double postulation. Let us turn once again to the 'Overture' of *The Raw and the Cooked*, where it seems clear that if this postulation is double, it is because it is a question here of a language on language:

> If critics reproach me with not having carried out an exhaustive inventory of South American myths before analyzing them, they are making a grave mistake about the nature and function of these documents. The total body of myth belonging to a given community is comparable to its speech. Unless the population dies out physically or morally, this totality is never complete. You might as well criticise a linguist for compiling the grammar of a language without having complete records of the words pronounced since the language came into being, and without knowing what will be said in it during the future part of its existence. Experience proves that a linguist can work out the grammar of a given language from a remarkably small number of sentences . . . . And even a partial grammar or outline grammar is a precious acquisition when we are dealing with unknown languages. Syntax does not become evident only after a (theoretically limitless) series of events has been recorded and examined, because it is

itself the body of rules governing their production. What I have tried to give is an outline of the syntax of South American mythology. Should fresh data come to hand, they will be used to check or modify the formulation of certain grammatical laws, so that some are abandoned and replaced by new ones. But in no instance would I feel constrained to accept the arbitrary demand for a total mythological pattern, since, as has been shown, such a requirement has no meaning.[11]

Totalization, therefore, is sometimes defined as *useless*, and sometimes as *imposs-ible*. This is no doubt due to the fact that there are two ways of conceiving the limit of totalization. And I assert once more that these two determinations coexist implicitly in Lévi-Strauss's, discourse. Totalization can be judged impossible in the classical style: one then refers to the empirical endeavour of either a subject or a finite richness which it can never master. There is too much, more than one can say. But nontotalization can also be determined in another way: no longer from the standpoint of a concept of finitude as relegation to the empirical, but from the standpoint of the concept of *play*. If totalization no longer has any meaning, it is not because the infiniteness of a field cannot be covered by a finite glance or a finite dis-course, but because the nature of the field — that is, language and a finite language — excludes totalization. This field is in effect that of *play*, that is to say, a field of infinite substitutions only because it is finite, that is to say, because instead of being an inexhaustible field, as in the classical hypothesis, instead of being too large, there is something missing from it: a centre which arrests and grounds the play of substitutions. One could say — rigorously using that word whose scandalous signification is always obliterated in French — that this movement of play, permitted by the lack or absence of a centre or origin, is the movement of *supplementarity*. One cannot determine the centre and exhaust totalization because the sign which replaces the centre, which supplements it, taking the centre's place in its absence — this sign is added, occurs as a surplus, as a *supplement*.[12] The movement of signification adds something, which results in the fact that there is always more, but this addition is a floating one because it comes to perform a vicarious function, to supplement a lack on the part of the signified. Although Lévi-Strauss in his use of the word 'supplementary' never emphasises, as I do here, the two directions of meaning which are so strangely compounded within it, it is not by chance that he uses this word twice in his 'Introduction to the Work of Marcel Mauss,' at one point where he is speaking of the 'overabundance of sign-ifier, in relation to the signifieds to which this overabundance can refer':

> In his endeavour to understand the world, man therefore always has at his disposal a surplus of signification (which he shares out amongst things according to the laws of symbolic thought — which is the task of ethnologists and linguists to study). This dis-tribution of a *supplementary* allowance [*ration supplémentaire*] — if it is permissible to put it that way — is absolutely necessary in order that on the whole the available signifier and the signified it aims at may remain in the relationship of complementarity which is the very condition of the use of symbolic thought.'[13]

(It could no doubt be demonstrated that this *ration supplémentaire* of signification is the origin of the *ratio* itself.) The word reappears a little further on, after Lévi-Strauss has mentioned 'this floating signifier, which is the servitude of all finite thought':

> In other words — and taking as our guide Mauss's precept that all social phenomena

can be assimilated to language — we see in *mana, Wakau, oranda* and other notions of the same type, the conscious expression of a semantic function, whose role it is to permit symbolic thought to operate in spite of the contradiction which is proper to it. In this way are explained the apparently insoluble antinomies attached to this notion . . . . At one and the same time force and action, quality and state, noun and verb; abstract and concrete, omnipresent and localised — *mana* is in effect all these things. But is it not precisely because it is none of these things that *mana* is a simple form, or more exactly, a symbol in the pure state, and therefore capable of becoming charged with any sort of symbolic content whatever? In the system of symbols constituted by all cosmologies, *mana* would simply be a zero symbolic value, that is to say, a sign marking the necessity of a symbolic content *supplementary* [my italics] to that with which the signified is already loaded, but which can take on any value required, provided only that this value still remains part of the available reserve and is not, as phonologists put it, a 'group-term.'

Lévi-Strauss adds the note:

'Linguists have already been led to formulate hypotheses of this type. For example: "A zero phoneme is opposed to all the other phonemes in French in that it entails no differential characters and no constant phonetic value. On the contrary, the proper function of the zero phoneme is to be opposed to phoneme absence." (R. Jakobson and J. Lutz, 'Notes on the French Phonemic Pattern,' *Word* 5, no. 2 [August 1949]: 155). Similarly, if we schematize the conception I am proposing here, it could almost be said that the function of notions like *mana* is to be opposed to the absence of signification, without entailing by itself any particular signification.'[14]

The *overabundance* of the signifier, its *supplementary* character, is thus the result of a finitude, that is to say, the result of a lack which must be *supplemented*.

It can now be understood why the concept of play is important in Lévi-Strauss. His references to all sorts of games, notably to roulette, are very frequent, especially in his *Conversations*,[15] in *Race and History*,[16] and in *The Savage Mind*. Further, the reference to play is always caught up in tension.

Tension with history, first of all. This is a classical problem, objections to which are now well worn. I shall simply indicate what seems to me the formality of the problem: by reducing history, Lévi-Strauss had treated as it deserves a concept which has always been in complicity with a teleological and eschatological metaphysics, in other words, paradoxically, in complicity with that philosophy of presence to which it was believed history could be opposed. The thematic of historicity, although it seems to be a somewhat late arrival in philosophy, has always been required by the determination of Being as presence. With or without etymology, and despite the classic antagonism which opposes these significations throughout all of classical thought, it could be shown that the concept of *epistémé* has always called forth that of *historia*, if history is always the unity of a becoming, as the tradition of truth or the development of science or knowledge oriented toward the appropriation of truth in presence and self-presence, toward knowledge in consciousness-of-self. History has always been conceived as the movement of a resumption of history, as a detour between two presences. But if it is legitimate to suspect this concept of history, there is a risk, if it is reduced without an explicit statement of the problem I am indicating here, of falling back into an ahistoricism of a classical type, that is to say, into a determined moment of the history of metaphysics. Such is the algebraic formality of the problem as I see it. More concretely, in the work of Lévi-Strauss it must be recognized that the respect for structurality, for the internal originality of the structure, compels a neutralisation of time and history. For example, the appearance of a new structure, of an original system, always comes about — and this is the very condition of its structural specificity — by a rupture with its past, its origin, and its cause. Therefore one can describe what is peculiar to the structural organization only by not taking into account, in the very moment of this description, its past conditions: by omitting to posit the problem of the transition from one structure to another, by putting history between brackets. In this 'structuralist' moment, the concepts of chance and discontinuity are indispensable. And Lévi-Strauss does in fact often appeal to them, for example, as concerns that structure of structures, language, of which he says in the 'Introduction to the Work of Marcel Mauss' that it 'could only have been born in one fell swoop':

> Whatever may have been the moment and the circumstances of its appearance on the scale of animal life; language could only have been born in one fell swoop. Things could not have set about acquiring signification progressively. Following a transformation the study of which is not the concern of the social sciences, but rather of biology and psychology, a transition came about from a stage where nothing had a meaning to another where everything possessed it.[17]

This standpoint does not prevent Lévi-Strauss from recognizing the slowness, the process of maturing, the continuous toil of factual transformations, history (for example, *Race and History*). But, in accordance with a gesture which was also Rousseau's and Husserl's, he must 'set aside all the facts' at the moment when he wishes to recapture the specificity of a structure. Like Rousseau, he must always conceive of the origin of a new structure on the model of catastrophe — an overturning of nature in nature, a natural interruption of the natural sequence, a setting aside *of* nature.

Besides the tension between play and history, there is also the tension between play and presence. Play is the disruption of presence. The presence of an element is always a signifying and substitutive reference inscribed in a system of differences and the movement of a chain. Play is always play of absence and presence, but if it is to be thought radically, play must be conceived of before the alternative of presence and absence. Being must be conceived as presence or absence on the basis of the possibility of play and not the other way around. If Lévi-Strauss, better than any other, has brought to light the play of repetition and the repetition of play, one no less perceives in his work a sort of ethic of presence, an ethic of nostalgia for origins, an ethic of archaic and natural innocence, of a purity of presence and self-presence in speech — an ethic, nostalgia, and even remorse, which he often presents as the motivation of the ethnological project when he moves toward the archaic societies which are exemplary societies in his eyes. These texts are well known.[18]

Turned towards the lost or impossible presence of the absent origin, this structuralist thematic of broken immediacy is therefore the saddened, *negative*, nostalgic, guilty, Rousseauistic side of the thinking of play whose other side would be the Nietzschean *affirmation*, that is the joyous affirmation of the play of the world and of the innocence of becoming, the affirmation of a world of signs without fault, without truth, and without origin which is offered to an active interpretation. *This affirmation then determines the noncentre otherwise than as loss of the centre.* And it plays without security. For there is a *sure* play: that which is limited to the *substitution* of *giving* and *existing, present*, pieces. In absolute chance, affirmation also surrenders itself to *genetic* indetermination, to the *seminal* adventure of the trace.

There are thus interpretations of interpretation, of structure, of sign, of play. The one seeks to decipher, dreams of deciphering a truth or an origin which escapes play and the order to the sign, and which lives the necessity of interpretation as an exile. The other, which is no longer turned toward the origin, affirms play and tries to pass beyond man and humanism, the name of man being the name of that being who, throughout the history of metaphysics or of ontotheology — in other words, throughout his entire history — has dreamed of full presence, the reassuring foundation, the origin and the end of play. The second interpretation of interpretation, to which Nietzsche pointed the way, does not seek in ethnography, as Lévi-Strauss does, the 'inspiration of a new humanism' (again citing the 'Introduction to the Work of Marcel Mauss').

There are more than enough indications today to suggest we might perceive that these two interpretations of interpretation — which are absolutely irreconcilable even if we live them simultaneously and reconcile them in an obscure economy — together share the field which we call, in such a problematic fashion, the social sciences.

For my part, although these two interpretations must acknowledge and accentuate their difference and define their irreducibility, I do not believe that today there is any question of *choosing* — in the first place because here we are in a region (let us say, provisionally, a region of historicity) where the category of choice seems particularly trivial; and in the second, because we must first try to conceive of the common ground, and the *différance* of this irreducible difference. Here there is a kind of question, let us still call it historical, whose *conception, formation, gestation,* and *labour* we are only catching a glimpse of today. I employ these words, I admit, with a glance toward the operations of childbearing — but also with a glance toward those who, in a society from which I do not exclude myself, turn their eyes away when faced by the as yet unnamable which is proclaiming itself and which can do so, as is necessary whenever a birth is in the offing, only under the species of the nonspecies, in the formless, mute, infant, and terrifying form of monstrosity.

Notes:

1. The reference, in a restricted sense, is to the Freudian theory of neurotic symptoms and of dream interpretation in which a given symbol is understood contradictorily as both the desire to fulfil an impulse and the desire to suppress the impulse. In a general sense the reference is to Derrida's thesis that logic and coherence themselves can only be understood contradictorily, since they presuppose the suppression of *différance*, 'writing' in the sense of the general economy. Cf. 'La pharmacie de Platon,' in *La dissemination*, pp. 125–26, where Derrida uses the Freudian model of dream interpretation in order to clarify the contractions embedded in philosophical coherence. [Translator's note.]
2. *The Raw and the Cooked*, trans. John and Doreen Wightman (New York: Harper and Row, 1969), p. 14. [Translation somewhat modified.]
3. *The Elementary Structures of Kinship*, trans. James Bell, John von Sturmer and Rodney Needham (Boston: Beacon Press, 1969), p. 8.
4. Ibid., p. 3.

5. *The Savage Mind* (London: George Weidenfeld and Nicolson; Chicago: The University of Chicago Press, 1966), p. 247.

6. Ibid., p. 17.

7. *The Raw and the Cooked*, p. 2.

8. Ibid., pp. 5–6.

9. Ibid., p. 12.

10. Ibid., pp. 17–18.

11. Ibid., pp. 7–8.

12. This double sense of supplement — to supply something which is missing, or to supply something additional — is at the centre of Derrida's deconstruction of traditional linguistics in *De la grammatologie*. In a chapter entitled 'The Violence of the Letter: From Lévi-Strauss to Rousseau' (pp. 149ff.), Derrida expands the analysis of Lévi-Strauss begun in this essay in order further to clarify the ways in which the contradictions of traditional logic 'program' the most modern conceptual apparatuses of linguistics and the social sciences. [Translator's note.]

13. 'Introduction à l'oeuvre de Marcel Mauss,' in Marcel Mauss, *Sociologie et anthropologie* (Paris: P.U.F., 1950), p. xlix.

14. Ibid., pp. xlix–l.

15. George Charbonnier, *Entretiens avec Claude Lévi-Strauss* (Paris: Plon, 1961).

16. *Race and History* (Paris: Unesco Publications, 1958).

17. 'Introduction à l'oeuvre de Marcel Mauss,' p. xlvi.

18. The reference is to *Tristes tropiques*, trans. John Russell (London: Hutchinson and Co., 1961). [Translator's note.]

Frank Kermode,
'Wuthering Heights'

I begin, then, with a partial reading of *Wuthering Heights* which represents a straightforward encounter between a competent modern reader (the notion of competence is, I think, essential, however much you may think this demonstration falls short of it) and a classic text. However, in assuming this role, I could not avoid noticing some remarks that are not in the novel at all, but in Charlotte Brontë's Biographical Notice of her sisters, in which she singles out a contemporary critic as the only one who got her sister's book right. 'Too often,' she says, 'do reviewers remind us of the mob of Astrologers, Chaldeans and Soothsayers gathered before the "writing on the wall", and unable to read the characters or make known the interpretation.' One, however, has accurately read 'the Mene, Mene, Tekel, Upharsin of an original mind' and 'can say with confidence, "This is the interpretation thereof" '. This latterday Daniel was Sidney Dobell, but a modern reader who looks him up in the hope of coming upon what would after all be a very valuable piece of information is likely to be disappointed. Very few would dream of doing so; most would mistrust the critic for whom such claims were made, or the book which lent itself to them. Few would believe that such an interpretation exists, however frequently the critics produce new 'keys'. For we don't think of the novel as a code, or a nut, that can be broken; which contains or refers to a meaning all will agree upon if it can once be presented *en clair*. We need little persuasion to believe that a good novel is not a message at all. We assume in principle the rightness of the plurality of interpretations to which I now, in ignorance of all the others, but reasonably confident that I won't repeat them, now contribute.

When Lockwood first visits Wuthering Heights he notices, among otherwise irrelevant decorations carved above the door, the date *1500* and the name *Hareton Earnshaw*. It is quite clear that everybody read and reads this (on p. 2) as a sort of promise of something else to come. It is part of what is nowadays called a 'hermeneutic code'; something that promises, and perhaps after some delay provides, explanation. There is, of course, likely to be some measure of peripeteia or trick; you would be surprised if the explanation were not, in some way, surprising, or at any rate, at this stage unpredictable. And so it proves. The expectations aroused by these inscriptions are strictly *generic*; you must know things of this kind before you can entertain expectations of the sort I mention. Genre in this sense is what Leonard Meyer (writing of music) calls 'an internalized probability system'.[1] Such a system could, but perhaps shouldn't, be thought of as constituting some sort of contract between reader and writer. Either way, the inscriptions can be seen as something other than simple elements in a series of one damned thing after another, or even of events relative to a story as such. They reduce the range of probabilities, reduce randomness, and are expected to recur. There will be 'feedback'. This may not extinguish all the informational possibilities in the original stimulus, which may be, and in this case is, obscurer than we thought, 'higher', as the information theorists say, 'in entropy'. The narrative is more than merely a lengthy delay, after which a true descendant of Hareton Earnshaw reoccupies the ancestral house; though there is little delay before we hear about him, and we can make a guess if we want.

When Hareton is first discussed, Nelly Dean rather oddly describes him as 'the late Mrs. Linton's nephew'. Why not 'the late Mr. Earnshaw's son'? It is only in the previous sentence that we have first heard the name Linton, when the family of that name is mentioned as having previously occupied Thrushcross Grange. Perhaps we are to wonder how Mrs. Linton came to have a nephew named Earnshaw. At any rate, Nelly's obliquity thus serves to associate Hareton, in a hazy way, with the house on which his name is *not* carved, and with a family no longer in evidence. Only later do we discover that he is the direct Earnshaw line, in fact, as Nelly says, 'the last of them'. So begins the provision of information which both fulfils and qualifies the early 'hermeneutic' promise; because, of course, Hareton, his inheritance restored, goes to live at the Grange. The two principal characters remaining at the end are Mr. and Mrs. Hareton Earnshaw. The other names, which have intruded on Earnshaw — Linton and Heathcliff — are extinct. In between there have been significant recursions to the original inscription — in Chapter XX Hareton cannot read it; in XXIV he can read the name but not the date.

We could say, I suppose, that this so far tells us nothing about *Wuthering Heights* that couldn't, with appropriate changes, be said of most novels. All of them contain the equivalent of such inscriptions; indeed all writing is a sort of inscription, cut memorably into the uncaused flux of event; and inscriptions of the kind I am talking about are interesting secondary clues about the nature of the writing in which they occur. They draw attention to the literariness of what we are reading, indicate that the story is a story, perhaps with beneficial effects on our normal powers of perception; above all they distinguish a *literary* system which has no constant relation to readers with interests and expectations altered by long passages of time. Or, to put it another way, Emily Brontë's contemporaries operated different probability systems from ours, and might well ignore whatever in a text did not comply with their generic expectations, dismissing the rest somehow — by skipping, by accusations of bad craftsmanship, inexperience, or the like. In short, their internalized probability systems survive them in altered and less stringent forms; we can read more of the text than they could, and of course read it differently. In fact, the only works we value enough to call classic are those which, and they demonstrate by surviving, are complex and indeterminate enough to allow us our necessary pluralities. That 'Mene, Mene, Tekel, Upharsin' has now many interpretations. It is in the nature of works of art to be open, in so far as they are 'good'; though it is in the nature of authors, and of readers, to close them.

The openness of *Wuthering Heights* might be somewhat more extensively illustrated by an inquiry into the passage describing Lockwood's bad night at the house, when, on his second visit, he was cut off from Thrushcross Grange by a storm. He is given an odd sort of bed in a bedroom-within-a-bedroom; Catherine Earnshaw slept in it and later Heathcliff would die in it. Both the bed and the lattice are subjects of very elaborate 'play'; but I want rather to consider the inscriptions Lockwood examines before retiring. There is writing on the wall, or on the ledge by his bed: it 'was nothing but a name repeated in all kinds of characters, large and small — *Catherine Earnshaw*, here and there varied to *Catherine Heathcliff*, and then again to *Catherine Linton*'. When he closes his eyes Lockwood is assailed by white letters 'which started from the dark, as vivid as spectres — the air swarmed with Catherines'. He has no idea whatever to whom these names belong, yet the expression 'nothing but a name' seems to suggest that they all belong to one person. Waking from a doze he finds the name *Catherine Earnshaw* inscribed in a book his candle has scorched.

It is true that Lockwood has earlier met a Mrs. Heathcliff, and got into a tangle about who she was, taking first Heathcliff and then Hareton Earnshaw for her husband, as indeed, we discover she, in a different sense, had also done or was to do. For she had a merely apparent kinship relation with Heathcliff — bearing his name as the wife of his impotent son and having to tolerate his ironic claim to fatherhood — as a prelude to the restoration of her true name, Earnshaw; it is her mother's story reversed. But Lockwood was not told her first name. Soon he is to encounter a ghost called Catherine Linton; but if the scribbled names signify one person he and we are obviously going to have to wait to find out who it is. Soon we learn that Mrs. Heathcliff is Heathcliff's daughter-in-law, *née* Catherine Linton, and obviously not the ghost. Later it becomes evident that the scratcher must have been Catherine Earnshaw, later Linton, a girl long dead who might well have been Catherine Heathcliff, but wasn't.

When you have processed all the information you have been waiting for you see the point of the order of the scribbled names, as Lockwood gives them: *Catherine Earnshaw, Catherine Heathcliff, Catherine Linton*. Read from left to right they recapitulate Catherine Earnshaw's story; read from right to left, the story of her daughter, Catherine Linton. The names Catherine and Earnshaw begin and end the narrative. Of course some of the events needed to complete this pattern had not occurred when Lockwood slept in the little bedroom; indeed the marriage of Hareton and Catherine is still in the future when the novel ends. Still, this is an account of the movement of the book: away from Earnshaw and back, like the movement of the house itself. And all the movements must be *through* Heathcliff.

Charlotte Brontë remarks, from her own experience, that the writer says more than he knows, and was emphatic that this was so with Emily. 'Having formed these beings, she did not know what she had done.' Of course this strikes us as no more than common sense; though Charlotte chooses to attribute it to Emily's ignorance of the world. A narrative is not a transcription of something pre-existent. And this is precisely the situation represented by Lockwood's play with the names he does not understand, his constituting, out of many scribbles, a rebus for the plot of the novel he's in. The situation indicates the kind of work we must do when a narrative opens itself to us, and contains information in excess of what generic probability requires.

Consider the names again; of course they reflect the isolation of the society under consideration, but still it is remarkable that in a story whose principal characters all marry there are effectively only three surnames, all of which each Catherine assumes. Furthermore, the Earnshaw family makes do with only three Christian names, Catherine, Hindley, Hareton. Heathcliff is a family name also, but parsimoniously, serving as both Christian name and surname; always lacking one or the other, he wears his name as an indication of his difference, and this persists after death since his tombstone is inscribed with the one word *Heathcliff*. Like Frances, briefly the wife of Hindley, he is simply a sort of interruption in the Earnshaw system.

Heathcliff is then as it were between names, as between families (he is the door through which Earnshaw passes into Linton, and out again to Earnshaw). He is often introduced, as if characteristically, standing outside, or entering, or leaving, a door. He is in and out of the Earnshaw family simultaneously; servant and child of the family (like Hareton, whom he puts in the same position, he helps to indicate the archaic nature of the house's society, the lack of sharp social division, which is not characteristic of the Grange). His origins are equally betwixt and between: the gutter or the royal origin imagined for him by Nelly; prince or pauper, American or Lascar, child of God or devil. This betweenness persists, I think: Heathcliff, for instance, fluctuates between poverty and riches; also between virility and impotence. To Catherine he is between brother and lover; he slept with her as a child, and again in death, but not between latency and extinction. He has much force, yet fathers an exceptionally puny child. Domestic yet savage like the dogs, bleak yet full of fire like the house, he bestrides the great opposites: love and death (the necrophiliac confession), culture and nature ('half-civilized ferocity') in a posture that certainly cannot be explained by any generic formula ('Byronic' or 'Gothic').

He stands also between a past and a future; when his force expires the old Earnshaw family moves into the future associated with the civilized Grange, where the insane authoritarianism of the Heights is a thing of the past, where there are cultivated distinctions between gentle and simple — a new world in the more civil south. It was the Grange that first separated Heathcliff from Catherine, so that Earnshaws might eventually live there. Of the children — Hareton, Cathy, and Linton — none physically resembles Heathcliff; the first two have Catherine's eyes (XXXIII) and the other is, as his first name implies, a Linton. Cathy's two cousin-marriages, constituting an endogamous route to the civilized exogamy of the south — are the consequence of Heathcliff's standing between Earnshaw and Linton, north and south; earlier he had involuntarily saved the life of the baby Hareton. His ghost and Catherine's, at the end, are of interest only to the superstitious, the indigenous now to be dispossessed by a more rational culture.

If we look, once more, at Lockwood's inscriptions, we may read them thus (see facing page).

Earnshaws persist, but they must eventually do so within the Linton culture. Catherine burns up in her transit from left to right. The quasi-Earnshaw union of Heathcliff and Isabella leaves the younger Cathy an easier passage; she has only to get through Linton Heathcliff, who is replaced by Hareton Earnshaw, Hareton has suffered part of Heathcliff's fate, moved, as it were, from Earnshaw to Heathcliff, and replaced him as son-servant, as gratuitously cruel; but he is the last of the Earnshaws, and Cathy can both restore to him the house on which his name is carved, and take him on the now smooth path to Thrushcross Grange.

Novels, even this one, were read in houses more like the Grange than the Heights, as the emphasis on the ferocious piety of the Earnshaw library suggests. The order of the novel is a civilized order; it presupposes a reader in the midst of an educated family and habituated to novel reading; a reader, moreover, who

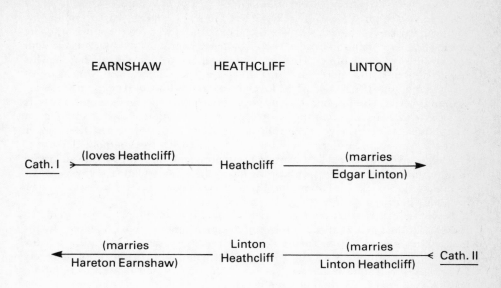

N.B. Heathcliff stands between Earnshaw and Linton as having Earnshaw origins but marrying Isabella Linton. He could also be represented as moving from left to right and right to left — into the Linton column, and then back to the Earnshaw when he usurps the hereditary position of Hareton. Hareton himself might be represented as having first been forced out of the Earnshaw column into the intermediate position when Heathcliff reduces him to a position resembling the one he himself started from, a savage and inferior member of the family. But he returns to the Earnshaw column with Cath. II. Finally they move together (without passing through the intermediate position, which has been abolished) from left to right, from Wuthering Heights to Thrushcross Grange.

believes in the possibility of effective ethical choices. And because this is the case, the author can allow herself to meet his proper expectations without imposing on the text or on him absolute generic control. She need not, that is, know all that she is saying. She can, in all manner of ways, invite the reader to collaborate, leave to him the supply of meaning where the text is indeterminate or discontinuous, where explanations are required to fill narrative lacunae.

Instances of this are provided by some of the dreams in the book.[2] Lockwood's brief dream of the spectral letters is followed by another about an interminable sermon, which develops from hints about Joseph in Catherine's Bible. The purport of this dream is obscure. The preacher Jabes Branderham takes a hint from his text and expands the seven deadly sins into seventy times seven plus one. It is when he reaches the last section that Lockwood's patience runs out, and he protests, with his own allusion to the Bible: 'He shall return no more to his house, neither shall his place know him any more.' Dreams in stories are usually given a measure of oneiric ambiguity, but stay fairly close to the narrative line, or if not, convey information otherwise useful; but this one does not appear to do so, except in so far as that text may bear obscurely and incorrectly on the question of where Hareton will end up. It is, however, given a naturalistic explanation: the rapping of the preacher on the pulpit is a dream version of the rapping of the fir tree on the window.

Lockwood once more falls asleep, but dreams again, and 'if possible, still more disagreeably than before'. Once more he hears the fir-bough, and rises to silence it; he breaks the window and finds himself clutching the cold hand of a child who calls herself Catherine Linton.

He speaks of this as a dream, indeed he ascribes to it 'the intense horror of nightmare', and the blood that runs down into the bedclothes may be explained by his having cut his hand as he broke the glass, but he does not say so, attributing it to his own cruelty in rubbing the child's wrist on the pane; and Heathcliff immediately makes it obvious that of the two choices the text has so far allowed us the more acceptable is that Lockwood was not dreaming at all.

So we cannot dismiss this dream as 'Gothic' ornament or commentary, or even as the kind of dream Lockwood has just had, in which the same fir-bough produced a comically extended dream-explanation of its presence. There remain all manner of puzzles: why is the visitant a child and, if a child, why Catherine *Linton*? The explanation, that this name got into Lockwood's dream from a scribble in the Bible is one even he finds hard to accept. He hovers between an explanation involving 'ghosts and goblins', and the simpler one of nightmare; though he has no more doubt than Heathcliff that 'it' — the child — was trying to enter. For good measure he is greeted, on going downstairs, by a cat, a brindled cat, with its echo of Shakespearian witchcraft.

It seems plain, then, that the dream is not simply a transformation of the narrative, a commentary on another level, but an integral part of it. The Branderham dream is, in a sense, a trick, suggesting a measure of rationality in the earlier dream which we might want to transfer to the later experience, as Lockwood partly does. When we see that there is a considerable conflict in the clues as to how we should read the second tapping and relate it to the first we grow aware of further contrasts between the two, for the first is a comic treatment of 491 specific and resistible sins for which Lockwood is about to be punished by exile from his home, and the second is a more horrible spectral invasion of the womb-like or tomb-like room in which he is housed. There are doubtless many other observations to be made; it is not a question of deciding which is the single right reading, but of dealing, as reader, with a series of indeterminacies which the text will not resolve.

Nelly Dean refuses to listen to Catherine's dream, one of those which went through and through her 'like wine through water'; and of those dreams we hear nothing save this account of their power. 'We're dismal enough without conjuring up ghosts and visions to perplex us,' says Nelly — another speaking silence in the text, for it is implied that we are here denied relevant information. But she herself suffers a dream or vision. After Heathcliff's return she finds herself at the signpost: engraved in its sandstone — with all the permanence that Hareton's name has on the house — are 'Wuthering Heights' to the north, 'Gimmerton' to the east, and 'Thrushcross Grange' to the south. Soft south, harsh north, and the rough civility of the market town (something like that of Nelly herself) in between. As before, these inscriptions provoke a dream apparition, a vision of Hindley as a child. Fearing that he has come to harm, she rushes to the Heights and again sees the spectral child, but it turns out to be Hareton, Hindley's son. His appearance betwixt and between the Heights and the Grange was proleptic; now he is back at the Heights, a stone in his hand, threatening his old nurse, rejecting the Grange. And as Hindley turned into Hareton, so Hareton turns into Heathcliff, for the figure that appears in the doorway is Heathcliff.

This is very like a real dream in its transformations and displacements. It has no simple narrative function whatever, and an abridgement might leave it out. But the confusion of generations, and the double usurpation of Hindley by his son and Heathcliff, all three of them variants of the incivility of the Heights, gives a new relation to the agents, and qualifies our sense of all narrative explanations offered in the text. For it is worth remarking that no naturalistic explanation of Nelly's experience is offered; in this it is unlike the treatment of the later vision, when the little boy sees the ghost of Heathcliff and 'a woman', a passage which is a preparation for further ambiguities in the ending. Dreams, visions, ghosts — the whole pneumatology of the book is only indeterminately related to the 'natural' narrative. And this serves to muddle routine 'single' readings, to confound explanation and expectation, and to make necessary a full recognition of the intrinsic plurality of the text.

Would it be reasonable to say this: that the mingling of generic opposites — daylight and dream narratives — creates a need, which we must supply, for something that will mediate between them? If so, we can go on to argue that the text in our response to it is a provision of such mediators, between life and death, the barbaric and the civilized, family and sexual relations. The principal instrument of mediation may well be Heathcliff: neither inside nor out, neither wholly master nor wholly servant, the husband who is no husband, the brother who is no brother, the father who abuses his changeling child, the cousin without kin. And that the chain of narrators serve to mediate between the barbarism of the story and the civility of the reader — making the text itself an intermediate term between archaic and modern — must surely have been pointed out.

What we must not forget, however, is that it is in the completion of the text by the reader that these adjustments are made; and each reader will make them differently. Plurality is here not a prescription but a fact. There is so much that is blurred and tentative, incapable of decisive explanation; however we set about our reading, with a sociological or a pneumatological, a cultural or a narrative code uppermost in our minds, we must fall into division and discrepancy; the doors of communication are sometimes locked, sometimes open, and Heathcliff may be astride the threshold, opening, closing, breaking. And it is surely evident that the possibilities of interpretation increase as time goes on. The constraints of a period culture dissolve, generic presumptions which concealed gaps disappear, and we now see that the book, as James thought novels should, truly 'glories in a gap', a hermeneutic gap in which the reader's imagination must operate, so that he speaks continuously in the text. For these reasons the rebus — *Catherine Earnshaw, Catherine Heathcliff, Catherine Linton* — has exemplary significance. It is a riddle that the text answers only silently; for example it will neither urge nor forbid you to remember that it resembles the riddle of the Sphinx — what manner of person exists in these three forms? — to which the single acceptable and probable answer involves incest and ruin.

I have not found it possible to speak of *Wuthering Heights* in this light without, from time to time, hinting — in a word here, or a trick of procedure there — at the new French criticism. I am glad to acknowledge this affinity, but it also seems important to dissent from the opinion that such 'classic' texts as this — and the French will call them so, but with pejorative intent — are essentially naïve, and become in a measure plural only by accident. The number of choices is simply too large; it is impossible that even two competent readers should agree on an authorized naïve version. It is because texts are so naïve that they can become classics. It is true, as I have said, that time opens them up; if readers were immortal the classic would be much closer to changelessness; their deaths do, in an important sense, liberate the texts. But to attribute the entire *potential* of plurality to that cause (or to the wisdom and cunning of later readers) is to fall into a mistake. The 'Catherines' of Lockwood's inscriptions may not have been attended to, but there they were in the text, just as ambiguous and plural as they are now. What happens is that methods of repairing such indeterminacy change; and, as Wolfgang Iser's neat formula has it, 'the repair of indeterminacy' is what gives rise 'to the generation of meaning'.[3]

Having meditated thus on *Wuthering Heights* I passed to the second part of my enterprise and began to read what people have been saying about the book. I discovered without surprise that no two readers saw it exactly alike; some seemed foolish and some clever, but whether they were for the party that claims to elucidate Emily Brontë's intention, or libertarians whose purpose is to astonish us, all were different. This secondary material is voluminous, but any hesitation I might have had about selecting from it was ended when I came upon an essay which in its mature authority dwarfs all the others: Q. D. Leavis's 'A Fresh Approach to *Wuthering Heights*'.[4]

Long-meditated, rich in insights, this work has a sober force that nothing I say could, or is intended to, diminish. Mrs. Leavis remarks at the outset that merely to *assert* the classic status of such a book as *Wuthering Heights* is useless; that the task is not to be accomplished by ignoring 'recalcitrant elements' or providing sophistical explanations of them. One has to show 'the nature of its success'; and this, she at once proposes, means giving up some parts of the text. 'Of course, in general one attempts to achieve a reading of a text which includes all its elements, but here I believe we must be satisfied with being able to account for some of them and concentrate on what remains.' And she decides that Emily Brontë through inexperience, and trying to do too much, leaves in the final version vestiges of earlier creations, 'unregenerate writing', which is discordant with the true 'realistic novel' we should attend to.

She speaks of an earlier version deriving from *King Lear*, with Heathcliff as an Edmund figure, and attributes to this layer some contrived and unconvincing

scenes of cruelty. Another layer is the fairy-story, Heathcliff as the prince transformed into a beast; another is the Romantic incest-story: Heathcliff as brother-
lover; and nearer the surface, a sociological novel, of which she has no difficulty in
providing, with material from the text, a skilful account. These vestiges explain
some of the incongruities and inconsistencies of the novel — for example, the
ambiguity of the Catherine-Heathcliff relationship — and have the effect of
obscuring its 'human centrality'. To summarise a long and substantial argument,
this real novel, which we come upon clearly when the rest is cut away, is founded on
the contrast between the two Catherines, the one willing her own destruction, the
other educated by experience and avoiding the same fate. Not only does this cast a
new light on such characters as Joseph and Nelly Dean as representatives of a culture that, as well as severity, inculcates a kind of natural piety, but enables us to see
Emily Brontë as 'a true novelist . . . whose material was real life and whose concern was to promote a fine awareness of human relations and the problem of maturity'. And we can't see this unless we reject a good deal of the text as belonging
more to 'self-indulgent story' than to the 'responsible piece of work' Emily was
eventually able to perform. Heathcliff we are to regard as 'merely a convenience';
in a striking comparison with Dostoevsky's Stavrogin, Mrs. Leavis argues that he
is 'enigmatic . . . only by reason of his creator's indecision', and that to find reasons for thinking otherwise is 'misguided critical industry'. By the same token the
famous passages about Catherine's love for Heathcliff are dismissed as rhetorical
excesses, obstacles to the 'real novel enacted so richly for us to grasp in all its
complexity'.[5]

Now it seems very clear to me that the 'real novel' Mrs. Leavis describes *is* there,
in the text. It is also clear that she is aware of the danger in her own procedures, for
she explains how easy it would be to account for *Wuthering Heights* as a sociological
novel by discarding certain elements and concentrating on others, which, she says,
would be 'misconceiving the novel and slighting it'. What she will not admit is that
there is a sense in which all these versions are not only present but have a claim on
our attention. She creates a hierarchy of elements, and does so by a peculiar
archaeology of her own, for there is no *evidence* that the novel existed in the earlier
forms which are supposed to have left vestiges in the only text we have, and there is
no reason why the kind of speculation and conjecture on which her historical argument depends could not be practised with equal right by proponents of quite other
theories. Nor can I explain why it seemed to her that the only way to establish hers
as the central reading of the book was to explain the rest away; for there, after all,
the others *are*. Digging and carbon-dating simply have no equivalents here; there is
no way of distinguishing old signs from new; among readings which attend to the
text it cannot be argued that one attends to a truer text than all the others.

It is true that 'a fine awareness of human relations', and a certain maturity, may
be postulated as classic characteristics; Eliot found them in Virgil. But it is also true
that the coexistence in a single text of a plurality of significances from which, in the
nature of human attentiveness, every reader misses some — and, in the nature of
human individuality, prefers one — is, empirically, a requirement and a distinguishing feature of the survivor, *centum qui perfecit annos*. All those little critics, each
with his piece to say about *King Lear* or *Wuthering Heights*, may be touched by a
venal professional despair, but at least their numbers and their variety serve to
testify to the plurality of the documents on which they swarm; and though they

may lack authority, sometimes perhaps even sense, many of them do point to what is *there* and ought not to be wished away.

A recognition of this plurality relieves us of the necessity of a *Wuthering Heights* without a Heathcliff, just as it does of a *Wuthering Heights* that 'really' ends with the death of Catherine, or for that matter an *Aeneid* which breaks off, as some of the moral allegorists would perhaps have liked it to, at the end of Book VI. A reading such as that with which I began Chapter 1 is of course extremely selective, but it has the negative virtue that it does not excommunicate from the text the material it does not employ; indeed, it assumes that it is one of the very large number of readings that may be generated from the text of the novel. They will of course overlap, as mine in some small measure does with that of Mrs. Leavis.

And this brings me to the point: Mrs. Leavis's reading is privileged; what conforms with it is complex, what does not is confused; and presumably all others would be more or less wrong, in so far as they treated the rejected portions as proper objects of attention. On the other hand, the view I propose does not in any way require me to reject Mrs. Leavis's insights. It supposes that the reader's share in the novel is not so much a matter of knowing, by heroic efforts of intelligence and divination, what Emily Brontë really meant — knowing it, quite in the manner of Schleiermacher, better than she did — as of responding creatively to indeterminacies of meaning inherent in the text and possibly enlarged by the action of time.

We are entering, as you see, a familiar zone of dispute. Mrs. Leavis is rightly concerned with what is 'timeless' in the classic, but for her this involves the detection and rejection of what exists, it seems to her irrelevantly or even damagingly, in the aspect of time. She is left, in the end, with something that, in her view, has not changed between the first writing and her reading. I, on the other hand, claimed to be reading a text that might well signify differently to different generations, and different persons within those generations. It is a less attractive view, I see; an encouragement to foolishness, a stick that might be used, quite illicitly as it happens, to beat history, and sever our communications with the dead. But it happens that I set a high value on these, and wish to preserve them. I think there is a substance that prevails, however powerful the agents of change; that *King Lear*, underlying a thousand dispositions, subsists in change, prevails, by being patient of interpretation; that my *Wuthering Heights*, sketchy and provocative as it is, relates as disposition to essence quite as surely as if I had tried to argue that it was Emily Brontë's authorized version, or rather what she intended and could not perfectly execute.

This 'tolerance to a wide variety of readings' is attacked, with considerable determination, by E. D. Hirsch, committed as he is to the doctrine that the object of interpretation is the verbal meaning of the author; I think he would be against me in all details of the present argument. For example, he says quite firmly that interpretations must be judged entire, that they stand or fall as wholes; so that he could not choose, as I do, both to accept Mrs. Leavis's 'realist' reading and to reject her treatment of Heathcliff.[6] But as I said in Chapter 2, Hirsch makes a mistake when he allows that the 'determinations' (*bestimmungen*) of literary texts are more constrained than those of legal texts; and a further difficulty arises over his too sharp distinction between criticism and interpretation. In any case he does not convince me that tolerance in these matters represents 'abject intellectual surrender'; and I was cheered to find him in a more eirenic mood in his later paper. He is surely right to allow, in the matter of meaning, some element of personal preference; the 'best meaning' is not uniform for all.

This being so one sees why it is thought possible, in theory at any rate, to practise what is called 'literary science' as distinct from criticism or interpretation: to consider the structure of a text as a system of signifiers, as in some sense 'empty', as what, by the intervention of the reader, takes on many possible significances.[7] To put this in a different way, one may speak of the text as a system of signifiers which always shows a surplus after meeting any particular restricted reading. It was Lévi-Strauss who first spoke of a 'surplus of signifier' in relation to shamanism, meaning that the patient is cured because the symbols and rituals of the doctor offer him not a specific cure but rather a language 'by means of which unexpressed, and otherwise inexpressible, psychic states can be immediately expressed'.[8] Lévi-Strauss goes on to make an elaborate comparison with modern psychoanalysis. But as Fredric Jameson remarks, the importance of the concept lies rather in its claim for the priority of the signifier over the signified: a change which itself seems to have offered a shamanistic opportunity for the expression of thoughts formerly repressed.[9]

The consequences for literary texts are much too large for me to enter on here; among them, of course, is the by-passing of all the old arguments about 'intention'. And even if we may hesitate to accept the semiological method in its entirety we can allow, I think, for the intuitive rightness of its rules about plurality. The gap between text and meaning, in which the reader operates, is always present and always different in extent.[10] It is true that authors try, or used to try, to close it; curiously enough, Barthes reserves the term 'classic' for texts in which they more or less succeed, thus limiting plurality and offering the reader, save as accident prevents him, merely a product, a consumable. In fact what Barthes call 'modern' is very close to what I am calling 'classic', and what he calls 'classic' is very close to what I call 'dead'.***

Notes:

1. Leonard B. Meyer, *Music, the Arts and Ideas*, 1967, 8 (speaking of musical styles).
2. My subsequent reading in *Wuthering Heights* criticism (which has certainly substantiated my vague sense that there was a lot of it about) has taught me that the carved names, and Lockwood's dreams, have attracted earlier comment. Dorothy Van Ghent's distinguished essay asks why Lockwood, of all people, should experience such a dream as that of the ghost-child, and decides that the nature of the dreamer — 'a man who has shut out the powers of darkness' — is what gives force to our sense of powers 'existing autonomously' both without and within. (*The English Novel: Form and Function*, 1953.) Ronald E. Fine suggests that the dreams are 'spasms of realism' and that Emily Brontë arranged the story to fit them, or as he says, lets the dreams generate the story. He emphasizes their sexual significance, and the structural relations between them, explained by the generative force of a basic dream of two lovers seeking to be reunited ('Lockwood's Dream and the Key to *Wuthering Heights*', *Nineteenth-Century Fiction*, xxiv, 1969–70, 16–30). Ingeborg Nixon suggests that 'the names must have been written by Catherine after her first visit to Thrushcross Grange as a child . . . but they form a silent summary of the whole tragic dilemma'; they indicate three possibilities for Catherine, who of course chooses *Linton*. This is to give the inscriptions the most limited possible 'hermeneutic' sense, reading them back into a possible chronology and ignoring their larger function as literary or defamiliarising signs ('A note on the Pattern of *Wuthering Heights*', *English Studies*, xlv, 1964). Cecil W. Davies notices that 'Heathcliff' is an

Earnshaw name, and argues that this makes him 'in a real, though non-legal sense, a true inheritor of Wuthering Heights' ('A Reading of *Wuthering Heights*', *Essays in Criticism*, xix, 1969). Doubtless C. P. Sanger's justly celebrated essay ('The Structure of *Wuthering Heights*' [1926]) is partly responsible for the general desire to fit everything that can be fitted into legal and chronological schemes; but the effect is often to miss half the point. All these essays are reprinted, in whole or in part, in the Penguin Critical Anthology, *Emily Brontë*, ed. J.-P. Petit, 1973. Other collections include one by Miriam Allott in the Macmillan Casebook series (1970), Thomas A. Vogler's *Twentieth-Century Interpretations of 'Wuthering Heights'* (1965) and William A. Sale's Norton edition (1963).

3. 'Indeterminacy and the Reader's Response', in *Aspects of Narrative*, ed. J. Hillis Miller, 1971, 42.
4. F. R. Leavis and Q. D. Leavis, *Lectures in America*, 1969, 83–152.
5. For a different approach to Mrs. Leavis's reading see D. Donoghue, 'Emily Brontë: On the Latitude of Interpretation', *Harvard English Studies*, i, ed. M. W. Bloomfield, 1970; reprinted in *Emily Brontë*, ed. J.-P. Petit, 1973, 296–314, 316.
6. *Validity in Interpretation*, 168.
7. F. Jameson, *The Prison-House of Language*, 1972, 195, compares the Frege-Carnap distinction between *Sinn* (unchanging formal organisation) and *Bedeutung* (the unchanging significance given to the text by successive generations of readers).
8. *Structural Anthropology*, 1968, 198.
9. Jameson, 1972, 196.
10. '. . . commentaries or interpretations are generated out of an ontological lack in the text itself . . . a text can have no ultimate meaning . . . the process of interpretation . . . is properly an infinite one' (Jameson, 176, paraphrasing Jacques Derrida).

Section Five

INTERPRETATIONS, CONTEXTS AND READERS

1. Stanley E. Fish, 'Interpreting the *Variorum*' (1976)
2. E. D. Hirsch, Jr., 'The Politics of Theories of Interpretation' (1982)
3. Jerome J. McGann, 'The Text, The Poem, and the Problem of Historical Method' (1981)

Points of information

1. The essays by Stanley Fish and E. D. Hirsch were first published in *Critical Inquiry* from where they are reprinted. Jerome McGann's essay first appeared in *New Literary History*. It is reprinted in this version from his *The Beauty of Inflections* (1985).

2. The 'Robertsonian' critics mentioned by both Fish and Hirsch are used as an example of a rather traditionally-minded scholastic criticism. D. W. Robertson is a medieval scholar. For an example of his theoretical position see 'Some Observations on Method in Literary Studies', *New Literary History*, 1 (1969).

3. The Latin phrase used by Hirsch on p. 176 means (roughly): 'There should be nothing in the interpretation that is not previously in the design (or schema)'.

This section examines some work in a broad area of theoretical debate which usually goes by the name of 'hermeneutics'. Hermeneutics is a philosophical term which refers to the science, or art, of interpretation, and the essays in this section all address some fundamental questions concerning this activity. For instance: is meaning located in the mind of the interpreter or in the thing interpreted? Are there ways in which we can validate interpretations? Is it possible to discover the original meanings of written texts? Clearly these questions are central to all of the criticism examined so far in this book. To respond to them requires an alert sense of philosophical issues as well as a command of the literary materials and these essays are for that reason demanding in argument and implication.

In a sense the scope of these questions return us to the New Critical arguments on the intentional and affective fallacies described in the introduction to Section 2. The New Critics focused their attention on 'the poem itself' and ruled out of account as unknowable or hopelessly relativistic both the author's original intention and the reader's response. Neither of these could provide useful critical standpoints. In New Critical accounts the literary work was seen as an autonomous entity, and the metaphors they used for it, and their views on language, encouraged the reader to see it as leading a life independent in a sense of both the reader and creator.

The writers represented here — all American — take issue with this view in various ways. Both E. D. Hirsch (b. 1928) and Jerome McGann (b. 1937), from different standpoints, hold that it is possible to recover contexts, either philosophically, or historically, or by way of both, which will ground interpretive validity. Stanley Fish (b. 1938), on the other hand, sees meaning not as a paraphrasable *thing* to be taken from a literary work, but an event in which the reader's experience of reading is paramount. All three critics respond more or less directly to New Critical theories; but they are also aware of the development of arguments in the wake of structuralism and it is worthwhile making a few additional remarks on these before proceeding.

As we have seen, the analysis of language and meaning developed by structuralist and post-structuralist theory poses major problems for the interpretive activities of literary critics. In post-structuralism meanings are unstable textual effects; there can be no possibility of an anchoring intention or origin which will forestall their textual play. In one of his most frequently cited essays — a kind of companion piece to 'From Work to Text' — Roland Barthes welcomes 'The Death of the Author'. In one sense, therefore, post-structuralist thinking resembles the New Critical attack on the intentional fallacy. In another sense, though, it runs counter to New Critical theory, for some post-structuralist critics salute the interpretive virtuosity of readers. In Barthes this appears as a kind of textual hedonism whereby attention to hermeneutical complexity is a pleasure to be relished above the repressive gratifications to be obtained from sealing and delivering a closed meaning. Amongst the essays here both Hirsch and McGann attack aspects of this free-wheeling textual pluralism.

The structuralist approach to hermeneutical problems is more cautious. A controlling structure can be identified which permits individual meanings to appear. Meanings are thus analysed either through the structural conditions which obtain in the work itself, or, in an alternative version, through the structures which govern the interpretive activity. These are located in the mind of the interpreter or, rather, in the conventions of interpretation within which the interpreter works. Jonathan Culler has offered an influential version of this theory in his *Structuralist Poetics* and elsewhere, though his interpretive schema is a great deal more sophisticated than what follows.

Culler speaks of an interpreter's 'competence'; that is, his or her familiarity with the interpretive procedures relevant to the object under scrutiny. For example, we may take the first line of Burns's famous poem:

O, my Luve's like a red, red rose

A hypothetical naive reader may look at the meaning-possibilities in this statement and come up with conflicting, multiple options. The speaker may be informing the reader that his or her love is beautiful, healthy, blooming, sweet-smelling and so on. Alternatively, the reader could imagine another paradigmatic set: the speaker's love is short-lived, immobile and unpleasantly covered in small green insects. S/he could even think the love was a Lancastrian, or Lancashire itself, or a member of the Labour Party, or the Party itself since it adopted the red rose as its symbol.

In fact, though, most readers of this line possess a competence, acquired through schooling or wide reading, which closes such possibilities down and enables them to select a suitable interpretive framework. S/he will be familiar, for example, with the ways of metaphor and simile, with the conventions of lover's compliments in lyric poetry, with the fact that Burns was Scottish and therefore unlikely to write about Lancashire in that way (though he could be being ironic), and with the fact that he lived before the Labour Party chose its present symbol.

Such an example perhaps makes these interpretive problems appear unproblematic, but it is not hard to see the difficulties which will occur when cases become more complex. For the theoretical stance still places the burden of meaning and decision on readers; and readers are notoriously disputatious (and rightly so) when it comes to assessing the meanings of literary works. They will stubbornly insist that their readings are correct and those of others aren't. So there are still insistent questions, for who is to adjudicate amongst divergent readings (in for instance examination answers) without appeal to something beyond his or her interpretive frameworks?

Stanley Fish's essay printed here is a sophisticated extension of the overall trajectory of these ideas and Fish, in some senses, shares adjacent conceptual frameworks with some structuralist and post-structuralist theory. However, though he has written interestingly and illuminatingly about Derrida, this is not a case of direct influence or development of ideas. Fish established his reputation with two pioneering books on Renaissance poetry and has consistently developed the thinking which began there in theoretical directions.

In Fish's work, more than most perhaps, it is difficult to separate theoretical concerns from actual interpretive instances. For, for him, the discovery of meaning is bound in with the experience of reading. Like some post-structuralist, though not structuralist, writers Fish rejects spatial, formalist or diagramatic models and metaphors for textual understanding. As the essay here demonstrates, he regards meaning as something that unfolds in time and not as something that is arrived at after the event in one whole cognitive action.

Nevertheless, Fish rejects the outright subjectivism this may seem to imply. For Fish, too, readers are more or less competent to meet the demands the text makes of them. This, though, does not mean that the text itself legitimates a 'correct' reading. Rather what texts engage are questions of belief rather than validation; and what in turn gives authority to any individual interpretation is the 'interpretive community' to which the reader belongs; though the critic him– or herself does not choose this (compare E. D. Hirsch's view in his essay here). The interpretive community inhabited by the individual reader will determine criteria of adequacy — though these are not adequate in any ultimate sense. In this way Fish overcomes the twin dangers — as he sees it — of subjectivism and objectivism both of which paralyse the interpretive encounter. Though quite what the boundaries of these interpretive communities are, in any specific social sense, is left unremarked.

Fish is a formidable and witty controversialist and an attractive, persuasive stylist who is generally regarded as a leading figure in a wider critical movement in America known as 'Reader Response Criticism'. This includes diverse critical practices and theories, some of which are orientated to a more overt subjectivism and consideration of the psychological effects and responses of readers.

E. D. Hirsch's first substantial statement on these kinds of hermeneutical problems was in his book *Validity in Interpretation* in 1967, though his essay here, from 1982, is placed after Stanley Fish's because in part it responds to his work. *Validity* challenges the New Critical insistence that intentional meanings must be forever unknown.

When Hirsch claims that it is possible to recover solid authorial intentions to ground interpretive validity he does not have in mind the simple evidences of authorial statements. Rather he insists that literary works are public statements and thus share normative inter-subjective rules. They are not wayward utterances, but are produced within generic and conventional frameworks which render them comprehensible by others even across time. An idea — or meaning — 'type' can thus be posited for a work and progressively refined against its details.

For example, a poet writes an epic poem. Such an undertaking commits him or her to certain conventions and frameworks. When a critic comes to interpret this poem s/he will then be able to assess the functioning of these conventions in the actual epic to hand. S/he will also be able to register the amendments made to them, or deviations made from them, and this will give a reliable sense of the grounding intention of the work in the particular case. Though these will only be probability judgements they will, as in other areas of human knowledge, be sufficient to justify clear, adequate, formal statement.

The next stage in Hirsch's theory is to distinguish between 'interpretation' and 'significance' (though he has since abandoned this as being in practice unworkable). Interpretation is the process outlined above. The discussion of significance is a separate activity which assesses meanings in broader contexts. We might, for instance, wish to ask whether the portrayal of heroism in the epic is an adequate one from whatever human, social, political or other criteria we may choose, even anachronistically, to bring to bear. By locating the burden of initial interpretive meaning in the text in this way, Hirsch can avoid the problems which might be thought to lie in wait for hermeneutical theories which take the reader as the locus of meaning.

Hirsch's second theoretical work, *The Aims of Interpretation* (1976), contains some adjustments to his original position, and in part responds to post-structuralist theory. The essay printed here also takes issue with these lines of thought and attempts to draw out the implications of this trend in thinking for criticism as a general cultural activity. It attacks what Hirsch sees as the *a-priori* reasoning of much contemporary theory, its commitment to high abstraction and steam-rollering rhetorical demands. It defends the humane validity of human choices when the cultural stakes are so high. His belief in the possibility of legitimate discrimination amongst values, which need not be thought of as always determined by structures controllingly beyond the individual, might usefully be compared to some of the positions represented in Sections 3 and 4, as well as some of the marxist thinking in the following section. For these reasons Hirsch is sometimes thought of as being a rather traditionally-minded thinker of a liberal and humanistic cast.

Jerome McGann, too, takes exception to the post-structuralist emphasis on textuality which he sees as another mode of 'intrinsic' criticism which, because it is committed only to the words on the page, cannot develop adequate accounts of contextual meaning and hence interpretive rules appropriate to the social and historical nature of the object. McGann's is a more explicitly socially-grounded theory than that of Hirsch. As such it, too, looks forward to the next section.

McGann has great respect for historical particularity and the cognitive value of historical difference (we perceive ourselves by trying to understand others). He is a textual scholar — in the sense of one who establishes the texts of those words on the page from which discussion proceeds — of high reputation in the Romantic period. In this essay he brings this textual scrupulousness into relation with 'extrinsic' contexts and discusses the consequences of this for some rival theories.

Finally, it should be stressed that the line of argument offered here is only one strand amongst many in this area. We have noted in passing the varieties of American 'Reader Response' theory. There is also a powerful body of German thought which requires attention. Known as 'Reception Theory' it takes its impetus from the Phenomenological school of philosophy which has also influenced Derrida. See below for introductory reading.

Further reading:

Many of Stanley Fish's theoretical essays are collected in *Is There a Text in this Class? The Authority of Interpretive Communities* (1982). Also of interest are two of his books on seventeenth-century writing *Surprised By Sin: The Reader in Paradise Lost* (1967) and *Self-Consuming Artefacts: The Experience of Seventeenth-Century Literature* (1972). His essay on Derrida, 'With the Compliments of the Author', is to be found in *Critical Inquiry, 8* (1982).

E. D. Hirsch's two theoretical books are *Validity in Interpretation* (1967) and *The Aims of Interpretation* (1976).

Jerome J. McGann's *The Beauty of Inflections: Literary Investigations in Historical Method and Theory* (1985) contains much of theoretical interest, as does his *The Romantic Ideology: A Critical Investigation* (1983). The primary focus of both of these is on writing in the Romantic period. The latter contains an interesting chapter on Wordsworth.

There are two very useful anthologies of 'Reader Response' criticism: *The Reader in the Text: Essays on Audience and Interpretation*, ed. Susan R. Suleiman and Inge Crossman (1980), and *Reader Response Criticism: From Formalism to Post-structuralism*, ed. Jane P. Tompkins (1980). Both include some European work and both have excellent bibliographies.

Robert C. Holub, *Reception Theory: A Critical Introduction* (1984) focusses on German theory but touches on the material offered here and is relevant to discussion of the broader issues, as is Christopher Butler, *Interpretation, Deconstruction and Ideology* (1984). Frank Lentricchia, *After the New Criticism* (1980) and William Ray, *Literary Meaning: From Phenomenology to Deconstruction* (1984) are both key discussions of American hermeneutical debates. Lentricchia has a chapter on Hirsch, and Ray chapters on Hirsch and Fish.

There is an essay on Fish's work in Jonathan Culler's *The Pursuit of Signs* (1981). Frank Kermode discusses Hirsch in his *Essays on Fiction* (1983), and Walter Benn Michaels responds to Hirsch's essay here in 'Is There a Politics of Interpretation?', *Critical Inquiry*, 9 (1982). *Critical Inquiry* contains many interesting discussions of hermeneutical questions. The reader might look especially at volumes 8 and 9.

1

Stanley E. Fish,
'Interpreting the Variorum *'*

I

The first two volumes of the Milton *Variorum Commentary* have now appeared, and I find them endlessly fascinating. My interest, however, is not in the questions they manage to resolve (although these are many) but in the theoretical assumptions which are responsible for their occasional failures. These failures constitute a pattern, one in which a host of commentators — separated by as much as two hundred and seventy years but contemporaries in their shared concerns — are lined up on either side of an interpretive crux. Some of these are famous, even infamous: what is the two-handed engine in *Lycidas*? what is the meaning of Haemony in *Comus*? Others, like the identity of whoever or whatever comes to the window in *L'Allegro*, line 46, are only slightly less notorious. Still others are of interest largely to those who make editions: matters of pronoun referents, lexical ambiguities, punctuation. In each instance, however, the pattern is consistent: every position taken is supported by wholly convincing evidence — in the case of *L'Allegro* and the coming to the window there is a persuasive champion for every proper noun within a radius of ten lines — and the editorial procedure always ends either in the graceful throwing up of hands, or in the recording of a disagreement between the two editors themselves. In short, these are problems that apparently cannot be solved, at least not by the methods traditionally brought to bear on them. What I would like to argue is that they are not *meant* to be solved, but to be experienced (they signify), and that consequently any procedure that attempts to determine which of a number of readings is correct will necessarily fail. What this means is that the commentators and editors have been asking the wrong questions and that a new set of questions based on new assumptions must be formulated. I would like at least to make a beginning in that direction by examining some of the points in dispute in Milton's sonnets. I choose the sonnets because they are brief and because one can move easily from them to the theoretical issues with which this paper is finally concerned.

Milton's twentieth sonnet — 'Lawrence of virtuous father virtuous son' — has been the subject of relatively little commentary. In it the poet invites a friend to join him in some distinctly Horatian pleasures — a neat repast intermixed with conversation, wine, and song; a respite from labour all the more enjoyable because outside the earth is frozen and the day sullen. The only controversy the sonnet has inspired concerns its final two lines:

155

> Lawrence of virtuous father virtuous son,
>> Now that the fields are dank, and ways are mire,
>> Where shall we sometimes meet, and by the fire
>> Help waste a sullen day; what may be won
> 5 From the hard season gaining; time will run
>> On smoother, till Favonius reinspire
>> The frozen earth; and clothe in fresh attire
>> The lily and rose, that neither sowed nor spun.
> What neat repast shall feast us, light and choice,
> 10 Of Attic taste, with wine, whence we may rise
>> To hear the lute well touched, or artful voice
> Warble immortal notes and Tuscan air?
>> He who of those delights can judge, and spare
>> To interpose them oft, is not unwise.[1]

The focus of the controversy is the word 'spare,' for which two readings have been proposed: leave time for and refrain from. Obviously the point is crucial if one is to resolve the sense of the lines. In one reading 'those delights' are being recommended — he who can leave time for them is not unwise; in the other, they are the subject of a warning — he who knows when to refrain from them is not unwise. The proponents of the two interpretations cite as evidence both English and Latin syntax, various sources and analogues, Milton's 'known attitudes' as they are found in his other writings, and the unambiguously expressed sentiments of the following sonnet on the same question. Surveying these arguments, A. S. P. Woodhouse roundly declares: 'It is plain that all the honours rest with' the meaning 'refrain from' or 'forbear to.' This declaration is followed immediately by a bracketed paragraph initialled D. B. for Douglas Bush, who, writing presumably after Woodhouse has died, begins 'In spite of the array of scholarly names the case for "forbear to" may be thought much weaker, and the case for "spare time for" much stronger, than Woodhouse found them.'[2] Bush then proceeds to review much of the evidence marshaled by Woodhouse and to draw from it exactly the opposite conclusion. If it does nothing else, this curious performance anticipates a point I shall make in a few moments: evidence brought to bear in the course of formalist analyses — that is, analyses generated by the assumption that meaning is embedded in the artifact — will always point in as many directions as there are interpreters; that is, not only will it prove something, it will prove anything.

It would appear then that we are back at square one, with a controversy that cannot be settled because the evidence is inconclusive. But what if that controversy is *itself* regarded as evidence, not of an ambiguity that must be removed, but of an ambiguity that readers have always experienced? What, in other words, if for the question 'what does "spare" mean?' we substitute the question 'what does the fact that the meaning of "spare" has always been an issue mean'? The advantage of this question is that it can be answered. Indeed it has already been answered by the readers who are cited in the *Variorum Commentary*. What these readers debate is the judgment the poem makes on the delights of recreation; what their debate indicates is that the judgment is blurred by a verb that can be made to participate in contradictory readings. (Thus the important thing about the evidence surveyed in the *Variorum* is not how it is marshaled, but that it could be marshaled at all, because it then becomes evidence of the equal availability of both interpretations.) In other words, the lines first generate a pressure for judgment — 'he who of those delights can judge' — and then decline to deliver it; the pressure, however, still exists, and it is transferred from the words on the page to the reader (the reader is 'he who'), who comes away from the poem not with a statement, but with a responsibility, the responsibility of deciding when and how often — if at all — to indulge in 'those delights' (they remain delights in either case). This transferring of responsibility from the text to its readers is what the lines ask us to do — it is the essence of their experience — and in my terms it is therefore what the lines *mean*. It is a meaning the *Variorum* critics attest to even as they resist it, for what they are labouring so mightily to do by fixing the sense of the lines is to give the responsibility back. The text, however, will not accept it and remains determinedly evasive, even in its last two words, 'not unwise.' In their position these words confirm the impossibility of extracting from the poem a moral formula, for the assertion (certainly too strong a word) they complete is of the form, 'He who does such and such, of him it cannot be said that he is unwise'; but of course neither can it be said that he is wise. Thus what Bush correctly terms the 'defensive' 'not unwise' operates to prevent us from attaching the label 'wise' to any action, including *either* of the actions — leaving time for or refraining from — represented by the ambiguity of 'spare.' Not only is the pressure of judgment taken off the poem, it is taken off the activity the poem at first pretended to judge. The issue is finally not the moral status of 'those delights — they become in seventeenth-century terms 'things indifferent' — but on the good or bad uses to which they can be put by readers who are left, as Milton always leaves them, to choose and manage by themselves.

Let us step back for a moment and see how far we've come. We began with an apparently insoluble problem and proceeded, not to solve it, but to make it signify; first by regarding it as evidence of an experience and then by specifying for that experience a meaning. Moreover, the configurations of that experience, when they are made available by a reader-oriented analysis, serve as a check against the endlessly inconclusive adducing of evidence which characterizes formalist analysis. That is to say, any determination of what 'spare' means (in a positivist or literal sense) is liable to be upset by the bringing forward of another analogue, or by a more complete computation of statistical frequencies, or by the discovery of new biographical information, or by anything else; but if we first determine that everything in the line before 'spare' creates the expectation of an imminent judgment, then the ambiguity of 'spare' can be assigned a significance in the context of that expectation. (It disappoints it and transfers the pressure of judgment to us.) That context is experiential, and it is within its contours and constraints that significances are established (both in the act of reading and in the analysis of that act). In formalist analyses the only constraints are the notoriously open-ended possibilities and combination of possibilities that emerge when one begins to consult dictionaries and grammars and histories; to consult dictionaries, grammars, and histories is to assume that meanings can be specified independently of the activity of reading; what the example of 'spare' shows is that it is in and by that activity that meanings — experiential, not positivist — are created.

In other words, it is the structure of the reader's experience rather than any structures available on the page that should be the object of description. In the case of Sonnet XX, that experiential structure was uncovered when an examination of formal structures led to an impasse; and the pressure to remove that impasse led to the substitution of one set of questions for another. It will more often be the case that the pressure of a spectacular failure will be absent. The sins of formalist-positivist analysis are primarily sins of omission, not an inability to explain phenomena, but an inability to see that they are there because its assumptions make it inevitable that they will be overlooked or suppressed. Consider, for example, the concluding lines of another of Milton's sonnets, 'Avenge O Lord thy slaughtered saints.'

> Avenge O Lord thy slaughtered saints, whose bones
> Lie scattered on the Alpine mountains cold,
> Even them who kept thy truth so pure of old
> When all our fathers worshipped stocks and stones,
> 5   Forget not: in thy book record their groans
> Who were thy sheep and in their ancient fold
> Slain by the bloody Piedmontese that rolled
> Mother with infant down the rocks. Their moans
> The vales redoubled to the hills, and they
> 10   To heaven. Their martyred blood and ashes sow
> O'er all the Italian fields where still doth sway
> The triple Tyrant: that from these may grow
> A hundredfold, who having learnt thy way
> Early may fly the Babylonian woe.

In this sonnet, the poet simultaneously petitions God and wonders aloud about the justice of allowing the faithful — 'Even them who kept thy truth' — to be so brutally slaughtered. The note struck is alternately one of plea and complaint, and there is more than a hint that God is being called to account for what has happened to the Waldensians. It is generally agreed, however, that the note of complaint is less and less sounded and that the poem ends with an affirmation of faith in the ultimate operation of God's justice. In this reading, the final lines are taken to be saying something like this: From the blood of these martyred, O God, raise up a new and more numerous people, who, by virtue of an early education in thy law, will escape destruction by fleeing the Babylonian woe. Babylonian woe has been variously glossed[3]; but whatever it is taken to mean it is always read as part of a statement that specifies a set of conditions for the escaping of destruction or punishment; it is a warning to the reader as well as a petition to God. As a warning, however, it is oddly situated since the conditions it seems to specify were in fact met by the Waldensians, who of all men most followed God's laws. In other words, the details of their story would seem to undercut the affirmative moral the speaker proposes to draw from it. It is further undercut by a reading that is fleetingly available, although no one has acknowledged it because it is a function, not of the words on the page, but of the experience of the reader. In that experience, line 13 will for a moment be accepted as a complete sense unit and the emphasis of the line will fall on 'thy way' (a phrase that has received absolutely no attention in the commentaries). At this point 'thy way' can refer only to the way in which God has dealt with the Waldensians. That is, 'thy way' seems to pick up the note of outrage with which the poem began, and if we continue to so interpret it, the conclusion of the poem will be a grim one indeed: since by this example it appears that God rains down punishment indiscriminately, it would be best perhaps to withdraw from the arena of his service, and thereby hope at least to be safely out of the line of fire. This is not the conclusion we carry away, because as line 14 unfolds, another reading of 'thy way' becomes available, a reading in which 'early' qualifies 'learnt' and refers to something the faithful should do (learn thy way at an early age) rather than to something God has failed to do (save the Waldensians). These two readings are answerable to the pull exerted by the beginning and ending of the poem: the outrage expressed in the opening lines generates a pressure for an explanation, and the grimmer reading is answerable to that pressure (even if it is also distrubing); the ending of the poem, the forward and upward movement of lines 10–14, creates the expectation of an affirmation, and the second reading fulfills that expectation. The criticism shows that in the end we settle on the more optimistic reading — it feels better — but even so the other has been a part of our experience, and because it has been a part of our experience, it *means*. What it means is that while we may be able to extract from the poem a statement affirming God's justice, we are not allowed to forget the evidence (of things seen) that makes the extraction so difficult (both for the speaker and for us). It is a difficulty we experience in the act of reading, even though a criticism which takes no account of that act has, as we have seen, suppressed it.

II

In each of the sonnets we have considered, the significant word or phrase occurs at a line break where a reader is invited to place it first in one and then in another structure of syntax and sense. This moment of hesitation, of semantic or syntactic slide, is crucial to the experience the verse provides, but, in a formalist analysis, that moment will disappear, either because it has been flattened out and made into an (insoluble) interpretive crux, or because it has been eliminated in the course of a procedure that is incapable of finding value in temporal phenomena. In the case of 'When I consider how my light is spent,' these two failures are combined.

> When I consider how my light is spent,
>   Ere half my days, in this dark world and wide,
>   And that one talent which is death to hide,
>   Lodged with me useless, though my soul more bent
> 5 To serve therewith my maker, and present
>   My true account, lest he returning chide,
>   Doth God exact day-labour, light denied,
>   I fondly ask; but Patience to prevent
> That murmur, soon replies, God doth not need
> 10 Either man's work or his own gifts, who best
>   Bear his mild yoke, they serve him best, his state
> Is kingly. Thousands at his bidding speed
>   And post o'er land and ocean without rest:
>   They also serve who only stand and wait.

The interpretive crux once again concerns the final line: 'They also serve who only stand and wait.' For some this is an unqualified acceptance of God's will, while for others the note of affirmation is muted or even forced. The usual kinds of evidence are marshaled by the opposing parties, and the usual inconclusiveness is the result. There are some areas of agreement. 'All the interpretations,' Woodhouse remarks, 'recognize that the sonnet commences from a mood of depression, frustration [and] impatience.'[4] The object of impatience is a God who would first demand service and then take away the means of serving, and the oft noted allusion to the parable of the talents lends scriptural support to the accusation the poet is implicitly making: you have cast the wrong servant into unprofitable darkness. It has also been observed that the syntax and rhythm of these early lines, and especially of lines 6–8, are rough and uncertain; the speaker is struggling with his agitated thoughts and he changes direction abruptly, with no regard for the line as a unit of sense. The poem, says one critic, 'seems almost out of control.'[5]

The question I would ask is 'whose control?'; for what these formal descriptions point to (but do not acknowledge) is the extraordinary number of adjustments required of readers who would negotiate these lines. The first adjustment is the result of the expectations created by the second half of line 6 — 'lest he returning chide.' Since there is no full stop after 'chide,' it is natural to assume that this will be an introduction to reported speech, and to assume further that what will be reported is the poet's anticipation of the voice of God as it calls him, to an unfair accounting. This assumption does not survive line 7 — 'Doth God exact day-labour, light denied' — which rather than chiding the poet for his inactivity seems to rebuke him for having expected that chiding. The accents are precisely those heard so often in the Old Testament when God answers a reluctant Gideon, or a disputatious Moses, or a self-justifying Job: do you presume to judge my ways or to appoint my motives? Do you think I would exact day labour, light denied? In other words, the poem seems to turn at this point from a questioning of God to a questioning of that questioning; or, rather, the reader turns from the one to the other in the act of revising his projection of what line 7 will say and do. As it turns out, however, that revision must itself be revised because it had been made within the assumption that what we are hearing is the voice of God. This assumption falls before the very next phrase 'I fondly ask,' which requires not one, but two adjustments. Since the speaker of line 7 is firmly identified as the poet, the line must be reinterpreted as a continuation of his complaint — Is that the way you operate, God, denying light, but exacting labour? — but even as that interpretation emerges, the poet withdraws from it by inserting the adverb 'fondly,' and once again the line slips out of the reader's control.

In a matter of seconds, then, line 7 has led four experiential lives, one as we anticipate it, another as that anticipation is revised, a third when we retroactively identify its speaker, and a fourth when that speaker disclaims it. What changes in each of these lives is the status of the poet's murmurings — they are alternately expressed, rejected, reinstated, and qualified — and as the sequence ends, the reader is without a firm perspective on the question of record: does God deal justly with his servants?

A firm perspective appears to be provided by Patience, whose entrance into the poem, the critics tell us, gives it both argumentative and metrical stability. But in fact the presence of Patience in the poem finally assures its continuing instability by making it impossible to specify the degree to which the speaker approves, or even participates in, the affirmation of the final line: 'They also serve who only stand and wait.' We know that Patience to prevent the poet's murmur soon replies (not soon enough however to prevent the murmur from registering), but we do not know when that reply ends. Does Patience fall silent in line 12, after 'kingly'? or at the conclusion of line 13? or not at all? Does the poet appropriate these lines or share them or simply listen to them, as we do? These questions are unanswerable, and it is because they remain unanswerable that the poem ends uncertainly. The uncertainty is not in the statement it makes — in isolation line 14 is unequi-vocal — but in our inability to assign that statement to either the poet or to Patience. Were the final line marked unambiguously for the poet, then we would receive it as a resolution of his earlier doubts; and were it marked for Patience, it would be a sign that those doubts were still very much in force. It is marked for neither, and therefore we are without the satisfaction that a firmly conclusive end-ing (in *any* direction) would have provided. In short, we leave the poem unsure, and our unsureness is the realization (in our experience) of the unsureness with which the affirmation of the final line is, or is not, made. (This unsureness also ope-rates to actualize the two possible readings of 'wait': wait in the sense of expecting, that is waiting for an opportunity to serve actively; or wait in the sense of waiting *in* service, a waiting that is itself fully satisfying because the impulse to self-glorifying action has been stilled.)

The question debated in the *Variorum Commentary* is, how far from the mood of frustration and impatience does the poem finally move? The answer given by an experiential analysis is that you can't tell, and the fact that you can't tell is respon-sible for the uneasiness the poem has always inspired. It is that uneasiness which the critics inadvertently acknowledge when they argue about the force of the last line, but they are unable to make analytical use of what they acknowledge because they have no way of dealing with or even recognizing experiential (that is, tem-poral) structures. In fact, more than one editor has eliminated those structures by punctuating them out of existence: first by putting a full stop at the end of line 6 and thereby making it unlikely that the reader will assign line 7 to God (there will no longer be an expectation of reported speech), and then by supplying quotation marks for the sestet in order to remove any doubts one might have as to who is speaking. There is of course no warrant for these emendations, and in 1791 Thomas Warton had the grace and honesty to admit as much. 'I have,' he said, 'introduced the turned commas both in the question and answer, not from any authority, but because they seem absolutely necessary to the sense.'[6]

III

Editorial practices like these are only the most obvious manifestations of the assumptions to which I stand opposed: the assumption that there *is* a sense, that it is embedded or encoded in the text, and that it can be taken in at a single glance. These assumptions are, in order, positivist, holistic, and spatial, and to have them is to be committed both to a goal and to a procedure. The goal is to settle on a mean-ing, and the procedure involves first stepping back from the text, and then putting together or otherwise calculating the discrete units of significance it contains. My quarrel with this procedure (and with the assumptions that generate it) is that in the course of following it through the reader's activities are at once ignored and devalued. They are ignored because the text is taken to be self-sufficient — every-thing is *in* it — and they are devalued because when they are thought of at all, they are thought of as the disposable machinery of extraction. In the procedures I would urge, the reader's activities are at the centre of attention, where they are regarded, not as leading to meaning, but as *having* meaning. The meaning they have is a consequence of their not being empty; for they include the making and revising of assumptions, the rendering and regretting of judgments, the coming to and abandoning of conclusions, the giving and withdrawing of approval, the specifying of causes, the asking of questions, the supplying of answers, the solving of puzzles. In a word, these activities are interpretive — rather than being preliminary to questions of value they are at every moment settling and resettling questions of value — and because they are interpretive, a description of them will also be, and without any additional step, an interpretation, not after the fact, but of the fact (of experiencing). It will be a description of a moving field of concerns, at once wholly present (not waiting for meaning, but constituting meaning) and continually in the act of reconstituting itself.

As a project such a description presents enormous difficulties, and there is hardly time to consider them here;[7] but it should be obvious from my brief examples how different it is from the positivist-formalist project. Everything depends on the temporal dimension, and as a consequence the notion of a mistake, at least as something to be avoided, disappears. In a sequence where a reader first structures the field he inhabits and then is asked to restructure it (by changing an assignment of speaker or realigning attitudes and positions) there is no question of priority among his structurings; no one of them, even if it is the last, has privilege; each is equally legitimate, each equally the proper object of analysis, because each is equally an event in his experience.

The firm assertiveness of this paragraph only calls attention to the questions it avoids. Who is this reader? How can I presume to describe his experiences, and what do I say to readers who report that they do not have the experiences I describe? Let me answer these questions or rather make a beginning at answering them in the context of another example, this time from Milton's *Comus*. In line 46 of *Comus* we are introduced to the villain by way of genealogy:

> Bacchus that first from out the purple grape,
> Crushed the sweet poison of misused wine.

In almost any edition of this poem, a footnote will tell you that Bacchus is the god of wine. Of course most readers already know that, and because they know it, they will be anticipating the appearance of 'wine' long before they come upon it in the final position. Moreover, they will also be anticipating a negative judgment on it, in part because of the association of Bacchus with revelry and excess, and especially because the phrase 'sweet poison' suggests that the judgment has already been made. At an early point then, we will have both filled in the form of the assertion and made a decision about its moral content. That decision is upset by the word 'misused'; for what 'misused' asks us to do is transfer the pressure of judgment from wine (where we have already placed it) to the abusers of wine, and therefore when 'wine' finally appears, we must declare it innocent of the charges we have ourselves made.

This, then, is the structure of the reader's experience — the transferring of a moral label from a thing to those who appropriate it. It is an experience that depends on a reader for whom the name Bacchus has precise and immediate associations; another reader, a reader for whom those associations are less precise will not have that experience because he will not have rushed to a conclusion in relation to which the word 'misused' will stand as a challenge. Obviously I am discriminating between these two readers and between the two equally real experiences they will have. It is not a discrimination based simply on information, because what is important is not the information itself, but the action of the mind which its possession makes possible for one reader and impossible for the other. One might discriminate further between them by noting that the point at issue — whether value is a function of objects and actions or of intentions — is at the heart of the seventeenth-century debate over 'things indifferent.' A reader who is aware of that debate will not only *have* the experience I describe; he will recognize at the end of it that he has been asked to take a position on one side of a continuing controversy; and that recognition (also a part of his experience) will be part of the disposition with which he moves into the lines that follow.

It would be possible to continue with this profile of the optimal reader, but I would not get very far before someone would point out that what I am really describing is the intended reader, the reader whose education, opinions, concerns, linguistic competences, etc. make him capable of having the experience the author wished to provide. I would not resist this characterization because it seems obvious that the efforts of readers are always efforts to discern and therefore to realize (in the sense of becoming) an author's intention. I would only object if that realization were conceived narrowly, as the single act of comprehending an author's purpose rather than (as I would conceive it) as the succession of acts readers perform in the continuing assumption that they are dealing with intentional beings. In this view discerning an intention is no more or less than understanding, and understanding includes (is constituted by) all the activities which make up what I call the structure of the reader's experience. To describe that experience is therefore to describe the reader's efforts at understanding, and to describe the reader's efforts at understanding is to describe his realization (in two senses) of an author's intention. Or to put it another way, what my analyses amount to are descriptions of a succession of decisions made by readers about an author's intention; decisions that are not limited to the specifying of purpose but include the specifying of every aspect of successively intended worlds; decisions that are precisely the shape, because they are the content, of the reader's activities.

Having said this, however, it would appear that I am open to two objections. The first is that the procedure is a circular one. I describe the experience of a reader who in his strategies is answerable to an author's intention, and I specify the author's intention by pointing to the strategies employed by that same reader. But this objection would have force only if it were possible to specify one independently of the other. What is being specified from either perspective are the conditions of utterance, of what could have been understood to have been meant by what was said. That is, intention and understanding are two ends of a conventional act, each of which necessarily stipulates (includes, defines, specifies) the other. To construct the profile of the informed or at-home reader is at the same time to characterize the author's intention and vice versa, because to do either is to specify the *contemporary* conditions of utterance, to identify, by becoming a member of, a community made up of those who share interpretive strategies.

The second objection is another version of the first: if the content of the reader's experience is the succession of acts he performs in search of an author's intentions, and if he performs those acts at the bidding of the text, does not the text then produce or contain everything — intention *and* experience — and have I not compromised my antiformalist position? The objection will have force only if the formal patterns of the text are assumed to exist independently of the reader's experience, for only then can priority be claimed for them. Indeed, the claims of independence and priority are one and the same; when they are separated it is so that they can give circular and illegitimate support to each other. The question 'do formal features exist independently?' is usually answered by pointing to their priority: they are 'in' the text before the reader comes to it. The question 'are formal features prior?' is usually answered by pointing to their independent status: they are 'in' the text before the reader comes to it. What looks like a step in an argument is actually the spectacle of an assertion supporting itself. It follows then that an attack on the independence of formal features will also be an attack on their priority (and vice versa), and I would like to mount such an attack in the context of two short passages from *Lycidas*.

The first passage (actually the second in the poem's sequence) begins at line 42:

> The willows and the hazel copses green
> Shall now no more be seen,
> Fanning their joyous leaves to thy soft lays.
> (Ll. 42–44)

It is my thesis that the reader is always making sense (I intend 'making' to have its literal force), and in the case of these lines the sense he makes will involve the assumption (and therefore the creation) of a completed assertion after the word 'seen,' to wit, the death of Lycidas has so affected the willows and the hazel copses green that, in sympathy, they will wither and die (will no more by seen by *anyone*). In other words at the end of line 43 the reader will have hazarded an interpretation, or performed an act of perceptual closure, or made a decision as to what is being asserted. I do not mean that he has done four things, but that he has done one thing the description of which might take any one of four forms — making sense, interpreting, performing perceptual closure, deciding about what is intended. (The importance of this point will become clear later.) Whatever he has done (that is, however we characterize it) he will undo it in the act of reading the next line; for here he discovers that his closure, or making of sense, was premature and that he must make a new one in which the relationship between man and nature is exactly the reverse of what was first assumed. The willows and the hazel copses green will in fact be seen, but they will not seen by Lycidas. It is he who will be no more, while they go on as before, fanning their joyous leaves to someone else's soft lays (the whole of line 44 is now perceived as modifying and removing the absoluteness of 'seen'). Nature is not sympathetic, but indifferent, and the notion of her sympathy is one of those 'false surmises' that the poem is continually encouraging and then disallowing.

The previous sentence shows how easy it is to surrender to the bias of our critical language and begin to talk as if poems, not readers or interpreters, did things. Words like 'encourage' and 'disallow' (and others I have used in this paper) imply agents, and it is only 'natural' to assign agency first to an author's intentions and then to the forms that assumedly embody them. What really happens, I think, is something quite different: rather than intention and its formal realization producing interpretation (the 'normal' picture), interpretation creates intention and its formal realization by creating the conditions in which it becomes possible to pick them out. In other words, in the analysis of these lines from *Lycidas* I did what critics always do: I 'saw' what my interpretive principles permitted or directed me to see, and then I turned around and attributed what I had 'seen' to a text and an intention. What my principles direct me to 'see' are readers performing acts; the points at which I find (or to be more precise, declare) those acts to have been performed become (by a sleight of hand) demarcations *in* the text; those demarcations are then available for the designation 'formal features,' and as formal features they can be (illegitimately) assigned the responsibility for producing the interpretation which in fact produced them. In this case, the demarcation my interpretation calls into being is placed at the end of line 42; but of course the end of that (or any other) line is worth noticing or pointing out only because my model *demands* (the word is not too strong) perceptual closures and therefore locations at which they occur; in that model this point will be one of those locations, although (1) it needn't have been (not every line ending occasions a closure) and (2) in another model, one that does not give value to the activities of readers, the possibility of its being one would not have arisen.

What I am suggesting is that formal units are always a function of the interpretative model one brings to bear; they are not 'in' the text, and I would make the same argument for intentions. That is, intention is no more embodied 'in' the text than are formal units; rather an intention, like a formal unit, is made when perceptual or interpretive closure is hazarded; it is verified by an interpretive act, and I would add, it is not verifiable in any other way. This last assertion is too large to be fully considered here, but I can sketch out the argumentative sequence I would follow were I to consider it: intention is known when and only when it is recognized; it is recognized as soon as you decided about it; you decide about it as soon as you make a sense; and you make a sense (or so my model claims) as soon as you can.

Let me tie up the threads of my argument with a final example from *Lycidas*:

> He must not float upon his wat'ry bier
> Unwept . . .
>
> (Ll. 13–14)

Here the reader's experience has much the same career as it does in lines 42–44: at the end of line 13 perceptual closure is hazarded, and a sense is made in which the line is taken to be a resolution bordering on a promise: that is, there is now an expectation that something will be done about this unfortunate situation, and the reader anticipates a call to action, perhaps even a program for the undertaking of a rescue mission. With 'Unwept,' however, that expectation and anticipation are disappointed, and the realization of that disappointment will be inseparable from the making of a new (and less comforting) sense: nothing will be done; Lycidas will continue to float upon his wat'ry bier, and the only action taken will be the lamenting of the fact that no action will be efficacious, including the actions of speaking and listening to this lament (which in line 15 will receive the meretricious and self-mocking designation 'melodious tear'). Three 'structures' come into view at precisely the same moment, the moment when the reader having resolved a sense unresolves it and makes a new one; that moment will also be the moment of picking out a formal pattern or unit, end of line/beginning of line, and it will also be the moment at which the reader having decided about the speaker's intention, about what is meant by what has been said, will make the decision again and in so doing will make another intention.

This, then, is my thesis: that the form of the reader's experience, formal units, and the structure of intention are one, that they come into view simultaneously, and that therefore the questions of priority and independence do not arise. What does arise is another question: what produces *them*? That is, if intention, form, and the shape of the reader's experience are simply different ways of referring to (different perspectives on) the same interpretive act, what is that act an interpretation *of*? I cannot answer that question, but neither, I would claim, can anyone else, although formalists try to answer it by pointing to patterns and claiming that they are available independently of (prior to) interpretation. These patterns vary according to the procedures that yield them: they may be statistical (number of two-syllable words per hundred words), grammatical (ratio of passive to active constructions, or of right-branching to left-branching sentences, or of anything else); but whatever they are I would argue that they do not lie innocently in the world but are themselves constituted by an interpretive act, even if, as is often the case, that act is unacknowledged. Of course, this is as true of my analyses as it is of anyone else's. In the examples offered here I appropriate the notion 'line ending' and treat it as a fact of nature; and one might conclude that as a fact it is responsible for the reading experience I describe. The truth I think is exactly the reverse: line endings exist by virtue of perceptual strategies rather than the other way around. Historically, the strategy that we know as 'reading (or hearing) poetry' has included paying attention to the line as a unit, but it is precisely that attention which has made the line as a unit (either of print or of aural duration) available. A reader so practised in paying that attention that he regards the line as a brute fact rather than as a convention will have a great deal of difficulty with concrete poetry; if he overcomes that difficulty, it will not be because he has learned to ignore the line as a unit but because he will have acquired a new set of interpretive strategies (the strategies constitutive of 'concrete poetry reading') in the context of which the line as a unit no longer exists. In short, what is noticed is what has been *made* noticeable, not by a clear and undistorting glass, but by an interpretive strategy.

This may be hard to see when the strategy has become so habitual that the forms it yields seem part of the world. We find it easy to assume that alliteration as an effect depends on a 'fact' that exists independently of any interpretive 'use' one might make of it, the fact that words in proximity begin with the same letter. But it takes only a moment's reflection to realize that the sameness, far from being natural, is enforced by an orthographic convention; that is to say, it is the product of an interpretation. Were we to substitute phonetic conventions for orthographic ones (a 'reform' traditionally urged by purists), the supposedly 'objective' basis for alliteration would disappear because a phonetic transcription would require that we distinguish between the initial sounds of those very words that enter into alliterative relationships; rather than conforming to those relationships the rules of spelling make them. One might reply that, since alliteration is an aural rather than a visual phenomenon when poetry is heard, we have unmediated access to the physical sounds themselves and hear 'real' similarities. But phonological 'facts' are no more uninterpreted (or less conventional) than the 'facts' of orthography; the distinctive features that make articulation and reception possible are the product of a system of differences that must be *imposed* before it can be recognized; the patterns the ear hears (like the patterns the eye sees) are the patterns its perceptual habits make available.

One can extend this analysis forever, even to the 'facts' of grammar. The history of linguistics is the history of competing paradigms each of which offers a different account of the constituents of language. Verbs, nouns, cleft sentences, transformations, deep and surface structures, semes, rhemes, tagmemes — now you see them, now you don't, depending on the descriptive apparatus you employ. The critic who confidently rests his analyses on the bedrock of syntactic descriptions is resting on an interpretation; the facts he points to *are* there, but only as a consequence of the interpretive (man-made) model that has called them into being.

The moral is clear: the choice is never between objectivity and interpretation but between an interpretation that is unacknowledged as such and an interpretation that is at least aware of itself. It is this awareness that I am claiming for myself, although in doing so I must give up the claims implicitly made in the first part of this paper. There I argue that a bad (because spatial) model has suppressed what was really happening, but by my own declared principles the notion 'really happening' is just one more interpretation.

IV

It seems then that the price one pays for denying the priority of either forms or intentions is an inability to say how it is that one ever begins. Yet we do begin, and we continue, and because we do there arises an immediate counter-objection to the preceding pages. If interpretive acts are the source of forms rather than the other way around, why isn't it the case that readers are always performing the same acts or a sequence of random acts, and therefore creating the same forms or a random succession of forms? How, in short, does one explain these two 'facts' of reading?: (1) the same reader will perform differently when reading two 'different' (the word is in quotation marks because its status is precisely what is at issue) texts; and (2) different readers will perform similarly when reading the 'same' (in quotes for the same reason) text. That is to say, both the stability of interpretation among readers and the variety of interpretation in the career of a single reader would seem to argue for the existence of something independent of and prior to interpretive acts, something which produces them. I will answer this challenge by asserting that both the stability and the variety are functions of interpretive strategies rather than of texts.

Let us suppose that I am reading *Lycidas*. What is it that I am doing? First of all, what I am not doing is 'simply reading,' an activity in which I do not believe because it implies the possibility of pure (that is, disinterested) perception. Rather, I am proceeding on the basis of (at least) two interpretive decisions: (1) that *Lycidas* is a pastoral and (2) that it was written by Milton. (I should add that the notions 'pastoral' and 'Milton' are also interpretations; that is they do not stand for a set of indisputable, objective facts; if they did, a great many books would not now be getting written.) Once these decisions have been made (and if I had not made these I would have made others, and they would be consequential in the same way), I am immediately predisposed to perform certain acts, to 'find,' by looking for, themes (the relationship between natural processes and the careers of men, the efficacy of poetry or of any other action), to confer significances (on flowers, streams, shepherds, pagan deities), to mark out 'formal' units (the lament, the consolation, the turn, the affirmation of faith, etc.). My disposition to perform these acts (and others; the list is not meant to be exhaustive) constitutes a set of interpretive strategies, which, when they are put into execution, become the large act of reading. That is to say, interpretive strategies are not put into execution after reading (the pure act of perception in which I do not believe); they are the shape of reading, and because they are the shape of reading, they give texts their shape, making them rather than, as it is usually assumed, arising from them. Several important things follow from this account:

1. I did not have to execute this particular set of interpretive strategies because I did not have to make those particular interpretive (pre-reading) decisions. I could have decided, for example, that *Lycidas* was a text in which a set of fantasies and defenses find expression. These decisions would have entailed the assumption of another set of interpretive strategies (perhaps like that put forward by Norman Holland in *The Dynamics of Literary Response*) and the execution of that set would have made another text.

2. I could execute this same set of strategies when presented with texts that did not bear the title (again a notion which is itself an interpretation) *Lycidas, A Pastoral Monody*. . . . I could decide (it is a decision some have made) that *Adam Bede* is a pastoral written by an author who consciously modeled herself on Milton (still remembering that 'pastoral' and 'Milton' are interpretations, not facts in the public domain); or I could decide, as Empson did, that a great many things not usually considered pastoral were in fact to be so read; and either decision would give rise to a set of interpretive strategies, which, when put into action, would *write* the text I write when reading *Lycidas*. (Are you with me?)

3. A reader other than myself who, when presented with *Lycidas*, proceeds to put into execution a set of interpretive strategies similar to mine (how he could do so is a question I will take up later), will perform the same (or at least a similar) succession of interpretive acts. He and I then might be tempted to say that we agree about the poem (thereby assuming that the poem exists independently of the acts either of us performs); but what we really would agree about is the way to write it.

4. A reader other than myself who, when presented with *Lycidas* (please keep in mind that the status of *Lycidas* is what is at issue), puts into execution a different set of interpretive strategies will perform a different succession of interpretive acts. (I am assuming, it is the article of my faith, that a reader will always execute some set of interpretive strategies and therefore perform some succession of interpretive acts.) One of us might then be tempted to complain to the other that we could not possibly be reading the same poem (literary criticism is full of such complaints) and he would be right; for each of us would be reading the poem he had made.

The large conclusion that follows from these four smaller ones is that the notions of the 'same' or 'different' texts are fictions. If I read *Lycidas* and *The Waste Land* differently (in fact I do not), it will not be because the formal structures of the two poems (to term them such is also an interpretive decision) call forth different interpretive strategies but because my predisposition to execute different interpretive strategies will *produce* different formal structures. That is, the two poems are different because I have decided that they will be. The proof of this is the possibility of doing the reverse (that is why point 2 is so important). That is to say, the answer to the question 'why do different texts give rise to different sequences of interpretive acts?' is that *they don't have to*, an answer which implies strongly that 'they' don't exist. Indeed it has always been possible to put into action interpretive strategies designed to make all texts one, or to put it more accurately, to be forever making the same text. Augustine urges just such a strategy, for example, in *On Christian Doctrine* where he delivers the 'rule of faith' which is of course a rule of interpretation. It is dazzlingly simple: everything in the Scriptures, and indeed in the world when it is properly read, points to (bears the meaning of) God's love for us and our answering responsibility to love our fellow creatures for His sake. If only you should come upon something which does not at first seem to bear this meaning, that 'does not literally pertain to virtuous behavior or to the truth of faith,' you are then to take it 'to be figurative' and proceed to scrutinize it 'until an interpretation contributing to the reign of charity is produced.' This then is both a stipulation of what meaning there is and a set of directions for finding it, which is of course a set of directions — of interpretive strategies — for making it, that is, for the endless reproduction of the same text. Whatever one may think of this interpretive program, its success and ease of execution are attested to by centuries of Christian exegesis. It is my contention that any interpretive program, any set of interpretive strategies, can have a similar success, although few have been as spectacularly successful as this one. (For some time now, for at least three hundred years, the most successful interpretive program has gone under the name 'ordinary language.') In our own discipline programs with the same characteristic of always reproducing one text include psychoanalytic criticism, Robertsonianism (always threatening to extend its sway into later and later periods), numerology (a sameness based on the assumption of innumerable fixed differences).

The other challenging question — 'why will different readers execute the same interpretive strategy when faced with the "same" text?' — can be handled in the same way. The answer is again that *they don't have to*, and my evidence is the entire history of literary criticism. And again this answer implies that the notion 'same text' is the product of the possession by two or more readers of similar interpretive strategies.

But why should this ever happen? Why should two or more readers ever agree, and why should regular, that is, habitual, differences in the career of a single reader ever occur? What is the explanation on the one hand of the stability of interpretation (at least among certain groups at certain times) and on the other of the orderly variety of interpretation if it is not the stability and variety of texts? The answer to all of these questions is to be found in a notion that has been implicit in my argument, the notion of *interpretive communities*. Interpretive communities are made up of those who share interpretive strategies not for reading (in the conventional sense) but for writing texts, for constituting their properties and assigning their intentions. In other words these strategies exist prior to the act of reading and therefore determine the shape of what is read rather than, as is usually assumed, the other way around. If it is an article of faith in a particular community that there are a variety of texts, its members will boast a repertoire of strategies for making them. And if a community believes in the existence of only one text, then the single strategy its members employ will be forever writing it. The first community will accuse the members of the second of being reductive, and they in turn will call their accusers superficial. The assumption in each community will be that the other is not correctly perceiving the 'true text,' but the truth will be that each perceives the text (or texts) its interpretive strategies demand and call into being. This, then, is the explanation both for the stability of interpretation among different readers (they belong to the same community) and for the regularity with which a single reader will employ different interpretive strategies and thus make different texts (he belongs to different communities). It also explains why there are disagreements and why they can be debated in a principled way: not because of a stability in texts, but because of a stability in the makeup of interpretive communities and therefore in the opposing positions they make possible. Of course this stability is always temporary (unlike the longed for and timeless stability of the text). Interpretive communities grow larger and decline, and individuals move from one to another; thus while the alignments are not permanent, they are always there, providing just enough stability for the interpretive battles to go on, and just enough shift and slippage to assure that they will never be settled. The notion of interpretive communities thus stands between an impossible ideal and the fear which leads so many to maintain it. The ideal is of perfect agreement and it would require texts to have a status independent of interpretation. The fear is of interpretive anarchy, but it would only be realized if interpretation (text making) were completely random. It is the fragile but real consolidation of interpretive communities that allows us to talk to one another, but with no hope or fear of ever being able to stop.

In other words interpretive communities are no more stable than texts because interpretive strategies are not natural or universal, but *learned*. This does not mean that there is a point at which an individual has not yet learned any. The ability to interpret is not acquired; it is constitutive of being human. What is acquired are the ways of interpreting and those same ways can also be forgotten or supplanted, or complicated or dropped from favour ('no one reads that way anymore'). When any of these things happens, there is a corresponding change in texts, not because they are being read differently, but because they are being written differently.

The only stability, then, inheres in the fact (at least in my model) that interpretive strategies are always being deployed, and this means that communication is a much more chancy affair than we are accustomed to think it. For if there are no fixed texts, but only interpretive strategies making them; and if interpretive strategies are not natural, but learned (and are therefore unavailable to a finite description), what is it that utterers (speakers, authors, critics, me, you) do? In the old model utterers are in the business of handing over ready made or prefabricated meanings. These meanings are said to be encoded, and the code is assumed to be in the world independently of the individuals who are obliged to attach themselves to it (if they do not they run the danger of being declared deviant). In my model, however, meanings are not extracted but made and made not by encoded forms but by interpretive strategies that call forms into being. It follows then that what utterers do is give hearers and readers the opportunity to make meanings (and texts) by inviting them to put into execution a set of strategies. It is presumed that the invitation will be recognized, and that presumption rests on a projection on the part of a speaker or author of the moves *he* would make if confronted by the sounds or marks he is uttering or setting down.

It would seem at first that this account of things simply reintroduces the old objection; for isn't this an admission that there is after all a formal encoding, not perhaps of meanings, but of the directions for making them, for executing interpretive strategies? The answer is that they will only *be* directions to those who already have the interpretive strategies in the first place. Rather than producing interpretive acts, they are the product of one. An author hazards his projection, not because of something 'in' the marks, but because of something he assumes to be in his reader. The very existence of the 'marks' is a function of an interpretive community, for they will be recognized (that is, made) only by its members. Those outside that community will be deploying a different set of interpretive strategies (interpretation cannot be withheld) and will therefore be making different marks.

So once again I have made the text disappear, but unfortunately the problems do not disappear with it. If everyone is continually executing interpretive strategies and in that act constituting texts, intentions, speakers, and authors, how can any one of us know whether or not he is a member of the same interpretive community as any other of us? The answer is that he can't, since any evidence brought forward to support the claim would itself be an interpretation (especially if the 'other' were an author long dead). The only 'proof' of membership is fellowship, the nod of recognition from someone in the same community, someone who says to you what neither of us could ever prove to a third party: 'we know.' I say it to you now, knowing full well that you will agree with me (that is, understand) only if you already agree with me.

Notes:

1. All references are to *The Poems of John Milton*, ed. John Carey and Alastair Fowler (London, 1968).
2. *A Variorum Commentary on the Poems of John Milton*, vol. 2, pt. 2, ed. A. S. P. Woodhouse and Douglas Bush (New York, 1972), p. 475.
3. It is first of all a reference to the city of iniquity from which the Hebrews are urged to flee in Isaiah and Jeremiah. In Protestant polemics Babylon is identified with the Roman Church whose destruction is prophesied in the book of Revelation. And in some Puritan tracts, Babylon is the name for Augustine's earthly city, from which the faithful are to flee inwardly in order to escape the fate awaiting the unregenerate. See *Variorum Commentary*, pp. 440–41.
4. *Variorum Commentary*, p. 469.
5. Ibid., p. 457.
6. *Poems Upon Several Occasions, English, Italian, And Latin, With Translations, By John Milton*, ed. Thomas Warton (London, 1791), p. 352.
7. See my *Surprised by Sin: The Reader in* Paradise Lost (London and New York, 1967); *Self-consuming Artifacts: The Experience of Seventeenth-Century Literature* (Berkeley, 1972); 'What Is Stylistics and Why are They Saying Such Terrible Things About It?' in *Approaches to Poetics*, ed. Seymour Chatman (New York, 1973), pp. 109–52; 'How Ordinary Is Ordinary Language?' in *New Literary History*, 5 (Autumn, 1973): 41–54; 'Facts and Fictions: A Reply to Ralph Rader,' *Critical Inquiry*, 1 (June 1975): 883–91.

2

E. D. Hirsch, Jr.,
'The Politics of Theories of Interpretation'

All interpretations originate in politics, which is to say, in values. As in other human affairs, we choose one activity over another because we have values or habits which could be termed, in the broadest sense, 'political.' Scientific interpretations are no exception. Scientists prosecute many more interpretations in medicine than in astrophysics for reasons that are not themselves scientific. But even if our interpretations do originate in politics, must it follow that their final character is also politically predetermined? Not necessarily. Although we may ask an interpretive question for political reasons, its answer may not necessarily be dictated by those same reasons. If we ask whether laetrile cures cancer, our question is political in origin and could have a politically predetermined answer. But we might be more interested in getting at the truth of the case. Some scientific interpreters might be much more interested in the truth about laetrile than in having the answer come out on one side or the other. Their main political interest might be in getting the answer right, getting the interpretation right.

No doubt an interpretation can be politically predetermined. That would happen if the interpreter cared more about fostering a particular result than about being right. A proponent of political predetermination could object that the aim of being right is also a political aim which usually masks a conservative, status-quo ideology. That could be so, for who would deny that the aim of being right is itself an ideology and therefore political? On the other hand, isn't it also the case that the ideology of truth is structurally different from any other political ideology? Under other political ideologies, we desire and sometimes predetermine a particular result. Under the ideology of truth, our desire for a particular result is subordinated to our desire to be right. Our orientation is a posteriori, not a priori. We decide after the fact, not before the fact. And even if an interpreter is told that there are no disinterested, theory-free facts, the ideologue of truth still *tries* to operate under the control of some 'other,' of some reality beyond predisposition and preference.

This choice between predetermined and revisable, postdetermined interpretations has an importance beyond textual exegesis. Interpretation is the central activity of cognition. Our perceived meanings or, metaphorically, our objects-in-the-world are always interpreted constructs, that is, they are always other than the 'language' of vibrations (light, sound, heat, and so on) through which we perceive them. We always perceive (construct) something other than the language through which we know that thing. This constructive process is interpretation. Since our interpretations are always other than the language by which they are construed, a space of uncertainty exists between the vehicle (our language of cognition) and the meanings (or objects) interpreted from it. This gap, which cannot be overcome, is a space in which different interpretations can be played out. Hence there is always an element of uncertainty in every possible sphere of interpretation. This gap of uncertainty is the defining feature of interpretation — the gap between the vibrations and the object, between the vehicle and the meaning, between the sign and the signified.

One of the most influential ideas of our time, which is drawn from Kant, is that the form of our interpretive constructs is predetermined from within, rather than imposed from without. This is the doctrine of the synthetic a priori. Since Kant, the most significant development of the a priori has been its application to the changing realm of culture rather than just to the permanent structures of our minds.[1] This cultural Kantianism has had an immense influence on the popular mind as well as on recent theories of interpretation. Language, for instance, is said to predetermine the forms and limits of our ideas. Culture, in a still larger sense, is said to predetermine the forms and limits of all realities in our world. Ideology is said to predetermine the results of our inquiries, and politics (the extension of ideology) is said unconsciously to predetermine our interpretations.[2]

The staying power of the synthetic a priori comes partly from the impossibility of refuting it. Any empirical counterclaim advanced against the a priori can always be seen as occurring within its predetermined forms. Thus, even Kant's original claims about the a priori character of causality and Euclidian space, though long since called into doubt by physics, still leads a vigorous life in science and philosophy — on the grounds that such 'refutations' already take place within an a priori structure. But the impossibility of refuting the a priori also means the impossibility of confirming it. Therefore, the a posteriori is also alive and well in the sciences, if not in the humanities. Philosophically speaking, the *revisability* of interpretations is an idea just as impregnable as the predetermination of interpretations. The a priori claim than a revision 'always already' occurs within a predetermining scheme can be met by the counterclaim that the scheme itself is revisable. Revisability is as reasonable an ultimate as predetermination. Thus, neither the a priori nor the a posteriori could ever be definitively proved or falsified. Both are 'metaphysical' concepts. The political a priori is a metaphysical doctrine that, like all forms of cultural Kantianism, has no compelling logical application to practice. Psychologically, of course, it strongly influences practice, as do all metaphysical beliefs. But, logically, the doctrine of the synthetic a priori is neutral with regard to politics. Any and all interpretive choices are equally governed by its imperial force. If a political a priorist tried to distinguish between authentic and inauthentic interpretations, his theory would lose its epistemological generality and would then be seen to be what it really is: rhetorical exhortation. Exhortations imply choices; metaphysical a priori theories imply universal necessity. A priorism is, in Hegel's phrase, 'the night in which all cows are black.'

The only philosophical theory that could describe the politics of interpretation would be one that described interpretive choice as a theoretical ultimate. This, cultural Kantianism fails to do. Its political efficacy lies in its secondary rhetorical effect — in its suggesting that we do not *really* have ultimate interpretive choices, in its showing that we cannot *really* prosecute 'objective' interpretations, and so on.

My contrary thesis here is that interpretive choice can be described in ultimate theoretical terms and that interpreters can and should resist the rhetorical force of the a priori if they want to make those genuine political choices. I wish to expose the sheer rhetoricity of a priori theories and at the same time explore the most basic political choices governing interpretation.

Let me start with a simple example. Suppose that we are interpreting Blake's well-known poem 'The Lamb'. According to most a priori theories, we are not fully able to recover the original meaning of that poem. My efforts at historical reconstruction would necessarily be filtered through my own prior cultural or political categories. Since that secondary filtering cannot be overcome, the attempt to do so is an illusioned charade. To this, the ideologue of truth replies: 'Maybe; but in light of multiple vectors of evidence, and continual revision, we might some-times achieve an accurate reconstruction, despite our cultural predispositions.' One of the interpretive questions that has been asked of 'The Lamb' is whether its original meaning was sentimental or ironic.[3] Many readers take the poem to be straightforward, while Harold Bloom and others take it to be ironic. So far, that is an argument about how *Blake* meant the poem to be taken. It is, therefore, the typ-ical, old-fashioned kind of question to which historical interpretation has always dedicated its energies. Can we, should we, try to resolve that historical question?

In providing this example, I do not intend to discuss the merits of ironic versus nonironic historical interpretations of 'The Lamb'. I use it to focus instead on another kind of choice. A mere disagreement between ironic and nonironic readings is a disagreement about the nature of an historical event, namely, Blake's original purpose. But there is another and more fundamental kind of disagreement which underlies the real politics of interpretation. It is a disagreement about the norm of interpretation itself. Whatever may be said for choosing an ironic versus nonironic reading of 'The Lamb', the choice would usually be governed by the attempt to reconstruct an historical event. But a very different kind of norm would be invoked if the interpreter decided to choose whatever meaning seemed preferable quite apart from its historicality. I shall argue that *this*, rather than disagreements about an historical event, is the ultimate political choice in interpretation.

To explain this basic choice, it will be convenient to steer a detour around all the irrelevant questions that have been raised concerning authorial intent. I confess to feeling personally responsible for some of the irrelevancies surrounding this issue, and I am at work on a book that tries to untangle those interesting problems. But that is another topic. In order to perceive the political essence of interpretive norms, we can circumvent the whole question of author psychology by adopting a semiotic account of interpretation.[4] Instead of referring an interpretation back to an original author, we could just for the moment refer it back to an original code or convention system. Let us say that the historical interpretation is the one that applies an earlier code system to the text. For instance, one historical problem in interpreting 'The Lamb' would then be whether the original code system made the poem ironic or not. This semiotic account can be simplified still further if, instead of talking about particular conventions, we talk about the choice between different convention systems and we pretend that the choice is controlled by the selection of a particular 'cypher key.' Under this semiotic account, then, the political choices of interpretation have to do with the choice of a cypher key.

This model for dealing with the matter has another advantage besides simplicity. It not only avoids digressive issues connected with author psychology, it avoids confusions about the social and conventional character of linguistic meaning. Those who attack the author norm, or some other individualistic version of interpretation, rightly observe that no one could ever impose an arbitrary linguistic mode of interpretation. Nobody can act quite as Humpty-Dumpty did when he told Alice that he could make a word mean whatever he wanted it to mean. But the real political question does not concern the conventionality versus the individuality of interpretation; it concerns, rather, the locus of authority. *Who* chooses the cypher key?

It would be wrong to see this as anything but a political question. When Alice asked Humpty-Dumpty whether he really could apply any arbitrary meaning to a text, Humpty replied, 'The question is, which is to be master — that's all.' Although the choice of cypher keys in not unlimited, as Humpty-Dumpty claimed, that fact does not have the theoretical importance which some theorists have attached to it. Much more important is the fact that several conventional codes can be applied to any text. That being so, Humpty-Dumpty's question, *Who* shall be master? *Who* shall choose the cypher key? is the ultimate political question in interpretation.

In the a priori view, the real chooser of norms is, of course, willy-nilly the reader. So, the short answer to the question, Who chooses the cypher key? is the reader chooses. But this short answer hides an important detail, namely, that the reader can decide to let somebody other than the reader choose the cypher key. Under that kind of arrangement, the reader, like the ideologue of truth, would take an a posteriori approach. The reader would accept whatever cypher key seemed, on the evidence, to be one that governed a past event. That kind of interpretation is inherently and necessarily historical, since it always refers back to a decision made in the past. Therefore, the structure of the historical norm, which is always open to revision, is different from the structure of a norm based on ad hoc reader preferences, which are open only to change by whim.

This distinction between a reader's present, ad hoc choice of a cypher key and the reader's decision to accept somebody's past choice of a cypher key is applicable to every act of interpretation whether of speech or of writing. Let us call the reader's choice of his or her own preferred cypher key a 'self-governing' or 'autocratic' norm. In contrast, let us call the reader's decision to defer to past choice of a cypher key an 'other-governing' or 'allocratic' norm.

This distinction is more general and useful than 'author-norm' and 'reader-norm,' since 'author' usually refers to an original author and to one single historical event, and that is not the only important kind of historical interpretation in the humanities. Take this example of nonauthorial yet historical interpretation. Suppose I say that my goal is to interpret 'The Lamb' not as Blake understood it but as Bloom did. It is true that I would then conceive of Bloom as a kind of secondary author, and so I would still be conducting an interpretation under a kind of authorial norm. Structurally speaking, to conduct an accurate historical interpretation of Bloom's 'Lamb', I would follow the same sort of allocratic procedure as I would in conducting an historical interpretation of Blake's.[5] Both would be historical a posteriori investigations, and evidence relevant to either historical event would help provisionally in choosing the cypher key to be applied. The historical, allocratic norm would govern both, thus giving that term a greater generality than authorial norm.

This autocratic/allocratic distinction holds also for those interpretive communities celebrated by Stanley Fish. In the example just mentioned, I might choose to belong either to the Blakean community or the Bloomian community, but in both cases I would have to look back to an historical act of choice by which the community adopted some cypher key which defines it as an interpretive community. On the other hand, if I decided to disregard *anybody's* choice of a cypher key and chose the one that I preferred, or that seemed right to me, or that was always already given to me, I then would be following the autocratic norm. It's true that such a norm is not merely an individualistic one, since the cypher key I have chosen consists of social conventions. Moreover it's true that other people might independently choose as I do, thus making me a member of a transindividual interpretive community. But the only way anyone could deliberately join me in that community would be to practise an historical, allocratic interpretation in order to find out what the cypher key of my community was. To do that they would have to engage in straightforward allocratic, historical interpretation.

From the standpoint of logical coherence and even legitimacy, I do not think there is anything to choose between an autocratic or allocratic norm of interpretation. I must not object that the autocratic norm is linguistically implausible, since any choice of any cypher key would actualize some existing conventional, legitimate system. But this very plurality of legitimate code systems requires an interpreter to choose one cypher key rather than another, without having any *logical* reason for choosing one over another. So, the decision between the autocratic and the allocratic norm is at bottom an ethical and political choice, and only that. Against Fish's insistence that interpretation is always already autocratic (whether we know it or not) must be set P. D. Juhl's insistence that interpretation is always already allocratic (whether we know it or not).[6] Both of these monolithic descriptions are rhetorical exhortations masked as theory (whether they know it or not). For the claim that we have no choice between the autocratic and allocratic norms is in practice an exhortation to make one choice rather than another; the political choice itself is very real. Ironically, the a priori theory that interpretations are always already politically predetermined is an evasion of the very real political choice between the autocratic and allocratic norms.

Let me briefly summarize the analysis to this point. First, the politics of interpretation resides in the choice between the autocratic and allocratic norm. Under the autocratic norm, authority resides in the reader, while under the allocratic norm, the reader delegates authority to the reconstructed historical act of another person or community. Second, autocratic interpretation is not in principle revisable except by accidental change of preference, whereas allocratic interpretation is revisable ex post facto on the basis of changing theories and evidence about a determinative historical event. Hence the autocratic norm is a priori and incorrigible; the allocratic norm is a posteriori and revisable. The authority to choose one of these norms lies with the reader, and this choice, being free, is ethical or political in nature; it is entirely unconstrained by epistemological considerations. I will now amplify this last point.

Broadly speaking, those who claim that all interpretations are prestructured by cultural schemas may be called 'idealists': Nihil in interpretatione nisi prius in schema. In the deepest sense, in this view, interpretation is always already auto-cratic, that is, always constituted by the reader's predetermining schemas, whether cultural, political, or what have you. The contrasting view, that interpretation can be either autocratic or allocratic, assumes that the truth about an historical event (say, another person's choice of a cypher key) is something that might be objec-tively known despite the influence of cultural schemas. Those who hold this latter view may be called 'realists.' (In recent polemics, they are called 'naive realists' with 'naive' being a nonseparable prefix.) This contrast between realism and idea-lism seems to be the epistemological bottom line between the autocratic-a priori and the allocratic-a posteriori principles in interpretation. As Richard Rorty has pointed out, the rise of a prioristic, post-modern literary theory is a resurgence of nineteenth-century cognitive idealism — in a new guise.[7]

In calling the views of Foucault, Fish, Derrida, and De Man 'idealistic,' I do not suppose that I score a telling point. Quite the contrary. Idealism is one of the dur-able positions in epistemology. Furthermore, when I assume the philosophical respectability of cognitive realism, I do not suppose that philosophical problems are circumvented merely by appealing to the universal realism of common sense. The realist position, like the idealist, is beset by embarrassments (though they happen to embarrass me less than the idealist ones). My observation that post-modern theorists are idealists has a practical, not a philosophical, motivation. I want to claim that *neither* epistemological idealism nor epistemological realism has any direct practical bearing on the politics of interpretation. Ultimately, nothing argued at the grandiose level of epistemology, such as the turn from 'logocentrism' (Derrida), 'the historical a priori' (Foucault), 'the political unconscious' (Jameson) — none of these high-level generalizations can decide the issue between autocratic and allocratic norms of interpretation.

This truth is acknowledged by both idealist and realist arguments in their more thoughtful forms. A sophisticated idealist would never deny that we can act like realists — that is, act *as though* our beliefs were indefinitely revisable and *as though* they sometimes corresponded to reality. The idealist simply proposes that these beliefs are either wrong or unjustifiable. A sophisticated realist, on the other side, would not deny that our beliefs might, at some unknown, ultimate, not-yet-defined level be unrevisable, nor that we couldn't sometimes *act* like idealists if we wanted to. People do act like realists even if the idealist position should (in some undemonstrable way) be right; they can go on acting like idealists, at least in the sphere of intellectual affairs, even if the realist position should (in some unde-monstrable way) be right. This influence on action constitutes what I would call the 'rhetoricity' of interpretive theories. In short, even a sophisticated idealist would grant that we can *act* as though we have a choice between autocratic and allocratic interpretation, and action is the medium of politics and ethical choice.

Thus, to be a realist or idealist in an ultimate epistemological sense is rather like being a theist or an atheist. Such metaphysical belief is a psychological sanction for action rather than a position that can be proved or demolished. Neither position is certainly decidable. As Pascal once observed with regard to religious belief: 'We are incapable of knowing either what He is or whether He exists. This being so, who will be so rash as to decide?'[8] Yet, in practical terms, as Pascal also observed, we are put into the position of having to choose, that is, having to act. Pascal proposed, therefore, the further question: How shall we act in the absence of any decisive grounding for theism or atheism? He argued that in the end such a decision had to be a gamble: 'Let us weigh the gain and loss in calling heads — that God exists. Let us estimate the two chances. If you win, you win everything. If you lose, you lose nothing. Do not hesitate then, gamble on His existence.'

The analogy between Pascal's famous wager and the situation of the interpreter is this: no philosopher, including whichever current sage one chances to revere — Foucault, Heidegger, Rorty, Derrida — has put forward a decisive argument for preferring an idealist over a realist view. As with theism versus atheism, no decisive ground could be put forward. This fact has led Rorty, for example, to adopt what he calls a 'pragmatist' (in my view, an idealist) position. But the same facts and arguments which lead Rorty to repudiate traditional epistemology can, following Pascal's argument, lead to a different imperative, namely: choose that position among the two undecidable ones which sanctions the most desired or desirable practice. The modern version of Pascal's wager would be: Let us weigh the practical gain and loss in calling heads — that is, that objective historical truth exists. Let us estimate the two chances. If you win, you win something. If you lose, you lose nothing. Do not hesitate then, gamble on the existence of objective truth.

How does that wager play itself out in the sphere of interpretive practice? I have suggested that the realist (a posteriori) viewpoint sanctions the possibility that we might sometimes know the objective truth about the following historical question: What was the code of conventions that somebody chose at some historical moment to apply to this text? To the extent that this historical question might be answered correctly, historical, allocratic interpretation might be carried out correctly. Allocratic interpretation, moreover, is the only sort that can in principle be revised, and thus make practical use of scholarship, evidence, logical argument, and could even look to the possibility of empirical progress. Allocratic interpretation, then, offers the possibility of being wrong. Autocratic interpretation, by contrast, is always right or, more exactly, could be neither right nor wrong; it offers itself no external standard with respect to which it could be one or the other. That doesn't nullify autocratic interpretation, which in a particular circumstance could serve the more valuable purpose.[9] But such a value judgment would be a practical, not a theoretical, decision. It would be a genuine political decision.

What have I tried to achieve with this Pascalian argument? First, a negative goal — I want to remove the delusion that philosophers, theorists, and cultural sages could ever definitively show that objective truth is impossible or that accurate historical interpretation is a delusion. They have not shown this, and they cannot do so. This means that the field of interpretation is, in its large theoretical structure (and despite some genuine technical advances), more or less where it was 100 years ago. That is where big theoretical issues are likely to remain, along with the big epistemological questions to which they are allied — forever in the realm of the never-surely-decidable. I have argued that the practical consequence of this theoretical aporia is not to subordinate the politics of interpretation to big theory but rather to subordinate big theory to politics. In the end, the debate between autocratic and allocratic interpretation is a political, not an epistemological, issue. And the political issue is: What sort of culture do we want to foster?

When I was first starting on a career in scholarship, I was thrilled to read Max Weber's lecture to young scholars called 'Wissenschaft als Beruf,' 'Science as a

Vocation.' No one will venture to contend that Weber neglected or under-estimated the cultural, personal, social, and political influences that impinge upon the seeking of objective truth. He was the master of that subject. Yet no one has spoken of the goal of objective truth — *Wissenschaft* — with more impressive and infectious fervour than Weber did in that 1919 lecture. His message to young scholars was: In the academy beware of politics as an adjunct to science and, equally, beware of science as an adjunct to politics. Fourteen years later, in 1933, Ernst Krieck, the first Nazi rector of the University of Frankfurt, pronounced in his inaugural address a different view: 'Nowadays the task of the universities is not to cultivate objective science, but soldier-like, militant science' — a succinct state-ment of the politics of interpretation.[10]

The word 'science' (*Wissenschaft*) of course meant to Weber more than the word 'science' can convey in English, since *Wissenschaft* embraces the humane as well as the natural sciences. Indeed the interpretation of texts was one of the memorable examples Weber used in his lecture to illustrate what he meant by science:

> Whoever lacks the capacity . . . to come up to the idea that the fate of his soul depends upon whether or not he makes the correct conjecture at this passage of this manuscript may as well stay away from science. He will never have what one may call the 'personal experience' of science. If you lack this strange intoxication, ridiculed by every outsider, if you lack this passion . . . you have no calling for science and should do something else. For nothing is worthy of man as man unless he can pursue it with passionate devotion.[11]

In the 1980s, we who find ourselves in the profession of textual interpretation cannot respond wholeheartedly to Weber's example. Too many children of science have already pored over too few canonical texts with just the intensity that Weber so inspiringly described. The allocratic exegesis of our major canonical texts has pretty much reached a dead end because our texts are few and our interpreters, over the years, have been many. The allocratic exegesis of Chaucer, Shakespeare, Spenser, and Milton on narrow literary principles cannot provide us with an endless frontier, and it is the closing down of that New Critical frontier rather than 'advances' in epistemology which now draws our profession toward autocratic interpretation (for which the frontier no doubt seems endless, even if intellectually uninteresting). But it is doubtful that autocratic interpretation will long continue to satisfy either its practitioners or its readers.

Unfortunately, the forty-year-old doctrine that textual exegesis (interpretation in the New Critical sense) is our only legitimate critical activity still holds sway in the academy. It is the hidden assumption that joins allocrats and autocrats together; it is the common bond of Derridians and Robertsonians. But without this assumption that only interpretation of the 'literary work' is legitimate, would we still feel an institutional pressure to continue to produce new readings whether autocratic or allocratic? Does not this restriction of our activity to interpretation in a narrow sense betray a certain habit-bound lack of imagination? What is needed for the future is a genuinely new frontier for allocratic, historical interpretation — interpretation with an object, but with a new kind of object.

This can be found only in history. And it will have to be found beyond the narrow boundaries of the aesthetic and the text-in-itself. Interpretation, as the general term for cognition, is hardly limited to the boundaries of texts or to the arbitrary confines of fiction and poetry. Historical interpretation is the humanistic pursuit par excellence and embraces not just texts but contexts. On this score, the contextual urgings of Foucault (minus his a priori obfuscations) are all in the right direction.

Whether professors of literature shall find new objects of historical inquiry is a political, not a theoretical, question, even though in a large perspective it is perhaps an insignificant political question. Sometimes, however, academic humanists do enter the sphere of significant politics in addition to their considerable influence in the classroom. Once in a while some professor in the humanities is named to an important panel or called on to testify before a legislative committee. When that happens, the humanist is never asked to put forward an autocratic interpretation of texts or of the world. The humanist is called on to tell, as far as possible, the objective historical truth about some facet of reality that he or she has closely studied. Nobody outside the academy is interested in autocratic interpretations, even when they follow the conventions of some established interpretive community. Interpretation is intellectually interesting inside the academy mainly when it is trying to determine some objective historical truth. It is politically significant outside the academy *only* when it is trying to determine some objective historical truth. Whether or not an interpretation *is* telling the historical truth is a question that nobody can answer. Nonetheless, the interpreter's decision to try to tell this truth is a genuine political decision, too important to be yielded by default to the rhetoricity of interpretive theories.

Notes:

1. The term 'a priori' is of course familiar to readers in philosophy. Taken loosely and in a broad sense it sometimes means the totality of prior givens which enable us to interpret experience: such prior cognitive frameworks as space, time, object, person, and so on. These givens 'ground' our experience; we never confront experience with an innocent eye — on that point all parties agree, including empirical psychologists of various schools. The more specific doctrine that I call the 'a priori' here is a Kantian form of idealism which holds that we cannot change our formative givens in a fundamental way. Thus, I use the term a priori to specify the doctrine of the *unrevisability* of our cognitive givens. This unrevisability doctrine, central to Kant, is held, *mutatis mutandis*, by the cultural Kantians of our time. The a posteriorist, by contrast, while not contesting the idea of cognitive frameworks, does contest the idea of their unrevisability. There is no limit in principle to the revisability and corrigibility of our interpreted constructs. The a posteriorist regards our prior givens as provisional rather than as ultimate. For extended discussion, see Arthur Pap, *The A Priori in Physical Theory* (New York, 1946), and the recent translation of Hans Reichenbach's path-breaking book of 1919, *The Theory of Relativity and A Priori Knowledge*. ed. and trans. Maria Reichenbach (Berkeley, 1965).
2. See, e.g., Fredric Jameson, *The Political Unconscious* (Ithaca, N. Y., 1981), p. 17: 'This book will argue the priority of the literary interpretation of literary texts. It conceives of the political perspective not as some supplementary method, not as an optional auxiliary to other interpretive methods current today . . . but rather as the absolute horizon of all reading and all interpretation.'
3. The a priorist would quickly observe that these questions themselves fall within a predetermined scheme. Yes, they do. The more fundamental issue is whether these pre-given questions (or frameworks) are themselves revisable. If so, they are predetermining only in a 'Pickwickian' sense, that is, not absolutely predetermining at all.
4. By no means do I consider semiotics to be an adequate account by itself, nor have I abandoned the principle of authorial intent. I have simply set aside that issue for the moment in order to focus on the nature of basic political choices in interpretation.
5. I have noted before that a priorist, autocratic critics invite us to pursue an allocratic interpretation

of their own writings — thus recognizing implicitly the reality of the autocratic/allocratic choice — by their actions if not by their theories.

6. Stanley Fish: 'No longer is the critic the humble [allocratic] servant of texts whose glories exist independently of anything he might do; it is what he [autocratically] does, within the constraints embedded in the literary institution, that brings texts into being and makes them available for analysis and appreciation' (*Is There a Text in This Class?* [Cambridge, Mass., 1980], p. 368). P. D. Juhl: 'There is a logical connection between statements about the meaning of a literary work and [allocratic] statements about the author's intention such that a statement about the meaning of a work *is* a statement about the author's intention' (*Interpretation* [Princeton, N. J., 1980], p. 12).

7. See Richard Rorty, 'Nineteenth-Century Idealism and Twentieth-Century Textualism,' *The Monist* 64 (1981): 155–74.

8. Pascal, *The 'Pensées,'* trans. J. M. Cohen (Harmondsworth, 1961), no. 451.

9. For instance, we might prefer to interpret Benjamin Frankin's proverb 'A rolling stone gathers no moss' *autocratically* as an admonishment to keep out of a rut, rather than allocratically as his admonishment to stay put. In this case my own preference is for the autocratic interpretation, and I would be willing to argue that in certain contexts it is the more valuable one. But in making that political choice, I haven't the slightest need of epistemological theories.

10. Gerald Graff has quoted Mussolini in a similar vein in *Literature Against Itself* ([Chicago, 1979], p. 188), and the two examples together show pretty well that the politics of interpretation, though now espoused by the intellectual Left, is not the exclusive property of any political group. Nor is it only a characteristic of the Right to take on the cloak of realism and 'spurious objectivity.' A political leftist can be an ideologue of truth and a realist-objectivist — such was Lenin. See the account of Lenin's realism and objectivism in Roger Trigg, *Reality at Risk: A Defense of Realism in Philosophy and the Sciences* (New York, 1980), pp. 27–39. See also the spirited defence of realism by a thinker whom nobody would call conservative, Paul Feyerabend, especially in his 'Realism and Instrumentalism,' *Realism, Rationalism, and Scientific Method: Philosophical Papers* (Cambridge, 1981), pp. 176–202. Another example would be the cohabitation of realism with Maoism in Hilary Putnam a few years back (see Putnam, *Philosophical Papers*, 2 vols. [London, 1975]). All of this further documents a primary thesis of this essay: that politics and epistemology are independent variables and that the attempt to sanction either of them by the other is basically a rhetorical (political) manoeuvre.

11. Max Weber, 'Science as a Vocation,' *From Max Weber: Essays in Sociology*, ed. and trans. H. H. Gerth and C. W. Mills (New York, 1946), p. 131.

3

Jerome J. McGann,
'The Text, the Poem, and the Problem of Historical Method'

I

At this point in academic time, the problem of historical method emerges most dramatically at the elementary levels of textual interpretation. The problem appears in two typical forms which are inversely related to each other. On the one hand, intrinsic critics cannot see that historical studies go to the heart of literary objects. Since the latter appear to address problems (and people) which are not historically limited, the 'problem' with historical studies is that they continue to be pursued at all. Why should works which transcend their originary moment require historical analysis and commentary?

On the other hand, historical method is also a problem for scholars and critics who work in any of the areas of extrinsic criticism: in bibliography and textual criticism, in philology, in biography and literary history, and so forth. In this case, the difficulty is that the scholar's work so often does seem irrelevant to the understanding and appreciation of poetry. What is most disturbing about this situation is that so few scholars even acknowledge that their methods require a theoretical grounding in hermeneutics.

These brief remarks will come as news to no one. We are all aware of the situation. Before I try to suggest how we might try to deal with these issues, however, permit me another brief essay into familiar territory. For I believe that we can best come to grips with these problems of historical method if we see more clearly how they came to assume their present form.

It is well known that the most advanced literary studies in the nineteenth century were those which developed and modified the enormous advances in theory and method made in classical and biblical philology and textual criticism. Wolf and Eichhorn are only the most familiar names among that group of brilliant, predominantly German, critics of the late eighteenth century who made the initial breakthrough in transforming literary studies into a modern scientific discipline. These are the scholars who created both the Lower (or textual) Criticism and the Higher (or philological) Criticism. Historical philology in the nineteenth century brought analytic techniques to bear upon previously synthesized material in order to see more clearly the strokes of the tulip and the parts of the rainbow. The most advanced of such critics — in England, men like Coleridge and Arnold — hoped to enlist these analytic techniques in the service of a new and higher synthesis: to

182

adapt Coleridge's famous declaration, by dissolving, diffusing, and dissipating, 'to recreate . . . to idealize and to unify'.

In the twentieth century, however, the historical methods of the Lower and Higher Criticism gave way before the advance of several sorts of form criticism and structural analysis. As we know, the principal impetus behind these critical movements came from language study and especially from linguistics. What Wolf, Lachmann, and Strauss were to nineteenth-century literary criticism, Saussure and Hjelmslev have been to the twentieth century. Hjelmslev's lucid *Prolegomena to a Theory of Language* (1943) accurately describes the shift which took place as a deliberate effort to break free of the descriptive, atomistic, and empirical approaches which flourished in the nineteenth century. 'The study of literature and the study of art', Hjelmslev says, had been carried out under 'historically descriptive rather than systematizing disciplines', and his project, which explicitly follows Saussure, proposes a systematic rather than an empirical analytic of humanistic phenomena. '*A priori* it would seem to be a generally valid thesis that for every *process* there is a corresponding *system*, by which the process can be analyzed and described by means of a limited number of premises. It must be assumed that any process can be analyzed into a limited number of elements recurring in various combinations.'[1] In this passage Hjelmslev prepares the ground for a systematic linguistics, but his words clearly underwrite any number of other twentieth-century programmes of a formal or structural sort (Bultmann in biblical criticism, Lévi-Strauss in anthropology, Propp, Greimas, and many others in literary studies). These new semiological methods can be applied in all humanistic disciplines, as Hjelmslev well knew.

The shift from an empirical to a structural analytic has deeply influenced twentieth-century approaches to literary works, with far-reaching consequences. Before I turn to them, however, and thus reconnect with my initial two-handed 'problem of historical method', let me point out an interesting peripheral remark in Hjelmslev's book. When he attacks the empirical methods of the nineteenth century, its anti-systematic bias, he also explains the particular aesthetic position which underlies that

> humanistic tradition which, in various dress, has till now predominated . . . According to this view, humanistic, as opposed to natural, phenomena, are non-recurrent and for that very reason cannot, like natural phenomena, be subjected to exact and generalizing treatment. In the field of the humanities, consequently, there would have to be a different method — namely, mere description, which would be nearer to poetry than to exact science — or, at any event, a method that restricts itself to a discursive form of presentation, in which the phenomena pass by, one by one, without being interpreted through a system (pp. 8–9).

As far as the appreciation of poetry is concerned, the nineteenth century's 'humanistic' methods sought to preserve and illuminate the uniqueness of the poetic object. We would do well to remember this fact about nineteenth-century philology, for in the modern period — as we survey those prelapsarian Germanic tomes of dryasdust scholarship — we do not always recall (indeed, their authors do not always recall) the aesthetic phenomena those critical procedures were designed to illuminate. Our preoccupation with the minute particularities of poetical works emerged from the philological traditions which gave us 'textual criticism'. The contemporary vulgarization of this philological term eloquently demonstrates the position that modern literary studies takes in relation to its immediate forebears.

The structural and semiological approaches to language and, in particular, to literature provided modern critics with operational procedures for analysing literature in a Kantian mode. In the *Critique of Judgement*, Kant offered a novel philosophy of art grounded in the notion that aesthetic works were integral phenomena whose finality was exhausted in the individual's experience of the work. The modern concept of 'the poem itself' as a self-referential linguistic system is fundamentally Kantian, though twentieth-century developments in linguistics provided this Kantian approach with its basic procedural rules for an actual critical practice.

These procedural rules operated under one fundamental premise: that literary works are special sorts of linguistic 'texts', that every poem is coextensive with its linguistic structure. Twentieth-century literary criticism contains a rich variety of schools and methods — analytical, structural, rhetorical, stylistic — but for all their important differences, they tend to share the conviction that poems are self-subsistent linguistic systems. The function of criticism is to illuminate the operations of those linguistic structures which we now like to call 'text'. According to the classic formulation of Roman Jakobson: 'Poetics deals with problems of verbal structure . . . Since linguistics is the global science of verbal structure, poetics may be regarded as an integral part of linguistics.'[2]

This idea of the poem as verbal object is so commonplace in modern criticism that we may seem perverse to question it. Still we must do so, for the 'problem of historical method' — whether we approach it from an 'intrinsic' or an 'extrinsic' point of view — will never be opened to solutions until we see one of the signal failures of modern criticism: its inability to distinguish clearly between a concept of the *poem* and a concept of the *text*. Indeed, when we recover this essential analytic distinction, we will begin to reacquire some other, equally crucial distinctions which have fallen into disuse: for example, the distinction between concepts of *poem* and of *poetical work*. For the present I will concentrate on the first of these distinctions, and my analysis will proceed through a series of illustrative examples.[3]

II

When Byron sent the manuscript of *Don Juan* Cantos I and II to his publisher John Murray late in 1818, the poet was not only, with Goethe, the most famous writer in the Western world, his works were the most saleable products on the English literary market. He was not an author Murray wanted to lose. But this new work set Murray back on his heels. He was filled with wonder at its genius and with loathing at its immorality — at its obscenity, its blasphemy, its libellous attacks upon the poet laureate, and its seditious attitude toward the English government's policies at home and abroad.[4]

In the struggle that ensued, Murray and his London circle (which included some of Byron's best and oldest friends) pressed the poet either to withdraw the poem altogether or to revise it drastically and remove its objectionable parts. Byron agreed to some revisions, but his final line of retreat still seemed a fearful one to his publisher. When Byron threatened to take his poem elsewhere, Murray agreed to publish; he did not, however, tell his celebrated author precisely *how* he would publish.

For Murray, the problem was how to issue this inflammatory work without provoking a legal action against himself either by the government directly or by the notorious Society for the Suppression of Vice. His plan of action was ingenious but, in the end, self-defeating. Murray decided to issue a short run (1,500 copies) of the poem in a sumptuous quarto edition and to print it without either Byron's name as author or even his own as publisher. The price — £1 11s. 6d. — was set high in order to ensure a circulation limited alike in numbers and in social class.

The immediate effect of this manoeuvre was successful, for *Don Juan* stole into the world without provoking any moral outcry. The earliest reviewers were generally quite favourable, even from entrenched conservative quarters like *The Literary Gazette*.

But Murray's plan for avoiding the censors failed, in the end, because it was, in the words of Hugh J. Luke, Jr., 'a contradictory one'.[5] Murray avoided prosecution for issuing *Don Juan*, but his method of publication ensured a widespread piratical printing of the poem in the radical press. Thousands of copies of *Don Juan* were issued in cheap pirated editions, and as the work received wider celebrity and distribution, so the moral outcry against it was raised, and spread.

The significance which this story holds for my present purposes — i.e. for my aim to elucidate the problematics of the 'text' — is neatly explained by an anonymous article (possibly by Southey) printed in the conservative *Quarterly Review* in April 1822. In its quarto form, the reviewer notes, *Don Juan*

> would have been confined by its price to a class of readers with whom its faults might have been somewhat compensated by its merits; with whom the ridicule, which it endeavors to throw upon virtue, might have been partially balanced by that with which it covers vice, particularly the vice to which the class of readers to whom we are alluding are most subject — that which pleads romantic sensibility, or ungovernable passion; to readers, in short, who would have turned with disgust from its indecencies, and remembered only its poetry and its wit.[6]

But the poem was issued in numerous cheap piracies and therein lay the mischief, 'some publishing it with obscene engravings, others in weekly numbers, and all in a shape that brought it within the reach of purchasers on whom its poison would operate without mitigation — who would search its pages for images to pamper a depraved imagination, and for a sanction for the insensibility to the sufferings of others, which is often one of the most unhappy results of their own.' In short, as the reviewer says so well: ' "Don Juan" in quarto and on hotpressed paper would have been almost innocent — in a whity-brown duodecimo it was one of the worst of the mischievous publications that have made the press a snare.'

Several important conclusions follow from this eventful narrative. In the first place, the example illustrates how different texts, in the bibliographical sense, embody different poems (in the aesthetic sense) despite the fact that both are linguistically identical. In the second place, the example also suggests that the method of printing or publishing a literary work carries with it enormous cultural and aesthetic significance for the work itself. Finally, we can begin to see, through this example, that the essential character of a work of art is not determined *sui generis* but is, rather, the result of a process involving the actions and interactions of a specific and socially integrated group of people.[7]

The contemporary fashion of calling literary works 'texts' carries at least one unhappy critical result: it suggests that poems and works of fiction possess their integrity *as poems and works of fiction* totally aside from the events and materials describable in their bibliographies. In this usage we are dealing with 'texts' which transcend their concrete and actual textualities. This usage of the word *text* does not mean anything written or printed in an actual physical state; rather, it means the opposite: it points to an *Ur*-poem or meta-work whose existence is the Idea that can be abstracted out of all concrete and written texts which have ever existed or which ever will exist.[8] All these different texts are what can be called — Ideally — 'The Text'.

This Ideal Text is the object of almost all the critical scrutiny produced in the New Critical and post-New Critical traditions, whether formal, stylistic, or structural.[9] To arrive at such a Text, however, the critic normally obligates himself to make certain that his physical text is 'correct', which is to say that it corresponds, linguistically, to the author's final intentions about what editors call his work's substantive and accidental features. By meeting this obligation the critic pays his dues to the philological traditions of the last three hundred years. At the same time, the critic places himself in a position from which he can treat the literary work as if it were a timeless object, unconnected with history. The Text is viewed *sub specie aeternitatis*, and modern criticism approaches it much as the pre-critical scholar of Sacred Scripture approached the Word of God.

But in fact not even a linguistic uniformity sanctioned by philology can deliver over to us a final, definitive Text which will be the timeless object of critical interpretation and analysis. The example from Byron suggests this, clearly, but that case is merely paradigmatic. No literary work is definable purely in linguistic terms, and the illustration from Byron could easily be replaced by examples from any writer one might choose. It would not be very difficult to show, from the works of William Blake, that linguistic uniformity will hardly serve to establish a definitive Text. Of course everyone knows that Blake's *words* do not comprehend Blake's 'poetical works', so that (Ideally) critics recognize the necessity of 'reading' Blake in facsimile editions; and, in fact, facsimile editions do deliver more of Blake's work to the reader. But a Blake text comprising both words and illustrative matter still falls short of delivering this artist's work to an audience today.

Since Blake's work operates in an integrated verbal and visual medium, we are forced to see that the 'linguistic level' of this work corresponds to the entire mixed medium and not merely to the verbal one. But that Blake's 'poetical works' are not finished and complete in some Ideal mixed-medium Text is apparent if we simply recall the character of Blake's original methods of 'publication'. He is probably the most private and individualistic artist ever to emerge from England, and each of his engraved works was a unique publication by itself. It was part of Blake's artistic project that each of his works *be* unique, and he in fact achieved his purpose — most notoriously, I suppose, in his masterwork *Jerusalem*. Fewer than ten original copies of this work survive, and each is quite distinct. To speak of the Text of *Jerusalem*, then, as if that term comprehended some particular concrete reality rather than a heuristic idea, is manifestly to talk nonsense. One might as well try to speak of the Text of Emily Dickinson's verse. In reality, there is no such Text; there are only texts, of various kinds, prepared by various people (some by the author), at various periods, for particular and various purposes.

Yet the example of Blake carries a moral which takes us beyond the insight that an artist's work is not equivalent to an Ideal Text, nor even to some particular text or edition (say, an especially meticulous one prepared by a skilled editor). For every work of art is the product of an interaction between the artist, on the one hand, and a variety of social determinants on the other. Even the simplest textual problem — establishing a work's *linguistic* correctness — can involve other problems that are, quite literally, insoluble. Keats, we recall, wrote two distinct and finished versions of 'La Belle Dame Sans Merci'.[10] But even if one were to set aside these special problems and assume that we can establish 'the author's final intentions' toward the language or even the entire format of a work, we would still have, as readers, merely one text of the work, or — as scholars — the means for producing a number of possible editions, or texts.

The fact is that the works of an artist are produced, at various times and places, and by many different sorts of people, in a variety of different textual constitutions (some better than others). Each of these texts is the locus of a process of artistic production and consumption involving the originary author, other people (his audience[s], his publisher, etc.), and certain social institutions. Blake's special way of creating his works emphasizes the presence of these impinging social factors precisely because Blake strove so resolutely, even so obsessively, to produce work that was wholly his own. Each original copy of *Jerusalem* is unique, and in them Blake has achieved an extraordinary degree of artistic freedom. Had his work been reproduced through the procedures maintained by the ordinary publishing institutions of his day, it would have been a very different product altogether (it would have been reviewed, for example, and it would have fallen into many people's hands).[11] Nor are these differences merely accidental, and unimportant for the 'meaning' of Blake's work. Certainly to Blake they seemed immensely consequential; indeed — and he was quite right — they seemed definitive of the difference between one sort of art (free, creative) and another (commonplace, generalized).

In his own day Blake insisted upon having his artistic freedom, and the proper measure of his success in this aim — ironic though it seems — lies in his contemporary artistic anonymity. Yet the social life of an artist transcends his particular historical moment, and so Blake, lost to his own age, was 'discovered' by the Pre-Raphaelites, who initiated the process of full social integration which his work has since achieved. Blake's unique works, in consequence, would become mass-produced, and his fierce individuality would itself become deeply integrated into various ideologies and social institutions. We may well see an irony in this event. Even more, however, should we see how it illustrates a fundamental fact about all art: that it is a social product with various, and changing, social functions to perform.

The initial example from Byron and the general case of Blake illustrate very clearly, I think, that a work of art — a poem, in this case — is no more the isolate creation of an artist than 'the poem itself' is defined either by some particular text on the one hand, or by the Ideal Text on the other. Poems are artistic works produced, and maintained, under specific socialized conditions. It is the business of analytic criticism to isolate and categorize the various social factors which meet and interact in various works of art, and finally, to explain those interactions.

In attempting to show how different poetical works have acquired different textual constitutions, I have drawn attention to certain physical characteristics of some texts of *Don Juan* and *Jerusalem*. The physical differences between the several texts stand as signs of a productive process which is different in each case, and which, consequently, produces several different artistic works. The first two cantos of *Don Juan*, as issued by Murray, are not the same work as the first two cantos as issued by the pirates. The fact that Byron's *Don Juan* should have called out these two sorts of edition is one sign of its creative power, just as the poem's long and complex bibliographical history has testified to its trans-historical character and relevance.

Let there be no confusion in this matter, however: when we see that an author's work exists in many different textual constitutions, we do not mean to suggest that, for example, there are as many poems called *Jerusalem* as there are texts or editions. We must resist the modern fashion of referring to poems as 'texts' precisely because this vulgar usage confuses the fundamental difference between a poem's *text* — which is one thing — and a poem — which is quite another. Preserving this distinction is crucial for purposes of critical method, since the distinction facilitates a clear view of a poem's changing life in human society. Speaking of poems as 'texts' implicitly affirms an idea of literary works which involves two contradictory propositions: (1) that a poem is equivalent to its linguistic constitution and (2) that the textual differences in a poem's bibliographical history have no necessary relation to issues of literary criticism as such. The poem-as-text, then, is a critical idea which at once reduces poetry to a verbal construct and inflates it to the level of an immaterial, non-particular pure Idea (the poem as Ideal Text). This result seems paradoxical, but in fact it is the necessary consequence of a view of literary works which is founded on a contradiction.

The example of *Don Juan* must not be taken to suggest, however, that a poetical work is the product of a social engagement entered into, voluntarily or otherwise, by author, printer, and publisher alone. Rather, the local publishing relationship among these three persons is itself a sign needing critical analysis. The fact that Blake deliberately avoided any involvement in this, the normal publishing relationship of his day, is of immense critical significance for his work and especially for a late work like *Jerusalem*. To know the publishing options taken (and refused) by Chaucer, or Donne, or Pope, or Blake, or Byron enables the critic to explain the often less visible, but more fundamental, social engagements which meet in and generate the work in question.

The illustration from Byron is especially illuminating because it brings to our attention another crucial productive figure (anterior to the audience of consumers) who participates in the artistic process initiated by the artist. I mean, of course, the reviewer (or critic), who is the final mediating force between author and audience. It is the function of the (contemporary) reviewer and (subsequent) critic to make explicit the lines of interpretation which exist *in potentia* in their respective audiences. Critics and reviewers — to adapt a phrase from Shelley — imagine what students and audiences already know about the works they are to read.

III

At this point in the analysis, though we have, I believe, established the generic functional usefulness of preserving distinctions among texts, poems, and poetical works, the specific value of such distinctions for literary criticism is still unclear. Are these the sort of distinctions which, in the end, make no difference?

In the example which follows I mean to illustrate two related points: first (on the negative side), that the failure to maintain these distinctions creates a procedural error which necessarily threatens any subsequent practical criticism with disaster; and second (on the positive side), that the pursuit and elucidation of such distinctions sharply increases our understanding of poetry and poems in both the theoretical and the practical spheres. This second aspect of the demonstration will return us to the 'problem of historical method' which was raised at the outset. By framing these historically self-conscious demonstrations along the traditional 'intrinsic' lines of formal and thematic analysis, I propose to show: (1) that poems are, by the nature of the case (or, as Kant might say, 'transcendentally'), time- and place-specific; (2) that historical analysis is, therefore, a necessary and essential function of any advanced practical criticism.

The case I propose to consider is Allen Tate's famous interpretation of Emily Dickinson's poem 'Because I could not Stop for Death'.[12] His discussion raises, once again, the whole range of unresolved problems which lie in wait for any critical method which cannot make serious distinctions between texts and poems.

Tate begins by quoting the poem in full and declaring it to be 'one of the greatest in the English language' and 'one of the perfect poems in English'. His argument for these judgements rests upon T. S. Eliot's famous discussion of the 'dissociation of sensibility'. Dickinson's poem is 'perfect' because it displays a perfect 'fusion of sensibility and thought': 'The framework of the poem is, in fact, the two abstractions, mortality and eternity, which are made to associate in equality with images: she sees the ideas, and thinks the perceptions. She did, of course, nothing of the sort; but we must use the logical distinctions, even to the extent of paradox, if we are to form any notion of this rare quality of mind' (p. 161). Tate argues for this general position by instancing what he sees as the poem's precision and tight structure of rhythm, image, and theme. The poem has nothing to excess; it is marked throughout by 'a restraint that keeps the poet from carrying' her dramatic images too far. As for the poem's ideas, they are something altogether different from 'the feeble poetry of moral ideals that flourished in New England in the eighties':

> The terror of death is objictified through this figure of the genteel driver, who is made ironically to serve the end of Immortality. This is the heart of the poem: she has presented a typical Christian theme in its final irresolution, without making any final statements about it. There is no solution to the problem; there can be only a presentation of it in the full context of intellect and feeling. A construction of the human will, elaborated with all the abstracting powers of the mind, is put to the concrete test of experience: the idea of immortality is confronted with the fact of physical disintegration. We are not told what to think; we are told to look at the situation. (p. 161)

In evaluating this criticism we begin with the text quoted by Tate. When he calls the poem 'The Chariot', as he does at the beginning of his discussion, he tells us what his text shows: Tate is reading the work printed in 1890 by Todd and Higginson. But of course, 'The Chariot' is not what Dickinson wrote, at any time; rather, it is a text which her first editors produced when they carefully worked over the (untitled) text written by the author. Among other, less significant changes, an entire stanza was removed (the fourth) and several lines underwent major alteration.[13] Since Tate's argument for the greatness of the poem depends heavily upon his view of its linguistic perfection, we are faced with a rather awkward situation. Under the circumstances, one would not find it very difficult to embarrass Tate's reading by subjecting it to an ironical inquisition on the subject of textual criticism.

Of course, Tate had no access to the text Dickinson actually wrote. Nevertheless, his critical judgement ought to have been warned that textual problems existed since he did have available to him another — and, as it happens, more accurate — text of Dickinson's work. This text appeared in Martha Dickinson Bianchi's 1924 edition of *The Complete Poems*, and it is the one cited by Yvor Winters in the critique of Tate's essay first published by Winters in *Maule's Curse*.[14] But Tate's critical method could not prepare him to deal with problems in textual criticism. Indeed, he could not even *see* such problems, much less analyse their critical relevance. In this case, the impoverished historical sense of his general critical method appears as an inability to make critical judgements about poetic texts, to make distinctions between poems and their texts, and to relate those judgements and distinctions to the final business of literary criticism.

We have no call, nor any desire, to ridicule Tate's essay on this matter. Nevertheless, the issue must be faced squarely, for the problems raised by Tate's lack of textual scrupulousness appear at other points, and in other forms, in his discussion, and his example typifies the sorts of problem that remain widespread in Western modes of formal, stylistic, structural, and post-structural procedures. We may observe the congruence of his critical practice — the symmetry between his lack of interest in textual matters and his general interpretive approach — by examining his remarks on the poem's thematic concerns. We shall notice two matters here: first, a tendency to overread the poem at the linguistic level; and second, a reluctance to take seriously, or even notice, either the fact or the importance of the poem's ideological attitudes. In each case we are dealing with something fundamental to Tate's literary criticism and to twentieth-century interpretive approaches generally: their attempt to lift the poem out of its original historical context and to erase the distance between that original context and the immediate context of the critical act.

In this next phase of my analysis, then, I am proposing to extend the discussion from its specific interest in 'the problem of the text' to the more general issue which that problem localizes. Critics who do not or cannot distinguish between the different concrete texts which a poem assumes in its historical passage are equally disinclined to study the aesthetic significance of a poem's topical dimensions, or its didactic, ethical, or ideological materials. Poems that have no textual histories have, at the thematic level, only those meanings and references which 'transcend' the particulars of time and place. The poetry of poems, in this view, is a function not of specific ideology or topical matters but of 'universal' themes and references — and the *most* universal of these universals are a poem's formal, stylistic, or structural excellences. The ultimate consequence of such approaches is that the present critic loses altogether his awareness that his own criticism is historically limited and time-bound in very specific ways. Losing a critical sense of the past, the interpreter necessarily loses his ability to see his own work in a critical light.

Let me return to Tate's analysis and the Dickinson poem, however, where we can study these problems as they emerge in concrete forms. When Tate says, for example, that the poem presents 'the problems of immortality . . . confronted with the fact of physical disintegration', we observe a critical move characteristic of twentieth-century criticism: that is, the habit of dealing with poetry's substantive concerns at the most abstract and generalized thematic levels. I will have more to say about this sort of critical abstraction in a moment. For now we want most to query Tate's interpretation of the thematic aspects of the Dickinson poem. When he argues, for example, that the poem does not treat 'moral ideas', and that it takes a non-committal ('unresolved') stance toward a serious intellectual problem, we

are surely justified in demurring. The civil kindliness of Death is of course ironically presented, but the irony operates at the expense of those who — foolishly,
the poem implies — regard Death as a fearful thing and who give all their attention to their mortal affairs ('My labor, and my leisure too') either because of their
fear or as a consequence of it. Like the poem's speaker before Death 'stopped' for
her, the readers of the poem are assumed to be fearful of Death and too busy with
the affairs of their lives to 'stop' for him.[15] The poem does indeed have a 'a moral',
and it appears in an unmistakable form in the final stanza:

> Since then — 'tis Centuries — and yet
> Feels shorter than the Day
> I first surmised the Horses Heads
> Were toward Eternity —

'We are not told what to think' by the poem, Tate asserts, but his position is only
technically correct. Of course the poem does not *tell* us what to think, but its message about the benevolence of Death is plain enough. This message, however, like
the poem which carries it, is no simple-minded pronouncement; the message is rich
and affecting because it is delivered in human rather than abstract space.
Dickinson's poem locates a set of relationships in which Dickinson, her fictive
speaker, and her invited readers engage with each other in various emotional and
intellectual ways.[16] The focus of these engagements is the poem's commonplace
Christian theme: that people who are too busily involved with their worldly affairs
give little serious thought to Death and the Afterlife. Criticizing such thought-
lessness, the poem encourages its readers to ponder Death and the Afterlife in a
positive way. Its procedure for doing so involves the assumption of another thematic commonplace — that people fear to think about Death — and then undermining its force by a play of wit.

The wit appears most plainly in the rhetorical structure of the poem, which
pretends to be spoken by a person already dead. Like some Christian Blessed
Damozel from New England, Dickinson's speaker addresses this world from the
other side, as it were, and lets us know that Death leads us not to oblivion but to
'Eternity' and 'Immortality'.[17] But the wit goes deeper, for Dickinson does not
present her fiction as anything *but* fiction. The playfulness of the poem — which is
especially evident in the final stanza, whose quiet good humour has been remarked
upon frequently — is the work's most persuasive argument that Death can be con-
templated not merely without fear but — more positively — with feelings of civilized affection. The kindliness and civility of the carriage driver are qualities we
recognize in the *voice* of the poem's speaker and in the *wit* of its maker.

When we speak of the poem's wit, however, we should not lose ourselves in a
hypnotic fascination with its verbal reality alone. The wit is at least as much a function of Dickinson's perspicuous observations of, and comments upon, social reality
as it is of her facility with language. We may see this more clearly if we recall the
standard critical idea that the figure of Death in this poem is — in the words of a
recent critic — a 'gentlemanly suitor'.[18] Tate seems to have initiated this reading
when he spoke of the driver as 'a gentleman taking a lady out for a drive', and when
he proceeded to notice the 'erotic motive' associated with 'this figure of the genteel
driver'. His commentary shows an acute awareness of one of the poem's subtlest

and least explicit aspects, but it also displays a failure to see a more obvious but no less important fact about the driver.

This man is not a suitor but an undertaker, as we see quite clearly in the penultimate line's reference to 'Horses Heads'.[19] This small matter of fact has considerable importance for anyone wishing to develop an accurate critical account of the poem. It forces us to see, for example, that the journey being presented is not some unspecified drive in the country, but a funeral ride which is located quite specifically in relation to Emily Dickinson and her Amherst world. The hearse in the poem is on its way out from Pleasant Street, past Emily Dickinson's house, to the cemetery located at the northern edge of the town just beyond the Dickinson homestead.[20] Of course, these details are not verbalized into the Dickinson poem as explicit description. They are only present implicitly, as an originally evoked context which we — at our historical remove — can (and must) reconstitute if we wish to focus and explain the special emotional character of the work.

Consider once again, for example, the undertaker who appears in the poem. The behaviour of this man — his correctness, his rather stiff but kindly formality, his manner of driving the carriage — defines a character-type well-known in nineteenth-century culture, and a favourite one with contemporary caricaturists.[21] Behind the civility and kindly formal behaviour of Emily Dickinson's undertaker lies a tradition which saw in this man a figure of grotesque obsequiousness, as we know from Mark Twain's memorable scene in *Huckleberry Finn*. Indeed, I do not see how one could fully appreciate the finesse of what Tate calls the 'erotic motive' without also seeing just how the poem plays with it, and how Dickinson's poetic style both *re*presents and quietly modifies the contemporary stereotype of this important social functionary so well known to the inhabitants of towns like Amherst. The poem's general ideology, as a work of Christian consolation, would be merely religious claptrap without these 'poetic'[22] elements; and such elements can only escape the critical method which does not seek to grasp the poem at a level more comprehensive than a merely lingusitic one.

The power of the poem, then, rests in its ability to show us not merely the thoughts and feelings of Dickinson and her fictive speaker, but the attitudes of her implied readers as well. For all her notorious privacy, Emily Dickinson is, like every poet, a creator of those structures of social energy which we call poems. 'Because I could not Stop for Death' locates not merely an expressive lyrical act, but a significant relationship between the poet and her readers which we, as still later readers, are meant to recognize, enter into, and (finally) extend. Our sympathy with the poem may not be the same as that felt by a Christian reader, whether contemporary with the poem or not; nevertheless, it is *continuous* with the sympathy of such readers (who are consciously and explicitly assumed by the poem) because it takes those readers as seriously as it takes Emily Dickinson and her fictive speaker. Indeed, it must do this, for all are part of the poem in question. Later readers may not share the ideologies of the people represented by this poem, but they cannot read it without recognizing and respecting those ideologies — without, in fact, perpetuating them in a critical human memory whose sympathetic powers are drawn from a historical consciousness.

Having discussed the 'ideological set' of this poem — its poetically rendered 'message' — let us return to Allen Tate's essay, where an absence of ideological commitments is imputed to Dickinson's work. We return to ask why Tate should insist upon 'misreading' the poem as he has done.

The reason emerges when we ponder carefully Tate's use of T. S. Eliot. Tate's interpretation shows that he shares Eliot's ideas about how moral concepts should appear in verse (not 'didactically' but dramatically); that he prizes Eliot's views on Metaphysical verse and its excellences; and that he is anxious to deliver his praise of Dickinson's poem in critical terms that will draw her into the company of those poets who illustrate Eliot's standards. In short, Tate reads Emily Dickinson in the same spirit that Eliot read Donne and the Metaphysicals. *Why* Tate, and Eliot before him, should have taken such a position toward the moral aspects of poetry — and especially of Christian poetry in its various forms — is beyond the scope of this analysis, though scholars recognize that the answer lies in the historical factors which generated modernism and its various ideologies.[23]

I have not dwelt upon Tate's discussion in order to debunk it, but rather in order to show the consonance between his interpretation of the Dickinson poem and his ignorance of its textual problems. Tate's eye is no more focused upon Dickinson's poem than it is on the 1890 text of 'The Chariot'. Rather, Tate has 'taken "The Chariot" for his text', as we might say of one who delivers a sermon or a moral lesson. 'The Chariot' is the occasion for his ideological polemic on behalf of certain aesthetic criteria.

One important lesson to be drawn from this investigation of Tate's essay is that literary criticism — and even the analysis of poems — is not fundamentally a study of verbal structure *per se*. The very existence of Tate's influential and justly admired essay demonstrates that fact. Literary criticism must study poetic texts — the 'verbal structures' of poems — but the analysis of these verbal structures does not comprehend a poetic analysis. This paradox of critical method emerges forcibly in Tate's essay, which dramatizes, in its very limitations, the distinction between text and poem — a distinction, indeed, which Tate's analysis is incapable of making. Yet the distinction must be made — and textual criticism, in the traditional sense, must be revived among literary critics — if our received works of literature are to regain their full human resources — that is to say, if the entire history of poetry and all the potential of specific poems are to be made known and available to each new generation. Poetry and poems are, in this sense, transhistorical, but they acquire this perpetuity by virtue of the particular historical adventures which their texts undergo from their first appearance before their author's eyes through all their subsequent constitutions.

The textual histories of poems, in other words, are paradigm instances of the historically specific character of all poetry. By clarifying the distinction between a poem and its various texts, the examples from Byron and Blake illustrate the need for a systematic theory and method of historical criticism. On the other hand, the example from Dickinson argues, at the level of practical criticism, the specific critical powers inherent in a historical method. These powers appear as a special capacity for elucidating, in a systematic way, whatever in a poem is most concrete, local, and particular to it. Criticism cannot analyse poems, or reveal their special characteristics and values, if it abstracts away from their so-called accidental features. Attending merely to the formal or linguistic phenomena of poems constitutes an initial and massive act of absraction from what are some of the most crucial particulars of all poems.

Facing the poem and its texts, then, historical criticism tries to define what is most peculiar and distinctive in specific poetical works. Moreover, in specifying these unique features and sets of relationships, it transcends the concept of the-poem-as-verbal-object to reveal the poem as a special sort of communication event. This new understanding of poems takes place precisely because the critical act, occurring in a self-conscious present, can turn to look upon poems created in the past not as fixed objects but as the locus of certain past human experiences. Some of these are dramatized *in* the poems, while others are preserved *through* the poetical works, which embody various human experiences *with* the poems, beginning with the author's own experiences. In this way does a historical criticism define poetry not as a formal structure or immediate event but as a continuing human process. That *act* of definition is the fundamental *fact* of literary criticism.

The new fact about *historical* criticism, however, is that it systematically opposes its own reification. Being first of all an *act* of definition rather than a *set* of definitions, historical criticism calls attention to the time-specific and heuristic character of its abstraction. Like the poetry it studies, criticism is always tendentious because it always seeks to define and preserve human values. One of the special values of historical criticism, to my view at any rate, lies in its eagerness to specify and examine its polemical positions. This self-critical aspect of an historical approach seems to be a direct function of its basic method, for in attempting to specify historical distinctions, we set a gulf between our past and our present. It is this gulf which enables us to judge and criticize the past, but it is equally this gulf which enables the past — so rich in its achievements — to judge and criticize us. Thus in our differences do we learn about, and create, a community.

Notes:

1. Louis Hjelmslev, *Prolegomena to a Theory of Language*, trans. Francis J. Whitfield, Madison, 1961, p. 9.
2. Roman Jakobson, 'Linguistics and Poetics', in *Style in Language*, ed. T. A. Sebeok, Cambridge, Mass., 1960, p. 350. In the latest, post-structural phase of these traditions the models are more generically semiological than linguistic. The shift in emphasis — from specific 'text' to the process of 'textuality' — marks the increased self-consciousness in this tradition, but not a departure from its fundamental premises.
3. Literary criticism in general would benefit if certain clear distinctions were preserved when using words (and concepts) like *text, poem*, and *poetical work*. In the present essay, the word *text* is used as a purely bibliographical concept which means to deal with the material of poetry in a purely physical or impersonal frame of reference. The term deliberately abstracts away the critic's or the reader's immediate (social) point of view. Poetry is a social phenomenon, but the concept of *text* withholds from consideration all matters that relate to the involvement of reader or audience in the reproduction of the work. It does so, of course, for analytic purposes, and *only provisionally*. I propose that we use the term *text* when we deal with poems as they are part of a productive (or reproductive) process, but when we are withholding from consideration all matters that relate to the process of consumption. *Poem*, on the other hand, is the term I will use to refer to the work as it is the locus of a specific process of production (or reproduction) and consumption. *Poetical work* is my term for the global history of some particular work's process of production/reproduction and consumption. I use the term *poetry* to refer generically to imaginative literary works without respect to any specific social or historical factors. The terms *text* and *Ideal Text* also appear in this essay, and these refer to various (non-historical and non-sociological) twentieth-century critical concepts.

    I hope it is clear that these distinctions mean to counter the semiological approach to the concepts of *text* and *textuality*. A paradigm example of the latter approach will be found in Roland Barthes' famous essay 'From Work to Text'.

4. See *Don Juan: A Variorum Edition*, ed. T. G. Steffan and W. W. Pratt, Austin, 1957, i. 11–32 and iv. 293–308.

5. 'The Publishing of *Don Juan*', PMLA lxxx (June 1965), p. 200.

6. For the *Quarterly Review* quotations see ibid., p. 202.

7. Cf. Levin Schüking, *The Sociology of Literary Taste*, London, 1966.

8. Post-structural critiques of their own (formalist) tradition have been widespread during the past ten years and have contributed to the break-up of the academic consensus which developed between 1935 and 1965. See John Fekete, *The Critical Twilight*, London, 1978. The attacks upon the New Criticism have tended to accuse it of an arrogant and technocratic empiricism, with its insistence upon taking the poem as *sui generis*. These attacks — see Richard Palmer, *Hermeneutics* (Evanston, 1969), for example — charge the New Criticism with a crude theory of the poem as 'object' or 'thing'. This sort of attack is deeply misguided and misses entirely the fundamental Idealism of both the New Criticism in particular and its later formalist context in general. A revisionist commentator like Gerald Graff has been able to see the mistake in such critiques and to suggest what is in fact the case: that New Criticism and its academic inheritors (including many of its recent antagonists) are part of a single tradition (*Literature Against Itself*, Chicago, 1979, chap. 5). As Graff notes, New Criticism was marked throughout by contradictions along an Ideal/Empirical fault-line; nor could it have been otherwise with a fundamentally Idealist theory which was seeking to establish its authority in a scientific, rational, and technological world. Graff's views have been anticipated by a number of trenchant critiques put out from relatively orthodox Marxist writers: see, e.g. Robert Weimann, 'Past Significance and Present Meaning in Literary History', in *New Directions in Literary History*, ed. Ralph Cohen, Baltimore, 1974, esp. pp. 43–50.

9. That an Ideal Text is the object of contemporary 'textual' interpreters is patent; see also Tony Bennett, *Formalism and Marxism*, London, 1979, pp. 70–1.

10. For a more thorough discussion see McGann, 'Keats and the Historical Method in Literary Criticism' in *The Beauty of Inflections* (Oxford, Clarendon Press, 1985).

11. As is well known, Blake purchased his artistic freedom at a fearful personal cost, for his conscious artistic policies ensured his contemporary isolation. Appealing to what Byron called 'the Avenger, Time', Blake's work had to wait for the justice of history. Cf. the discussion in J. W. Saunders, *The Profession of Letters*, London, 1964, pp. 146–73 *passim* and, on Blake particularly, pp. 164–6; see also Jerome J. McGann, *A Critique of Modern Textual Criticism*, Chicago, 1983, pp. 44–7.

12. This is poem no. 172 in *The Poems of Emily Dickinson*, ed. Thomas H. Johnson, Cambridge, Mass., 1955, ii. 546–7. For Tate's discussion, see his 'New England Culture and Emily Dickinson', in *The Recognition of Emily Dickinson*, ed. C. E. Blake and C. F. Wells, Ann Arbor, 1968, pp. 153–67, esp. pp. 160–2, from which the quotations below are taken.

13. See *Poems by Emily Dickinson*, ed. Mabel Loomis Todd and Thomas W. Higginson, Boston, 1890. Also see Johnson's edition, where the textual issues are succinctly presented.

14. Winters's essay is reprinted in *The Recognition of Emily Dickinson*; see esp. pp. 192–3.

15. This motif is an ancient one in the tradition of Christian art and poetry. For its biblical sources see Matt. 24:43 and 1 Thess. 5:2–4. An excellent contemporary example is to be found in Alan Dugan's 'Tribute to Kafka for Someone Taken'.

16. See V. N. Volosinov (i.e. M. M. Bakhtin), 'Discourse in Life and Discourse in Art', in *Freudianism, A Marxist Critique*, trans. I. R. Titunik, New York, 1976, where Bakhtin distinguishes among the author, the reader, and the figure he calls 'the hero' or the 'third participant'.

17. In adopting this rhetorical model, Dickinson was following a literary practice that had grown extremely popular in the nineteenth century. See Ann Douglas, 'Heaven Our Home: Consolation Literature in the Northern United States 1830–1880', in *Death in America*, ed. Daniel Stannard, Philadelphia, 1974; see esp. pp. 58–9, 61–2. But the procedure is deeply traditional: see also Rosemary Woolf, *English Religious Lyric in the Middle Ages*, Oxford, 1963, chap. 9 *passim*.

18. Robert Weisbuch, *Emily Dickinson's Poetry*, Chicago, 1972, p. 114.

19. That is to say, a suitor's carriage would have had only one horse.

20. The hearse's journey to the Amherst cemetery — one of the new, so-called rural cemeteries — must have been appallingly familiar to Emily Dickinson. The mortality rate in Amherst was high, and Emily Dickinson's room overlooked the cemetery route. See Millicent Todd Bingham, *Emily Dickinson's Home*, New York, 1955, the map facing p. 62 and pp. 179–80; also Jay Leyda, *The Years and Hours of Emily Dickinson*, New Haven, 1960, ii. 2–3. Emily Dickinson's bedroom was the best vantage in the house for observing the stately procession of the funeral hearse as it moved out from Pleasant Street to the cemetery. The special location of the Dickinson house meant that the funeral hearse would always pass by, no matter where the deceased

person had lived in town. One should also note that the poem's references to the 'School' and the 'Fields of Gazing Grain' are precise. In point of fact, 'Because I could not Stop for Death' narrates the imagined (not imaginary) journey of the hearse from somewhere in the central part of Amherst out along Pleasant Street, past the schoolhouse on the left, and out to the beginning of the 'Fields of Gazing Grain', at which point the undertaker would have turned to the right and driven past more fields to the gravesite. For a general discussion of the rural cemetery see Neil Harris, 'The Cemetery Beautiful', in *Passing: The Vision of Death in America*, ed. Charles O. Jackson, Westport, 1977, pp. 103–11.

21. See Alfred Scott Warthen, 'The Period of Caricature' and 'The Modern Dance of Death', in *The Physician of the Dance of Death*, New York, 1934. Twain was fond of presenting the undertaker from a comic point of view. See *Huckleberry Finn*, chap. 27, and his essay 'The Undertaker's Chat'.

22. What makes them 'poetic' is their ability to dramatise the relationships which exist between specific social realities and a complex set of related — and often antagonistic — ideological attitudes and formations.

23. See Richard Ohmann, 'Studying Literature at the End of Ideology' in *The Politics of Literature*, ed. Louis Kampf and Paul Lauter, New York, 1973, esp. pp. 134–59; Renato Poggioli, *The Theory of the Avant-Garde*, trans. Gerald Fitzgerald, New York, 1971; and see nn. 3 and 8 above and McGann, 'The Religious Poetry of Christina Rossetti' in *The Beauty of Inflections*.

Section Six

LITERATURE AND SOCIETY: MARXIST APPROACHES

1. Karl Marx, from the 'Preface' to *A Contribution to the Critique of Political Economy* (1859).
2. Raymond Williams, 'Base and Superstructure in Marxist Cultural Theory' (1973).
3. Raymond Williams, 'The Multiplicity of Writing' (1977).
4. Terry Eagleton, 'T. S. Eliot' (1976).

Points of Information

1. Marx's 'Preface' is reprinted from *Selected Works* (1968).

2. Williams's 'Base and Superstructure' essay was first published in *New Left Review*. It is reprinted here from his *Problems in Materialism and Culture* (1980). 'The Multiplicity of Writing' is a chapter from his *Marxism and Literature*.

3. Terry Eagleton's account of T. S. Eliot forms one section of chapter 4 of his *Criticism and Ideology*. The chapter also includes accounts of Arnold, George Eliot, Dickens, Conrad, James, Yeats, Joyce, and Lawrence. It is prefaced here by a short account from chapter 3 of Pierre Macherey's ideas, and the introduction to chapter 4.

As a sustained attempt to explore a set of founding theoretical concepts marxist literary theory has — perhaps surprisingly — the longest history amongst the leading critical schools who have formed our present theoretical horizons. In its earliest forms however, in Marx and Engels themselves, marxist approaches to literature consist of provocative theoretical orientations rather than a theory fully adequate to its object of study. Though Marx and Engels were informed and intelligent readers of literature they had more pressing work to do, and their influence is felt through their placing of literature within their general social and cultural theory rather than in individual readings or studies, suggestive though some of their occasional comments are. The passage from Marx printed here conveniently and briefly sets out the terms of the general theory as it bears upon literary studies.

Marxist literary theory is a *relational* theory. If we start with literature — though this of course is to reverse Marx's own order of priorities — the theory expands in stages through enlarged categories. Thus any literary work is seen in relation to the literary culture of which it is a part; this, in turn, is then seen as a part of a society's overall culture (including both its art and its general ways of life); and the overall culture is then seen as produced by the modes of economic and material production in that society. By 'modes of production' Marx means both the physical means and the relations of production between the social classes. Much subsequent work, including Marx and Engels's own later writings, have attempted to refine and clarify these elements in the theory, though the basic orientations are clear enough in the passage below.

Marxism is also a *deterministic* theory. That is, each of these phenomena is determined (ie formed and conditioned) by the larger category of which it is a part, except the last which, in complex ways, determines all the others. In the passage here Marx expresses this in an architectural metaphor: the cultural superstructure is based upon the material foundations, just as a building is held up by its foundations. Thus culture depends upon its economic base, and the nature of the base will determine the shape of the cultural forms it supports. It can therefore be said that society determines the production of literary texts, though in a complex, mediated way.

The key mediating term in this process is *ideology*. Society's ruling groups — those who own and control the modes of production — seek to dominate the perceptions of individuals and groups who live within that society in order to obtain their consent to the status quo. There are many ways this can be gained, but one powerful way is through culture itself. Because culture is resourced and formed by the economic base, it will tend to reflect the interests of the groups which control the base. Individual cultural productions will, therefore, be disposed towards these interests. (Though in minority cases, they will also be oppositional.) Ideology is the name usually given in marxist theory to the ideas, images and belief sets which reflect the interests of social groups.

Marxist students of literature will therefore be interested in, for instance, the social and historical conditions of the *production* of kinds of writing. They will also be interested, when they come to look at individual works, in the ideological belief sets (which may be unconscious on the author's part) which structure literary representations of life at historically specific moments. Marxist critics may also be interested in the *reception* of literary works; for works can be recirculated in later periods to achieve ideological ends, though again these can also be oppositional in intention. As a result marxist critics will also be interested in the history of criticism, for criticism can be seen as a powerful medium for spreading ideological messages about literature, about education, and about culture and society itself.

That said, the level of abstraction at which Marx pitches his introductory account of his theory of culture can seem rather rigid and remote when set against, for example, the complex, densely-realised world of a nineteenth-century novel. Indeed the frustration sometimes experienced by critics when confronted by this aspect of marxism (especially as marxist ideas are transmitted to us through a complex and difficult political history) can be seen in the early work of the second writer printed here, Raymond Williams.

Williams (b. 1921) is a socialist critic who has come late to a sustained engagement with marxist theoretical concepts, and his early work shows an impatience with them: the chapter on 'Marxism and Culture' in his *Culture and Society* (1958) is an example. His 'Base and Superstructure' essay printed here, though, shows his willingness, over the past dozen years or so, to re-encounter marxism and develop its insights. The essay is set within the classical terms of the theoretical problem. However it attempts to rework these terms to produce a more subtle and nuanced account in the light of marxist work produced since Marx. In one sense it is a survey article but it also stretches the conceptual endeavour.

Marxist theory invites us to consider fundamental questions about literary studies. It asks us to think carefully about our understanding of what literature is and does, particularly as the idea of it regularly becomes value-laden. It also asks us to readjust our perceptions of the connections we make amongst cultural material. Such questions are the subjects of Williams's second piece here. In it he considers definitions of literature or 'literariness', not, as in formalist or some structuralist thought, as a term descriptive of certain kinds of language use, but as an evaluative and even restrictive category which limits our conception of the material to be studied. For, if one basic term of analysis is the concept of ideology, then it must become necessary to examine other literary or non-literary material to see how ideas, forms and styles are used and developed in relationship to each other in the context in which they are produced or received. This will give an alert sense of the historical and social processes alive·within a whole culture and will not restrict analysis to selected (by whom?) masterpieces cut adrift from these contexts. Further, Williams sees the *idea* of literature itself as being an ideologically-produced category influencing the dispositions and aims of criticism; just as, say, conceptions of personality or social roles influence the production of a literary text. In response to these restrictions some marxist work has encouraged the study of neglected or downgraded writing, for instance that of working-class writers.

Marxism, then, sees literature as a relational entity within a cultural totality where individual features are determined by larger structures. Putting matters in this way makes it easy to see the possibility of an arresting theoretical connection between marxism and structuralism, though, as has been noted in earlier introductions, structuralism has a difficulty in attending to historical processes. (The bald outlines of the marxist conception of historical change is given at the close of the passage by Marx.) The fourth piece printed here, by Terry Eagleton, emerges from the encounter of marxism with structuralism which occurred in some British and American criticism in the 1970s.

Like Williams, Eagleton (b. 1943) has developed his work in various directions in response to new theoretical initiatives. Specifically, in *Criticism and Ideology*, he is responding to structuralist developments of marxism which took place in France in the 1960s. These were principally associated with the work of Louis Althusser and his colleague Pierre Macherey, who developed and extended Althusser's ideas in relation to literature. Eagleton briefly introduces Macherey's work in this extract. This structuralist marxism emphasised the massive coercive power of ideology in the cultural processes. Althusser's influential essay 'Ideology and Ideological State Apparatuses' (1969) portrays individuals as being 'hailed' and received into alloted social and ideological roles. They are given even their very identities by this process. In doing so Althusser makes use of some aspects of structuralist and, especially, psychoanalytic theory.

Althusserian marxism has subsequently come under heavy criticism in Britain (for instance by the historian E. P. Thompson) for its totalising theoretical ambitions, and certainly it seems to lead to a functionalist and monolithic conception of human identities and experiences. In literary studies however its ideas are suggestive for critics interested in the ideological composition of texts as Eagleton here describes. His reading of Eliot pithily indicates the ideological tradition Eliot inhabits, and the difficulties and contradictions which his work both conceals and reveals. It is an interesting rethinking of some of the material collected in Sections 1 and 2.

The marxist approach to literature has a long history which cannot be encompassed in a short section. There are many divergent developments and arguments that are not represented here from a field that offers theoretical challenges and perspectives which sometimes appear united only by broad political allegiances. An indication of possible further reading will be found in many of the books listed below and the relevant chapters of the general introductory accounts of literary theory by Eagleton, Jefferson and Robey, and Seldon.

Further reading:

Marx and Engels's original writings on literature and culture are widely scattered and it's probably best to approach them in anthologies such as *Selected Writings* (1968) and *Marx and Engels on Literature and Art* (1973). David McLellan's *The Thought of Karl Marx* (1980) is a useful collection of extracts with commentary. There is also a general anthology of *Marxists on Literature*, ed. David Craig (1975).

There are a number of introductions to marxist criticism including Terry Eagleton's very helpful *Marxism and Literary Criticism* (1976) and Dave Laing, *The Marxist Theory of Art: An Introductory Survey* (1978). Perry Anderson succinctly sets out western developments of marxism in *Considerations on Western Marxism* (1976).

Raymond Williams is a prolific writer and all of his work is of great interest; see, for instance, from a theoretical point of view: *Culture and Society* (1958), which contains essays on Eliot, Richards and Leavis as well as marxism; *The Long Revolution* (1961); *Marxism and Literature* (1977); *Culture* (1981); *Problems in Materialism and Culture* (1980) and *Writing in Society* (n.d.). The last two are collections of essays. Section four of *Writing and Society* presents Williams's thoughts on the contemporary situation in literary studies. *The English Novel from Dickens to Lawrence* (1970) contains an essay on the Brontës.

There is a short monograph on Williams by J. P. Ward, *Raymond Williams* (1981) and several essays have dealt with his work. These include a highly critical one on his early work by Terry Eagleton (chapter 1 of *Criticism and Ideology*) and Patrick Parrinder, 'The Accents of Raymond Williams', *Critical Quarterly*, 26

(1984). Probably, though, the best way into Williams's thinking is through his *Politics and Letters: Interviews with New Left Review* (1979), a 450-page book of argument and response which reviews his career.

Terry Eagleton's work includes, in addition to *Criticism and Ideology*, *Walter Benjamin, or Towards a Revolutionary Criticism* (1981) and *The Function of Criticism* (1984). He has a stimulating essay on *Wuthering Heights* in his *Myths of Power: A Marxist Study of the Brontës* (1975).

Louis Althusser's structuralist-influenced marxism can be approached in his collection *Lenin and Philosophy* (1971). This contains 'Ideology and Ideological State Apparatuses'. Pierre Macherey's principal work on literature is *A Theory of Literary Production* (1966). There are several interesting responses to this and other work in *On Ideology*, ed. Bill Schwarz *et al.* (1977); *Culture, Media, Language*, ed. Stuart Hall *et al.* (1980); and Fredric Jameson's demanding *The Political Unconscious* (1981). See also Tony Bennett, *Formalism and Marxism* (1979); Catherine Belsey, *Critical Practice* (1980); and Rosalind Coward and John Ellis, *Language and Materialism* (1977). E. P. Thompson's critique of Althusser is to be found in his *The Poverty of Theory* (1978).

1

Karl Marx,

from the 'Preface' to A Contribution to the Critique of Political Economy

In the social production of their life, men enter into definite relations that are indispensable and independent of their will, relations of production which correspond to a definite stage of development of their material productive forces. The sum total of these relations of production constitutes the economic structure of society, the real foundation, on which rises a legal and political superstructure and to which correspond definite forms of social consciousness. The mode of production of material life conditions the social, political and intellectual life process in general. It is not the consciousness of men that determines their being, but, on the contrary, their social being that determines their consciousness. At a certain stage of their development, the material productive forces of society come in conflict with the existing relations of production, or — what is but a legal expression for the same thing — with the property relations within which they have been at work hitherto. From forms of development of the productive forces these relations turn into their fetters. Then begins an epoch of social revolution. With the change of the economic foundation the entire immense superstructure is more or less rapidly transformed. In considering such transformations a distinction should always be made between the material transformation of the economic conditions of production, which can be determined with the precision of natural science, and the legal, political, religious, aesthetic or philosophic — in short, ideological forms in which men become conscious of this conflict and fight it out. Just as our opinion of an individual is not based on what he thinks of himself, so can we not judge of such a period of transformation by its own consciousness; on the contrary, this consciousness must be explained rather from the contradictions of material life, from the existing conflict between the social productive forces and the relations of production. No social order ever perishes before all the productive forces for which there is room in it have developed; and new, higher relations of production never appear before the material conditions of their existence have matured in the womb of the old society itself. Therefore mankind always sets itself only such tasks as it can solve; since, looking at the matter more closely, it will always be found that the task itself arises only when the material conditions for its solution already exist or are at least in the process of formation. In broad outlines Asiatic, ancient, feudal, and modern bourgeois modes of production can be designated as progressive epochs in the economic formation of society. The bourgeois relations of production are the last antagonistic form of the social process of production — antagonistic not in the sense of individual antagonism, but of one arising from the social conditions of life of the individuals; at the same time the productive forces developing in the womb of bourgeois society create the material conditions for the solution of that antagonism. This social formation brings, therefore, the prehistory of human society to a close.

2

Raymond Williams,
'Base and Superstructure in Marxist Cultural Theory'

Any modern approach to a Marxist theory of culture must begin by considering the proposition of a determining base and a determined superstructure. From a strictly theoretical point of view this is not, in fact, where we might choose to begin. It would be in many ways preferable if we could begin from a proposition which originally was equally central, equally authentic: namely the proposition that social being determines consciousness. It is not that the two propositions necessarily deny each other or are in contradiction. But the proposition of base and superstructure, with its figurative element, with its suggestion of a fixed and definite spatial relationship, constitutes, at least in certain hands, a very specialized and at times unacceptable version of the other proposition. Yet in the transition from Marx to Marxism, and in the development of mainstream Marxism itself, the proposition of the determining base and the determined superstructure has been commonly held to be the key to Marxist cultural analysis.

It is important, as we try to analyse this proposition, to be aware that the term of relationship which is involved, that is to say 'determines', is of great linguistic and theoretical complexity. The language of determination and even more of determinism was inherited from idealist and especially theological accounts of the world and man. It is significant that it is in one of his familiar inversions, his contradictions of received propositions, that Marx uses the word which becomes, in English translation, 'determines' (the usual but not invariable German word is *bestimmen*). He is opposing an ideology that had been insistent on the power of certain forces outside man, or, in its secular version, on an abstract determining consciousness. Marx's own proposition explicitly denies this, and puts the origin of determination in men's own activities. Nevertheless, the particular history and continuity of the term serves to remind us that there are, within ordinary use — and this is true of most of the major European languages — quite different possible meanings and implications of the word 'determine'. There is, on the one hand, from its theological inheritance, the notion of an external cause which totally predicts or prefigures, indeed totally controls a subsequent activity. But there is also, from the experience of social practice, a notion of determination as setting limits, exerting pressures.

Now there is clearly a difference between a process of setting limits and exerting pressures, whether by some external force or by the internal laws of a particular development, and that other process in which a subsequent content is essentially

204

prefigured, predicted and controlled by a pre-existing external force. Yet it is fair to say, looking at many applications of Marxist cultural analysis, that it is the second sense, the notion of prefiguration, prediction or control, which has often explicitly or implicitly been used.

Superstructure: Qualifications and Amendments

The term of relationship is then the first thing that we have to examine in this proposition, but we have to do this by going on to look at the related terms themselves. 'Superstructure' (*Überbau*) has had most attention. In common usage, after Marx, it acquired a main sense of a unitary 'area' within which all cultural and ideological activities could be placed. But already in Marx himself, in the later correspondence of Engels, and at many points in the subsequent Marxist tradition, qualifications were made about the determined character of certain superstructural activities. The first kind of qualification had to do with delays in time, with complications, and with certain indirect or relatively distant relationships. The simplest notion of a superstructure, which is still by no means entirely abandoned, had been the reflection, the imitation or the reproduction of the reality of the base in the superstructure in a more or less direct way. Positivist notions of reflection and reproduction of course directly supported this. But since in many real cultural activities this relationship cannot be found, or cannot be found without effort or even violence to the material or practice being studied, the notion was introduced of delays in time, the famous lags; of various technical complications; and of indirectness, in which certain kinds of activity in the cultural sphere — philosophy, for example — were situated at a greater distance from the primary economic activities. That was the first stage of qualification of the notion of superstructure: in effect, an operational qualification. The second stage was related but more fundamental, in that the process of the relationship itself was more substantially looked at. This was the kind of reconsideration which gave rise to the modern notion of 'mediation', in which something more than simple reflection or reproduction — indeed something radically different from either reflection or reproduction — actively occurs. In the later twentieth century there is the notion of 'homologous structures', where there may be no direct or easily apparent similarity, and certainly nothing like reflection or reproduction, between the superstructural process and the reality of the base, but in which there is an essential homology or correspondence of structures, which can be discovered by analysis. This is not the same notion as 'mediation', but it is the same kind of amendment in that the relationship between the base and the superstructure is not supposed to be direct, nor simply operationally subject to lags and complications and indirectnesses, but that of its nature it is not direct reproduction.

These qualifications and amendments are important. But it seems to me that what has not been looked at with equal care is the received notion of the 'base' (*Basis, Grundlage*). And indeed I would argue that the base is the more important concept to look at if we are to understand the realities of cultural process. In many uses of the proposition of base and superstructure, as a matter of verbal habit, 'the base' has come to be considered virtually as an object, or in less crude cases, it has been considered in essentially uniform and usually static ways. 'The base' is the real social existence of man. 'The base' is the real relations of production corresponding to a stage of development of the material productive forces. 'The base' is a mode of production at a particular stage of its development. We make and repeat propositions of this kind, but the usage is then very different from Marx's emphasis on productive activities, in particular structural relations, constituting the foundation of all other activities. For while a particular stage of the development of production can be discovered and made precise by analysis, it is never in practice either uniform or static. It is indeed one of the central propositions of Marx's sense of history that there are deep contradictions in the relationship of production and in the consequent social relationships. There is therefore the continual possibility of the dynamic variation of these forces. Moreover, when these forces are considered, as Marx always considers them, as the specific activities and relationships of real men, they mean something very much more active, more complicated and more contradictory than the developed metaphorical notion of 'the base' could possibly allow us to realize.

The Base and the Productive Forces

So we have to say that when we talk of 'the base', we are talking of a process and not a state. And we cannot ascribe to that process certain fixed properties for subsequent translation to the variable processes of the superstructure. Most people who have wanted to make the ordinary proposition more reasonable have concentrated on refining the notion of superstructure. But I would say that each term of the proposition has to be revalued in a particular direction. We have to revalue 'determination' towards the setting of limits and the exertion of pressure, and away from a predicted, prefigured and controlled content. We have to revalue 'superstructure' towards a related range of cultural practices, and away from a reflected, reproduced or specifically dependent content. And, crucially, we have to revalue 'the base' away from the notion of a fixed economic or technological abstraction, and towards the specific activities of men in real social and economic relationships, containing fundamental contradictions and variations and therefore always in a state of dynamic process.

It is worth observing one further implication behind the customary definitions. 'The base' has come to include, especially in certain twentieth-century developments, a strong and limiting sense of basic industry. The emphasis on heavy industry, even, has played a certain cultural role. And this raises a more general problem, for we find ourselves forced to look again at the ordinary notion of 'productive forces'. Clearly what we are examining in the base is primary productive forces. Yet some very crucial distinctions have to be made here. It is true that in his analysis of capitalist production Marx considered 'productive work' in a very particular and specialized sense corresponding to that mode of production. There is a difficult passage in the *Grundrisse* in which he argues that while the man who makes a piano is a productive worker, there is a real question whether the man who distributes the piano is also a productive worker; but he probably is, since he contributes to the realization of surplus value. Yet when it comes to the man who plays the piano, whether to himself or to others, there is no question: he is not a productive worker at all. So piano-maker is base, but pianist superstructure. As a way of considering cultural activity, and incidentally the economics of modern cultural activity, this is very clearly a dead-end. But for any theoretical clarification it is crucial to recognize that Marx was there engaged in an analysis of a particular kind of production, that is capitalist commodity production. Within his analysis of this mode,

he had to give to the notion of 'productive labour' and 'productive forces' a specialized sense of primary work on materials in a form which produced commodities.
But this has narrowed remarkably, and in a cultural context very damagingly,
from his more central notion of *productive forces*, in which, to give just brief
reminders, the most important thing a worker ever produces is himself, himself in
the fact of that kind of labour, or the broader historical emphasis of men producing
themselves, themselves and their history. Now when we talk of the base, and of
primary productive forces, it matters very much whether we are referring, as in
one degenerate form of this proposition became habitual, to primary production
within the terms of capitalist economic relationships, or to the primary production
of society itself, and of men themselves, the material production and reproduction
of real life. If we have the broad sense of productive forces, we look at the whole
question of the base differently, and we are then less tempted to dismiss as superstructural, and in that sense as merely secondary, certain vital productive social
forces, which are in the broad sense, from the beginning, basic.

Uses of Totality

Yet, because of the difficulties of the ordinary proposition of base and superstructure, there was an alternative and very important development, an emphasis primarily associated with Lukács, on a social 'totality'. The totality of social practices
was opposed to this layered notion of base and a consequent superstructure. This
concept of a totality of practices is compatible with the notion of social being determining consciousness, but it does not necessarily interpret this process in terms of a
base and a superstructure. Now the language of totality has become common, and
it is indeed in many ways more acceptable than the notion of base and superstructure. But with one very important reservation. It is very easy for the notion of
totality to empty of its essential content the original Marxist proposition. For if we
come to say that society is composed of a large number of social practices which
form a concrete social whole, and if we give to each practice a certain specific recognition, adding only that they interact, relate and combine in very complicated
ways, we are at one level much more obviously talking about reality, but we are at
another level withdrawing from the claim that there is any process of determination. And this I, for one, would be very unwilling to do. Indeed, the key question to
ask about any notion of totality in cultural theory is this: whether the notion of
totality includes the notion of intention.

If totality is simply concrete, if it is simply the recognition of a large variety of
miscellaneous and contemporaneous practices, then it is essentially empty of any
content that could be called Marxist. Intention, the notion of intention, restores
the key question, or rather the key emphasis. For while it true that any society is a
complex whole of such practices, it is also true that any society has a specific organization, a specific structure, and that the principles of this organization and structure can be seen as directly related to certain social intentions, intentions by which
we define the society, intentions which in all our experience have been the rule of a
particular class. One of the unexpected consequences of the crudeness of the
base/superstructure model has been the too easy acceptance of models which
appear less crude — models of totality or of a complex whole — but which exclude
the facts of social intention, the class character of a particular society and so on.
And this reminds us of how much we lose if we abandon the superstructural

emphasis altogether. Thus I have great difficulty in seeing processes of art and thought as superstructural in the sense of the formula as it is commonly used. But in many areas of social and political thought — certain kinds of ratifying theory, certain kinds of law, certain kinds of institution, which after all in Marx's original formulations were very much part of the superstructure — in all that kind of social apparatus, and in a decisive area of political and ideological activity and construction, if we fail to see a superstructural element we fail to recognize reality at all. These laws, constitutions, theories, ideologies, which are so often claimed as natural, or as having universal validity or significance, simply have to be seen as expressing and ratifying the domination of a particular class. Indeed the difficulty of revising the formula of base and superstructure has had much to do with the perception of many militants — who have to fight such institutions and notions as well as fighting economic battles — that if these institutions and their ideologies are not perceived as having that kind of dependent and ratifying relationship, if their claims to universal validity or legitimacy are not denied and fought, then the class character of the society can no longer be seen. And this has been the effect of some versions of totality as the description of cultural process. Indeed I think we can properly use the notion of totality only when we combine it with that other crucial Marxist concept of 'hegemony'.

The Complexity of Hegemony

It is Gramsci's great contribution to have emphasized hegemony, and also to have understood it at a depth which is, I think, rare. For hegemony supposes the existence of something which is truly total, which is not merely secondary or superstructural, like the weak sense of ideology, but which is lived at such a depth, which saturates the society to such an extent, and which, as Gramsci put it, even constitutes the substance and limit of common sense for most people under its sway, that it corresponds to the reality of social experience very much more clearly than any notions derived from the formula of base and superstructure. For if ideology were merely some abstract, imposed set of notions, if our social and political and cultural ideas and assumptions and habits were merely the result of specific manipulation, of a kind of overt training which might be simply ended or withdrawn, then the society would be very much easier to move and to change than in practice it has even been or is. This notion of hegemony as deeply saturating the consciousness of a society seems to me to be fundamental. And hegemony has the advantage over general notions of totality, that it at the same time emphasizes the facts of domination.

Yet there are times when I hear discussions of hegemony and feel that it too, as a concept, is being dragged back to the relatively simple, uniform and static notion which 'superstructure' in ordinary use had become. Indeed I think that we have to give a very complex account of hegemony if we are talking about any real social formation. Above all we have to give an account which allows for its elements of real and constant change. We have to emphasize that hegemony is not singular; indeed that its own internal structures are highly complex, and have continually to be renewed, recreated and defended; and by the same token, that they can be continually challenged and in certain respects modified. That is why instead of speaking simply of 'the hegemony', 'a hegemony', I would propose a model which allows for this kind of variation and contradiction, its sets of alternatives and its processes of change.

For one thing that is evident in some of the best Marxist cultural analysis is that it is very much more at home in what one might call *epochal* questions than in what one has to call *historical* questions. That is to say, it is usually very much better at distinguishing the large features of different epochs of society, as commonly between feudal and bourgeois, than at distinguishing between different phases of bourgeois society, and different moments within these phases: that true historical process which demands a much greater precision and delicacy of analysis than the always striking epochal analysis which is concerned with main lineaments and features.

The theoretical model which I have been trying to work with is this. I would say first that in any society, in any particular period, there is a central system of practices, meanings and values, which we can properly call dominant and effective. This implies no presumption about its value. All I am saying is that it is central. Indeed I would call it a corporate system, but this might be confusing, since Gramsci uses 'corporate' to mean the subordinate as opposed to the general and dominant elements of hegemony. In any case what I have in mind is the central, effective and dominant system of meanings and values, which are not merely abstract but which are organized and lived. That is why hegemony is not to be understood at the level of mere opinion or mere manipulation. It is a whole body of practices and expectations; our assignments of energy, our ordinary understanding of the nature of man and of his world. It is a set of meanings and values which as they are experienced as practices appear as reciprocally confirming. It thus constitutes a sense of reality for most people in the society, a sense of absolute because experienced reality beyond which it is very difficult for most members of the society to move, in most areas of their lives. But this is not, except in the operation of a moment of abstract analysis, in any sense a static system. On the contrary we can only understand an effective and dominant culture if we understand the real social process on which it depends: I mean the process of incorporation. The modes of incorporation are of great social significance. The educational institutions are usually the main agencies of the transmission of an effective dominant culture, and this is now a major economic as well as a cultural activity; indeed it is both in the same moment. Moreover, at a philosophical level, at the true level of theory and at the level of the history of various practices, there is a process which I call the *selective tradition*: that which, within the terms of an effective dominant culture, is always passed off as '*the* tradition', '*the* significant past'. But always the selectivity is the point; the way in which from a whole possible area of past and present, certain meanings and practices are chosen for emphasis, certain other meanings and practices are neglected and excluded. Even more crucially, some of these meanings and practices are reinterpreted, diluted, or put into forms which support or at least do not contradict other elements within the effective dominant culture. The processes of education; the processes of a much wider social training within institutions like the family; the practical definitions and organization of work; the selective tradition at an intellectual and theoretical level: all these forces are involved in a continual making and remaking of an effective dominant culture, and on them, as experienced, as built into our living, its reality depends. If what we learn there were merely an imposed ideology, or if it were only the isolable meanings and practices of the ruling class, or of a section of the ruling class, which gets imposed on others, occupying merely the top of our minds, it would be — and one would be glad — a very much easier thing to overthrow.

It is not only the depths to which this process reaches, selecting and organizing and interpreting our experience. It is also that it is continually active and adjusting; it isn't just the past, the dry husks of ideology which we can easily discard. And this can only be so, in a complex society, if it is something more substantial and more flexible than any abstract imposed ideology. Thus we have to recognize the alternative meanings and values, the alternative opinions and attitudes, even some alternative senses of the world, which can be accommodated and tolerated within a particular effective and dominant culture. This has been much under-emphasized in our notions of a superstructure, and even in some notions of hegemony. And the under-emphasis opens the way for retreat to an indifferent complexity. In the practice of politics, for example, there are certain truly incorporated modes of what are nevertheless, within those terms, real oppositions, that are felt and fought out. Their existence within the incorporation is recognizable by the fact that, whatever the degree of internal conflict or internal variation, they do not in practice go beyond the limits of the central effective and dominant definitions. This is true, for example, of the practice of parliamentary politics, though its internal oppositions are real. It is true about a whole range of practices and arguments, in any real society, which can by no means be reduced to an ideological cover, but which can nevertheless be properly analysed as in my sense corporate, if we find that, whatever the degree of internal controversy and variation, they do not in the end exceed the limits of the central corporate definitions.

But if we are to say this, we have to think again about the sources of that which is not corporate; of those practices, experiences, meanings, values which are not part of the effective dominant culture. We can express this in two ways. There is clearly something that we can call alternative to the effective dominant culture, and there is something else that we can call oppositional, in a true sense. The degree of existence of these alternative and oppositional forms is itself a matter of constant historical variation in real circumstances. In certain societies it is possible to find areas of social life in which quite real alternatives are at least left alone. (If they are made available, of course, they are part of the corporate organization.) The existence of the possibility of opposition, and of its articulation, its degree of openness, and so on, again depends on very precise social and political forces. The facts of alternative and oppositional forms of social life and culture, in relation to the effective and dominant culture, have then to be recognized as subject to historical variation, and as having sources which are very significant as a fact about the dominant culture itself.

Residual and Emergent Cultures

I have next to introduce a further distinction, between *residual* and *emergent* forms, both of alternative and of oppositional culture. By 'residual' I mean that some experiences, meanings and values, which cannot be verified or cannot be expressed in terms of the dominant culture, are nevertheless lived and practised on the basis of the residue — cultural as well as social — of some previous social formation. There is a real case of this in certain religious values, by contrast with the very evident incorporation of most religious meanings and values into the dominant system. The same is true, in a culture like Britain, of certain notions derived from a rural past, which have a very significant popularity. A residual culture is usually at some distance from the effective dominant culture, but one has to recognize that, in real cultural activities, it may get incorporated into it. This is because some part of it, some version of it — and especially if the residue is from some major area of the past — will in many cases have had to be incorporated if the effective dominant culture is to make sense in those areas. It is also because at certain points a dominant culture cannot allow too much of this kind of practice and experience outside itself, at least without risk. Thus the pressures are real, but certain genuinely residual meanings and practices in some important cases survive.

By 'emergent' I mean, first, that new meanings and values, new practices, new significances and experiences, are continually being created. But there is then a much earlier attempt to incorporate them, just because they are part — and yet not a defined part — of effective contemporary practice. Indeed it is significant in our own period how very early this attempt is, how alert the dominant culture now is to anything that can be seen as emergent. We have then to see, first, as it were a temporal relation between a dominant culture and on the one hand a residual and on the other hand an emergent culture. But we can only understand this if we can make distinctions, that usually require very precise analysis, between residual-incorporated and residual not incorporated, and between emergent-incorporated and emergent not incorporated. It is an important fact about any particular society, how far it reaches into the whole range of human practices and experiences in an attempt at incorporation. It may be true of some earlier phases of bourgeois society, for example, that there were some areas of experience which it was willing to dispense with, which it was prepared to assign as the sphere of private or artistic life, and as being no particular business of society or the state. This went along with certain kinds of political tolerance, even if the reality of that tolerance was malign neglect. But I am sure it is true of the society that has come into existence since the last war, that progressively, because of developments in the social character of labour, in the social character of communications, and in the social character of decision, it extends much further than ever before in capitalist society into certain hitherto resigned areas of experience and practice and meaning. Thus the effective decision, as to whether a practice is alternative or oppositional, is often now made within a very much narrower scope. There is a simple theoretical distinction between alternative and oppositional, that is to say between someone who simply finds a different way to live and wishes to be left alone with it, and someone who finds a different way to live and wants to change the society in its light. This is usually the difference between individual and small-group solutions to social crisis and those solutions which properly belong to political and ultimately revolutionary practice. But it is often a very narrow line, in reality, between alternative and oppositional. A meaning or a practice may be tolerated as a deviation, and yet still be seen only as another particular way to live. But as the necessary area of effective dominance extends, the same meanings and practices can be seen by the dominant culture, not merely as disregarding or despising it, but as challenging it.

Now it is crucial to any Marxist theory of culture that it can give an adequate explanation of the sources of these practices and meanings. We can understand, from an ordinary historical approach, at least some of the sources of residual meanings and practices. These are the results of earlier social formations, in which certain real meanings and values were generated. In the subsequent default of a particular phase of a dominant culture, there is then a reaching back to those meanings and values which were created in real societies in the past, and which still seem to have some significance because they represent areas of human experience, aspiration and achievement, which the dominant culture under-values or opposes, or even cannot recognize. But our hardest task, theoretically, is to find a non-metaphysical and non-subjectivist explanation of emergent cultural practice. Moreover, part of our answer to this question bears on the process of persistence of residual practices.

Class and Human Practice

We have indeed one source to hand from the central body of Marxist theory. We have the formation of a new class, the coming to consciousness of a new class. This remains, without doubt, quite centrally important. Of course, in itself, this process of formation complicates any simple model of base and superstructure. It also complicates some of the ordinary versions of hegemony, although it was Gramsci's whole purpose to see and to create by organization that hegemony of a proletarian kind which would be capable of challenging the bourgeois hegemony. We have then one central source of new practice, in the emergence of a new class. But we have also to recognize certain other kinds of source, and in cultural practice some of these are very important. I would say that we can recognize them on the basis of this proposition: that no mode of production, and therefore no dominant society or order of society, and therefore no dominant culture, in reality exhausts the full range of human practice, human energy, human intention (this range is not the inventory of some original 'human nature' but, on the contrary, is that extraordinary range of variations, both practised and imagined, of which human beings are and have shown themselves to be capable). Indeed it seems to me that this emphasis is not merely a negative proposition, allowing us to account for certain things which happen outside the dominant mode. On the contrary, it is a fact about the modes of domination that they select from and consequently exclude the full range of actual and possible human practice. The difficulties of human practice outside or against the dominant mode are, of course, real. It depends very much whether it is in an area in which the dominant class and the dominant culture have an interest and a stake. If the interest and the stake are explicit, many new practices will be reached for, and if possible incorporated, or else extirpated with extraordinary vigour. But in certain areas, there will be in certain periods practices and meanings which are not reached for. There will be areas of practice and meaning which, almost by definition from its own limited character, or in its profound deformation, the dominant culture is unable in any real terms to recognize. This gives us a bearing on the observable difference between, for example, the practices of a capitalist state and a state like the contemporary Soviet Union in relation to writers. Since from the whole Marxist tradition literature was seen as an important activity, indeed a crucial activity, the Soviet state is very much sharper in investigating areas where different versions of practice, different meanings and values, are being attempted and expressed. In capitalist practice, if the thing is not making a profit, or if it is not being widely circulated, then it can for some time be overlooked, at least while it remains alternative. When it becomes oppositional in an explicit way, it does, of course, get approached or attacked.

I am saying then that in relation to the full range of human practice at any one time, the dominant mode is a conscious selection and organization. At least in its fully formed state it is conscious. But there are always sources of actual human practice which it neglects or excludes. And these can be different in quality from the developing and articulate interests of a rising class. They can include, for example, alternative perceptions of others, in immediate personal relationships, or new perceptions of material and media, in art and science, and within certain limits these new perceptions can be practised. The relations between the two kinds of source — the emerging class and either the dominatively excluded or the more generally new practices — are by no means necessarily contradictory. At times they can be very close, and on the relations between them much in political practice depends. But culturally and as a matter of theory the areas can be seen as distinct.

Now if we go back to the cultural question in its most usual form — what are the relations between art and society, or literature and society? — in the light of the preceding discussion, we have to say first that there are no relations between literature and society in that abstracted way. The literature is there from the beginning as a practice in the society. Indeed until it and all other practices are present, the society cannot be seen as fully formed. A society is not fully available for analysis until each of its practices is included. But if we make that emphasis we must make a corresponding emphasis: that we cannot separate literature and art from other kinds of social practice, in such a way as to make them subject to quite special and distinct laws. They may have quite specific features as practices, but they cannot be separated from the general social process. Indeed one way of emphasizing this is to say, to insist, that literature is not restricted to operating in any one of the sectors I have been seeking to describe in this model. It would be easy to say, it is a familiar rhetoric, that literature operates in the emergent cultural sector, that it represents the new feelings, the new meanings, the new values. We might persuade ourselves of this theoretically, by abstract argument, but when we read much literature, over the whole range, without the sleight-of-hand of calling Literature only that which we have already selected as embodying certain meanings and values at a certain scale of intensity, we are bound to recognize that the act of writing, the practices of discourse in writing and speech, the making of novels and poems and plays and theories, all this activity takes place in all areas of the culture.

Literature appears by no means only in the emergent sector, which is always, in fact, quite rare. A great deal of writing is of a residual kind, and this has been deeply true of much English literature in the last half-century. Some of its fundamental meanings and values have belonged to the cultural achievements of long-past stages of society. So widespread is this fact, and the habits of mind it supports, that in many minds 'literature' and 'the past' acquire a certain identity, and it is then said that there is now no literature: all that glory is over. Yet most writing, in any period, including our own, is a form of contribution to the effective dominant culture. Indeed many of the specific qualities of literature — its capacity to embody and enact and perform certain meanings and values, or to create in single particular ways what would be otherwise merely general truths — enable it to fulfil this effective function with great power. To literature, of course, we must add the visual arts and music, and in our own society the powerful arts of film and of broadcasting. But the general theoretical point should be clear. If we are looking for the relations between literature and society, we cannot either separate out this one practice from a formed body of other practices, nor when we have identified a particular practice can we give it a uniform, static and ahistorical relation to some abstract social formation. The arts of writing and the arts of creation and performance, over their whole range, are parts of the cultural process in all the different ways, the different sectors, that I have been seeking to describe. They contribute to the effective dominant culture and are a central articulation of it. They embody residual meanings and values, not all of which are incorporated, though many are. They express also and significantly some emergent practices and meanings, yet some of these may eventually be incorporated, as they reach people and begin to move them. Thus it was very evident in the sixties, in some of the emergent arts of performance, that the dominant culture reached out to transform, or seek to transform, them. In this process, of course, the dominant culture itself changes, not in its central formation, but in many of its articulated features. But then in a modern society it must always change in this way, if it is to remain dominant, if it is still to be felt as in real ways central in all our many activities and interests.

Critical Theory as Consumption

What then are the implications of this general analysis for the analysis of particular works of art? This is the question towards which most discussion of cultural theory seems to be directed: the discovery of a method, perhaps even a methodology, through which particular works of art can be understood and described. I would not myself agree that this is the central use of cultural theory, but let us for a moment consider it. What seems to me very striking is that nearly all forms of contemporary critical theory are theories of *consumption*. That is to say, they are concerned with understanding an object in such a way that it can profitably or correctly be consumed. The earliest stage of consumption theory was the theory of 'taste', where the link between the practice and the theory was direct in the metaphor. From taste there came the more elevated notion of 'sensibility', in which it was the consumption by sensibility of elevated or insightful works that was held to be the essential practice of reading, and critical activity was then a function of this sensibility. There were then more developed theories, in the 1920s with I. A. Richards, and later in New Criticism, in which the effects of consumption were studied directly. The language of the work of art as object then became more overt. 'What effect does this work ("the poem" as it was ordinarily described) have on me?' Or, 'what impact does it have on me?', as it was later to be put in a much wider area of communication studies. Naturally enough, the notion of the work of art as *object*, as *text*, as an isolated artefact, became central in all these later consumption theories. It was not only that the practices of *production* were then overlooked, though this fused with the notion that most important literature anyway was from the past. The real social conditions of production were in any case neglected because they were believed to be at best secondary. The true relationship was seen always as between the taste, the sensibility or the training of the reader and this isolated work, this object 'as in itself it really is', as most people came to put it. But the notion of the work of art as object had a further larger theoretical effect. If you ask questions about the work of art seen as object, they may include questions about the components of its production. Now, as it happened, there was a use of the formula of base and superstructure which was precisely in line with this. The components of a work of art were the real activities of the base, and you could study the object to discover these components. Sometimes you even studied the components and then projected the object. But in any case the relationship that was looked for was one between an object and its components. But this was not only true of Marxist suppositions of a base and a superstructure. It was true also of various kinds of psychological theory, whether in the form of archetypes, or the images of the collective unconscious, or the myths and symbols which were seen as the *components* of particular works of art. Or again there was biography, or psycho-biography and its like, where the components were in the man's life and the work of art was an object in which components of this kind were discovered. Even in some of the more rigorous forms of New Criticism and of structuralist criticism, this essential procedure of regarding the work as an object which has to be reduced to its components, even if later it may be reconstituted, came to persist.

Objects and Practices

Now I think the true crisis in cultural theory, in our own time, is between this view of the work of art as object and the alternative view of art as a practice. Of course it is at once argued that the work of art *is* an object: that various works have survived from the past, particular sculptures, particular paintings, particular buildings, and these are objects. This is of course true, but the same way of thinking is applied to works which have no such singular existence. There is no *Hamlet*, no *Brothers Karamazov*, no *Wuthering Heights*, in the sense that there is a particular great painting. There is no *Fifth Symphony*, there is no work in the whole area of music and dance and performance, which is an object in any way comparable to those works in the visual arts which have survived. And yet the habit of treating all such works as objects has persisted because this is a basic theoretical and practical presupposition. But in literature (especially in drama), in music and in a very wide area of the performing arts, what we permanently have are not objects but *notations*. These notations have then to be interpreted in an active way, according to the particular conventions. But indeed this is true over an even wider field. The relationship between the making of a work of art and its reception is always active, and subject to conventions, which in themselves are forms of (changing) social organization and relationship, and this is radically different from the production and consumption of an object. It is indeed an activity and a practice, and in its accessible forms, although it may in some arts have the character of a singular object, it is still only accessible through active perception and interpretation. This makes the case of notation, in arts like drama and literature and music, only a special case of a much wider truth. What this can show us here about the practice of analysis is that we have to break from the common procedure of isolating the object and then discovering its components. On the contrary we have to discover the nature of a practice and then its conditions.

Often these two procedures may in part resemble each other, but in many other cases they are of radically different kinds, and I would conclude with an observation on the way this distinction bears on the Marxist tradition of the relation between primary economic and social practices, and cultural practices. It we suppose that what is produced in cultural practice is a series of objects, we shall, as in most current forms of sociological-critical procedure, set about discovering their components. Within a Marxist emphasis these components will be from what we have been in the habit of calling the base. We then isolate certain features which we can so to say recognize *in component form*, or we ask what processes of transformation or mediation these components have gone through before they arrived in this accessible state.

But I am saying that we should look not for the components of a product but for the conditions of a practice. When we find ourselves looking at a particular work, or group of works, often realizing, as we do so, their essential community as well as their irreducible individuality, we should find ourselves attending first to the reality of their practice and the conditions of the practice as it was then executed. And from this I think we ask essentially different questions. Take for example the way in which an object — 'a text' — is related to a genre, in orthodox criticism. We identify it by certain leading features, we then assign it to a larger category, the genre, and then we may find the components of the genre in a particular social history (although in some variants of criticism not even that is done, and the genre is supposed to be some permanent category of the mind).

It is not that way of proceeding that is now required. The recognition of the relation of a collective mode and an individual project — and these are the only categories that we can initially presume — is a recognition of related practices. That is to say, the irreducibly individual projects that particular works are, may come in experience and in analysis to show resemblances which allow us to group them into collective modes. These are by no means always genres. They may exist as resemblances within and across genres. They may be the practice of a group in a period, rather than the practice of a phase in a genre. But as we discover the nature of a particular practice, and the nature of the relation between an individual project and a collective mode, we find that we are analysing, as two forms of the same process, both its active composition and its conditions of composition, and in either direction this is a complex of extending active relationships. This means, of course, that we have no built-in procedure of the kind which is indicated by the fixed character of an object. We have the principles of the relations of practices, within a discoverably intentional organization, and we have the available hypotheses of dominant, residual and emergent. But what we are actively seeking is the true practice which has been alienated to an object, and the true conditions of practice — whether as literary conventions or as social relationships — which have been alienated to components or mere background.

As a general proposition this is only an emphasis, but it seems to me to suggest at once the point of break and the point of departure, in practical and theoretical work, within an active and self-renewing Marxist cultural tradition.

Raymond Williams,
'The Multiplicity of Writing'

Literary theory cannot be separated from cultural theory, though it may be distinguished within it. This is the central challenge of any social theory of culture. Yet while this challenge has to be sustained at every point, in general and in detail, it is necessary to be precise about the modes of distinction which then follow. Some of these become modes of effective separation, with important theoretical and practical consequences. But there is equal danger in an opposite kind of error, in which the generalizing and connecting impulse is so strong that we lose sight of real specificities and distinctions of practice, which are then neglected or reduced to simulations of more general forms.

The theoretical problem is that two very powerful modes of distinction are deeply implanted in modern culture. These are the supposedly distinctive categories of 'literature' and of 'the aesthetic'. Each, of course, is historically specific: a formulation of bourgeois culture at a definite period of its development, from the mid-eighteenth to the mid-nineteenth century. But we cannot say this merely dismissively. In each mode of distinction, and in many of the consequent particular definitions, there are elements which cannot be surrendered, either to historical reaction or to a confused projective generalization. Rather, we have to try to analyse the very complicated pressures and limits which, in their weakest forms, these definitions falsely stabilized, yet which, in their strongest forms, they sought to emphasize as new cultural practice.

We have already examined the historical development of the concept of 'literature': from its connections with literacy to an emphasis on polite learning and on printed books, and then, in its most interesting phase, to an emphasis on 'creative' or 'imaginative' writing as a special and indispensable kind of cultural practice. It is important that elements of this new definition of literature were dragged back to older concepts, as in the attempted isolation of 'the literary tradition' as a form of tradition of 'polite learning'. But it is more important that the most active elements of the new definition were both specialized and contained, in quite new ways.

The specialization was the interpretation of 'creative' or 'imaginative' writing through the weak and ambiguous concept of 'fiction', or through the grander but even more questionable concepts of 'imagination' and 'myth'. The containment partly followed from this specialization, but was decisively reinforced by the concept of 'criticism': in part the operative procedure of a selecting and containing 'tradition'; in part also the key shift from creativity and imagination as active productive processes to categorical abstractions demonstrated and ratified by conspicuous humanistic consumption: criticism as 'cultivation', 'discrimination', or 'taste'.

Neither the specialization nor the containment has ever been completed. Indeed, in the continuing reality of the practice of writing this is strictly impossible. But each has done significant harm, and in their domination of literary theory have become major obstacles to the understanding of both theory and practice. It is still difficult, for example, to prevent any attempt at literary theory from being turned, almost *a priori*, into critical theory, as if the only major questions about literary production were variations on the question 'how do we *judge*?' At the same time, in looking at actual writing, the crippling categorizations and dichotomies of 'fact' and 'fiction', or of 'discursive' and 'imaginative' or 'referential' and 'emotive', stand regularly not only between works and readers (whence they feed back, miserably, into the complications of 'critical theory') but between writers and works, at a still active and shaping stage.

The multiplicity of writing is its second most evident characteristic, the first being its distinctive practice of the objectified material composition of language. But of course this multiplicity is a matter of interpretation as well as of fact. Indeed multiplicity can be realized in weak ways as often as strong. Where the specializing and containing categories operate at an early stage, multiplicity is little more than a recognition of varying 'forms of literature' — poetry, drama, novel — or of forms within these forms — 'lyric', 'epic', 'narrative', and so on. The point is not that these recognitions of variation are unimportant; on the contrary they are necessary, though not always in these received and often residual forms. The really severe limitation is the line drawn between all these variations and other 'non-literary' forms of writing. Pre-bourgeois categorization was normally in terms of the writing itself, as in the relatively evident distinction between verse and other forms of composition, usually drawn in characteristically feudal or aristocratic terms of 'elevation' or 'dignity'. It is significant that while that distinction held, verse normally included what would now be called 'historical' or 'philosophical' or 'descriptive' or 'didactic' or even 'instructional' writing, as well as what would now be called 'imaginative' or 'dramatic' or 'fictional' or 'personal' writing and experience.

The bourgeois drawing and redrawing of all these lines was a complex process. On the one hand it was the result, or more strictly the means, of a decisive secularization, rationalization, and eventually popularization of a wide area of experience. Different values can be attached to each of these processes at different stages, but in history, philosophy, and social and scientific description it is clear that new kinds of distinction about forms and methods of writing were radically connected with new kinds of distinction and intention. 'Elevation' and 'dignity' gave place, inevitably, in certain selected fields, to 'practicality', 'effectiveness', or 'accuracy'. Intentions other than these were either willingly conceded or contemptuously dismissed. 'Literature' as a body of 'polite learning' was still used to unite these varying intentions, but under pressure, especially in the late eighteenth and early nineteenth centuries, this broke down. 'Literature' became either the conceded or the contemptuous alternative — the sphere of imagination or fancy, or of emotional substance and effect — or, at the insistence of its practitioners, the relatively removed but again 'higher' dimension — the creative as distinguished from the rational or the practical. In this complex interaction it is of course significant that the separated literature itself changed, in many of its immediate forms. In the 'realist' novel, especially in its distinction from 'romance', in the new drama (socially extended, secular and contemporary), and in the new special forms of biography and autobiography, many of the same secular, rational, or popular impulses changed particular forms of writing from the inside, or created new literary forms.

Two major consequences followed from this. There was a falsification — false distancing — of the 'fictional' or the 'imaginary' (and connected with these the 'subjective'). And there was a related suppression of the fact of writing — active signifying composition — in what was distinguished as the 'practical', the 'factual', or the 'discursive'. These consequences are profoundly related. To move, by definition, from the 'creative' to the 'fictional', or from the 'imaginative' to the 'imaginary', is to deform the real practices of writing under the pressure of the interpretation of certain specific forms. The extreme negative definition of 'fiction' (or of 'myth') — an account of 'what did not (really) happen' — depends, evidently, on a pseudo-positive isolation of the contrasting definition, 'fact'. The real range in the major forms — epic, romance, drama, narrative — in which this question of 'fact' and 'fiction' arises is the more complex series: what really happened; what might (could) have happened; what really happens; what might happen; what essentially (typically) happened/happens. Similarly the extreme negative definition of 'imaginary persons' — 'who did not/do not exist' — modulates in practice into the series: who existed in this way; who might (could) have existed; who might (could) exist; who essentially (typically) exist. The range of actual writing makes use, implicitly or explicitly, of all these propositions, but not only in the forms that are historically specialized as 'literature'. The characteristically 'difficult' forms (difficult because of the defomed definition) of history, memoir, and biography use a significant part of each series, and given the use of real characters and events in much major epic, romance, drama, and narrative, the substantial overlap — indeed in many areas the substantial community — is undeniable.

The range of actual writing similarly surpasses any reduction of 'creative imagination' to the 'subjective', with its dependent propositions: 'literature' as 'internal' or 'inner' truth; other forms of writing as 'external' truth. These depend, ultimately, on the characteristic bourgeois separation of 'individual' and 'society' and on the older idealist separation of 'mind' and 'world'. The range of writing, in most forms, crosses these artificial categories again and again, and the extremes can even be stated in an opposite way: autobiography ('what I experienced', 'what happened to me') is 'subjective' but (ideally) 'factual' writing; realist fiction or naturalist drama ('people as they are', 'the world as it is') is 'objective' (the narrator or even the fact of narrative occluded in the form) but (ideally) 'creative' writing.

The full range of writing extends even further. Argument, for example, can be distinguished from narrative or characterizing forms, but in practice certain forms of narrative (exemplary instances) or forms of characterization (this kind or person, this kind of behaviour) are radically embedded in many forms of argument. Moreover, the very fact of address — a crucial element in argument — is a *stance* (at times sustained, at times varying) strictly comparable to elements that are elsewhere isolated as narrative or dramatic. This is true even of the apparently extreme case, in which the stance is 'impersonal' (the scientific paper), where it is the practical mode of writing that establishes this (conventional) absence of personality, in the interest of the necessary creation of the 'impersonal observer'. Thus over a practical range from stance to selection, and in the employment of the vast variety of explicit or implicit propositions which define and control composition, this real multiplicity of writing is continually evident, and much of what has been known as literary theory is a way either of confusing or of diminishing it. The first task of any social theory is then to analyse the forms which have determined certain (interpreted) inclusions and certain (categorical) exclusions. Subject always to the effect of residual categorization, the development of these forms is in the end a social history. The dichotomies fact/fiction and objective/subjective are then the theoretical and historical keys to the basic bourgeois theory of literature, which has controlled and specialized the actual multiplicity of writing.

Yet there is another necessary key. The multiplicity of productive practice was in one way acknowledged, and then effectively occluded, by a transfer of interest from intention to. effect. The replacement of the disciplines of grammar and rhetoric (which speak to the multiplicities of intention and performance) by the discipline of criticism (which speaks of effect, and only through effect to intention and performance) is a central intellectual movement of the bourgeois period. Each kind of discipline moved, in the period of change, to a particular pole: grammar and rhetoric to writing; criticism to reading. Any social theory, by contrast, requires the activation of both poles: not merely their interaction — movement from one fixed point, stance, or intention to and from another; but their profound interlocking in actual composition. Something of this kind is now being attempted in what is known (but residually) as communication theory and aesthetics.

And it is on the delineation of 'aesthetics' that we have first to fix our attention. From the description of a theory of perception aesthetics became, in the eighteenth and especially the nineteenth century, a new specializing form of description of the response to 'art' (itself newly generalized from skill to 'imaginative' skill). What emerged in bourgeois economics as the 'consumer' — the abstract figure corresponding to the abstraction of (market and commodity) 'production' — emerged in cultural theory as 'aesthetics' and 'the aesthetic response'. All problems of the multiplicities of intention and performance could then be undercut, or bypassed, by the transfer of energy to this other pole. Art, including literature, was to be defined by its capacity to evoke this special response: initially the perception of beauty; then the pure contemplation of an object, for its own sake and without other ('external') considerations; then also the perception and contemplation of the 'making' of an object: its language, its skill of construction, its 'aesthetic properties'. Such response (power to evoke response) could be as present in a work of history or philosophy as in a play or poem or novel (and all were then 'literature'). Equally, it could be absent in this play or this poem or this novel (and these were then 'not literature' or 'not really literature' or 'bad literature'). The specializing concept of 'literature', in its modern forms, is thus a central example of the controlling and categorizing specialization of 'the aesthetic'.

4

Terry Eagleton,
'T. S. Eliot'

***It is important to grasp here the closeness of relation between the 'ideological' and the 'aesthetic'. The text does not merely 'take' ideological conflicts in order to 'resolve' them aesthetically, for the character of those conflicts is itself overdetermined by the textual modes in which they are produced. The text's mode of resolving a particular ideological conflict may then produce textual conflicts elsewhere — at other levels of the text, for example — which need in turn to be 'processed'. But here the work is 'processing' ideological conflict under the form of resolving specifically *aesthetic* problems, so that the problem-solving process of the text is never merely a matter of its reference outwards to certain pre-existent ideological cruxes. It is, rather, a matter of the 'ideological' presenting itself in the form of the 'aesthetic' and *vice versa* — of an 'aesthetic' solution to ideological conflict producing in its turn an aesthetic problem which demands ideological resolution, and so on. It is not simply that ideology furnishes the 'materials' for the text's formal aesthetic operations; the textual process is, rather, a complex mutual articulation of the two, whereby aesthetic modes so define and determine ideological problems as to be able to continue to reproduce themselves, but only within the limits and subject to the problems which their own overdetermination of the ideological sets. This is one sense in which the processes of conflict and resolution are synchronic rather than diachronic. Every phrase, every image of the text, in so far as it is both in general determined by and exerts a determination on the whole, in so far as it is always both product and producer, destination and departure, is at once an 'answer' and a 'question', mobilising new possibilities of conflict in the very moment of taking the weight of a provisional 'solution'. We may say, then, that the text in this sense 'produces itself' — but produces itself in constant relation to the ideology which permits it such relative autonomy, so that this ceaseless elaboration and recovery of its own lines of meaning is simultaneously the production of a determining ideology. One might say, too, that the text's *relation to itself* is problematical because it is simultaneously a relation to certain ideological problems. The text is thus never at one with itself, for if it were it would have absolutely nothing to say. It is, rather, a process of *becoming* at one with itself — an attempt to overcome the problem of itself, a problem produced by the fact that the text itself is the production, rather than reflection, of an ideological 'solution'.

It may be useful to refer once more at this point to the work of Pierre Macherey. Macherey claims that literary works are internally dissonant, and that this dissonance arises from their peculiar relation to ideology. The distance which separates

221

the work from ideology embodies itself in the internal distance which, so to speak, separates the work from itself, forces it into a ceaseless difference and division of meanings. In putting ideology to work, the text necessarily illuminates the absences, and begins to 'make speak' the silences, of that ideology. The literary text, far from constituting some unified plenitude of meaning, bears inscribed within it the marks of certain determinate absences which twist its various significations into conflict and contradiction. These absences — the '*not-said*' of the work — are precisely what bind it to its ideological problematic: ideology is present in the text in the form of its eloquent silences. The task of criticism, then, is not to situate itself within the same space as the text, allowing it to speak or completing what it necessarily leaves unsaid. On the contrary, its function is to install itself in the very incompleteness of the work in order to *theorise* it — to explain the ideological necessity of those '*not-saids*' which constitute the very principle of its identity. Its object is the *unconsciousness* of the work — that of which it is not, and cannot be, aware. What the text 'says' is not just this or that meaning, but precisely their difference and separation: it articulates the space which both divides and binds together the text's multiple sense. It is criticism's task to demonstrate how the text is thus 'hollowed' by its relation to ideology — how, in putting that ideology to work, it is driven up against those gaps and limits which are the product of ideology's relation to history. And ideology exists because there are certain things which must not be spoken of. In so putting ideology to work, the text begins to illuminate the absences which are the foundation of its articulate discourse. And in doing this, it helps to 'liberate' us from the ideology of which that discourse is the product. ***

I have tried in the preceding chapters to examine the critical situation in which this study intervenes, to outline a systematic conceptual topography of the field of study, and to provide a detailed analysis of the relations between text and ideology. I want now to study those relations as they manifest themselves in a particular sector of English literary history from Matthew Arnold to D. H. Lawrence.

Bourgeois ideology in nineteenth-century England confronted a severe problem. Nurtured in the sparse soil of Utilitarianism, it was unable to produce a set of potently affective mythologies which might permeate the texture of lived experience of English society. It needed, therefore, to have constant resort to the Romantic humanist heritage — to that nebulous compound of Burkean conservatism and German idealism, transmitted by the later Coleridge to Carlyle, Disraeli, Arnold and Ruskin, which has become known as the 'Culture and Society' tradition. It was a tradition which offered an idealist critique of bourgeois social relations, coupled with a consecration of the rights of capital. The peculiar complexity of English nineteenth-century ideology, founded on a complex conjuncture of bourgeois and aristocratic classes within the dominant bloc, lies in part in this contradictory unity between what Antonio Gramsci refers to as 'organic' and 'traditional' elements.[1] An impoverished empiricism, unable to rise to the level of an ideology proper, is driven to exploit the fertile symbolic resources of Romantic humanism, drawing on its metaphysical sanctions and quasi-feudalist social models to ratify bourgeois property relations. The 'Culture and Society' tradition is the literary record of this ideological conjuncture; John Stuart Mill, mechanistically harnessing Coleridge to Bentham in the late eighteen-thirties, provides one of its more palpable instances.[2]

Gramsci, indeed, has commented directly on this ideological formation in nineteenth-century England. 'There is a very extensive category of organic intellectuals — those, that is, who come into existence on the same industrial terrain as the economic group — but in the higher sphere we find that the old land-owning class preserves its position of virtual monopoly. It loses its economic supremacy and is assimilated as "traditional intellectuals" and as directive (*dirigente*) group by the new group in power. The old land-owning aristocracy is joined to the industrialists by a kind of suture which is precisely that which in other countries unites the traditional intellectuals with the new dominant classes.'[3]

One aspect of this assimilation can be seen in bourgeois ideology's growing dependence on 'organicist' concepts of society.[4] As Victorian capitalism assumes increasingly corporate forms, it turns to the social and aesthetic organicism of the Romantic humanist tradition, discovering in art models of totality and affectivity relevant to its ideological requirements. During the second half of the century, the initially poetic notion of 'organic form' becomes progressively extended to the dominant literary mode of the time, fiction. A serious aesthetics of fiction consequently develops, to discover its major ideologue at the end of the century in Henry James.[5] This essay will survey, in skeletal and schematic form, some relations between a sector of the major literature of the last century and the ideological formations in which it is set; it will do so by taking the concept of 'organic form' as one crucial nexus between history and literary production.[6]***

T. S. Eliot

Henry James's successor as a conservative American expatriate was T. S. Eliot, son of an 'aristocratic' St Louis family. The social and intellectual hegemony of the Eliots had been traumatically undermined in the early years of this century by revelations of the corrupt, boss-ridden system of St Louis — a corruption in which the Eliots were apparently implicated.[7] Spiritually disinherited like James by industrial capitalist America, able later to discover in America the 'blood', breeding and 'organic' regionalism he valued only in such phenomena as the right-wing neo-agrarian movement in Virginia, Eliot came to Europe with the historic mission of redefining the organic unity of its cultural traditions, and reinserting a culturally provincial England into that totality. He was, indeed, to become himself the focal-point of the organic consciousness of the 'European mind', that rich, unruptured entity mystically inherent in its complex simultaneity in every artist nourished by it. English literary culture, still in the grip of ideologically exhausted forms of liberal humanism and late Romanticism, was to be radically reconstructed into a classicism which would eradicate the last vestiges of 'Whiggism' (protestantism, liberalism, Romanticism, humanism). It would do so in the name of a higher, corporate ideological formation, defined by the surrender of 'personality' to order, reason, authority and tradition.

The wholesale demolition and salvage job which it was Eliot's historical task to carry out in the aesthetic region of English ideology was one for which he was historically peculiarly well-equipped, as an expatriate with a privileged, panoramic vantage-point on that area. He was sufficiently internal to it as a New Englander to judge 'authoritatively', yet as a 'European' American sufficiently external to identify its parochial limitations. Eliot's own description of his function is characteristically sham-casual: 'From time to time, every hundred years or so, it is desirable that a critic shall appear to review the past of our literature, and set the poets and the poem in a new order. This task is not one of revolution but of readjustment'.[8] It seems a modest description of what Graham Martin has rightly termed 'the most ambitious feat of cultural imperialism the century seems likely to produce';[9] but the bland unalarmist, evolutionary stress of Eliot's formulation is central to his project. Confronted with world imperialist crisis, severe economic depression and intensifying working-class militancy, English society in the early years of Eliot's career as poet and critic stood in urgent ideological need of precisely the values his literary classicism encapsulated. Yet the ideological potency of that classicism rested in its refusal of static, rationalist forms for an empiricist, historicist mould — rested, indeed, in the production of a classicism contradictorily united with the evolutionary organicism of the Romantic tradition. Eliot's 'Tradition' is a labile, self-transformative organism extended in space and time, constantly reorganized by the present; but this radical historical relativism is then endowed with the status of absolute classical authority. What Eliot does, in fact, is to adopt the aesthetic of a late phase of Romanticism (symbolism), with its view of the individual artefact as organic, impersonal and autonomous, and then project this doctrine into an authoritarian cultural ideology.[10]

By framing his classicist doctrine in the organicist terms of the Romantic tradition, Eliot is able to combine an idealist totality with the sensuous empiricism which is its other aspect. If the aesthetic region of ideology is to be effectively refashioned, poetic language must clutch and penetrate the turbulent, fragmentary character of contemporary experience, sinking its tentacular roots into the primordial structures of the collective unconsciousness. As such, poetry offers a paradigm of ideological affectivity in general: Eliot's ideal of the organic society is one in which a finely conscious élite transmits its values through rhythm, habit and resonance to the largely unconscious masses, infiltrating the nervous system rather than engaging the mind.[11] Hence the radical anti-intellectualism of the scholarly, esoteric Eliot: the nervous distrust of abstract ideas, the insistence on the poetic transmutation of thought into sense-experience, the imagist emphasis on the hard, precise image as 'containing' its concept, yoked to the symbolist preoccupation with poetry as music.

There is, however, a latent contradiction between Eliot's concern for art as organic order and his insistence on the sensuously mimetic properties of poetic language. The Olympian pontificator of *Tradition and the Individual Talent*, with his values of order and impersonality, is also the poet of *The Love-Song of J. Alfred Prufrock*, with its restlessly subjective universe of doomed emotions and discrete objects. Eliot attempts to surmount this contradiction in his recourse to the Metaphysical poets: for Donne represents the last *strained* and *tortuous* historical moment of organic coherence between mind and blood, senses and intellect, before the cataclysmic fall into the secularist disintegration of the seventeenth century — the defeat of royalism, the puritan emigration (including the Eliots from Somerset), the demise of the catholicity of the Church of England, the rise of scientific rationalism, the linguistic disaster of Milton, the accelerating decline to the Romantic cult of the errant ego. Donne creates organic wholes from experience while enacting its actual fragmentation; and this, presumably, is also the intention of *The Waste Land*. Yet the 'form' of that poem is in contradiction with its 'content': *The Waste Land*'s fragmentary content listlessly mimes the experience of cultural disintegration, while its totalising mythological forms silently allude to a transcendence of such collapse. The poem is opaque both because of its verbal complicity in that collapse, and in the esoteric allusions which attempt to construct an ideal order across it.

It is possible to trace in this aesthetic dissonance something of Eliot's own ambiguous relationship to the crisis of European bourgeois society which *The Waste Land* records. Indeed, the question of where Eliot stands in relation to the poem becomes the question of where he stands in relation to his adopted society. As an 'aristocratic' American expatriate preoccupied in the first place with a vision of organic cultural unity, Eliot's idealism partly dissevers him from the historical reality of the crisis he confronts. Yet the cosmopolitan *avant-garde* poet of the early work is also the industrious servant of Lloyd's bank, necessarily supporting the economic system which practically ensures, even while it 'spiritually' threatens, the conditions of élitist culture. It is in the blank space between the 'form' and 'content' of *The Waste Land*, between its cosmic detachment and guilty collusion, that the ideology which produces it is most visibly inscribed.

Yet *The Waste Land* produces an ideology, as well as being produced by one. It is not in the first place an ideology of 'cultural disintegration'; it is an ideology of *cultural knowledge*. What the poem signifies, indeed, is not 'the decay of Europe' or fertility cults but its own elaborate display of esoteric allusion — a display *enabled* by such arcane or panoramic motifs. The reader who finds his or her access to the poem's 'meaning' baulked by its inscrutable gesturing off-stage is already in possession of that 'meaning' without knowing it. Cultures collapse, but Culture survives, and its form is *The Waste Land*: this is the ideological gesture of the text, inscribed in the scandalous fact of its very existence. It is in this sense that the poem's signifying codes contradict their signifieds: for if history is indeed sterility then the work itself could not come into being, and if the work exists then it does so only as an implicit denial of its 'content'. The self-cancelling status of *The Waste Land* is the index of an ideological riddle of origins to which there is no material answer: if history is futile and exhausted, where does Culture come from? One may rephrase the riddle differently: if poetic signs have ideological potency only by virtue of being crammed with sensory experience, how are they to fulfil the ideologically vital role of *commenting* on the experience they enact? It is the same question in a different guise: where *within* the sphere of experience is the source of the discourse (Culture, ideology) needed to redeem it? It cannot be inside that sphere, for this would be to level its transcendental status; but it cannot be outside of it either, for this would be to rob it of 'experiential' force, rendering it as impotent as the spectatorial Tiresias. If, then, positive value can lie neither inside nor outside the poem, it must reside instead in the very limits of the text itself — in that which gives it its form. It must lie in that which can be shown but not spoken, which is nothing less than the 'fact' of the poem itself. The 'fact' of the poem is constituted by a set of 'progressive' devices which articulate discourse with discourse, refusing the allure of organic closure; the text's partial dissolution of its signs to its fragmentary situations, its mimetic denial of a 'totalising' overview, *is* its ideological affectivity. Such partial dissolution however, is in no sense a 'naturalising' of the sign: in its *articulated* discourses, the poem parades itself as a thoroughly constructed text, tempting a 'representational' reading which it simultaneously subverts by its exposed productive mechanisms. Yet this subversion turns out to be merely phenomenal: for behind the back of this ruptured, radically decentred poem runs an alternative text which is nothing less than the closed, coherent, authoritative discourse of the mythologies which frame it. The phenomenal text, to use one of Eliot's own metaphors, is merely the meat with which the burglar distracts the guard-dog while he proceeds with his stealthy business. The ideology of the text lies in the distance between these two discourses — in the fact that the 'phenomenal' text is able to 'show', but not *speak of*, the covert coherence which sustains it. For if that coherence is directly articulated, an ideological impact gained only through indirection is lost; yet it is important, none the less, that such impact should not be wholly dispersed to its phenomenal effects. It is for this reason that at the end of the poem the 'covert' text does, for once, speak, in the cryptic imperatives delivered by the voice of the thunder. It is not T. S. Eliot, or a character, or the 'phenomenal' text who speaks; it can only be an anonymous, conveniently hypostasized absolute. What the thunder enunciates is a withdrawn ascetic wisdom whose ideological implications are at odds with the 'progressive', pioneering, typographically-conscious forms of the poem itself; but it is precisely in this conjuncture of 'progressive form' and 'reactionary content' that the ideology of *The Waste Land* inheres. Both elements are united by a certain 'élitism': the 'avant-garde' experiments of a literary côterie match the conservative values of a ruling minority. The purpose of those experiments is precisely to put such values 'in train'; yet the effect of this is nothing less than a questioning of their efficacy, as the thunder's Olympian *fiats* are shown up for the hollow booming they are.

Eliot's early espousal of F. H. Bradley's neo-Hegelianism, with its insistence on the non-relational unity of immediate experience, provided him with a partial solution to his search for organic wholeness. But Bradley's dissolution of the self to the relations between its experiences, while counteracting that puritan individualism which was for Eliot the ideological enemy, by the same token merely confirmed the exile's sense of ruptured, deracinated identity. Similarly, though in Bradley the unity of immediate experience prefigures the supra-rational unity of an Absolute for which the early Eliot hungers, in practice all standpoints are reduced by that doctrine to total relativism. Eliot's Tradition 'historicises' Bradleyan organicism, as Bradley had dehistoricised Hegel; but in doing so it extends rather than escapes from a sealed, intersubjective circuit, replacing real history with a self-evolving idealist whole in which all time is eternally present, and so unredeemable. The purely phenomenological totality offered by Bradley is ideologically insufficient: Eliot moves beyond it to the royalist Anglican conservatism which will provide a social locus for such organicism. Ideally, that is; in fact, his pathetically nostalgic fantasies of a hierarchical Christian order, organically interfusing a devout populace with a clericist élite, are as historically obsolescent as Conrad's romanticising of the merchant code. 'Spiritual' wholeness must find its social correlative, yet in doing so merely reveals its social impotence. *Four Quartets* offers a spiritual totality which transcends a nugatory phenomenal world, yet must left-handedly imbue it with begrudged significance — a contradiction which will dislocate the very formal structures of Eliot's later drama, with its incongruous crossing and counterpointing of metaphysics and drawing-room comedy. Eliot 'advances' beyond Conrad and James to the point of locating the organic ideal in a concrete social institution, the Christian church;[12] if he could advance no further, it was because his solution was part of the problem.

Notes:

1. For Gramsci, 'organic' intellectuals are those who come into existence on the basis of an emergent social class, but who then confront — and need to vanquish and assimilate — those 'traditional' intellectual categories which survive from previous social conditions. Gramsci argues, significantly enough for the English tradition, that 'The popularised traditional type of intellectual is represented by the literary man, the philosopher, the artist' (*Selections from the Prison Notebooks*, p. 9). It is important to distinguish Gramsci's use of the term 'organic' from the meaning I assign to it in this essay.
2. See F. R. Leavis (ed.), *Mill on Bentham and Coleridge* (London, 1950). Eric Hobsbawm has noted the ideological limitations of 'pure' Utilitarianism — how its demystification of 'natural rights' could seriously weaken the force of 'metaphysical' sanctions in the defence of property, substituting for them the considerably less powerful, politically more volatile category of 'utility'. (*The Age of Revolution: Europe 1789–1848*, London, 1964, p. 236.)
3. *Selections from the Prison Notebooks*, ed. Quintin Hoare and Geoffrey Nowell Smith (London, 1971), p. 18.
4. I use 'organic' and 'organicism' to signify social and aesthetic formations with the supposedly spontaneous unity of natural life-forms, and more generally to denote symmetrically integrated systems characterised by the harmonious interdependence of their component elements.
5. The notion of fiction as organic form is not, however, a merely 'superstructural' matter. By the time of James, changes in the material mode of literary production meant a shift from the densely populated 'three-decker' novel, with its diffuse, multiple plots, to the more 'organic' single volume. We have here, indeed, a singularly complex instance of the conjuncture between the capitalist mode of production in general, the literary mode of production, 'aesthetic' ideology, and the demands of the dominant ideology.
6. I must apologise for the somewhat heterogeneous quality of the materials examined in this chapter, embracing as they do social criticism, fiction and poetry, as well as writers whose relation to English society may well seem highly tangential. Yet that tangentiality, as I hope will become apparent, is part of my point; and the unity of the materials studied here lies primarily in the *theme* of organicism. It is this thematic coherence which at one or two points dictates a reversal of literary chronology — as, for example, with James and Conrad, where James seems to me to extend organicist notions in new directions.
7. See Gabriel Pearson, 'Eliot: an American Use of Symbolism', in *Eliot in Perspective*, ed. Graham Martin (London, 1970), p. 98. My turning here from fiction to poetry itself reflects an historically significant shift; as we shall see, poetry for Eliot is itself a peculiarly resourceful and appropriate *ideological* medium, as it is in different ways for Yeats.
8. *The Use of Poetry and the Use of Criticism* (London, 1933), p. 108.
9. *Eliot in Persepective*, p. 22.
10. In a somewhat parallel way, the doctrine of the 'objective correlative' pivots on an arbitrary projection of subjective experience into formulae which are then merely *asserted* to be the 'objective', consistently identifiable codes for that experience.
11. See *The Idea of a Christian Society* (London, 1939) and *Notes towards the Definition of Culture* (1948). It is symptomatic of Eliot's political acumen that the regressive social utopianism of the former volume should be offered to the world on the very eve of the Second World War.
12. An institution which, incidently, exerted a significant fascination for both James and Conrad.

Section Seven

FEMINISM AND LITERATURE

1. Elaine Showalter, 'Towards a Feminist Poetics' (1979)
2. Sandra M. Gilbert and Susan Gubar, '*Wuthering Heights*' (1979)
3. Rachel Blau DuPlessis, 'For the Etruscans' (1979–80)

Points of information

1. 'Towards a Feminist Poetics' first appeared in *Women Writing and Writing About Women*, ed. Mary Jacobus. Gilbert and Gubar's account of *Wuthering Heights* is extracted from their *The Madwoman in the Attic* where the chapter on Emily Brontë was written by Sandra Gilbert. 'For the Etruscans' first appeared, in this version, in *The New Feminist Criticism*, ed. Elaine Showalter (1986). It is printed in its entirety.

2. Gilbert and Gubar refer to Urizen and Los, two characters from Blake's prophetic books. Roughly, Urizen represents the jealous god of conventional Christianity, and Los the principle of energy and change.

Like marxist criticism, feminist approaches to literature are part of a wider set of social perceptions. Both bodies of thought proceed from discernments of social disadvantage and their roots are to be found outside academic institutions. Unlike marxism, however, feminism has no central corpus of concepts or texts to focus its concerns, though this is by no means necessarily a disadvantage. It finds its origins in the experiences of many women in a culture organised by and for men. In this culture women and women's labour have been traditionally and systematically downgraded, suppressed, ignored or patronised. The usual name for this is patriarchy.

In many senses literature and literary studies can be seen as an apt place for feminist concerns. The discipline's origins — in its recognisably modern form — owe something to the demands for higher education made by women in the early years of the century. English was then seen as an appropriate subject with which to meet these. It could for instance be seen as 'suitably' polite, intellectually undemanding, socially harmless and emotionally and civically cultivating. Perhaps it is possible to speculate that some residue of these prejudices can, even now, be detected in the fact that the majority of students are women, whilst the majority of their teachers are men: a position which makes some women academics and students feel particularly vulnerable.

English is also a discipline in which women have made large contributions as writers, and the surge of interest in women's writing and feminist criticism has been aided by the production of contemporary literature of great quality and interest by women. Feminist criticism can thus go to work encouraged by a body of primary material appropriate to its concerns and supported by an infrastructure of journals and activist and self-help groups. The success of specialist women's publishers has provided outlets and opportunities for feminist critics and has spurred the recovery of women writers from the past whose work has been neglected. Feminist criticism is thus both analytically oppositional and celebratory. There is a flourishing diversity of feminist approaches to literature and a developing body of black and lesbian criticism. Feminist criticism is thus at the sharp end of many kinds of wider struggle.

The three pieces printed here are all by American critics though feminism is international in its endeavours and outlook. This internationalism, however, covers a wide range of emphases, as Elaine Showalter demonstrates in her 'taxonomy' of feminist criticisms here. Showalter (b.1941) has been one of the feminist critics principally interested in the recovery of a tradition of women's writing which rivals and sets askew the conventional male canon. Even when women writers have been included in the lists of major authors their concerns and procedures have been defined in terms which usually ignore their womanhood. Showalter's *A Literature of Their Own* (1978) argues for the existence of a tradition of women novelists in Britain from the Brontës to Doris Lessing. These novelists write in relation to this tradition and address themselves to concerns specific to it. This kind of work represents an important revision of more traditional kinds of literary history.

Lately, though, Showalter's work has been criticised by feminist colleagues. Sydney Janet Kaplan, for instance, has argued that Showalter overprivileges the theoretical at the expense of the experiential. For there are powerful arguments within feminism which insist that it is with women's *experiences* that feminism is distinctively concerned. Theory itself, in this account, is seen as a disablingly male activity, emphasising an overbearing rationalism and a labelling and partitioning of experience, not least that of women readers.

Toril Moi, on the other hand, has recently contended that, in the light of post-structuralist thinking, Showalter's conception of the literary work is theoretically naïve. It is based on an old-fashioned 'realist' aesthetics and assumes too close a correspondence between work and author. It ignores, in other words, the productiveness of 'modernist' textuality (see Section 4). Moi herself favours such writing and emphasises the contribution of recent French feminist theorists such as

Julia Kristeva, Hélène Cixous and Luce Irigaray who draw on Derrida and Lacan. Showalter's essay here, and these responses to her work, illustrate some of the principal issues with which feminist literary criticism is presently concerned, and also the combinations of perspective which are possible in the contemporary theoretical climate.

Sandra M. Gilbert and Susan Gubar's *The Madwoman in the Attic* resumes in some respects Elaine Showalter's concern with women's literary history. *The Madwoman in the Attic* is a long book subtitled 'The Woman Writer and the Nineteenth-Century Literary Imagination', which indicates its interest in relating women's writing to the conditions of its production alongside that of men. It contains long essays on Austen, Mary Shelley, the Brontës, George Eliot and some women poets particularly Emily Dickinson, Christina Rosetti and Elizabeth Barrett Browning. The conventionality of the selection is mitigated by the freshness of the analyses, the power of the authors' engagements and the challenge of the overall argument.

Like Showalter, Gilbert (b. 1936) and Gubar (b. 1944) argue for a distinctively female literary tradition which is formed amongst women writers and against male pressures. However, whereas Showalter sees development and change within this tradition — as she does in her essay here on criticism — Gilbert and Gubar posit a consistency and coherence amongst the aims and concerns of the nineteenth and twentieth-century writers they examine. All illustrate a struggle with the dominant male tradition, and all explore the consequences of the divisions in women's social and psychological experiences which result from patriarchal pressures. The radical edge to women's writing in these periods is thus understood in relation to both the literary and the social systems, though the centre of theoretical interest in the book is in the former. In the extract printed here, on *Wuthering Heights*, they focus on the representation of this split experience in the contradictions of the elder Catherine's situation and desires, though some traces of the larger argument are visible.

In arguing their case about the woman writer's relationship to the male tradition Gilbert and Gubar adapt Harold Bloom's influential theory of literary development, just as their account of *Wuthering Heights* draws something from psychoanalysis. Bloom is one of the American critics who have been influenced by Derridean deconstruction, particulary its conception of 'intertextuality' (see Section 4), though Bloom's work has a logic and direction of its own. In Bloom's theory literary history develops via enabling 'misreadings' by writers of 'strong' earlier writers. Action provokes reaction. Any piece of literature is situated intertextually against its predecessors, and in order to found its unique authority it has to 'swerve' away from over-dominant forebears in a kind of Freudian Oedipal drama whereby the father is killed to liberate the son. For example many Romantic poets needed (as they did) to come to terms with Milton to found their own epic ambitions. (See, for example, Wordsworth's 1814 'Preface' to *The Excursion*, Keats's reconsideration of his style in *Hyperion* and Shelley's comments on Milton's Satan in the 'Preface' to *Prometheus Unbound*.) Writing, in this way, is thus seen as intertextual re-writing.

Such a theory clearly has possibilities for feminist critics once freed of its masculine bias and overtones of the wrestling match. In *The Madwoman in the Attic* Gilbert and Gubar see women writers as engaged in similar quarrels with the male tradition. Women writers, however, have to struggle not only with the general 'anxiety of influence' (in Bloom's phrase) but also the fact that male literature tends to reflect male concerns and produce male messages. Women are further confined, in the literary sense, by what is thought proper for a 'female writer'. Hence nineteenth-century women writers often chose male or androgynous pen-names or narrative perspectives. They have no spontaneous access to literary forms or attitudes which reflect their interests and experiences. In the long chapter from which this extract comes (entitled 'How are we fall'n? Milton's Daughters'), Gilbert and Gubar situate their account of *Wuthering Heights* against Milton's patriarchal sensibility, as well as the sensibilities of those early nineteenth-century writers, like Blake, Mary Shelley and Byron, who challenge and redefine Milton's 'culture myths' of creation, fall and redemption.

One problem for Gilbert and Gubar's argument is that it appears to offer essentialist definitions of femaleness, and it is certainly the case that there is much anger and little joy in *The Madwoman in the Attic*; if, that is, one discounts — as one shouldn't — the exhilaration conveyed by the authors in encountering these writers. The third piece printed here, however, embraces the polarities and diversities in feminist criticism and women's experiences.

Whilst Showalter and Gilbert and Gubar are engaged in revising literary history, Rachel Blau DuPlessis's 'For the Etruscans' is more obviously experiential; though that does not mean that it is anti-theoretical. It is both celebratory and aware of the pressures and limits of that mode. In presenting the reader with different perspectives DuPlessis (b. 1941) constructs a more clearly dialectical criticism which brings together debates and experiences without seeking to resolve them in a finished theoretical programme. As such it parallels some versions of post-structuralism.

As we have noted in the introduction to Section 4, some post-structuralist critics are eager to break down the usual distinctions between 'the literary' and 'the critical' and to challenge what is seen as the illusory objectivity of criticism which pretends to factual critical statements. The deconstructionist critic Geoffrey Hartman thus describes his book *Criticism in the Wilderness* (1980) as one of 'experiences' rather than systematic explorations, and he increasingly writes in a personalised and self-conscious manner. (See for instance the essay 'The Interpreter: A Self-Analysis' in *The Fate of Reading* [1975].) Though some feminists have made deliberate use of deconstruction's possibilities for their work, it would be wrong, I feel, to assume too close a proximity in stance and outlook between DuPlessis and the deconstructionists. In any case the critical essay which proceeds from subjective responses has a long history, as for example in Romantic essayists like Hazlitt, Lamb or Coleridge.

'For the Etruscans' works through juxtapositions. It brings together — to list some of the more obvious features — the domestic and the professional, the personal and the social, the contemporary and the historical, the 'read' and the 'lived'. It traces a personal history and a cultural movement. It juxtaposes the familiar with the different or little-known (the Etruscans). At either pole, however, none of these differential categories can be left free-standing and self-validating, and that — I assume — is the point. Criss-crossed by history, mingling the personal and the general, shifting in time and place, creating myths and de-stabilising them, DuPlessis's essay can be seen as a version in criticism of the modernist aesthetics with which so much of this book's debate is concerned.

Further reading

Perhaps the best way to begin acquaintance with feminist criticism is in one of several excellent anthologies: Elizabeth Abel, ed., *Writing and Sexual Difference* (1982); Josephine Donovan, ed., *Feminist Literary Criticism: Explorations in Theory* (1975); Mary Eagleton, ed., *Feminist Literary Theory: A Reader* (1986) — this contains short extracts from many books and essays; Gayle Greene and Coppélia Kahn, eds., *Making a Difference: Feminist Literary Criticism* (1985); Mary Jacobus, ed., *Women Writing and Writing About Women* (1979); Elaine Showalter, ed., *The New Feminist Criticism: Essays on Women, Literature and Theory* (1986).

Elaine Marks and Isabelle Courtivron, eds., *New French Feminisms* (1980) is an anthology of material of a kind not represented here. Moi (below) gives an introduction to it. See also Juliet Mitchell, *Psychoanalysis and Feminism* (1974). Mitchell's collection *Women: The Longest Revolution: Essays in Feminism, Literature and Psychoanalysis* (1984) contains a reading of *Wuthering Heights*. Carol Ohmann, 'Emily Brontë in the Hands of Male Critics', *College English*, 32 (1971) is also of interest, as, on the representation of adolescence in *Wuthering Heights*, is Patricia Meyer Spacks, *The Female Imagination* (1976).

There are two helpful introductions to feminist criticism: K. K. Ruthven, *Feminist Literary Studies: An Introduction* (1984) and Toril Moi, *Sexual/Textual Politics* (1985). It should, though, be said that Ruthven is a man, and that his book is disapproved of in some feminist circles. John Goode's essay 'Woman and the Literary Text' in *The Rights and Wrongs of Women*, ed., Juliet Mitchell and Ann Oakley (1976) is also useful. See also Maggie Humm, *Feminist Criticism* (1986). The bibliographies in these, as well as the anthologies above, will guide additional reading. The criticisms of Elaine Showalter mentioned in the introduction are to be found in Greene and Kahn's anthology and Moi's book above.

Harold Bloom's theories of literary development are to be found in his *The Anxiety of Influence: A Theory of Poetry* (1973) and *A Map of Misreading* (1975). For feminist responses see, in addition to Gilbert and Gubar, Annette Kolodny, 'A Map of Misreading: Gender and the Interpretation of Literary Texts', which is reprinted in Showalter, ed., *The New Feminist Criticism*.

1

Elaine Showalter,
'Towards a Feminist Poetics'

In 1977, Leon Edel, the distinguished biographer of Henry James, contributed to a London symposium of essays by six male critics called *Contemporary Approaches to English Studies*. Professor Edel presented his essay as a dramatised discussion between three literary scholars who stand arguing about art on the steps of the British Museum:

> There was Criticus, a short, thick-bodied intellectual with spectacles, who clung to a pipe in his right hand. There was Poeticus, who cultivated a Yeatsian forelock, but without the eyeglasses and the ribbon. He made his living by reviewing and had come to the B. M. to look up something or other. Then there was Plutarchus, a lean and lanky biographer wearing a corduroy jacket.

As these three gentlemen are warming to their important subject, a taxi pulls up in front of them and releases 'an auburn-haired young woman, obviously American, who wore ear-rings and carried an armful of folders and an attaché case'. Into the Museum she dashes, leaving the trio momentarily wondering why femininity requires brainwork. They are still arguing when she comes out, twenty-one pages later.[1]

I suppose we should be grateful that at least one woman — let us call her Critica — makes an appearance in this gathering, even if she is not invited to join the debate. I imagine that she is a feminist critic — in fact if I could afford to take taxis to the British Museum, I would think they had perhaps seen me — and it is pleasing to think that while the men stand gossiping in the sun, she is inside hard at work. But these are scant satisfactions when we realise that of all the approaches to English studies current in the 1970s, feminist criticism is the most isolated and the least understood. Members of English departments who can remember what Harold Bloom means by *clinamen*, and who know the difference between Tartu and Barthian semiotics, will remark that they are against feminist criticism and consequently have never read any. Those who have read it, often seem to have read through a glass darkly, superimposing their stereotypes on the critical texts. In his introduction to Nina Auerbach's subtle feminist analysis of *Dombey and Son* in the *Dickens Studies Annual*, for example, Robert Partlow discusses the deplorable but non-existent essay of his own imagining:

> At first glance, Nina Auerbach's essay . . . might seem to be a case of special pleading, another piece of women's lib propaganda masquerading as literary criticism, but it is not quite that . . . such an essay could have been . . . ludicrous . . . it could have seen dark

phallic significance in curving railroad tracks and upright church pews — but it does not.[2]

In contrast to Partlow's caricature (feminist criticism will naturally be obsessed with the phallus), there are the belligerent assumptions of Robert Boyers, in the Winter 1977 issue of the influential American quarterly *Partisan Review*, that it will be obsessed with destroying great male artists. In 'A Case Against Feminist Criticism', Boyers used a single work, Joan Mellen's *Women and Their Sexuality in the New Film* (1973), as an example of feminist deficiency in 'intellectual honesty' and 'rigour'. He defines feminist criticism as the 'insistence on asking the same questions of every work and demanding ideologically satisfactory answers to those questions as a means of evaluating it', and concludes his diatribe thus:

> Though I do not think anyone has made a credible case for feminist criticism as a viable alternative to any other mode, no one can seriously object to feminists continuing to try. We ought to demand that such efforts be minimally distinguished by intellectual candour and some degree of precision. This I have failed to discover in most feminist criticism.[3]

Since his article makes its 'case' so recklessly that Joan Mellen brought charges for libel, and the *Partisan Review* was obliged to print a retraction in the following issue, Boyers hardly seems the ideal champion to enter the critical lists under the twin banners of honesty and rigour. Indeed, his terminology is best understood as a form of intimidation, intended to force women into using a discourse more acceptable to the academy, characterised by the 'rigour' which my dictionary defines as strictness, a severe or cruel act, or 'state of rigidity in living tissues or organs that prevents response to stimuli'. In formulating a feminist literary theory, one ought never to expect to appease a Robert Boyers. And yet these 'cases' cannot continue to be settled, one by one, out of court. The absence of a clearly articulated theory makes feminist criticism perpetually vulnerable to such attacks, and not even feminist critics seem to agree what it is that they mean to profess and defend.

A second obstacle to the articulation of a feminist critical practice is the activist's suspicion of theory, especially when the demand for clarification comes from sources as patently sexist as the egregiously named Boyers and Mailers of the literary quarterlies. Too many literary abstractions which claim to be universal have in fact described only male perceptions, experiences and options, and have falsified the social and personal contexts in which literature is produced and consumed. In women's fiction, the complacently precise and systematising male has often been the target of satire, especially when his subject is Woman. George Eliot's impotent structuralist Casaubon is a classic instance, as is Mr Ramsay, the self-pitying philosopher in Virginia Woolf's *To the Lighthouse*. More recently Doris Lessing's Professor Bloodrot in *The Golden Notebook* lectures confidently on orgasm in the female swan; as Bloodrot proceeds, the women in the audience rise one by one and leave. What women have found hard to take in such male characters is their self-deception, their pretence to objectivity, their emotion parading as reason. As Adrienne Rich comments in *Of Woman Born*, 'the term "rational" relegates to its opposite term all that it refuses to deal with, and thus ends by assuming itself to be purified of the nonrational, rather than searching to identify and assimilate its own surreal or nonlinear elements'.[4] For some radical feminists, methodology itself is an intellectual instrument of patriarchy, a tyrannical Methodolatry which sets implicit limits to what can be questioned and discussed. 'The God Method', writes Mary Daly,

> is in fact a subordinate deity, serving higher powers. These are social and cultural institutions whose survival depends upon the classification of disruptive and disturbing information as nondata. Under patriarchy, Method has wiped out women's questions so totally that even women have not been able to hear and formulate our own questions, to meet our own experiences.[5]

From this perspective, the academic demand for theory can only be heard as a threat to the feminist need for authenticity, and the visitor looking for a formula he or she can take away without personal encounter is not welcome. In the United States, where Women's Studies programmes offer degree options in nearly 300 colleges and universities, there are fears that feminist analysis has been co-opted by academia, and counter-demands that we resist the pressure to assimilate. Some believe that the activism and empiricism of feminist criticism is its greatest strength, and point to the flourishing international women's press, to new feminist publishing houses, and to writing collectives and manifestoes. They are afraid that if the theory is perfected, the movement will be dead. But these defensive responses may also be rationalisations of the psychic barriers to women's participation in theoretical discourse. Traditionally women have been cast in the supporting rather than the starring roles of literary scholarship. Whereas male critics in the twentieth century have moved to centre-stage, openly contesting for primacy with writers, establishing coteries and schools, speaking unabashedly (to quote Geoffrey Hartman) of their 'pen-envy',[6] women are still too often translators, editors, hostesses at the conference and the Festschrift, interpreters; to congratulate ourselves for working patiently and anonymously for the coming of Shakespeare's sister, as Virginia Woolf exhorted us to do in 1928, is in a sense to make a virtue of necessity. In this essay, therefore, I would like to outline a brief taxonomy, if not a poetics, of feminist criticism, in the hope that it will serve as an introduction to a body of work which needs to be considered both as a major contribution to English studies and as part of an interdisciplinary effort to reconstruct the social, political and cultural experience of women.

Feminist criticism can be divided into two distinct varieties. The first type is concerned with *woman as reader* — with woman as the consumer of male-produced literature, and with the way in which the hypothesis of a female reader changes our apprehension of a given text, awakening us to the significance of its sexual codes. I shall call this kind of analysis the *feminist critique*, and like other kinds of critique it is a historically grounded inquiry which probes the ideological assumptions of literary phenomena. Its subjects include the images and stereotypes of women in literature, the omissions and misconceptions about women in criticism, and the fissures in male-constructed literary history. It is also concerned with the exploitation and manipulation of the female audience, especially in popular culture and film; and with the analysis of woman-as-sign in semiotic systems. The second type of feminist criticism is concerned with *woman as writer* — with woman as the producer of textual meaning, with the history, themes, genres and structures of literature by women. Its subjects include the psychodynamics of female creativity; linguistics and the problem of a female language; the trajectory of the individual or collective female literary career; literary history; and, of course, studies of particular writers and works. No term exists in English for such a specialised discourse, and so I have adapted the French term *la gynocritique: 'gynocritics'* (although the significance of the male pseudonym in the history of women's writing also suggested the term 'georgics').

The feminist critique is essentially political and polemical, with theoretical affiliations to Marxist sociology and aesthetics; gynocritics is more self-contained and experimental, with connections to other modes of new feminist research. In a dialogue between these two positions, Carolyn Heilbrun, the writer, and Catherine Stimpson, editor of the American journal *Signs: Women in Culture and Society*, compare the feminist critique to the Old Testament, 'looking for the sins and errors of the past', and gynocritics to the New Testament, seeking 'the grace of imagination'. Both kinds are necessary, they explain, for only the Jeremiahs of the feminist critique can lead us out of the 'Egypt of female servitude' to the promised land of the feminist vision. That the discussion makes use of these Biblical metaphors points to the connections between feminist consciousness and conversion narratives which often appear in women's literature; Carolyn Heilbrun comments on her own text, 'when I talk about feminist criticism, I am amazed at how high a moral tone I take'.[7]

The Feminist Critique: Hardy

Let us take briefly as an example of the way a feminist critique might proceed, Thomas Hardy's *The Mayor of Casterbridge*, which begins with the famous scene of the drunken Michael Henchard selling his wife and infant daughter for five guineas at a country fair. In his study of Hardy, Irving Howe has praised the brilliance and power of this opening scene:

> To shake loose from one's wife; to discard that drooping rag of a woman, with her mute complaints and maddening passivity; to escape not by a slinking abandonment but through the public sale of her body to a stranger, as horses are sold at a fair; and thus to wrest, through sheer amoral wilfulness, a second chance out of life — it is with this stroke, so insidiously attractive to male fantasy, that *The Mayor of Casterbridge* begins.[8]

It is obvious that a woman, unless she has been indoctrinated into being very deeply identified indeed with male culture, will have a different experience of this scene. I quote Howe first to indicate how the fantasies of the male critic distort the text; for Hardy tells us very little about the relationship of Michael and Susan Henchard, and what we see in the early scenes does not suggest that she is drooping, complaining or passive. Her role, however, is a passive one; severely constrained by her womanhood, and further burdened by her child, there is no way that *she* can wrest a second chance out of life. She cannot master events, but only accommodate herself to them.

What Howe, like other male critics of Hardy, conveniently overlooks about the novel is that Henchard sells not only his wife but his child, a child who can only be female. Patriarchal societies do not readily sell their sons, but their daughters are all for sale sooner or later. Hardy wished to make the sale of the daughter emphatic and central; in early drafts of the novel Henchard has two daughters and sells only one, but Hardy revised to make it clearer that Henchard is symbolically selling his entire share in the world of women. Having severed his bonds with this female community of love and loyalty, Henchard has chosen to live in the male community, to define his human relationships by the male code of paternity, money and legal contract. His tragedy lies in realising the inadequacy of this system, and in his inability to repossess the loving bonds he comes desperately to need.

The emotional centre of *The Mayor of Casterbridge* is neither Henchard's relationship to his wife, nor his superficial romance with Lucetta Templeman, but his slow appreciation of the strength and dignity of his wife's daughter, Elizabeth-Jane. Like the other women in the book, she is governed by her own heart — man-made laws are not important to her until she is taught by Henchard himself to value legality, paternity, external definitions, and thus in the end to reject him. A self-proclaimed 'woman-hater', a man who has felt at best a 'supercilious pity' for womankind, Henchard is humbled and 'unmanned' by the collapse of his own virile facade, the loss of his mayor's chain, his master's authority, his father's rights. But in Henchard's alleged weakness and 'womanishness', breaking through in moments of tenderness, Hardy is really showing us the man at his best. Thus Hardy's female characters in *The Mayor of Casterbridge*, as in his other novels, are somewhat idealised and melancholy projections of a repressed male self.

As we see in this analysis, one of the problems of the feminist critique is that it is male-oriented. If we study stereotypes of women, the sexism of male critics, and the limited roles women play in literary history, we are not learning what women have felt and experienced, but only what men have thought women should be. In some fields of specialisation, this may require a long apprenticeship to the male theoretician, whether he be Althusser, Barthes, Macherey or Lacan; and then an application of the theory of signs or myths or the unconscious to male texts or films. The temporal and intellectual investment one makes in such a process increases resistance to questioning it, and to seeing its historical and ideological boundaries. The critique also has a tendency to naturalise women's victimisation, by making it the inevitable and obsessive topic of discussion. One sees, moreover, in works like Elizabeth Hardwick's *Seduction and Betrayal*, the bittersweet moral distinctions the critic makes between women merely betrayed by men, like Hetty in *Adam Bede*, and the heroines who make careers out of betrayal, like Hester Prynne in *The Scarlet Letter*. This comes dangerously close to a celebration of the opportunities of victimisation, the seduction *of* betrayal.[9]

Gynocritics and Female Culture

In contrast to this angry or loving fixation on male literature, the programme of gynocritics is to construct a female framework for the analysis of women's literature, to develop new models based on the study of female experience, rather than to adapt male models and theories. Gynocritics begins at the point when we free ourselves from the linear absolutes of male literary history, stop trying to fit women between the lines of the male tradition, and focus instead on the newly visible world of female culture. This is comparable to the ethnographer's effort to render the experience of the 'muted' female half of a society which is described in Shirley Ardener's collection, *Perceiving Women*.[10] Gynocritics is related to feminist research in history, anthropology, psychology and sociology, all of which have developed hypotheses of a female subculture including not only the ascribed status, and the internalised constructs of femininity, but also the occupations, interactions and consciousness of women. Anthropologists study the female subculture in the relationships between women, as mothers, daughters, sisters and friends; in sexuality, reproduction and ideas about the body; and in rites of initiation and passage, purification ceremonies, myths and taboos. Michelle Rosaldo writes in *Woman, Culture, and Society,*

> the very symbolic and social conceptions that appear to set women apart and to circumscribe their activities may be used by women as a basis for female solidarity and worth. When men live apart from women, they in fact cannot control them, and unwittingly they may provide them with the symbols and social resources on which to build a society of their own.[11]

Thus in some women's literature, feminine values penetrate and undermine the masculine systems which contain them; and women have imaginatively engaged the myths of the Amazons, and the fantasies of a separate female society, in genres from Victorian poetry to contemporary science fiction.

In the past two years, pioneering work by four young American feminist scholars has given us some new ways to interpret the culture of nineteenth-century American women, and the literature which was its primary expressive form. Carroll Smith-Rosenberg's essay 'The Female World of Love and Ritual' examines several archives of letters between women, and outlines the homosocial emotional world of the nineteenth century. Nancy Cott's *The Bonds of Womanhood: Woman's Sphere in New England 1780–1835* explores the paradox of a cultural bondage, a legacy of pain and submission, which none the less generates a sisterly solidarity, a bond of shared experience, loyalty and compassion. Ann Douglas's ambitious book, *The Feminization of American Culture*, boldly locates the genesis of American mass culture in the sentimental literature of women and clergymen, two allied and 'disestablished' post-industrial groups. These three are social historians; but Nina Auerbach's *Communities of Women: An Idea in Fiction* seeks the bonds of womanhood in women's literature, ranging from the matriarchal households of Louisa May Alcott and Mrs Gaskell to the women's schools and colleges of Dorothy Sayers, Sylvia Plath and Muriel Spark. Historical and literary studies like these, based on English women, are badly needed; and the manuscript and archival sources for them are both abundant and untouched.[12]

Gynocritics: Elizabeth Barrett Browning and Muriel Spark

Gynocritics must also take into account the different velocities and curves of political, social and personal histories in determining women's literary choices and careers. 'In dealing with women as writers,' Virginia Woolf wrote in her 1929 essay, 'Women and Fiction', 'as much elasticity as possible is desirable; it is necessary to leave oneself room to deal with other things besides their work, so much has that work been influenced by conditions that have nothing whatever to do with art.'[13] We might illustrate the need for this completeness by looking at Elizabeth Barrett Browning, whose verse-novel *Aurora Leigh* (1856) has recently been handsomely reprinted by the Women's Press. In her excellent introduction Cora Kaplan defines Barrett Browning's feminism as romantic and bourgeois, placing its faith in the transforming powers of love, art and Christian charity. Kaplan reviews Barrett Browning's dialogue with the artists and radicals of her time; with Tennyson and Clough, who had also written poems on the 'woman question'; with the Christian Socialism of Fourier, Owen, Kingsley and Maurice; and with such female predecessors as Madame de Staël and George Sand. But in this exploration of Barrett Browning's intellectual milieu, Kaplan omits discussion of the male poet whose influence on her work in the 1850s would have been most pervasive: Robert Browning. When we understand how susceptible women writers have always been to the aesthetic standards and values of the male tradition, and to male approval and validation, we can appreciate the complexity of a marriage between artists. Such a union has almost invariably meant internal conflicts, self-effacement, and finally obliteration for the women, except in the rare cases — Eliot and Lewes, the Woolfs — where the husband accepted a managerial rather than a competitive role. We can see in Barrett Browning's letters of the 1850s the painful, halting, familiar struggle between her womanly love and ambition for her husband and her conflicting commitment to her own work. There is a sense in which she *wants* him to be the better artist. At the beginning of the decade she was more famous than he; then she notes with pride a review in France which praises him more; his work on *Men and Women* goes well; her work on *Aurora Leigh* goes badly (she had a young child and was recovering from the most serious of her four miscarriages). In 1854 she writes to a woman friend,

> I am behind hand with my poem . . . Robert swears he shall have his book ready in spite of everything for print when we shall be in London for the purpose, but, as for mine, it must wait for the next spring I begin to see clearly. Also it may be better not to bring out the two works together.

And she adds wryly, 'If mine were ready I might not say so perhaps.'[14]

Without an understanding of the framework of the female subculture, we can miss or misinterpret the themes and structures of women's literature, fail to make necessary connections within a tradition. In 1852, in an eloquent passage from her autobiographical essay 'Cassandra', Florence Nightingale identified the pain of feminist awakening as its essence, as the guarantee of progress and free will. Protesting against the protected unconscious lives of middle-class Victorian women, Nightingale demanded the restoration of their suffering:

> Give us back our suffering, we cry to Heaven in our hearts — suffering rather than indifferentism — for out of suffering may come the cure. Better to have pain than paralysis: A hundred struggle and drown in the breakers. One discovers a new world.[15]

It is fascinating to see how Nightingale's metaphors anticipate not only her own medical career, but also the fate of the heroines of women's novels in the nineteenth and twentieth centuries. To waken from the drugged pleasant sleep of Victorian womanhood was agonising; in fiction it is much more likely to end in drowning than in discovery. It is usually associated with what George Eliot in *Middlemarch* calls 'the chill hours of a morning twilight', and the sudden appalled confrontation with the contingencies of adulthood. Eliot's Maggie Tulliver, Edith Wharton's Lily Barth, Olive Schreiner's Lyndall, Kate Chopin's Edna Pontellier wake to worlds which offer no places for the women they wish to become; and rather than struggling they die. Female suffering thus becomes a kind of literary commodity which both men and women consume. Even in these important women's novels — *The Mill on the Floss, Story of an African Farm, The House of Mirth* — the fulfilment of the plot is a visit to the heroine's grave by a male mourner.

According to Dame Rebecca West, unhappiness is still the keynote of contemporary fiction by English women.[16] Certainly the literary landscape is strewn with dead female bodies. In Fay Weldon's *Down Among the Women* and *Female*

Friends, suicide has come to be a kind of domestic accomplishment, carried out after the shopping and the washing-up. When Weldon's heroine turns on the gas, 'she feels that she has been half-dead for so long that the difference in state will not be very great'. In Muriel Spark's stunning short novel of 1970, *The Driver's Seat*, another half-dead and desperate heroine gathers all her force to hunt down a woman-hating psychopath, and persuades him to murder her. Garishly dressed in a purposely bought outfit of clashing purple, green and white — the colours of the suffragettes (and the colours of the school uniform in *The Prime of Miss Jean Brodie*) — Lise goes in search of her killer, lures him to a park, gives him the knife. But in Lise's careful selection of her death-dress, her patient pursuit of her assassin, Spark has given us the devastated postulates of feminine wisdom: that a woman creates her identity by choosing her clothes, that she creates her history by choosing her man. That, in the 1970s, Mr Right turns out to be Mr Goodbar, is not the sudden product of urban violence, but a latent truth which fiction exposes. Sparks asks whether men or women are in the driver's seat, and whether the power to choose one's destroyer is women's only form of self-assertion. To label the violence or self-destructiveness of these painful novels as neurotic expressions of a personal pathology, as many reviewers have done, is to ignore, Annette Kolodny suggests,

> the possibility that the worlds they inhabit may in fact be real, or true, and for them the only worlds available, and further, to deny the possibility that their apparently 'odd' or unusual responses may in fact be justifiable or even necessary.[17]

But women's literature must go beyond these scenarios of compromise, madness and death. Although the reclamation of suffering is the beginning, its purpose is to discover the new world. Happily, some recent women's literature, especially in the United States where novelists and poets have become vigorously involved in the women's liberation movement, has gone beyond reclaiming suffering to its re-investment. This newer writing relates the pain of transformation to history. 'If I'm lonely,' writes Adrienne Rich in 'Song',

> it must be the loneliness
> of waking first, of breathing
> dawn's first cold breath on the city
> of being the one awake
> in a house wrapped in sleep[18]

Rich is one of the spokeswomen for a new women's writing which explores the will to change. In her recent book, *Of Woman Born: Motherhood as Experience and Institution*, Rich challenges the alienation from and rejection of the mother that daughters have learned under patriarchy. Much women's literature in the past has dealt with 'matrophobia' or the fear of becoming one's mother.[19] In Sylvia Plath's *The Bell Jar*, for example, the heroine's mother is the target for the novel's most punishing contempt. When Esther announces to her therapist that she hates her mother, she is on the road to recovery. Hating one's mother was the feminist enlightenment of the fifties and sixties; but it is only a metaphor for hating oneself. Female literature of the 1970s goes beyond matrophobia to a courageously sustained quest for the mother, in such books at Margaret Atwood's *Surfacing*, and Lisa Alther's recent *Kinflicks*. As the death of the father has always been an archetypal rite of passage for the Western hero, now the death of the mother as witnessed and transcended by the daughter has become one of the most profound occasions of female literature. In analysing these purposeful awakenings, these reinvigorated mythologies of female culture, feminist criticism finds its most challenging, inspiriting and appropriate task.

Women and the Novel: the 'Precious Speciality'

The most consistent assumption of feminist reading has been the belief that women's special experience would assume and determine distinctive forms in art. In the nineteenth century, such a contribution was ambivalently valued. When Victorian reviewers like G. H. Lewes, Richard Hutton and Richard Simpson began to ask what the literature of women might mean, and what it might become, they focused on the educational, experiential and biological handicaps of the woman novelist, and this was also how most women conceptualised their situation. Some reviewers, granting women's sympathy, sentiment and powers of observation, thought that the novel would provide an appropriate, even a happy, outlet for female emotion and fantasy. In the United States, the popular novelist Fanny Fern understood that women had been granted access to the novel as a sort of repressive desublimation, a harmless channel for frustrations and drives that might otherwise threaten the family, the Church and the State. Fern recommended that women write as therapy, as a release from the stifling silence of the drawing-room, and as a rebellion against the indifference and insensitivity of the men closest to them:

> Look around, and see innumerable women, to whose barren and loveless lives this would be improvement and solace, and I say to them, write! write! It will be a safe outlet for thoughts and feelings that maybe the nearest friend you have has never dreamed had place in your heart and brain . . . it is not *safe* for the women of 1867 to shut down so much that cries out for sympathy and expression, because life is such a maelstrom of business or folly or both that those to whom they have bound themselves, body and soul, recognize only the needs of the former . . . One of these days, when that diary is found, when the hand that penned it shall be dust, with what amazement and remorse will many a husband or father exclaim, I never knew my wife or my child until this moment.[20]

Fern's scribbling woman spoke with fierce indirectness to the male audience, to the imagined husband or father; her purpose was to shock rather than to please, but the need to provoke masculine response was the controlling factor in her writing. At the turn of the century, members of the Women Writers Suffrage League, an important organisation of novelists and journalists, began to explore the psychological bondage of women's literature and its relationships to a male-dominated publishing industry. Elizabeth Robins, the first president of the League, a novelist and actress who had starred in early English productions of Ibsen, argued in 1908 that no woman writer had ever been free to explore female consciousness:

> The realization that she had access to a rich and as yet unrifled storehouse may have crossed her mind, but there were cogent reasons for concealing her knowledge. With that wariness of ages which has come to be instinct, she contented herself with echoing the old fables, presenting to a man-governed world puppets as nearly as possible like those that had from the beginning found such favour in men's sight.

> Contrary to the popular impression, to say in print what she thinks is the last thing the woman-novelist or journalist is so rash as to attempt. There even more than elsewhere

(unless she is reckless) she must wear the aspect that shall have the best chance of pleasing her brothers. Her publishers are not women.[21]

It was to combat this inhibiting commercial monopoly that nineteenth-century women began to organise their own publishing houses, beginning with Emily Faithfull's Victoria Press in the 1870s, and reaching a peak with the flourishing suffrage presses at the beginning of this century. One of the most fervent beliefs of the Women Writers Suffrage League was that the 'terra incognita' of the female psyche would find unique literary expression once women had overthrown male domination. In *A Room of One's Own*, Virginia Woolf argued that economic independence was the essential precondition of an autonomous women's art. Like George Eliot before her, Woolf also believed that women's literature held the promise of a 'precious speciality', a distinctly female vision.

Feminine, Feminist, Female

All of these themes have been important to feminist literary criticism in the 1960s and 1970s but we have approached them with more historical awareness. Before we can even begin to ask how the literature of women would be different and special, we need to reconstruct its past, to rediscover the scores of women novelists, poets and dramatists whose work has been obscured by time, and to establish the continuity of the female tradition from decade to decade, rather than from Great Woman to Great Woman. As we recreate the chain of writers in this tradition, the patterns of influence and response from one generation to the next, we can also begin to challenge the periodicity of orthodox literary history, and its enshrined canons of achievement. It is because we have studied women writers in isolation that we have never grasped the connections between them. When we go beyond Austen, the Brontës and Eliot, say, to look at a hundred and fifty or more of their sister novelists, we can see patterns and phases in the evolution of a female tradition which correspond to the developmental phases of any subcultural art. In my book on English women writers, *A Literature of Their Own*, I have called these the Feminine, Feminist and Female stages.[22] During the Feminine phase, dating from about 1840 to 1880, women wrote in an effort to equal the intellectual achievements of the male culture, and internalised its assumptions about female nature. The distinguishing sign of this period is the male pseudonym, introduced in England in the 1840s, and a national characteristic of English women writers. In addition to the famous names we all know — George Eliot, Currer, Ellis and Acton Bell — dozens of other women chose male pseudonyms as a way of coping with a double literary standard. This masculine disguise goes well beyond the title page; it exerts an irregular pressure on the narrative, affecting tone, diction, structure and characterisation. In contrast to the English male pseudonym, which signals such clear self-awareness of the liabilities of female authorship, American women during the same period adopted superfeminine, little-me pseudonyms (Fanny Fern, Grace Greenwood, Fanny Forester), disguising behind these nominal bouquets their boundless energy, powerful economic motives and keen professional skills. It is pleasing to discover the occasional Englishwoman who combines both these techniques, and creates the illusion of male authorship with a name that contains the encoded domestic message of femininity — such as Harriet Parr, who wrote under the pen name 'Holme Lee'. The feminist content of feminine art is typically oblique, displaced, ironic and subversive; one has to read it between the lines, in the missed possibilities of the text.

In the Feminist phase, from about 1880 to 1920, or the winning of the vote, women are historically enabled to reject the accomodating postures of femininity and to use literature to dramatize the ordeals of wronged womanhood. The personal sense of injustice which feminine novelists such as Elizabeth Gaskell and Frances Trollope expressed in their novels of class struggle and factory life become increasingly and explicity feminist in the 1880s, when a generation of New Women redefined the woman artist's role in terms of responsibility to suffering sisters. The purest examples of this phase are the Amazon Utopias of the 1890s, fantasies of perfected female societies set in an England or an America of the future, which were also protests against male government, male laws and male medicine. One author of Amazon Utopias, the American Charlotte Perkins Gilman, also analysed the preoccupations of masculine literature with sex and war, and the alternative possibilities of an emancipated feminist literature. Gilman's Utopian feminism carried George Eliot's idea of the 'precious speciality' to its matriarchal extremes. Comparing her view of sisterly collectivity to the beehive, she writes that

> the bees's fiction would be rich and broad, full of the complex tasks of comb-building and filling, the care and feeding of the young . . . It would treat of the vast fecundity of motherhood, the educative and selective processes of the group-mothers, and the passion of loyalty, of social service, which holds the hives together.[23]

This is Feminist Socialist Realism with a vengeance, but women novelists of the period — even Gilman, in her short stories — could not be limited to such didactic formulas, or such maternal topics.

In the Female phase, ongoing since 1920, women reject both imitation and protest — two forms of dependency — and turn instead to female experience as the source of an autonomous art, extending the feminist analysis of culture to the forms and techniques of literature. Representatives of the formal Female Aesthetic, such as Dorothy Richardson and Virginia Woolf, begin to think in terms of male and female sentences, and divide their work into 'masculine' journalism and 'feminine' fictions, redefining and sexualising external and internal experience. Their experiments were both enriching and imprisoning retreats into the celebration of consciousness; even in Woolf's famous definition of life: 'a luminous halo, a semi-transparent envelope surrounding us from the beginning of consciousness to the end',[24] there is a submerged metaphor of uterine withdrawal and containment. In this sense, the Room of One's Own becomes a kind of Amazon Utopia, population 1.

Feminist Criticism, Marxism and Structuralism

In trying to account for these complex permutations of the female tradition, feminist criticism has tried a variety of theoretical approaches. The most natural direction for feminist criticism to take has been the revision, and even the subversion of related ideologies, especially Marxist aesthetics and structuralism, altering their vocabularies and methods to include the variable of gender. I believe, however, that this thrifty feminine making do is ultimately unsatisfactory. Feminist criticism cannot go around forever in men's ill-fitting hand-me-downs, the Annie Hall of English studies; but must, as John Stuart Mill wrote about women's literature in 1869, 'emancipate itself from the influence of accepted models, and guide itself by its own impulses'[25] — as, I think, gynocritics is beginning to do. This is not to deny the necessity of using the terminology and techniques of our profession. But when we consider the historical conditions in which critical ideologies are produced, we see why feminist adaptations seem to have reached an impasse.

Both Marxism and structuralism see themselves as privileged critical discourse, and pre-empt the claim to superior places in the hierarchy of critical approaches. A key word in each system is 'science'; both claim to be sciences of literature, and repudiate the personal, fallible, interpretative reading. Marxist aesthetics offers a 'science of the text', in which the author becomes not the creator but the producer of a text whose components are historically and economically determined. Structuralism presents linguistically based models of textual permutations and combinations, offering a 'science of literary meaning', a grammar of genre. The assimilation of these positivist and evangelical literary criticisms by Anglo-American scholarship in the past fifteen years is not — I would argue — a spontaneous or accidental cultural phenomenon. In the Cold War atmosphere of the late 1950s, when European structuralism began to develop, the morale of the Anglo-American male academic humanist was at its nadir. This was the era of Sputnik, of scientific competition with the Soviet Union, of government money flowing to the laboratories and research centres. Northrop Frye has written about the plight of the male intellectual confronting

> the dismal sexist symbology surrounding the humanities which he meets everywhere, even in the university itself, from freshman classes to the president's office. This symbology, or whatever one should call it, says that the sciences, especially the physical sciences, are rugged, aggressive, out in the world doing things, and so symbolically male, whereas the literatures are narcissistic, intuitive, fanciful, staying at home and making the home more beautiful but not doing anything serious and are therefore symbolically female.[26]

Frye's own *Anatomy of Criticism*, published in 1957, presented the first postulates of a systematic critical theory, and the 'possibility of literary study's attaining the progressive, cumulative qualities of science'.[27]

The new sciences of the text based on linguistics, computers, genetic structuralism, deconstructionism, neo-formalism and deformalism, affective stylistics and psychoaesthetics, have offered literary critics the opportunity to demonstrate that the work they do is as manly and aggressive as nuclear physics — not intuitive, expressive and feminine, but strenuous, rigorous, impersonal and virile. In a shrinking job market, these new levels of professionalisation also function as discriminators between the marketable and the marginal lecturer. Literary science, in its manic generation of difficult terminology, its establishment of seminars and institutes of post-graduate study, creates an élite corps of specialists who spend more and more time mastering the theory, less and less time reading the books. We are moving towards a two-tiered system of 'higher' and 'lower' criticism, the higher concerned with the 'scientific' problems of form and structure, the 'lower' concerned with the 'humanistic' problems of content and interpretation. And these levels, it seems to me, are now taking on subtle gender identities, and assuming a sexual polarity — hermeneutics and hismeneutics. Ironically, the existence of a new criticism practised by women has made it even more possible for structuralism and Marxism to strive, Henchard-like, for systems of formal obliga-tion. Feminists writing in these modes, such as Hélène Cixous and the women con-tributors to *Diacritics*, risk being allotted the symbolic ghettoes of the special issue or the back of the book for their essays.

It is not only because the exchange between feminism, Marxism and structura-lism has hitherto been so one-sided, however, that I think attempts at syntheses have so far been unsuccessful. While scientific criticism struggles to purge itself of the subjective, feminist criticism is willing to assert (in the title of a recent antho-logy) *The Authority of Experience*.[28] The experience of women can easily disappear, become mute, invalid and invisible, lost in the diagrams of the structuralist or the class conflict of the Marxists. Experience is not emotion; we must protest now as in the nineteenth century against the equation of the feminine with the irrational. But we must also recognise that the questions we most need to ask go beyond those that science can answer. We must seek the repressed messages of women in history, in anthropology, in psychology, and in ourselves, before we can locate the feminine not-said, in the manner of Pierre Macherey, by probing the fissures of the female text.

Thus the current theoretical impasse in feminist criticism, I believe, is more than a problem of finding 'exacting definitions and a suitable terminology', or 'theorizing in the midst of a struggle'. It comes from our own divided conscious-ness, the split in each of us. We are both the daughters of the male tradition, of our teachers, our professors, our dissertation advisers and our publishers — a tradi-tion which asks us to be rational, marginal and grateful; and sisters in a new women's movement which engenders another kind of awareness and com-mitment, which demands that we renounce the pseudo-success of token woman-hood, and the ironic masks of academic debate. How much easier, how less lonely it is, not to awaken — to continue to be critics and teachers of male literature, anthropologists of male culture, and psychologists of male literary response, claiming all the while to be universal. Yet we cannot will ourselves to go back to sleep. As women scholars in the 1970s we have been given a great opportunity, a great intellectual challenge. The anatomy, the rhetoric, the poetics, the history, await our writing.

I am sure that this divided consciousness is sometimes experienced by men, but I think it unlikely that many male academics would have had the division in them-selves as succinctly and publicly labelled as they were for me in 1976 when my official title at the University of Delaware was Visiting Minority Professor. I am deeply aware of the struggle in myself between the professor, who wants to study major works by major writers, and to mediate impersonally between these works and the readings of other professors — and the minority, the woman who wants connections between my life and my work, and who is committed to a revolution of consciousness that would make my concerns those of the majority. There have been times when the Minority wishes to betray the Professor, by isolating herself in a female ghetto; or when the Professor wishes to betray the Minority by denying the troubling voice of difference and dissent. What I hope is that neither will betray the other, because neither can exist by itself. The task of feminist critics is to find a new language, a new way of reading that can integrate our intelligence and our experience, our reason and our suffering, our scepticism and our vision. This enterprise should not be confined to women; I invite Criticus, Poeticus and Plutarchus to share it with us. One thing is certain: feminist criticism is not visiting. It is here to stay, and we must make it a permanent home.

Notes:

I wish to thank Nina Auerbach, Kate Ellis, Mary Jacobus, Wendy Martin, Adrienne Rich, Helen Taylor, Martha Vicinus, Margaret Walters and Ruth Yeazell for sharing with me their ideas on feminist criticism.

1. Leon Edel, 'The Poetics of Biography' in Hilda Schiff (ed.), *Contemporary Approaches to English Studies* (London, 1977), p. 38. The other contributors to the symposium are George Steiner, Raymond Williams, Christopher Butler, Jonathan Culler and Terry Eagleton.
2. Robert Partlow, *Dickens Studies Annual*, vol. v (Carbondale, Southern Illinois, 1976), pp. xiv–xv. Nina Auerbach's essay is called 'Dickens and Dombey: A Daughter After All'.
3. Robert Boyers, 'A Case Against Feminist Criticism', *Partisan Review*, vol. xliv (Winter 1977), pp. 602, 610.
4. Adrienne Rich, *Of Woman Born: Motherhood as Experience and Institution* (New York, 1977), p. 62.
5. Mary Daly, *Beyond God the Father: Towards a Philosophy of Women's Liberation* (Boston, 1973), pp. 12–13.
6. ·Geoffrey Hartman, *The Fate of Reading* (Chicago, 1975), p. 3.
7. 'Theories of Feminist Criticism' in Josephine Donovan (ed.), *Feminist Literary Criticism: Explorations in Theory* (Lexington, 1976), pp. 64, 68, 72.
8. Irving Howe, *Thomas Hardy* (London, 1968), p. 84. For a more detailed discussion of this problem, see my essay 'The Unmanning of the Mayor of Casterbridge' in Dale Kramer (ed.), *Critical Approaches to Hardy* (London, 1979).
9. Elizabeth Hardwick, *Seduction and Betrayal* (New York, 1974).
10. Shirley Ardener (ed.), *Perceiving Women* (London, 1975).
11. 'Women, Culture, and Society: A Theoretical Overview' in Louise Lamphere and Michelle Rosaldo (eds.), *Women, Culture and Society* (Stanford, 1974), p. 39.
12. Carroll Smith-Rosenberg, 'The Female World of Love and Ritual: Relations Between Women in Nineteenth-Century America', *Signs: Journal of Women in Culture and Society*, vol. i (Autumn 1975), pp. 1–30; Nancy Cott, *The Bonds of Womanhood* (New Heaven, 1977); Ann Douglas, *The Feminization of American Culture* (New York, 1977); Nina Auerbach, *Communities of Women* (Cambridge, Mass., 1978).
13. 'Women and Fiction' in Virginia Woolf, *Collected Essays*, vol. ii (London, 1967), p. 141.
14. Peter N. Heydon and Philip Kelley (eds.), *Elizabeth Barrett Browning's Letters to Mrs. David Ogilvy* (London, 1974), p. 115.
15. 'Cassandra' in Ray Strachey (ed.), *The Cause* (London, 1928), p. 398.
16. Rebecca West, 'And They All Lived Unhappily Ever After', *TLS* (26 July 1974), p. 779.
17. Annette Kolodny, 'Some Notes on Defining a "Feminist Literary Criticism" ', *Critical Inquiry*, vol. ii (1975), p. 84. For an illuminating discussion of *The Driver's Seat*, see Auerbach, *Communities of Women*, p. 181.
18. Adrienne Rich, *Diving into the Wreck* (New York, 1973), p. 20.
19. The term 'matrophobia' has been coined by Lynn Sukenick; see Rich, *Of Woman Born*, pp. 235 ff.
20. Quoted in Ann Douglas Wood, 'The "Scribbling Women" and Fanny Fern: Why Women Wrote', *American Quarterly*, vol. xxiii (1971), pp 3–24.
21. Elizabeth Robins, *Woman's Secret*, WSPU pamphlet in the collection of the Museum of London, p. 6. Jane Marcus is preparing a full-length study of Elizabeth Robins.
22. Elaine Showalter, *A Literature of Their Own: British Women Novelists from Brontë to Lessing* (Princeton, New Jersey, 1977).
23. Charlotte Perkins Gilman, *The Man-made World* (London, 1911), pp. 101–2.
24. 'Modern Fiction', *Collected Essays*, vol. ii, p. 106.
25. J. S. Mill, *The Subjection of Women* (London, 1869), p. 133.
26. Northrop Frye, 'Expanding Eyes', *Critical Inquiry*, vol. ii (1975), pp. 201–2.
27. Robert Scholes, *Structuralism in Literature: An Introduction* (New Haven, 1974), p. 118.
28. Lee Edwards and Arlyn Diamond (eds.), *The Authority of Experience* (Amherst, Mass., 1977).

2

Sandra M. Gilbert and Susan Gubar, *'Wuthering Heights'*

***Catherine's fall, however, is caused by a patriarchal past and present, besides being associated with a patriarchal future. It is significant, then, that her problems begin — violently enough — when she literally falls down and is bitten by a male bulldog, a sort of guard/god from Thrushcross Grange. Though many readers overlook this point, Catherine does not *go* to the Grange when she is twelve years old. On the contrary, the Grange seizes her and 'holds [her] fast,' a metaphoric action which emphasizes the turbulent and inexorable nature of the psychosexual *rites de passage Wuthering Heights* describes, just as the ferociously masculine bull/dog — as a symbolic representative of Thrushcross Grange — contrasts strikingly with the ascendancy at the Heights of the hellish female bitch goddess alternately referred to as 'Madam' and 'Juno.' [1]

Realistically speaking, Catherine and Heathcliff have been driven in the direction of Thrushcross Grange by their own desire to escape not only the pietistic tortures Joseph inflicts but also, more urgently, just that sexual awareness irritatingly imposed by Hindley's romantic paradise. Neither sexuality nor its consequences can be evaded, however, and the farther the children run the closer they come to the very fate they secretly wish to avoid. Racing 'from the top of the Heights to the park without stopping,' they plunge from the periphery of Hindley's paradise (which was transforming their heaven into a hell) to the boundaries of a place that at first seems authentically heavenly, a place full of light and softness and colour, a 'splendid place carpeted with crimson . . . and [with] a pure white ceiling bordered by gold, a shower of glass-drops hanging in silver chains from the centre, and shimmering with little soft tapers' (chap. 6). Looking in the window, the outcasts speculate that if they were inside such a room 'we should have thought ourselves in heaven!' From the outside, at least, the Lintons' elegant haven appears paradisaical. But once the children have experienced its Urizenic interior, they know that in their terms this heaven is hell.

Because the first emissary of this heaven who greets them is the bulldog Skulker, a sort of hellhound posing as a hound of heaven, the wound this almost totemic animal inflicts upon Catherine is as symbolically suggestive as his role in the girl's forced passage from Wuthering Heights to Thrushcross Grange. Barefoot, as if to emphasize her 'wild child' innocence, Catherine is exceptionally vulnerable, as a wild child must inevitably be, and when the dog is 'throttled off, his huge, purple tongue hanging half a foot out of his mouth . . . his pendant lips [are] streaming with bloody slaver.' 'Look . . . how her foot bleeds,' Edgar Linton exclaims, and

'She may be lamed for life,' his mother anxiously notes (chap. 6). Obviously such bleeding has sexual connotations, especially when it occurs in a pubescent girl. Crippling injuries to the feet are equally resonant, moreover, almost always signifying symbolic castration, as in the stories of Oedipus, Achilles, and the Fisher King. Additionally, it hardly needs to be noted that Skulker's equipment for aggression — his huge purple tongue and pendant lips, for instance — sounds extraordinarily phallic. In a Freudian sense, then, the imagery of this brief but violent episode hints that Catherine has been simultaneously catapulted into adult female sexuality *and* castrated.

How can a girl 'become a woman' and be castrated (that is, desexed) at the same time? Considering how Freudian its iconographic assumptions are, the question is disingenuous, for not only in Freud's terms but in feminist terms, as Elizabeth Janeway and Juliet Mitchell have both observed, femaleness — implying 'penis envy' — quite reasonably *means* castration. 'No woman has been deprived of a penis; she never had one to begin with,' Janeway notes, commenting on Freud's crucial 'Female Sexuality' (1931).

> But she *has* been deprived of something else that men enjoy: namely, autonomy, freedom, and the power to control her destiny. By insisting, falsely, on female deprivation of the male organ, Freud is pointing to an actual deprivation and one of which he was clearly aware. In Freud's time the advantages enjoyed by the male sex over the inferior female were, of course, even greater than at present, and they were also accepted to a much larger extent, as being inevitable, inescapable. Women were evident *social* castrates, and the mutilation of their potentiality as achieving human creatures was quite analogous to the physical wound.[2]

But if such things were true in Freud's time, they were even truer in Emily Brontë's. And certainly the hypothesis that Catherine Earnshaw has become in some sense a 'social castrate,' that she has been 'lamed for life,' is borne out by her treatment at Thrushcross Grange — and by the treatment of her alter ego, Heathcliff. For, assuming that she is a 'young lady,' the entire Linton household cossets the wounded (but still healthy) girl as if she were truly an invalid. Indeed, feeding her their alien rich food — negus and cakes from their own table — washing her feet, combing her hair, dressing her in 'enormous slippers,' and wheeling her about like a doll, they seem to be enacting some sinister ritual of initiation, the sort of ritual that has traditionally weakened mythic heroines from Persephone to Snow White. And because he is 'a little Lascar, or an American or Spanish castaway,' the Lintons banish Heathcliff from their parlour, thereby separating Catherine from the lover/brother whom she herself defines as her strongest and most necessary 'self.' For five weeks now, she will be at the mercy of the Grange's heavenly gentility.

To say that Thrushcross Grange is genteel or cultured and that it therefore seems 'heavenly' is to say, of course, that it is the opposite of Wuthering Heights. And certainly at every point the two houses are opposed to each other, as if each in its self-assertion must absolutely deny the other's being. Like Milton and Blake, Emily Brontë thought in polarities. Thus, where Wuthering Heights is essentially a great parlourless room built around a huge central hearth, a furnace of dark energy like the fire of Los, Thrushcross Grange has a parlour notable not for heat but for light, for 'a pure white ceiling bordered by gold' with 'a shower of glass-drops' in the centre that seems to parody the 'sovran vital Lamp' (*Paradise Lost*,

3.22) which illuminates Milton's heaven of Right Reason. Where Wuthering Heights, moreover, is close to being naked or 'raw' in Lévi-Strauss' sense — its floors uncarpeted, most of its inhabitants barely literate, even the meat on its shelves open to inspection — Thrushcross Grange is clothed and 'cooked': carpeted in crimson, bookish, feeding on cakes and tea and negus.[3] It follows from this, then, that where Wuthering Heights is functional, even its dogs working sheepdogs or hunters, Thrushcross Grange (though guarded by bulldogs) appears to be decorative or aesthetic, the home of lapdogs as well as ladies. And finally therefore, Wuthering Heights in its stripped functional rawness is essentially anti-hierarchical and egalitarian as the aspirations of Eve and Satan, while Thrushcross Grange reproduces the hierarchical chain of being that Western culture traditionally proposes as heaven's decree.

For all these reasons, Catherine Earnshaw, together with her whip Heathcliff, has at Wuthering Heights what Emily Dickinson would call a 'Barefoot-Rank.'[4] But at Thrushcross Grange, clad first in enormous, crippling slippers and later in 'a long cloth habit which she [is] obliged to hold up with both hands' (chap. 7) in order to walk, she seems on the verge of becoming, again in Dickinson's words, a 'Lady [who] dare not lift her Veil/For fear it be dispelled'. For in comparison to Wuthering Heights, Thrushcross Grange is, finally, the home of concealment and doubleness, a place where, as we shall see, reflections are separated from their owners like souls from bodies, so that the lady in anxiety 'peers beyond her mesh — /And wishes — and denies — /Lest Interview — annul a want/That Image — satisfies.' And it is here, therefore, at heaven's mercy, that Catherine Earnshaw learns 'to adopt a double character without exactly intending to deceive anyone' (chap. 8).

In fact, for Catherine Earnshaw, Thrushcross Grange in those five fatal weeks becomes a Palace of Instruction, as Brontë ironically called the equivocal schools of life where her adolescent Gondals were often incarcerated. But rather than learning, like A. G. A. and her cohorts, to rule a powerful nation, Catherine must learn to rule herself, or so the Lintons and her brother decree. She must learn to repress her own impulses, must girdle her own energies with the iron stays of 'reason.' Having fallen into the decorous 'heaven' of femaleness, Catherine must become a lady. And just as her entrance into the world of Thrushcross Grange was forced and violent, so this process by which she is obliged to accommodate herself to that world is violent and painful, an unsentimental education recorded by a practiced, almost sadistically accurate observer. For the young Gondals, too, had had a difficult time of it in their Palace of Instruction: far from being wonderful Golden Rule days, their school days were spent mostly in dungeons and torture cells, where their elders starved them into submission or self-knowledge.

That education for Emily Brontë is almost always fearful, even agonizing, may reflect the Brontës' own traumatic experiences at the Clergy Daughters School and elsewhere.[5] But it may also reflect in a more general way the repressiveness with which the nineteenth century educated all its young ladies, strapping them to back-boards and forcing them to work for hours at didactic samplers until the more high-spirited girls — the Catherine Earnshaws and Catherine Morlands — must have felt, like the inhabitants of Kafka's penal colony, that the morals and maxims of patriarchy were being embroidered on their own skins. To mention Catherine Morland here is not to digress. As we have seen, Austen did not subject her heroine to education as a gothic/Gondalian torture, except parodically. Yet even Austen's parody suggests that for a girl like Catherine Morland the school of life inevitably inspires an almost instinctive fear, just as it would for A. G. A. 'Heavenly' Northanger Abbey may somehow conceal a prison cell, Catherine suspects, and she develops this notion by sensing (as Henry Tilney cannot) that the female romances she is reading are in some sense the disguised histories of her own life.

In Catherine Earnshaw's case, these points are made even more subtly than in the Gondal poems or in *Northanger Abbey*, for Catherine's education in doubleness, in ladylike decorum meaning also ladylike deceit, is marked by an actual doubling or fragmentation of her personality. Thus though it is ostensibly Catherine who is being educated, it is Heathcliff — her rebellious alter ego, her whip, her id — who is exiled to a prison cell, as if to implement delicate Isabella Linton's first horrified reaction to him: 'Frightful thing! Put him in the cellar' (chap. 6). Not in the cellar but in the garret, Heathcliff is locked up and, significantly, starved, while Catherine, daintily 'cutting up the wing of a goose,' practices table manners below. Even more significantly, however, she too is finally unable to eat her dinner and retreats under the table cloth to weep for her imprisoned playmate. To Catherine, Heathcliff is 'more myself than I am,' as she later famously tells Nelly, and so his literal starvation is symbolic of her more terrible because more dangerous spiritual starvation, just as her literal wound at Thrushcross Grange is also a metaphorical deathblow to *his* health and power. For divided from each other, the once androgynous Heathcliff-and-Catherine are now conquered by the concerted forces of patriarchy, the Lintons of Thrushcross Grange acting together with Hindley and Frances, their emissaries at the Heights.

It is, appropriately enough, during this period, that Frances gives birth to Hareton, the new patriarch-to-be, and dies, having fulfilled her painful function in the book and in the world. During this period, too, Catherine's education in lady-like self-denial causes her dutifully to deny her self and decide to marry Edgar. For when she says of Heathcliff that 'he's more myself than I am,' she means that as her exiled self the nameless 'gipsy' really does preserve in his body more of her original being than she retains: even in his deprivation he seems whole and sure, while she is now entirely absorbed in the ladylike wishing and denying Dickinson's poem describes. Thus, too, it is during this period of loss and transition that Catherine obsessively inscribes on her windowsill the crucial writing Lockwood finds, writing which announces from the first Emily Brontë's central concern with identity: 'a name repeated in all kinds of characters, large and small — Catherine Earnshaw, here and there varied to Catherine Heathcliff, and then again to Catherine Linton' (chap. 3). In the light of this repeated and varied name it is no wonder, finally, that Catherine knows Heathcliff is 'more myself than I am,' for he has only a single name, while she has so many that she may be said in a sense to have none. Just as triumphant self-discovery is the ultimate goal of the male *Bildungsroman*, anxious self-denial, Brontë suggests, is the ultimate product of a female education. What Catherine, or any girl, must learn is that she does not know her own name, and therefore cannot know either who she is or whom she is destined to be.

It has often been argued that Catherine's anxiety and uncertainty about her own identity represents a moral failing, a fatal flaw in her character which leads to her inability to choose between Edgar and Heathcliff. Heathcliff's reproachful 'Why did you betray your own heart, Cathy?' (chap. 15) represents a Blakeian form of this moral criticism, a contemptuous suggestion that 'those who restrain desire do so because theirs is weak enough to be restrained.'[6] The more vulgar and common-sensical attack of the Leavisites, on the other hand — the censorious notion that 'maturity' means being strong enough to choose not to have your cake and eat it too — represents what Mark Kinkead-Weeks calls 'the view from the Grange.'[7] To talk of morality in connection with Catherine's fall — and specifically in connection with her self-deceptive decision to marry Edgar — seems pointless, however, for morality only becomes a relevant term where there are meaningful choices.

As we have seen, Catherine has no meaningful choices. Driven from Wuthering Heights to Thrushcross Grange by her brother's marriage, seized by Thrushcross Grange and held fast in the jaws of reason, education, decorum, she cannot do otherwise than as she does, must marry Edgar because there is no one else for her to marry and a lady must marry. Indeed, her self-justifying description of her love for Edgar — 'I love the ground under his feet, and the air over his head, and every-thing he touches, and every word he says' (chap. 9) — is a bitter parody of a genteel romantic declaration which shows how effective her education has been in indoctrinating her with the literary romanticism deemed suitable for young ladies, the swooning 'femininity' that identifies all energies with the charisma of fathers/lovers/husbands. Her concomitant explanation that it would 'degrade' her to marry Heathcliff is an equally inevitable product of her education, for her fall into ladyhood has been accompanied by Heathcliff's reduction to an equivalent position of female powerlessness, and Catherine has learned, correctly, that if it is degrading to be a woman it is even more degrading to be *like* a woman. Just as Milton's Eve, therefore, being already fallen, had no meaningful choice despite Milton's best efforts to prove otherwise, so Catherine has no real choice. Given the patriarchal nature of culture, women must fall — that is, they are already fallen because doomed to fall.

In the shadow of this point, however, moral censorship is merely redundant, a sort of interrogative restatement of the novel's central fact. Heathcliff's Blakeian reproach is equally superfluous, except insofar as it is not moral but etiological, a question one part of Catherine asks another, like her later passionate 'Why am I so changed?' For as Catherine herself perceives, social and biological forces have fiercely combined against her. God as — in W. H. Auden's words — a 'Victorian papa' has hurled her from the equivocal natural paradise she calls 'heaven' and He calls 'hell' into His idea of 'heaven' where she will break her heart with weeping to come back to the Heights. Her speculative, tentative 'mad' speech to Nelly captures, finally, both the urgency and the inexorability of her fall. 'Sup-posing at twelve years old, I had been wrenched from the Heights . . . and my all in all, as Heathcliff was at that time, and been converted at a stroke into Mrs. Linton, the lady of Thrushcross Grange, and the wife of a stranger: an exile, and outcast, thenceforth, from what had been my world.' In terms of the psychodramatic action of *Wuthering Heights*, only Catherine's use of the word *supposing* is here a rhetorical strategy; the rest of her speech is absolutely accurate, and places her subsequent actions beyond good and evil, just as it suggests, in yet another Blakeian reversal of customary terms, that her madness may really be sanity.

Catherine Earnshaw Linton's decline follows Catherine Earnshaw's fall. Slow at first, it is eventually as rapid, sickening, and deadly as the course of Brontë's own consumption was to be. And the long slide toward death of the body begins with what appears to be an irreversible death of the soul — with Catherine's fatalistic acceptance of Edgar's offer and her consequent self-imprisonment in the role of 'Mrs. Linton, the lady of Thrushcross Grange.' It is, of course, her announcement of this decision to Nelly, overheard by Heathcliff, which leads to Heathcliff's self-exile from the Heights and thus definitively to Catherine's psychic fragmentation. And significantly, her response to the departure of her true self is a lapse into illness which both signals the beginning of her decline and foreshadows its mortal end. Her words to Nelly the morning after Heathcliff's departure are therefore symbolically as well as dramatically resonant: 'Shut the window, Nelly, I'm starving!' (chap. 9).

As Dorothy van Ghent has shown, windows in *Wuthering Heights* consistently represent openings into possibility, apertures through which subversive otherness can enter, or wounds out of which respectability can escape like flowing blood.[8] It is, after all, on the window ledge that Lockwood finds Catherine's different names obsessively inscribed, as if the girl had been trying to decide which self to let in the window or in which direction she ought to fly after making her own escape down the branches of the neighbouring pine. It is through the same window that the ghost of Catherine Linton extends her icy fingers to the horrified visitor. And it is a window at the Grange that Catherine, in her 'madness,' begs Nelly to open so that she can have one breath of the wind that 'comes straight down the moor' (chap. 12). 'Open the window again wide, fasten it open!' she cries, then rises and, predicting her own death, seems almost ready to start on her journey homeward up the moor. ('I could not trust her alone by the gaping lattice,' Nelly comments wisely.) But besides expressing a general wish to escape from 'this shattered prison' of her body, her marriage, her self, her life, Catherine's desire now to *open* the window refers specifically back to that moment three years earlier when she had chosen instead to close it, chosen to inflict on herself the imprisonment and starvation that as part of her education had been inflicted on her double, Heathcliff.

Imprisonment leads to madness, solipsism, paralysis, as Byron's *Prisoner of Chillon*, some of Brontë's Gondal poems, and countless other gothic and neo-gothic tales suggest. Starvation — both in the modern sense of malnutrition and the archaic Miltonic sense of freezing ('to starve in ice') — leads to weakness, immobility, death. During her decline, starting with both starvation and imprisonment, Catherine passes through all these grim stages of mental and physical decay. At first she seems (to Nelly anyway) merely somewhat 'headstrong.' Powerless without her whip, keenly conscious that she has lost the autonomy of her hardy and free girlhood, she gets her way by indulging in tantrums, wheedling, manipulating, so that Nelly's optimistic belief that she and Edgar 'were really in possession of a deep and growing happiness' contrasts ironically with the housekeeper's simultaneous admission that Catherine 'was never subject to depression of spirits before' the three interlocking events of Heathcliff's departure, her 'perilous illness', and her marriage (chap. 10). But Heathcliff's mysterious reappearance six months after her wedding intensifies rather than cures her symptoms. For his return does not in any way suggest a healing of the wound of femaleness that was inflicted at puberty. Instead, it signals the beginning of 'madness,' a sort of feverish infection of the wound. Catherine's marriage to Edgar has now inexorably locked her into a social system that denies her autonomy, and thus, as psychic symbolism, Heathcliff's return represents the return of her true self's desires without the rebirth of her former powers. And desire without power, as Freud and Blake both knew, inevitably engenders disease.

If we understand all the action that takes place at Thrushcross Grange between Edgar, Catherine, and Heathcliff from the moment of Heathcliff's reappearance until the time of Catherine's death to be ultimately psychodramatic, a grotesque playing out of Catherine's emotional fragmentation on a 'real' stage, then further discussion of her sometimes genteelly Victorian, sometimes fiercely Byronic decline becomes almost unnecessary, its meaning is so obvious. Edgar's autocratic hostility to Heathcliff — that is, to Catherine's desirous self, her independent will — manifests itself first in his attempt to have her entertain the returned 'gipsy' or 'plough boy' in the kitchen because he doesn't belong in the parlour. But soon Edgar's hatred results in a determination to expel Heathcliff entirely from his house because he fears the effects of this demonic intruder, with all he signifies, not only upon his wife but upon his sister. His fear is justified because, as we shall see, the Satanic rebellion Heathcliff introduces into the parlours of 'heaven' contains the germ of a terrible dis-ease with patriarchy that causes women like Catherine and Isabella to try to escape their imprisonment in roles and houses by running away, by starving themselves, and finally by dying.

Because Edgar is so often described as 'soft,' 'weak,' slim, fair-haired, even effeminate-looking, the specifically patriarchal nature of his feelings toward Heathcliff may not be immediately evident. Certainly many readers have been misled by his almost stylized angelic qualities to suppose that the rougher, darker Heathcliff incarnates masculinity in contrast to Linton's effeminacy. The returned Heathcliff, Nelly says, 'had grown a tall, athletic, well-formed man, beside whom my master seemed quite slender and youthlike. His upright carriage suggested the idea of his having been in the army' (chap. 10). She even seems to acquiesce in his superior maleness. But her constant, reflexive use of the phrase 'my master' for Edgar tells us otherwise, as do some of her other expressions. At this point in the novel, anyway, Heathcliff is always merely 'Heathcliff' while Edgar is variously 'Mr. Linton,' 'my master,' 'Mr. Edgar,' and 'the master,' all phrases conveying the power and status he has independent of his physical strength.

In fact, as Milton also did, Emily Brontë demonstrates that the power of the patriarch, Edgar's power, begins with words, for heaven is populated by '*spirits* Masculine,' and as above, so below. Edgar does not need a strong, conventionally masculine body, because his mastery is contained in books, wills, testaments, leases, titles, rentrolls, documents, languages, all the paraphernalia by which patriarchal culture is transmitted from one generation to the next. Indeed, even without Nelly's designation of him as 'the master,' his notable bookishness would define him as a patriarch, for he rules his house from his library as if to parody that male education in Latin and Greek, privilege and prerogative, which so infuriated Milton's daughters.[9] As a figure in the psychodrama of Catherine's decline, then, he incarnates the education in young ladyhood that has commanded her to learn her 'place.' In Freudian terms he would no doubt be described as her superego, the internalized guardian of morality and culture, with Heathcliff, his opposite, functioning as her childish and desirous id.

But at the same time, despite Edgar's superegoistic qualities, Emily Brontë shows that his patriarchal rule, like Thrushcross Grange itself, is based on physical as well as spiritual violence. For her, as for Blake, heaven *kills*. Thus, at a word from Thrushcross Grange, Skulker is let loose, and Edgar's magistrate father cries 'What prey, Robert?' to his manservant, explaining that he fears thieves because 'yesterday was my rent day.' Similarly, Edgar, having decided that he has 'humored' Catherine long enough, calls for two strong men servants to support his authority and descends into the kitchen to evict Heathcliff. The patriarch, Brontë notes, needs words, not muscles, and Heathcliff's derisive language paradoxically suggests understanding of the true male power Edgar's 'soft' exterior conceals: 'Cathy, this lamb of yours threatens like a bull!' (chap. 11). Even more significant, perhaps, is the fact that when Catherine locks Edgar in alone with her and Heathcliff — once more imprisoning herself while ostensibly imprisoning the hated master — this apparently effeminate, 'milk-blooded coward' frees himself by striking Heathcliff a breathtaking blow on the throat 'that would have levelled a slighter man.'

Edgar's victory once again recapitulates that earlier victory of Thrushcross Grange over Wuthering Heights which also meant the victory of a Urizenic 'heaven' over a delightful and energetic 'hell.' At the same time, it seals Catherine's doom, locking her into her downward spiral of self-starvation. And in doing this it finally explains what is perhaps Nelly's most puzzling remark about the relationship between Edgar and Catherine. In chapter 8, noting that the love-struck sixteen-year-old Edgar is 'doomed, and flies to his fate,' the housekeeper sardonically declares that 'the soft thing [Edgar] . . . possessed the power to depart [from Catherine] as much as a cat possesses the power to leave a mouse half killed or a bird half eaten.' At that point in the novel her metaphor seems odd. Is not headstrong Catherine the hungry cat, and 'soft' Edgar the half-eaten mouse? But in fact, as we now see, Edgar all along represented the devouring force that will gnaw and worry Catherine to death, consuming flesh and spirit together. For having fallen into 'heaven,' she has ultimately — to quote Sylvia Plath — 'fallen / Into the stomach of indifference,' a social physiology that urgently needs her not so much for herself as for her function.[10]

When we note the significance of such imagery of devouring, as well as the all-pervasive motif of self-starvation in *Wuthering Heights*, the kitchen setting of this crucial confrontation between Edgar and Heathcliff begins to seem more than coincidental. In any case, the episode is followed closely by what C. P. Sanger calls Catherine's 'hunger strike' and by her famous mad scene.[11] Another line of Plath's describes the feelings of self-lessness that seem to accompany Catherine's realization that she has been reduced to a role, a function, a sort of walking costume: 'I have no face, I have wanted to efface myself.'[12] For the weakening of Catherine's grasp on the world is most specifically shown by her inability to recognize her own face in the mirror during the mad scene. Explaining to Nelly that she is not mad, she notes that if she were 'I should believe you really *were* [a] withered hag, and I should think I *was* under Penistone Crag; and I'm conscious it's night and there are two candles on the table making the black press shine like jet.' Then she adds, 'It does appear odd — I see a face in it' (chap. 12). But of course, ironically, there is no 'black press' in the room, only a mirror in which Catherine sees and repudiates her own image. Her fragmentation has now gone so far beyond the psychic split betokened by her division from Heathcliff that body and image (or body and soul) have separated.

Q. D. Leavis would have us believe that this apparently gothic episode, with its allusion to 'dark superstitions about premonitions of death, about ghosts and primitive beliefs about the soul . . . is a proof of [Emily Brontë's] immaturity at the time of the original conception of *Wuthering Heights.*' Leo Bersani, on the other hand, suggests that the scene hints at 'the danger of being haunted by alien versions of the self.'[13] In a sense, however, the image Catherine sees in the mirror is neither gothic nor alien — though she is alienated from it — but hideously familiar, and further proof that her madness may really equal sanity. Catherine sees in the mirror an image of who and what she has really become in the world's terms: 'Mrs. Linton, the lady of Thrushcross Grange.' And oddly enough, this image appears to be stored like an article of clothing, a trousseau-treasure, or again in Plath's words 'a featureless, fine / Jew linen,'[14] in one of the cupboards of childhood, the black press from her old room at the Heights.

Because of this connection with childhood, part of the horror of Catherine's vision comes from the question it suggests: was the costume/face always there, waiting in a corner of the little girl's wardrobe? But to ask this question is to ask again, as Frankenstein does, whether Eve was created fallen, whether women are not Education's but 'Nature's fools,' doomed from the start to be exiles and outcasts despite their illusion that they are hardy and free. When Milton's Eve is for her own good led away from her own image by a superegoistic divine voice which tells her that 'What there thou sees fair creature is thyself' — *merely* thyself — does she not in a sense determine Catherine Earnshaw's fall? When, substituting Adam's superior image for her own, she concedes that female 'beauty is excell'd by manly grace/And wisdom' (*Paradise Lost*, 4. 490–91) does not her 'sane' submission outline the contours of Catherine Earnshaw's rebelliously Blakeian madness? Such questions are only implicit in Catherine's mad mirror vision of herself, but it is important to see that they are implied. Once again, where Shelley clarifies Milton, showing the monster's dutiful disgust with 'his' own self-image, Brontë repudiates him, showing how his teachings have doomed her protagonist to what dutiful Nelly considers an insane search for her lost true self. 'I'm sure I should be myself were I once more among the heather on those hills,' Catherine exlaims, meaning that only a journey back into the androgynous wholeness of childhood could heal the wound her mirror-image symbolizes, the fragmentation that began when she was separated from heather and Heathcliff, and 'laid alone' in the first fateful enclosure of her oak-panelled bed. For the mirror-image is one more symbol of the cell in which Catherine has been imprisoned by herself and by society.

To escape from the horrible mirror-enclosure, then, might be to escape from all domestic enclosures, or to begin to try to escape. It is significant that in her madness Catherine tears at her pillow with her teeth, begs Nelly to open the window, and seems 'to find childish diversion in pulling the feathers from the rents she [has] just made' (chap. 12). Liberating feathers from the prison where they had been reduced to objects of social utility, she imagines them reborn as the birds they once were, whole and free, and pictures them 'wheeling over our heads in the middle of the moor,' trying to get back to their nests. A moment later, standing by the window 'careless of the frosty air,' she imagines her own trip back across the moor to Wuthering Heights, noting that 'it's a rough journey, and a sad heart to travel it; and we must pass by Gimmerton Kirk to go that journey! . . . But Heathcliff, if I dare you now, will you venture? . . . I won't rest till you are with me. I never will!' (chap. 12). For a 'fallen' woman, trapped in the distorting mirrors of patriarchy, the journey into death is the only way out, Brontë suggests, and the *Liebestod* is not (as it would be for a male artist, like Keats or Wagner) a mystical but a practical solution. In the presence of death, after all, 'The mirrors are sheeted,' to quote Plath yet again.[15]

The masochism of this surrender to what A. Alvarez has called the 'savage god' of suicide is plain, not only from Catherine's own words and actions but also from the many thematic parallels between her speeches and Plath's poems.[16] But of course, taken together, self-starvation or anorexia nervosa, masochism, and suicide form a complex of psychoneurotic symptoms that is almost classically associated with female feelings of powerlessness and rage. Certainly the 'hunger strike' is a traditional tool of the powerless, as the history of the feminist movement (and many other movements of oppressed peoples) will attest. Anorexia nervosa, moreover, is a sort of mad corollary of the self-starvation that may be a sane strategy for survival. Clinically associated with 'a distorted concept of body size' — like Catherine Earnshaw's alienated/familiar image in the mirror — it is fed by the 'false sense of power that the faster derives from her starvation,' and is associated, psychologists speculate, with 'a struggle for control, for a sense of identity, competence, and effectiveness.'

But then in a more general sense it can surely be argued that all masochistic or even suicidal behaviour expresses the furious power hunger of the powerless. Catherine's whip — now meaning Heathcliff, her 'love' for Heathcliff, and also, more deeply, her desire for the autonomy her union with Heathcliff represented — turns against Catherine. She whips herself because she cannot whip the world; and she must whip something. Besides, in whipping herself does she not, perhaps, torment the world? Of this she is, in her powerlessness, uncertain, and her uncertainty leads to further madness, reinforcing the vicious cycle. 'O let me not be mad,' she might cry, like Lear, as she tears off her own socially prescribed costumes so that she can more certainly feel the descent of the whip she herself has raised. In her rebelliousness Catherine has earlier played alternately the parts of Cordelia and of Goneril and Regan to the Lear of her father and her husband. Now, in her powerlessness, she seems to have herself become a figure like Lear, mourning her lost kingdom and suicidally surrendering herself to the blasts that come straight down the moor.***

Notes:

1. Eagleton does discuss the Lintons' dogs from a Marxist perspective; see *Myths of Power* (New York and London, Macmillan, 1975), pp 106–7.
2. Elizabeth Janeway, 'On "Female Sexuality," ' in Jean Strouse, ed., *Women and Analysis* (New York, Grossman, 1974), p. 58.
3. See Claude Lévi-Straus, *The Raw and the Cooked: Introduction to a Science of Mythology*, vol. 1 (New York, Harper & Row, 1969).
4. Dickinson, *Letters*, (Cambridge, Mass., Harvard University Press, 1958), 2:408.
5. Charlotte Brontë elaborated upon the terrors of 'ladylike' education in *The Professor, Jane Eyre*, and *Villette*. For a factual account of the Cowan Bridge experience, see also Winifred Gérin, *Charlotte Brontë* (Oxford, OUP, 1967) pp. 1–16.
6. Blake, *The Marriage of Heaven and Hell*, plate 5.
7. Mark Kinkead-Weekes, 'The Place of Love in *Jane Eyre* and *Wuthering Heights*,' in *The Brontës: A*

Collection of Critical Essays, ed. Ian Gregor (Englewood Cliffs, Prentice-Hall, 1970), p. 86.

8. See Dorothy van Ghent, *The English Novel: Form and Function* (New York, Harper & Row, 1961), pp. 153–70.
9. As we noted in discussing the metaphor of literary paternity, Jean-Paul Sartre thought of books as embodiments of power, and it seems relevant here that he once called his grandfather's library 'the world caught in a mirror' (Marjorie Grene, *Sartre*, [New York, New Viewpoints, 1973], p. 11)
10. Sylvia Plath, 'The Stones,' in *The Colossus* (New York, Vintage, 1968), p. 82.
11. C. P. Sanger, 'The Structures of *Wuthering Heights*,' Norton Critical Edition of *Wuthering Heights* (New York, Norton, 1972), p. 288.
12. Plath, 'Tulips,' *Ariel* (New York, Harper and Row, 1966), p. 11.
13. Q. D. Leavis, 'A Fresh Approach to *Wuthering Heights*,' Norton Critical Edn., p. 309; Leo Bersani, *A Future for Astyanax* (Boston, Little, Brown, 1976), pp. 208–9.
14. Plath, 'Lady Lazarus,' *Ariel*, p. 6.
15. Plath, 'Contusion,' *Ariel*, p. 83.
16. See A. Alvarez, *The Savage God* (London, Weidenfeld & Nicolson, 1971).

3

Rachel Blau DuPlessis,
'For the Etruscans'

Thinking smugly, 'She shouldn't be working on Woolf.' 1964. 'Doesn't she know that she'd better not work on a woman?' Why was I lucky to know this. What was the threat? Dickinson? Marginality? Nin? I bought Nin's book, I threw it out. What! Didn't want it, might confront

> The great difficulties in understanding the language . . . not . . . from an inability to read the script, every letter of which is now clearly understood. It is as if books were discovered, printed in our own Roman letters, so that one could articulate the words without trouble, but written in an unknown language with no known parallels.[1]

myself. 1979. The general feeling (of the dream) was that I was free of the testers. However, I was entirely obligated to take and pass their test. My relationship to the testers is — ? 1965. My big ambition, my hemmed and nervous space. Her uncompromising, oracular poems. Her fluid, decisive writing. Her dream life, surfacing. Not even to read this? to read with contempt? 'This is a Blossom of the Brain — /A small — italic Seed' (Dickinson, no. 945).

What is going on here? 1968. Is the female aesthetic simply an (1978) enabling myth? Fish on one foot, hook on the other, angling for ourselves. Woolf: catching 'something about the body.'[2] Crash. MOM! WHAT! 'You never buy what I like! Only what YOU like! (Fig Newtons.)

* * *

A golden bough. The torch is passed on. His son clutches his hand, his crippled father clings to his back, three male generations leave the burning city. The wife, lost. Got lost in burning. No one knows what happened to her, when they became the Romans.

She became the Etruscans?

> Even so, there is nothing to prevent those with a special aptitude for cryptography from tackling Etruscan, which is the last of the important languages to require translating.[3]

Sheepish, I am sheepish and embarrassed to mention this

that for me it was always the herding. The herding, the bonding, the way you can speak their language but also have a different language or different needs so hard to

259

say this. Always: I have heard this story from many sources — they bond and clump outside your door and never 'ask you to lunch' or they talk and be wonderful, lambent, but when you walk up 'they turn away' or 'they turn on you, teasing, making sexual jokes'

all headed in the same direction, herding and glistening, of course some don't. But it has been difficult for these to separate from the rest. Probably the reward system?

To translate ourselves from our disguises. The enthralled sexuality, the knife-edge brilliance, the intellectual dowdiness, evasions, embarrassments, imprecisions, deferments; smug primness with which there is no dialogue. Combativeness straight into malice. Invisibility, visibility, crossing the legs, uncrossing them. Knights in shining amour. Daddy to the rescue. 'Imposing' sex on the situation. 'Not imposing' 'sex' on the 'situation.' 'Doesn't she know she'd better not work on a woman?' She'd better now work on a woman. 'I bid you take a wisp from the wool of their precious fleece.'[4] The golden fleece. The golden bough. The female quest?

Frankly, it was *The Golden Notebook* (1966). Which pierced my heart with its two-headed arrow.

How to be? How to be-have? I remember one preceptor who brought her little white dog to school and trotted it up and down the fourth floor of Hamilton Hall. What delightful, charming, adorable girls! The temptation of Eve was fruit, of Mary, lambs. Thinking that they followed *you* to school.

*   *   *

It is, after all, always the meaning, the reading of difference that matters, and meaning is culturally engendered and sustained. Not to consider the body as some absolute (milk, blood, breasts, clitoris) for no 'body' is unmediated. Not body but the 'body' of psychosocial fabrications of difference. Or again, of sameness. Or again, of their relation. The contexts in which are formed and reinforced gendered human beings, produced in the family, in institutions of gender development, in the forms of sexual preference, in the division of labor by gender, especially the structure of infant care, in the class and conditions of the families in which we are psychologically born, and in the social maintenance of the sexes through life's stages and in any historical era.[5] And as such, these differing experiences do surely produce (some) different consciousnesses, different cultural expressions, different relations to realms of symbols and symbol users. Different 'language,' metaphorical; different uses of the grammatical and expressive resources of language (verb parts, questions, intonation, pronouns).

> Stein says we no longer have the words people used to have so we have to make them new in some way but women haven't had them at all and how can you deconstruct a language you never constructed or it was never constructed by others like you, or with you in mind?[6]

> Frances Jaffer

And therefore there is female aesthetic, but not *a* female aesthetic, not one single constellation of strategies.

I am watering cattle, who are thirsty. A frisky Holstein, pointed face and horns with pink tips, pokes me, playful, calling attention to herself. I must establish that she is not male (1978). I pick up her little curtain. There. Fleshy pink udders, she is pink, black

and white. I have watered the cattle and they have given me a guide.

Etruscan, the last important language.

What holds civilization intact? The presence of apparently voiceless Others, 'thoughtless' Others, powerless Others against which the Law, the Main, the Center, even the Diffusions of power are defined.

> **Throughout the ages the problem of woman has puzzled people of every kind . . . You too will have pondered this question insofar as you are men. From the women among you that is not to be expected, for you yourselves are the riddle.**[7]

A special aptitude for cryptography. The only ones barred from the riddle. Ha ha. His gallantry is hardest to bear. Not to think about the riddle is to remain the riddle. To break with what I have been told I am, and I am able to? am unable disabled disbarred *un sous-développé, comme tu dis, un sous-capable*[8] The Etruscan language can be heard, if one chooses to mouth it, but not comprehended. Pondering is not to be expected, so why bother?

What happens at the historical moment when the voiceless and powerless seek to unravel their riddle? (For Caliban does seize his voice, reject the magician of civilization in Césaire's writing of Shakespeare's *Tempest*.) ANS.: We are cutting into the deep heart, the deepest heart of cultural compacts. They have already lost our allegiance. Something is finished.

Now did I go downstairs, now did I cut up a pear, eight strawberries, now did I add some cottage cheese thinking to get some more or even some ricotta at the Italian Market so that I could make lasagna so that when B. comes back from New York he would have something nice and so I wouldn't have to cook again for days; now did I put some sugar on the fruit and then fill the sugar bowl because it was almost empty; now did I hang two bath mats out on the line, they are washed only once a year and it was today that I washed them; now did I and do I wonder that there are words that repeat in a swaying repetitive motion. Deliberately breaking the flow of thought, when it comes to change, and with food, with dust. With food and dust.

> **must here snatch time to remark how discomposing it is for her biographer that this culmination and peroration should be dashed from us on a laugh casually like this; but the truth is that when we write of a woman, everything is out of place — culminations and perorations; the accent never falls where it does with a man.**[9]

I dreamed I was an artist; my medium was cottage cheese.

For the woman artist is not privileged or mandated to find her self-in-world except by facing (affronting?) and mounting an enormous struggle with the cultural fictions — myths, narratives, iconographies, languages — which heretofore have delimited the representation of women. And which are culturally and psychically saturating.

*   *   *

To define then. 'Female aesthetic': the production of formal, epistemological, and thematic strategies of members of the group Woman, strategies born in struggle with much of already existing culture, and overdetermined by two elements of sexual difference — by women's psychosocial experiences of gender asymmetry and by women's historical status in an (ambiguously) nonhegemonic group.

All the animals, and I knew they were thirsty. They were mine, and were very thirsty. I had to give them

Something I call an emotional texture, a structural expression of mutuality. Writers know their text as a form of intimacy, of personal contact, whether conversations with the reader or with the self. Letters, journals, voices are sources for this element,

> see 'no reason why one should not write as one speaks, familiarly, colloquially'[10]

expressing the porousness and nonhierarchic stances of intimate conversation in both structure and function. Like *Orlando*, like Griffin's *Voices*, like *The Golden Notebook*, these may be antiphonal many-voiced works, beguilingly, passionately subjective, seeing emotional commitment as an adventure. (As our form of adventure?)[11]

'What a secret language we talk, Undertones, overtones, nuances, abstractions, symbols. Then we return to Henry with an incandescence which frightens him.'[12]

'addressing the reader, making herself and her reader part of the narrative . . . an offhand, conversational manner'[13]

> *I find myself more and more attracted to the porous, the statement that permits interpretation (penetration?) rather than positing an absolute. Not vagueness — I want each component to be clear — but a whole that doesn't pretend to be ultimate, academic.*[14]

Not positing oneself as the only, sol(e) authority. Sheep of the sun. Meaning, a statement that is open to the reader, not better than the reader, not set apart from, not seeking the authority of the writer. Not even seeking the authority of the writing. (Reader could be writer, writer reader. Listener could be teacher.)

*   *   *

Assuming for the moment. That this description is true? or that we could find these traits and name them. One way of proving that the female aesthetic can exist would be to find reasons for the existence of this poetics in the gender experiences specific to women, in sexual difference. Deena Metzger speaks of a denial of competition and aggression in women, suggesting that these lead to nonhierarchic forms of mutuality.[15] But female competition of course exists (jealous, 'she's said it all'; sibling, 'she was there first'; smug, 'she should know better than choosing to work on a woman'), wherever there are special rewards for some women at the expense of others. Or just because we are no better than anyone else. Jean Baker Miller and Carol Gilligan argue similarly that roles and functions of women engender a different psychological orientation. Shaped by nurturance, women take both donor and recipient roles, using tactics of giving and receiving. Shaped by the interdependent and relational, women are led to 'a more contextual mode of judgment and a different moral understanding.'[16]

The second trait is both/and vision. This is the end of the either-or, dichotomized universe, proposing monism (is this really the name for what we are proposing? or is it dialectics?) in opposition to dualism, a dualism pernicious because it valorizes one side above another, and makes a hierarchy where there were simply twain.

> a ' "shapeless" shapeliness,' said Dorothy Richardson, the 'unique gift of the feminine psyche' 'Its power to do what the shapely mentalities of men appear incapable of doing for themselves, to act as a focus for divergent points of view. . . . The characteristic . . . of being all over the place and in all camps at once. . . .'[17]

A both/and vision born of shifts, contraries, negations, contradictions; linked to personal vulnerability and need. Essay and sermon. A both/and vision that embraces movement, situational. (I don't mean: opportunistic, slidy.) Structurally, such a writing might say different things, not settle on one, which is final. This is not a condition of 'not choosing,' since choice exists always in what to represent and in the rhythms of presentation. It is nonacademic; for in order to make a formal presentation, one must have chosen among theses: this is the rhetorical demand. Cannot, in formal argument, say both yes and no, if yes and no are given equal value under the same conditions. Either one or the other has to prevail. But say, in a family argument? where both, where all, are right? generates another model of discourse.

*   *   *

If one does not just rest silent, stuff the mouth with food.

*   *   *

Lessing has built 'Dialogue' on an either-or opposition which becomes a both / and vision of the female. He: the tower, is nihilism, the abyss, rigidity, isolation, and control; is courage, reason, and a sickness. She: the leaf, a vulval shape. She is infused with an irrational happiness, sensuality, pleasure, and openness to community. Has common sense, does not drive a philosophical position to the end and bind herself to it. This female mode of seeing holds to one side of a polarity (a 'feminine' side) yet is simultaneously that force which includes and transcends male nihilism and rationality.[18] A constellated integrative form. This vision contains feminine, transcends masculine, asserts female as synthesis. Makes me very nervous (are we 'just' valorizing our idealized selves?). This structure is parallel to the double status of Mrs. Ramsay in Lily's painting (and in Woolf's *To the Lighthouse*), as one side of the masculine-feminine polarity, fit only to be surpassed; at the same time, as that stroke in the middle, the one unifying lighthouse stroke, which is love and ambition, mother and child, death and pleasure: the female synthesis.

Of the voices of Woolf's essay *Three Guineas*, one takes the trial tone: rational, legalistic, logical. The other voice discourses loosely, inventive, chatty, exploring every nook and cranny. As for facts — anecdote is authority. But as the Antigone reference ripens, and we talk of women defying the laws of the state, both masculine and feminine are sublated in a heroic, intransigent but unauthoritarian voice which combines reason and emotion, logic and defiance. This is the non-contractual voice of the Outsiders, (ambiguously) nonhegemonic

who speak the last of the important languages to require translating.

A constant alternation between time and its 'truth,' identity and its loss, history and the timeless, signless, extraphenomenal things that produce it. An impossible dialectic: a permanent alternation: never the one without the other. It is not certain that anyone here and now is capable of it. A [psycho] analyst conscious of history and politics? A politician tuned into the unconscious? A woman perhaps . . .[19]

This both/and vision, the contradictory movement between the logically irreconcilable, must have several causes. Perhaps it is based on the bisexual oscillation within female psychosexual development. Nancy Chodorow shows how the Oedipal configuration occurs differently in girls and boys and that, because of the way the sexes are reproduced in the family, most women retain men as erotic objects and women as emotional objects. This oscillation between men and women, father and mother, pervades her emotional (and thus aesthetic) life. And do we also value the K-Mart version of this structure: conflict avoidance. Everybody is right. Feel like a chameleon, taking coloration

Insider-outsider social status will also help to dissolve an either-or dualism. For the woman finds she is irreconcilable things: an outsider by her gender position, by her relation to power; may be an insider by her social position, her class. She can be both. Her ontological, her psychic, her class position all cause doubleness. Doubled consciousness. Doubled understandings. How then could she neglect to invent a form which produces this incessant, critical, splitting motion. To invent this form. To invent the theory for this form.

Following, the 'female aesthetic' will produce artworks that incorporate contradiction and nonlinear movement into the heart of the text.

An art object may then be nonhierarchic, showing 'an organization of material in fragments,' breaking climactic structures, making an even display of elements over the surface with no climatic place or moment, since the materials are 'organized into many centers.'[20]

Monique Wittig's *Les Guérillères*, a form of verbal quilt. We hear her lists, her unstressed series, no punctuation even, no pauses, no setting apart, and so everything joined with no subordination, no ranking. It is radical parataxis. Something droning. Nothing epitomizes another. If fruits are mentioned, many are named, for unlike symbolism, where one stands for the many, here the many stand for the many. Hol-Stein, one of the thirsty animals.

May also be a form of sexualty, that multifocal female body and its orgasmic capacity, where orgasms vary startlingly and are multiple. And how we think about the body.

> She began to think about 'climax' and 'anticlimax' — what these mean in female and male associations.[21] The language of criticism: 'lean, dry, terse, powerful, strong, spare, linear, focused, explosive' — god forbid it should be 'limp'!! But — 'soft, moist, blurred, padded, irregular, going around in circles,' and other descriptions of **our** bodies — the very **abyss** of aesthetic judgment, danger, the wasteland for artists!
>
> Frances Jaffer

Multiclimactic, multiple centers of attention: *Orlando, Between the Acts* where the cows, the rain intervene in art, where the border between life and art is down, is down!

The anti-authoritarian ethics occurs on the level of structure. We call all this 'new' ('new form,' 'new book,' 'new way of writing,' layered and 'strudled,' Metzger says), that use of the word 'new' which, for centuries, has signaled antithesis to dominant values.[22] And which coincides with the thrilling ambition to write a great, encyclopedic, holistic work, the ambition to get everything in, inclusively, reflexively, monumentally.

Moreover there looms ahead of me the shadow of some kind of form which a diary might attain to. I might in the course of time learn what it is that one can make of this loose, drifting material of life; finding another use for it than the use I put it to, so much more consciously and scrupulously, in fiction. What sort of diary should I like mine to be? Something loose knit and yet not slovenly, so elastic that it will embrace anything, solemn, slight or beautiful that comes into my mind. I should like it to resemble some deep old desk, or capacious hold-all, in which one flings a mass of odds and ends without looking them through.[23]

The form of the desk, the tote bag, the journal. Interesting that for Woolf it was the form of a journal, and for Pound too it began as a 'rag bag,' a market mess of spilled fish, but became the form of *Analects*, of codes, a great man's laws. The *Cantos*. For Williams, it was the form of antiquarian history, local lore, wonders, layered in the City. *Paterson*. For both the male writers, a geopolitical stance, and this may have happened in a turn from the female, a reassertion of the polarized sexes. For the woman, it is a diary: her bag, her desk.

We intend to find ourselves. In the burning city.

The holistic sense of life without the exclusionary wholeness of art. These holistic forms: inclusion, apparent nonselection, because selection is censorship of the unknown, the between, the data, the germ, the interstitial, the bit of sighting that the writer cannot place. Holistic work: great tonal shifts, from polemic to essay to lyric. A self-questioning, the writer built into the center of the work, the questions at the center of the writer, the discourses doubling, retelling the same, differently. And not censored: love, politics, children, dreams, close talk. The first Tampax in world literature. A room where clippings paper the walls.

*   *   *

of course I am describing *The Golden Notebook* again.   Again.

The artwork produced with this poetics distinguishes itself by the fact that it claims a social function and puts moral change and emotional vulnerability at the center of the experience for the reader.[24]

A possible definition? 'female aesthetic' tackling Etruscan   the doubling of doubleness   cottage cheese   the riddle our riddle   sphinx to sphinx   sexual difference   artistic production   I am hungry — K-Mart   *The Golden Notebook*   (ambiguously) nonhegemonic

Artistic production. The making, the materials the artist faced, collected, resolved. A process of makings, human choice and necessity. Any work is made to meet itself at the crossroads. Any work is a strategy to resolve, transpose, reweight, dilute, arrange, substitute contradictory material from culture, from society, from personal life. And (the) female aesthetic? Various and possibly contradictory strategies of response and invention shared by women in response to gender experiences.

Take Nin. Her diary as form and process is a stratagem to solve a contradiction often present in acute form for women: between the desire to please, making woman an object, and the desire to reveal, making her a subject. The culturally sanctioned relationship to art and artists which Nin continually imagines (ornament, inspiration, sexual and psychic reward) is in conflict with the direct relationship she seeks as artist, colleague, fellow worker. And Nin's diary as fact and artifact transposes these conflicting forces, reveals and protects simultaneously, allowing her to please others (by showing male friends specially prepared sections) while writing to please herself. Double, sometimes duplicitous needs.

These experiences of difference which produce different consciousnesses, different cultural expression, different relation to realms of symbols and to symbol users.

And therefore, and therefore, there is female aesthetic

> 'from this [difference in priorities between men and women] spring not only marked differences of plot and incident, but infinite differences in selection, method and style'[25]

as there is male

> 'It is a commonplace of criticism that only the male myths are valid or interesting; a book as fine (and well-structured) as *Jane Eyre* fails *even to be seen* by many citics because it grows out of experiences — events, fantasies, wishes, fears, daydreams, images of self — entirely foreign to their own.'[26]

Female aesthetic begins when women take, investigate, the structures of feeling that are ours. And trying to take them, find also the conflict between these often

inchoate feelings (coded as resistances, coded as the thirsty animals) and patriarchal structures of feeling — romantic thralldom, fear of male anger, and of our
own weaknesses of nerve. Essentialist? No. We are making a creation; not a
discovery.[27]

Yet it is also clear that there would be many reasons not to see female work as
different. Why might someone object?

First, a desire to say that great art is not made by the factoring out of the sexes, is
'androgynous' as Woolf uses the term in the twenties. The desire to state that
greatness is (must be?) universal, that anything else is special pleading. The fear
that to notice gender in any way becomes destructive to women. Thus the disincen-
tive: if gender categories have always been used so destructively, our use of them, is
it not 'playing into their hands'? (There can be no greater proof of gender
difference than this argument.)

> 'Another reason women don't like their art to be seen through their bodies is that women
> have been sex objects all along and to let your art be seen that way is just falling right
> back into the same old rut.'[28]

Women may then respond with a strategy of self-chosen, proud ghettoization
(Richardson's 'feminine psyche') or may respond as Woolf did. In that (neo-
Freudian) context, Woolf's argument for androgyny is a situational triumph,
rejecting the ghettos, stating that woman's art contains the man, contains the
woman, has access to both.

Where then is (the) 'female aesthetic'? In both, in all these strategies of response to
difference. Even if, even when, contradictory.

Then, there is the desire at all costs to avoid special pleading, anything that looks
like women have gotten by because of our sex (ambiguous word: meaning, our
gender, meaning, our sexuality). This is a rejection of the stance of the courtesan
for the firm-chinned professional, who does not (in dress, in manner, in talk) call
attention to her 'sex'. She has her babies bravely between semesters. She fears
being ghettoized. Being patronized. But it happened anyway. Any way. And she
did not 'control' it.

Another fear: that any aesthetic is bound to be misused, misappropriated, and this
one is surely extremely vulnerable, with its blurring of all the elements we have
firmly regarded as setting art apart: blurring between art and life, blurring
between social creativity and 'high' art, blurring between one's journal and one's
poem, blurring between the artifact and the immersion in experience. Such exact
polarities.[29]

I am hungry. I am very very hungry. Have I always been this empty?

*I see that the next day I wrote in my journal. I would love someone (me?) to write a wonderful novel using
the aesthetics you speak of — that are in my little list — mutuality, porousness, intimacy, recontacting a
both/and, using both sides of the brain, nonhierarchic, anti- or multiclimatic, wholistic, lacking distance*

. . . perhaps didactic — but I think this person would have to be a particularly strong and careful artist. I have to tell you that I don't love one single novel that has come out of the 1960–70s women's movement. I don't think there is anyone concerned enough about either language or the real details of daily life. My sense is that everyone has been in a rush. (I feel in this rush too sometimes. Who wants to be a poor nobody at forty?) Sure there are wonderful moments here and there in different pieces of fiction. But no one has been concerned enough about FORM for me. None of this conflicts with what you said in our workshop. It's just another vantage point. Or perhaps also a corrective, in the sense that I fear too many women can take your aesthetic and churn out crap in three easy lessons. It's really like petit-point to get so close to one's subject, keep it porous, open, multiclimatic, and still keep it art.

Carol Ascher

The possible characteristics of a female aesthetic that you suggested seemed familiar and true certainly of my own work. Therefore I wanted to find out something else and maybe offer something else (if only doubts or impatience with the deterministic limitation of nonhierarchic, layered, 'porously intimate,' subjective, etc. work) but felt disappointed and thwarted.

Mira Schor

In my essays' psychic and speculative search for contradictions, for wholeness, linear and constelled forms coexist. The work is metonymic (based on juxtaposition) and metaphoric (based on resemblance).[30] It is at once analytic and associative, visceral and intellectual, law and body. The struggle with cultural hegemony, and the dilemmas of that struggle, are articulated in a voice that does not seek authority of tone or stasis of position but rather seeks to express the struggle in which it is immersed.

As for female aesthetic? this essay points to one set of responses. One. Only. One among several possibilities.[31] Of course, for descriptive purposes, the actual traits matter, but more important are the functions I postulate, the functioning of the traits to express, confirm, illuminate, distort, evade, situations that have a gender valence.

But to test whether this is true, whether what you are calling women's themes do appear in women's writing, would you not have to use objective methods, devise objective tests of this knowledge?.

Mirra Komarovsky

We have covered the whole range of the anxiety inherent in scientific methodology — from Mirra's comment that the individual scholar must prove her thesis to have validation for more than herself (by the 'objective,' 'scientific' method), to my concern that to define a female aesthetic is to establish a rigid norm of female creativity, which repeats the patriarchal tyranny of an 'objective' absolute way of doing things.

Lou Roberts

Can I prove it? I can prove that different social groups produce differences in cultural expression. I can prove that women are a social group. I can point to examples of differences in our relation to the symbolic order and in our cultural expression.

But I cannot prove that only women, that women only, use this aesthetic. And this failure is actually the strongest proof of all.

Women are (ambiguously) nonhegemonic because as a group, generally, we are outside the dominant systems of meaning, value, and power, as these saturate us, as they are 'organized and lived.'[32] To talk of society and culture as involving 'hegemonic' practices does not mean that a hegemony is a ten-ton stone falling from nowhere to crush you into some shape.

Hegemony is not to be understood at the level of mere opinion or mere manipulation. It is a whole body of practices and expectations; our assignments of energy, our ordinary understanding of the nature of [people] and of [their] world. It is a set of meanings and values which as they are experienced as practices appear as reciprocally confirming. It thus constitutes a sense of reality for most people in the society . . . but . . . is not, except in the operation of a moment of abstract analysis, in any sense a static system.[33]

A hegemony, as a set of practices, has 'continually to be renewed, recreated, defended and modified' as well as 'continually resisted, limited, altered, challenged.'[34]

Women, in a generally nonhegemonic position, barred from or quota'd into the cultural institutions of renewal, defense, and modification.

> *the 'mainstream' of European intellectual history was carried on without us. The clerical status of scholars in the Middle Ages automatically excluded women from the formal training which would fit them for the learned world, and as you know, this situation was not rectified in modern times until very recently. Moreover, self-study was for most women virtually impossible because the formal training was carried on in a highly technical Latin (and Greek after the humanist movement), unintelligible even to the ordinary literate lay person.*

Yet still (Margery of Kemp, Christine de Pisane)

> *At least once before in Western history, women did make a substantial contribution to the formation of what might — in the context of our workshop — be called a nonpatriarchal language, the 'mother-tongue' which they spoke in contrast to the formal language of scholars.*
>
> Jo Ann McNamara

While it is generally asserted and assumed that women belong to the majority, to hegemony, I could suggest that women are virtually always (ambiguously) non-hegemonic. A great number are formed by residual social practices: ethnic, kin-based, male- and child-centered female communities. Some may be emergent, 'alternative or oppositional to the dominant elements.'[35]

Why are women as a group (ambiguously) nonhegemonic? A woman may be joined to a dominant system of meanings and practices by her race (say, white), yet not by her gender; she may be joined via her class, but not by her gender; joined thru her sexual preference, but not her gender. May be oppositional, with many sources of alternative conditions (working-class, black), but still oriented in ideology and consciousness towards hegemonic norms. (June Jordan's poem 'If you saw a Negro lady' speaks of this possibility.)

(Ambiguously) nonhegemonic. For women, then, existing in the dominant system of meanings and values that structure culture and society may be a painful, or amusing, double dance, clicking in, clicking out — the divided consciousness. For this, the locus classicus is Woolf.

Again if one is a woman one is often surprised by a sudden splitting off of consciousness, say in walking down Whitehall, when from being the natural inheritor of that civilization, she becomes, on the contrary, outside of it, alien and critical.[36]

That shifting focus, bringing the world into different perspectives, is the onto-logical situation of women because it is our social situation, our relationship to power, our relationship to language.

What we here have been calling (the) female aesthetic turns out to be a specialized name for any practices available to those groups — nations, genders, sexualities, races, classes — all social practices which wish to criticize, to differentiate from, to overturn the dominant forms of knowing and understanding with which they are saturated.

Nineteenth-century Russian fiction has analogues with women's writing; both are nonhegemonic practices ' "pointless" or "plotless" narratives stuffed with strange minutiae, and not obeying the accepted laws of dramatic development, lyrical in the wrong places, condensed in the wrong places, overly emotional, obsessed with things we do not understand, perhaps even grotesque.'[37]

Négritude has analogues with women's aesthetic practices.

Consider then the white European standing before an object, before the exterior world, before Nature, before the *Other*. A man of will, a warrior, a bird of prey, a pure act of watching, the white European distinguishes himself from the object. He holds the object at a distance, he immobilizes it, he fixes it. Equipped with his instruments of precision, he dissects it in a cold analysis. Moved by the will to power, he kills the Other and, in a centripetal move-ment, he makes it a means to use for his own practical ends. He *assimilates* it. . . . The black African is first of all in his colour as if standing in the pri-mordial night. He does not see the object, he *feels* it. He is like one of those worms of the Third Day, a pure sensing field. Subjectively, at the end of his sensing organs, he discovers the Other. . . . So the black African sympathizes with, and identifies with the Other.[38]

For blacks excluded from a Western world of whiteness will affirm a connection to rhythms of earth, sensuality, intuition, subjectivity, and this will sound precisely as some women writers do.

High modernists are the most problematic nonhegemonic group, because they make a conservative, sometimes *fascisante* criticism of bourgeois culture, with 'positive' values ascribed to hierarchical social order, sometimes buttressed by religion, but also, astonishingly, linked to peasant-based agriculture (as opposed, of course, to our urban, industrial morass). These writers constitute themselves as a group-against, whose common bond is opposition to the social basis on which their world in fact rested. Modernists show the strength of a politicized culture based on a shared revulsion to World War I, on one hand, and to the Russian Revolution on the other. This set of individuals with residual values (Eliot, Pound, Yeats, Lewis, Lawrence) depends on responses to a once-existing, and somewhat mythologized, social basis in peasantry and patriarch. Aristocrat, head, *il capo*. A revolution from the right.

Literature by women, in its ethical and moral position, has analogues with the equally nonhegemonic modernism in its subversive critique of culture. (Most — Woolf, Lessing, H. D. — are in no way right-wing; this more than just an 'interesting observation.') In women's writing, as in modernist, there is a didactic element, related to the project of cultural transformation, of establishing values. In women's writing, as in modernist, there is an encyclopedic impulse, in which the writer invents a new and total culture, symbolized by and announced in a long work, like the modern long poem.

And contemporary women have produced just such works, often in the encyclopedic form of essay, compendia, polemic, collage, sacred and critical texts and images: Susan Griffin's *Woman and Nature*; Judy Chicago's *The Dinner Party*; Tillie Olsen's *Silences*; Mary Daly's *Gyn/Ecology*.[39]

Then, literature by women, in its phenomenological position, is associated with postmodernism, and with the democratic tolerance and realism of Williams, or the generative blankness and fecundity of Stevens. A list of the characteristics of postmodernism would be a list of the traits of women's writing: inwardness, illumination in the here and now (Levertov); use of the continuous present (Stein); the foregrounding of consciousness (Woolf); the muted, multiple, or absent *telos;* a fascination with process; a horizontal world; a decentered universe where 'man' (indeed) is no longer privileged. But women reject this position as soon as it becomes politically quietistic or shows ancient gender values. For when the phenomenological exploration of self-in-world turns up a world that devalues the female self, when that exploration moves along the tacit boundaries of a social status quo, she cannot just 'let it be,' but must transform values, rewrite culture, subvert structures.

As my political analysis became more sophisticated, as I became a Marxist shaped by the Frankfurt School and then a feminist, I was able to present a theoretical explanation for my intuitions **(they were mine, and were thirsty).** *I understood that, at least for middle-class Americans under late capitalism, the form (structure, 'language') of the culture is the sustaining force of social domination. But though I was implicated in those forms, I also knew — perhaps because of my somewhat marginal position as a woman, a petite bourgeoise?* **(She became the Etruscans?)** *— that I recognized these forms to be, not self-evident and natural, but intolerable and changeable, and that occasionally I discovered, and tried to transmit through my teaching and writing* **(printed in our Roman letters)**, *examples and visions of how things could be other and better. It's been clearer and clearer to me, since I've been a feminist* **(some ricotta at the Italian Market)** *that we women were never completely integrated into the structures of capitalism* **((ambiguously) nonhegemonic)** *and that our difference* **(a vulval shape)**, *whether only psychosocial or somehow biological as well, has given us a privileged position* **(horns with pink tips)** *from which to rebel and to envision alternatives. What's difficult, though, is to believe in those glimmers* **(entirely obligated to take and pass their test)**, *to hold fast to them, even more, to model them out and explore them. And this is the importance to me of women's writing* **(her diary, her bag, her desk).** *If it's really the forms, the language, which dominate us, then disrupting them as radically as possible can give us hope and possibilities. What I'd like to try to understand and explain to other people* **(you yourselves are the riddle)** *is how the form of women's writing is, if ambiguously* **(of double, sometimes duplicitious needs)** *nonetheless profoundly* *revolutionary (as are, in their confusing ways, modernism and postmodernism, also written from positions of marginality to the dominant culture).*

But I've also been thinking recently that we need a writer who would be for feminism what Brecht was for modernism — who understands, to put it a little crudely, that literature doesn't change things, people do **(a process of makings, human choice and necessity)**. *Our literature and thinking still seem quietistic to me, in that they require us to understand and respond, but not to act on our understanding, certainly not to act collectively* **(a room where clippings paper the walls)**. *Moreover, I think we haven't even grasped the most radical implications of feminism for a theory which mediates back to practice: that we have a vision which men have barely glimpsed of what dialectical thought is really about — about a total, specific, feeling and thinking subject, present in her interaction with 'objective' materials, overcoming the division between thought and action.* **(The golden bough. The golden fleece. The female quest?)**

I've been angry recently that, while theory proliferates, we have given up on what was compelling about the late sixties and early seventies — that feeling of infinite possibility which challenged us to think and live differently. So many of those experiments have fallen by the wayside, victim to the economic situation and our own discouragement and exhaustion.

Sara Lennox

Exploration not in service of reconciling self to world, but creating a new world for a new self

given our revolutionary desire (that feeling of infinite possibility) for a nonpatriarchal order, in the symbolic realm and in the realms of productive, personal, and political relations.

for the Etruscans

Notes:

'For the Etruscans' is a shortened and revised version of what was said at Workshop 9, Barnard College, Scholar and Feminist Conference in 1979, and what was published in *The Future of Difference: The Scholar and the Feminist*, ed. Hester Eisenstein and Alice Jardine (Boston: G. K. Hall, 1980). For this text, I have also drawn on the version written for delivery at SUNY-Buffalo early in 1980. I have avoided the anachronistic temptation to alter opinions or to respond to commentary on the work, though I have updated some of the notes.

  With special thanks to Carol Ascher, Frances Jaffer, Sara Lennox, Jo Ann McNamara, Lou Roberts, Mira Schor, and Louise Yelin for their own letters and notes on Workshop 9, not all of which are retained in this version of the essay.

  My source of inspiration for this kind of writing was Robert Duncan's *H. D. Book* (chapters scattered in little magazines through the past decades), Virginia Woolf's essays, and my own letters. But (and) many people have reinvented the essay.

1. Ellen Macnamara, *Everyday Life of the Etruscans* (London: B. T. Batsford, 1973), p. 181.
2. Virginia Woolf, 'Professions for Women,' *The Death of the Moth and Other Essays* (1942; reprint ed., New York: Harcourt Brace Jovanovich, 1974), p. 240.
3. James Wellard, *The Search for the Etruscans* (New York: Saturday Review Press, 1973), p. 192.
4. The second task of Psyche. See Erich Neumann, *Amor and Psyche: The Psychic Development of the Feminine: A Commentary on the Tale by Apuleius*, trans. Ralph Manheim (1952; reprint ed., Princeton, N. J.: Princeton University Press, 1971). See also Rachel Blau DuPlessis, 'Psyche, or Wholeness,' *Massachusetts Review* 20 (Spring 1979), 77–96.
5. Sources for this summary include Gayle Rubin, 'The Traffic in Women: Notes on the "Political Economy" of Sex,' in *Toward an Anthropology of Women*, ed. Rayna [Rapp] Reiter (New York: Monthly Review Press, 1975), pp. 157–210; Nancy Chodorow, *The Reproduction of Mothering:*

Psychoanalysis and the Sociology of Gender (Berkeley: University of California Press, 1978); Dorothy Dinnerstein, *The Mermaid and the Minotaur: Sexual Arrangements and Human Malaise* (New York: Harper & Row, 1976); Juliet Mitchell, *Psychoanalysis and Feminism: Freud, Reich, Laing, and Women* (New York: Vintage Books, 1975).

6. Frances Jaffer, 'Procedures for Having Lunch,' unpublished manuscript.

7. Sigmund Freud, *New Introductory Lectures on Psycho-Analysis,* trans. W. J. H. Sprott (New York: W. W. Norton, 1933), pp. 154–55.

8. Aimé Césaire, *Une tempête, Adaptation de 'La Tempête' de Shakespeare pour un théâtre nègre* (Paris: Editions du Seuil, 1969), p. 88.

9. Virginia Woolf, *Orlando* (1928; reprint ed., New York: New American Library, 1960), p. 204.

10. Virginia Woolf, 'Mrs. Thrale,' *The Moment and Other Essays* (1949, reprint ed., New York: Harcourt Brace Jovanovich, 1974), p. 52.

11. B. Ruby Rich, 'The Films of Yvonne Rainer,' *Chrysalis: A Magazine of Women's Culture,* no. 2 (1977), pp. 115–27.

12. Anaïs Nin, *The Diary of Anaïs Nin,* vol. 1, *1931–1934,* ed. Gunther Stuhlmann (New York: Swallow Press and Harcourt, Brace & World, 1966), p. 34.

13. Julia Penelope Stanley and Susan J. Wolfe (Robbins), 'Toward a Feminist Aesthetic,' *Chrysalis,* no. 6 (1978), p. 68.

14. Anita Barrows, 'Form and Fragment', typescript, pp. 7–8, in Lynda Koolish, 'A Whole New Poetry Beginning Here' (Ph.D. thesis, Stanford University, 1981), pp. 7–8.

15. Deena Metzger, 'In Her Image,' *Heresies* 1 (May 1977), 2.

16. Jean Baker Miller, *Toward a New Psychology of Women* (Boston: Beacon Press, 1976), p. 51; Carol Gilligan, *In a Different Voice: Psychological Theory and Women's Development* (Cambridge, Mass.: Harvard University Press, 1982), p. 22.

17. Dorothy Richardson, 'Leadership in Marriage,' *New Adelphi,* 2nd ser. 2 (June–August 1929), 247.

18. Doris Lessing, 'Dialogue', *A Man and Two Women* (New York: Popular Library, 1958).

19. Julia Kristeva, *About Chinese Women,* trans. Anita Barrows (New York: Urizen Books, 1977; first published in 1974), p. 38.

20. Sheila de Bretteville, cited in Metzger, 'In Her Image,' p. 5.

21. Combining two citations from Jaffer, the second from a letter in response to Workshop 9, the first, from a review of *Literary Women,* by Ellen Moers, *Chrysalis,* no. 1 (1977), p. 136.

22. Metzger, 'In Her Image,' p. 7.

23. Virginia Woolf, *A Writer's Diary,* ed. Leonard Woolf (New York: Harcourt, Brace, 1953), p. 13 (dated 1919).

24. At this point in the original essay, I discussed the mother-daughter relations and the imbedded fictional artwork in *Kunstlerromane* by women such as Lessing, Woolf, Gilman, Olsen, Stead. The argument was based on a (then unpublished) chapter of my *Writing Beyond the Ending: Narrative Strategies of Twentieth-Century Women Writers* (Bloomington: Indiana University Press, 1985); it can best be consulted there.

25. Virginia Woolf, 'Women Novelists,' *Contemporary Writers* (New York: Harcourt, Brace & World, 1965), p. 27. Review dates from 1918.

26. Joanna Russ, 'What Can a Heroine Do? Or Why Women Can't Write,' in *Images of Women in Fiction: Feminist Perspectives,* ed. Susan Koppelman Cornillon (Bowling Green, Ohio: Bowling Green University Popular Press, 1972), p. 14.

27. Analysis of 'Essentialism' as a philosophic concept made by Sybil Cohen to the Delaware Valley Women's Studies Consortium, April 1984.

28. Lucy Lippard, *From the Center: Feminist Essays on Women's Art* (New York: E. P. Dutton, 1976), p. 92.

29. Confirmation of these strategies in Barbara Currier Bell and Carol Ohmann, 'Virginia Woolf's Criticism: A Polemical Preface,' in *Feminist Literary Criticism: Exploration in Theory,* ed. Josephine Donovan (Lexington: University Press of Kentucky, 1975), pp. 48–60; and in Melissa Meyer and Miriam Schapiro, 'Waste Not/Want Not: Femmage,' *Heresies,* no. 4 (1978), pp. 66–69.

30. Roman Jakobson, 'Linguistics and Poetics,' in *Style in Language,* ed. Thomas A. Sebeok (Cambridge, Mass.: MIT Press, 1960), pp. 350–77.

31. Because locating just one set of strategies, my description is, necessarily, completely incomplete. It does not deal with an absolutely parallel, but aesthetically opposite use of the oracular, gnarled, compressed tactics, suggesting the difficulty of articulation, not its fluidity: Emily Dickinson, Marianne Moore, Laura Riding, Mina Loy. As Jeanne Kammer has said: 'There emerges a complex psychology of linguistic parsimony related to a professional identity. Haunted by the specter

of the sweet-singing 'poetess,' the woman poet may have come to the 'modern' style of the early decades of the twentieth century by a very different route than her male counterparts' ('The Art of Silence and the Forms of Women's Poetry,' in *Shakespeare's Sisters: Feminist Essays on Women Poets*, ed. Sandra Gilbert and Susan Gubar [Bloomington: Indiana University Press, 1979], p. 156).

32. Raymond Williams, 'Base and Superstructure in Marxist Cultural Theory,' *New Left Review* 82 (November-December 1973), 9.

33. Ibid.

34. Raymond Williams, *Marxism and Literature* (Oxford: Oxford University Press, 1977), p. 112.

35. Ibid, p. 124.

36. Virginia Woolf, *A Room of One's Own* (New York: Harcourt, Brace, 1929), p. 101. Compare Richard Wright's observation in 1956: 'First of all, my position is a split one. I'm black. I'm a man of the West. These hard facts condition, to some degree, my outlook. I see and understand the West; but I also see and understand the non- or anti-Western point of view. . . . This contradiction of being both Western and a man of color creates a distance, so to speak, between me and my environment. . . . Me and my environment are one, but that oneness has in it, at its very heart, a schism.' In *Présence Africaine*, no. 8–9–10 (November 1956), the proceedings of the First International Conference of Negro Writers and Artists, cited in *The Black Writer in Africa and the Americas*, ed. Lloyd W. Brown (Los Angeles: Hennessey & Ingalls, 1973), p. 27.

37. Russ, 'What Can a Heroine Do?' in Cornillon, pp. 14–15.

38. Léopold Sédar Senghor, *Liberté* I, cited in *Selected Poems/Poésies Choisies*, trans. and intro. C. Williamson (London: Rex Collings, 1976), pp. 12–13. *Négritude* (a black aesthetic) is a controversial concept: distinguished writers and critics oppose it (Wole Soyinka, Ralph Ellison) and embrace it (James Baldwin, Senghor).

39. Susan Griffin, *Woman and Nature: The Roaring Inside Her* (New York: Harper & Row, 1978); Judy Chicago, *The Dinner Party: A Symbol of Our Heritage* (Garden City, N.Y.: Anchor Press, 1979); Tillie Olsen, *Silences* (New York: Delacorte Press, 1978); Mary Daly, *Gyn/Ecology: The Metaethics of Radical Feminism* (Boston: Beacon Press, 1978).

References

Abel, Elizabeth, ed., *Writing and Sexual Difference*, London, University of Chicago Press, 1982

Abrams, M. H., *A Glossary of Literary Terms*, 4th edn., London, Holt, Rinehart and Winston, 1981

Ackroyd, Peter, *T. S. Eliot*, London, Hamish Hamilton, 1984

Althusser, Louis, *Lenin and Philosophy and Other Essays*, trans. Ben Brewster, London, New Left Books, 1971

Anderson, Perry, *Considerations on Western Marxism*, London, New Left Books, 1976

Baldick, Chris, *The Social Mission of English Criticism, 1848–1932*, Oxford, Clarendon Press, 1983

Bann, S. and Bowlt, J. E., eds., *Russian Formalism: A Collection of Articles and Texts in Translation*, Edinburgh, Scottish Academic Press, 1973

Barthes, Roland, *Mythologies* (1957) trans. Annette Lavers, London, Paladin, 1973
Elements of Semiology (1964) trans. Annette Lavers and Colin Smith, London, Jonathan Cape, 1967
Critical Essays (1964) trans. Richard Howard, Evanston, Northwestern University Press, 1972
S/Z (1970) trans. Richard Howard, New York, Hill and Wang, 1975
The Pleasure of the Text (1973) trans. Richard Howard, New York, Hill and Wang, 1975
Image-Music-Text, ed. and trans. Stephen Heath, London, Fontana, 1977
Barthes: Selected Writings, ed. Susan Sontag, London, Fontana, 1983

Belsey, Catherine, *Critical Practice*, London, Methuen, 1980

Bennett, Tony, *Formalism and Marxism*, London, Methuen, 1979

Bennett, Tony, Martin, Graham, Mercer, Colin, and Woolcott, Janet, eds., *Culture, Ideology and Social Process: A Reader*, London, Batsford and Open University Press, 1981

Benveniste, Emile, *Problems in General Linguistics*, trans. Mary Elizabeth Meek, Coral Gables, University of Miami Press, 1971

Bergonzi, Bernard, 'Leavis and Eliot: The Long Road to Rejection', *Critical Quarterly*, 26 (1984), 21–43

Blonsky, Marshall, ed., *On Signs: A Semiotics Reader*, Oxford, Blackwell, 1985

Bloom, Harold, *The Anxiety of Influence: A Theory of Poetry*, Oxford, OUP, 1973
A Map of Misreading, Oxford, OUP, 1975

Bloom, Harold, *et al.*, *Deconstruction and Criticism*, London, RKP, 1979

Brooks, Cleanth, *The Well Wrought Urn* (1947) London, Methuen, 1968
Modern Poetry and the Tradition, London, Editions Poetry, 1948

Buckley, Vincent, *Poetry and Morality: Studies in the Criticism of Matthew Arnold, T. S. Eliot and F. R. Leavis*, London, Chatto and Windus, 1959

Butler, Christopher, *Interpretation, Deconstruction and Ideology: An Introduction to Some Current Issues in Literary Theory*, Oxford, Clarendon Press, 1984

Casey, John, *The Language of Criticism*, London, Methuen, 1966

Coward, Rosalind and Ellis, John, *Language and Materialism: Developments in Semiology and the Theory of the Subject*, London, RKP, 1977

Craig, David, ed., *Marxists on Literature*, Harmondsworth, Penguin, 1975

Culler, Jonathan, *Structuralist Poetics: Structuralism, Linguistics and the Study of Literature*, London, RKP, 1975
Saussure, London, Fontana, 1976
The Pursuit of Signs: Semiotics, Literature, Deconstruction, London, RKP, 1981
On Deconstruction: Theory and Criticism after Structuralism, London, RKP, 1983
Barthes, London, Fontana, 1983

De Man, Paul, *Allegories of Reading*, London, Yale University Press, 1979
Blindness and Insight: Essays in the Rhetoric of Contemporary Criticism, 2nd edn., London, Methuen, 1983

Derrida, Jacques, *Of Grammatology* (1967) trans. Gayatri Chakravorty Spivak, London, Johns Hopkins University Press, 1976
Writing and Difference, trans. Alan Bass, London, RKP, 1978·

Donovan, Josephine, ed., *Feminist Literary Criticism: Explorations in Theory*, Lexington, University Press of Kentucky, 1975

Eagleton, Mary, ed., *Feminist Literary Theory: A Reader*, Oxford, Blackwell, 1986

Eagleton, Terry, *Myths of Power: A Marxist Study of the Brontës*, London, Macmillan, 1975
Marxism and Literary Criticism, London, Methuen, 1976
Criticism and Ideology: A Study in Marxist Literary Theory, London, New Left Books, 1976
Walter Benjamin, or Towards a Revolutionary Criticism, London, New Left Books, 1981
Literary Theory: An Introduction, Oxford, Blackwell, 1983
The Function of Criticism: From the Spectator to Post-Structuralism, London, New Left Books, 1984

Ehrmann, Jacques, ed., *Structuralism*, New York, Doubleday, 1970

Eliot, T. S., *Selected Essays* (1932) 3rd edn., London, Faber, 1951
Selected Prose of T. S. Eliot, ed. Frank Kermode, London, Faber, 1975

Empson, William, *Seven Types of Ambiguity: A Study of its Effects on English Verse* (1930) 3rd edn., London, Chatto and Windus, 1953

Erlich, Victor, *Russian Formalism: History-Doctrine*, 3rd edn., London, Yale University Press, 1965

Fekete, John, *The Critical Twilight: Explorations in the Ideology of Anglo-American Literary Theory from Eliot to McLuhan*, London, RKP, 1977

Fish, Stanley, E., *Surprised By Sin: The Reader in Paradise Lost*, Berkeley, University of California Press, 1967
Self-Consuming Artefacts: The Experience of Seventeenth-Century Literature, Berkeley, University of California Press, 1972
Is There a Text in this Class? The Authority of Interpretive Communities, London, Harvard University Press, 1982
'With the Compliments of the Author: Reflections on Austin and Derrida', *Critical Inquiry*, 8 (1982), 693–721

Fokkema, D. W. and Kunne-Ibsch, Elrud, *Theories of Literature in the Twentieth Century*, London, Hirst, 1977

Foucault, Michel, *The Foucault Reader*, ed. Paul Rabinow, Harmondsworth, Penguin, 1986

Galen, F. W., *Historic Structures: The Prague School Project, 1928–1946*, Austin, University of Texas Press, 1985

Genette, Gerard, *Figures of Literary Discourse* (1966–69) trans. Alan Sheridan, Oxford, Blackwell, 1982
Narrative Discourse: An Essay in Method (1972) trans. Jane E. Lewin, Oxford, Blackwell, 1982

Gilbert, Sandra M. and Gubar, Susan, *The Madwoman in the Attic: The Woman Writer and the Nineteenth-Century Literary Imagination*, London, Yale University Press, 1979

Greene, Gayle and Kahn, Coppélia, eds., *Making a Difference: Feminist Literary Criticism*, London, Methuen, 1985

Hall, Stuart, *et al.*, eds., *Culture, Media, Language: Working Papers in Cultural Studies, 1972–79*, London, Hutchinson, 1980

Harari, Josué, V., *Textual Strategies: Perspectives in Post-structuralist Criticism*, Ithaca, Cornell University Press, 1979

Hartman, Geoffrey, H., *The Fate of Reading and Other Essays*, London, University of Chicago Press, 1975
Criticism in the Wilderness: The Study of Literature Today, London, Yale University Press, 1980

Hawkes, Terence, *Structuralism and Semiotics*, London, Methuen, 1977

Hawthorn, Jeremy, ed., *Criticism and Critical Theory*, London, Edward Arnold, 1984

Hirsch, E. D., *Validity in Interpretation*, London, Yale University Press, 1967
The Aims of Interpretation, London, University of Chicago Press, 1976
'The Politics of Theories of Interpretation', *Critical Inquiry*, 9 (1982), 235–247

Holub, Robert C., *Reception Theory: A Critical Introduction*, London, Methuen, 1984

Humm, Maggie, *Feminist Criticism: Women as Contemporary Writers*, Brighton, Harvester, 1986

Innes, Robert E., ed., *Semiotics: An Introductory Reader*, London, Hutchinson, 1986.

Jacobus, Mary, ed., *Women Writing and Writing about Women*, London, Croom Helm, 1979

Jameson, Fredric, *The Prison-House of Language: A Critical Account of Structuralism and Russian Formalism*, Princeton, Princeton University Press, 1972
The Political Unconscious: Narrative as a Socially Symbolic Act, London, Methuen, 1981

Jefferson, Ann and Robey, David, eds., *Modern Literary Theory: A Comparative Introduction*, 2nd edn., London, Batsford, 1986

Kermode, Frank, *Romantic Image*, London, RKP, 1957
The Sense of an Ending: Studies in the Theory of Fiction, London, OUP, 1966
The Classic, London, Faber, 1975
The Genesis of Secrecy: On the Interpretation of Narrative, London, Harvard University Press, 1979
Essays on Fiction 1971–82, London, RKP, 1983

Kreiger, Murray, *The New Apologists for Poetry*, Minneapolis, University of Minnesota Press, 1956

Laing, Dave, *The Marxist Theory of Art: An Introductory Survey*, Brighton, Harvester, 1978

Lane, Michael, ed., *Structuralism: A Reader*, London, Jonathan Cape, 1970

Lavers, Annette, *Roland Barthes: Structuralism and After*, London, Methuen, 1982

Leach, Edmund, *Lévi-Strauss*, London, Fontana, 1970

Leavis, F. R., *New Bearings in English Poetry* (1932) Harmondsworth, Penguin, 1963
   Revaluation (1936) Harmondsworth, Penguin, 1964
   Education and the University, (1943) Cambridge, CUP, 1979
   The Great Tradition (1948) Harmondsworth, Penguin, 1962
   The Common Pursuit (1952) Harmondsworth, Penguin, 1962
   and Leavis, Q. D., *Lectures in America*, London, Chatto and Windus, 1969

Leavis, Q. D., *Fiction and the Reading Public* (1932) Harmondsworth, Penguin, 1979
   Collected Essays, 2 vols., ed. G. Singh, Cambridge, CUP, 1983

Leitch, Vincent B., *Deconstructive Criticism: An Advanced Introduction*, London, Hutchinson, 1983

Lemon, Lee T. and Reis, Marion J., eds., *Russian Formalist Criticism: Four Essays*, London, University of Nebraska Press, 1965

Lentricchia, Frank, *After the New Criticism*, London, The Athlone Press, 1980

Lepschy, Guilio, *A Survey of Structural Linguistics*, London, Faber, 1970

Lévi-Strauss, Claude, *Structural Anthropology*, vol. 1 (1958) trans. Claire Jacobson and Brooke Grundfast Schoepf, Harmondsworth, Penguin, 1968

Lodge, David, ed., *Twentieth-Century Literary Criticism: A Reader*, London, Longman, 1972
   The Modes of Modern Writing: Metaphor, Metonymy, and the Typology of Modern Literature, London, Edward Arnold, 1977
   Working With Structuralism: Essays and Reviews on Nineteenth- and Twentieth-Century Literature, London, RKP, 1981

Lyons, John, *Chomsky*, London, Fontana, 1970

MacCabe, Colin, *James Joyce and the Revolution of the Word*, London, Macmillan, 1978

MacCallum, Pamela, *Literature and Method: Towards a Critique of I. A. Richards, T. S. Eliot and F. R. Leavis*, Dublin, Gill and Macmillan, 1983

McDiarmid, Lucy, *Saving Civilisation: Yeats, Eliot and Auden Between the Wars*, Cambridge, CUP, 1984

McGann, Jerome J., *The Romantic Ideology: A Critical Investigation*, London, University of Chicago Press, 1983
   The Beauty of Inflections: Literary Investigations in Historical Method and Theory, Oxford, Clarendon Press, 1985

Macherey, Pierre, *A Theory of Literary Production* (1966) trans. Geoffrey Wall, London, RKP, 1978

Macksey, Richard, and Donato, Eugenio, eds., *The Structuralist Controversy: The Languages of Criticism and the Sciences of Man*, London, Johns Hopkins University Press, 1972

McLellan, David, *The Thought of Karl Marx: An Introduction*, 2nd edn., London, Macmillan, 1980

Marks, Elaine and Courtivron, Isabelle, eds., *New French Feminisms: An Anthology*, Brighton, Harvester, 1980

Martin, Graham, ed., *Eliot in Perspective: A Symposium*, London, Macmillan, 1970

Marx, Karl, and Engels, Frederick, *Selected Works*, London, Lawrence and Wishart, 1968
Marx and Engels on Literature and Art, ed. Lee Baxandall and Stefan Morawski, New York, International General, 1973

Matejka, L. and Pomorska, K., eds., *Readings in Russian Poetics: Formalist and Structuralist Views*, Cambridge, Mass., MIT Press, 1971

Merquior, J. L., *Foucault*, London, Fontana, 1985

Michaels, Walter Benn, 'Is There a Politics of Interpretation?', *Critical Inquiry*, 9 (1982), 248–58

Miller, J. Hillis, *Fiction and Repetition: Seven English Novels*, Oxford, Blackwell, 1982

Mitchell, Juliet, *Psychoanalysis and Feminism*, Harmondsworth, Penguin, 1974
Women: The Longest Revolution: Essays in Feminism, Literature and Psychoanalysis, London, Virago, 1984
and Oakley, Ann, eds., *The Rights and Wrongs of Women*, Harmondsworth, Penguin, 1976

Moi, Toril, *Sexual/Textual Politics: Feminist Literary Theory*, London, Methuen, 1985

Mulhern, Francis, *The Moment of 'Scrutiny'*, London, New Left Books, 1979

Nevo, Ruth, '*The Waste Land*: Ur-Text of Deconstruction', *New Literary History*, XIII (1982), 453–61

Norris, Christopher, *Deconstruction: Theory and Practice*, London, Methuen, 1982

Ohmann, Carol, 'Emily Brontë in the Hands of Male Critics', *College English*, 32 (1971), 906–13

Palmer, D. J., *The Rise of English Studies: An Account of the Study of English from its Origins to the Making of the Oxford English School*, London, OUP, 1965

Parrinder, Patrick, *Authors and Authority: A Study of English Literary Criticism and Its Relation to Culture 1750–1900*, London, RKP, 1977
'The Accents of Raymond Williams', *Critical Quarterly*, 26 (1984), 47–57

Piaget, Jean, *Structuralism* (1968) ed. and trans. Chaninah Maschler, London, RKP, 1971

Propp, Vladimir, *Morphology of the Folktale* (1928) trans. Lawrence Scott, London, University of Texas Press, 1958

Ransom, John Crowe, *The World's Body*, New York, Charles Scribner, 1938
The New Criticism, Norfolk, Conn., New Directions, 1941

Ray, William, *Literary Meaning: From Phenomenology to Deconstruction*, Oxford, Blackwell, 1984

Richards, I. A., *Principles of Literary Criticism* (1924) London, RKP, 1960
Science and Poetry, London, Kegan Paul, Trench, Trubner, 1926
Practical Criticism (1929) London, RKP, 1964

Robertson, D. W., Jr., 'Some Observations on Method in Literary Studies', *New Literary History*, 1 (1969), 21–33

Robey, David, ed., *Structuralism: An Introduction*, Oxford, Clarendon, Press, 1974

Ruthven, K. K., *Critical Assumptions*, Cambridge, CUP, 1979
Feminist Literary Studies: An Introduction, Cambridge, CUP, 1984

Said, Edward W., *Beginnings: Intention and Method*, New York, Basic Books, 1975
Orientalism, London, RKP, 1978

The World, The Text and The Critic, London, Faber, 1983

Saussure, Ferdinand de, *Course in General Linguistics* (1916) trans. Wade Baskin (1959) London, Fontana, 1974; trans. Roy Harris, London, Duckworth, 1983

Schiff, Hilda, ed., *Contemporary Approaches to English Studies*, London, Heineman, 1977

Scholes, Robert, *Structuralism in Literature: An Introduction*, London, Yale University Press, 1974

Schwartz, Bill, *et al.*, eds., *On Ideology*, London, Hutchinson, 1978

Sebeok, Thomas, ed., *Style in Language*, Cambridge, Mass., MIT Press, 1960

Selden, Raman, *A Reader's Guide to Contemporary Literary Theory*, Brighton, Harvester, 1985

Showalter, Elaine, *A Literature of Their Own: British Women Novelists from Brontë to Lessing*, London, Virago, 1979
    ed., *The New Feminist Criticism: Essays on Women, Literature and Theory*, London, Virago, 1986

Simpson, Lewis P., ed., *The Possibilities of Order: Cleanth Brooks and his Work*, Baton Rouge, Louisiana State University Press, 1976

Spacks, Patricia Meyer, *The Female Imagination: A Literary and Psychological Investigation*, London, Allen and Unwin, 1976

Sturrock, John, ed., *Structuralism and Since*, Oxford, OUP, 1979
    Structuralism, London, Paladin, 1986

Suleiman, Susan R., and Crossman, Inge, eds., *The Reader in the Text: Essays on Audience and Interpretation*, Princeton, Princeton University Press, 1980

Thompson, Denys, ed., *The Leavises: Recollections and Impressions*, Cambridge, CUP, 1984

Thompson, E. M., *Russian Formalism and Anglo-American New Criticism*, The Hague, Mouton, 1971

Thompson, E. P., *The Poverty of Theory and Other Essays*, London, Merlin, 1978

Timpanaro, Sebastiano, *On Materialism*, trans. Lawrence Garner, London, New Left Books, 1980

Tompkins, Jane P., ed., *Reader Response Criticism: From Formalism to Post-Structuralism*, London, Johns Hopkins University Press, 1980

Trilling, Lionel, *The Liberal Imagination* (1951) Harmondsworth, Penguin, 1970

Ward, J. P., *Raymond Williams*, Cardiff, University of Wales Press, 1981

Weimann, Robert, *Structure and Society in Literary History: Studies in the History and Theory of Historical Criticism*, London, Lawrence and Wishart, 1977

Wellek, René, *Concepts of Criticism*, ed. Stephen G. Nichols, London, Yale University Press, 1963
    The Attack on Literature and Other Essays, Brighton, Harvester, 1982
    and Warren, Austin, *Theory of Literature* (1949) Harmondsworth, Penguin, 1963

Widdowson, Peter, ed., *Re-Reading English*, London, Methuen, 1982

Williams, Raymond, *Culture and Society 1780–1950* (1958) Harmondsworth, Penguin, 1961
    The Long Revolution (1961) Harmondsworth, Penguin, 1965
    The English Novel from Dickens to Lawrence, London, Chatto and Windus, 1970
    Marxism and Literature, Oxford, OUP, 1977
    Politics and Letters: Interviews with New Left Review, London, New Left Books, 1979

Problems in Materialism and Culture, London, New Left Books, 1980

Culture, London, Fontana, 1981

Keywords: A Vocabulary of Culture and Society, 2nd edn., London, Fontana, 1983

Writing in Society, London, New Left Books, n.d.

Wimsatt, W. K., *The Verbal Icon: Studies in the Meaning of Poetry* (1954) London, Methuen, 1970

and Brooks, Cleanth, *Literary Criticism: A Short History*, 4 vols. (1957) London, RKP, 1970

Wright, Elizabeth, *Psychoanalytic Criticism: Theory in Practice*, London, Methuen, 1984

Young, Robert, ed., *Untying the Text: A Post-structuralist Reader*, London, RKP, 1981

Zabel, Morton D., ed., *Literary Opinion in America*, 2nd edn., New York, Harper, 1951

Index